P1

BOXIANA;

OR,

SKETCHES

OF

ANCIENT AND MODERN

PUGILISM,

FROM THE DAYS OF THE RENOWNED

BROUGHTON AND SLACK,

TO THE

CHAMPIONSHIP OF CRIBB

Volume 1

Elibron Classics
www.elibron.com

Elibron Classics series.

© 2006 Adamant Media Corporation.

ISBN 1-4021-8128-0 (paperback)
ISBN 1-4021-5476-3 (hardcover)

This Elibron Classics Replica Edition is an unabridged facsimile
of the edition published in 1830 by George Virtue, London.

THRIFTBOOKS
12 11839 144
144

THOMAS CRIBB.

The Champion of England

BOXIANA;

OR, Sketches of

Antient & Modern

PUGILISM.

LONDON.

Published by GEORGE VIRTUE, 26, Ivy Lane.

1829.

BOXIANA;

OR,

SKETCHES

OF

ANCIENT AND MODERN

𝕻𝔲𝔤𝔦𝔩𝔦𝔰𝔪,

FROM THE DAYS OF THE RENOWNED

BROUGHTON AND SLACK,

TO THE

CHAMPIONSHIP OF CRIBB.

BY PIERCE EGAN.

Θάρσει μηδέ τί πω δειδίσσεο.—HOMER.
Homo sum, humani nil à me alienum puto.—TERENCE.

DEDICATED TO
CAPTAIN BARCLAY.

VOL. I.

London:
Printed by C. BAYNES, Duke-street, Lincoln's-inn-fields.
PUBLISHED BY GEORGE VIRTUE, IVY LANE,
PATERNOSTER ROW.

1830.

TO

CAPTAIN BARCLAY.

————

Sir,

WITH the freedom of an English-man, and consistent with those genuine principles of liberty for which you are distinguished, I conceive that no apology is requisite in addressing you on a subject, in which a peculiar FEATURE OF THE TIMES we live in may be developed, if not handed down to posterity.

In viewing you, Sir, as a LOVER AND PATRON OF THOSE SPORTS that tend to invigorate the human frame, and inculcate those principles of generosity and heroism, by which the inhabitants of the English Nation are so eminently distinguished above every other country, is the sole reason of dedicating to the attention of Captain BARCLAY, the work entitled—BOXIANA; or, SKETCHES OF ANCIENT AND MODERN PUGILISM.

To those, Sir, who prefer *effeminacy* to hardihood—*assumed refinement* to rough Nature—and to whom *a shower of rain* can terrify their *polite* frames suffering from the unruly elements—or who would not mind Pugilism, if BOXING was not so shockingly *vulgar*—the following work can have no interest whatever. But to persons, Sir, who, like yourself, feel that Englishmen are not automata, and however the advantages of discipline may serve for the precision and movement of great bodies, that it would ultimately lose its effects, were it not animated by that native spirit, which has been found to originate, in a great measure, from what the fastidious term—*vulgar Sports*, BOX-IANA will convey amusement, if not information.

The *cause*, Sir, ought not to be lost sight of in the *effect*—and the alacrity of the TAR in serving his gun, the daring intrepidity of the BRITISH SOLDIER in mounting the Breach, producing those brilliant victories which have reflected so much honour on the English Nation—may be traced to something like these sources; sources which impart generosity to the mind, and humanity to the heart, by instilling those unalterable principles in the breast of every Briton, not to take an unfair advantage of his antagonist. This trait cannot be more *nationally* illustrated than in the instance of a British Sailor, at the taking of Fort Omoa, who, being in possession of two swords, and suddenly meeting an enemy destitute of any weapon of defence, with unparalleled manliness and generosity, *divided* the instruments of death with him, that he might have a fair chance for his life !

SPORTS, Sir, which can produce *thorough-bred* actions like the above, will outlive all the sneers of the fastidious, and *cant* of the hyper-critics.

I remain, SIR,

With every consideration

and manly respect,

Your humble Servant,

P. EGAN.

July 29, 1812.

CONTENTS.

BOXIANA.

THE ART OF TRAINING.

INTRODUCTION.

ITS IMPORTANCE IN ATHLETIC CONTESTS. MORAL EFFECTS CONDUCE TO VICTORY. JOCKEYS, PEDESTRIANS, WRESTLERS, HOW DIFFERING FROM PUGILISTIC TRAINING. OF THE OLD-SCHOOL TRAINING AND WRITTEN TREATISES; COMMON ERROR OF ALL. TRAINING DOWN FAT AND FLESH; THICK BLOOD AND SLOW. SCURVICAL HABITS, GENERAL OBSERVANCES. OF TRAINING UPWARDS. CAPTAIN BARCLAY.

A SUBJECT of so much importance as enabling a man to use his best exertions in any affair that requires the employment of his *greatest capabilities*, yet previously impaired by irregularity, can be of no mean consideration to the pugilist, who has to contend against another, possibly more wary and circumspect than himself in this species of preparation for the strife. He sees his antagonist stripped, *showing the muscle* distinctly, and reflects with despondency at first

B

sight on the disparity of his own condition;* for the
victory is as often obtained by moral conviction of
success, as by actual superiority of strength and skill
residing in the same *quantity* of stuff, to say nothing
of that quickness of perception which *the mind*
acquires when the body (its habitation) is in good
condition.   If all has been done that can be effected
towards attaining this end, the combatant has at least
one consideration to cheer his prospects, that *nothing
has been neglected* on the part of his friends to secure
a *fair chance* of victory.   But would they go farther,
and practise a few precautions, founded on reason and
experience, they may more securely reckon upon the
attainment of their wishes, and thus undertake, as
matter of profit, that trouble which they would avoid
simply for sake of victory.   The jockey and the pedestrian train with very different views, as both do
differ with the pugilist in matter of feeling as well as
in the prize to be obtained.   The first seeks to reduce
his *weight* merely, without regarding the remains of
strength which he may retain; and although this
otherwise desirable quality may be improved by *his
training* (which always tends downwards), yet, if he
lasts five or six minutes' hard work, this is all he
requires.   *Should he fail, the horse is blamed.*   The
pedestrian engages against *Time*, generally; and if *the
old fellow* be not beaten, his impersonality comes not
to upbraid the *athletic* with superior *condition;* it is

---

* In 1811, when Cribb and Molineux entered the ring the latter
declared himself abashed at the fine condition of his opponent,
whom he expected to find " full of blubber," or loose flesh.

the *pugilist* only who suffers in his feelings by defective comparison with his opponent; and upon him
lies most incumbent the duty of attending to the precepts of older and wiser, if not equally interested,
persons, with himself. He may fail to win the fame
of *a conqueror*, but his backers will lose all *the blunt*.
In some respects, *wrestlers* require similar treatment
with *pugilists*, but the similarity extends no farther
than perhaps insomuch as the two species of undertaking may be considered alike, or than wrestling is a
subservient auxiliary to boxing. However, doubts
having arisen in some good minds, whether real pugilists should be allowed to close and wrestle for the
throw in any case, the consideration of this secondary
art is postponed to a subsequent page. Several persons verbally, and some *in writing*, have recommended
certain observances to *the men* of the ring about to
engage in battle, as to what they should do to acquire
most bodily strength. Both kinds of persons speak
to points of regimen; but all have erred, or rather
hit short of the *mark* of excellence, by supposing *all
the men* who require training to be in one and the
same condition previously to going into training.
Three doses of salts, three sweats, and three vomits,
accompanied by three other things not worthy mention, for three weeks, with victuals three quarters
dressed, constitute the most intelligent rationale of
training recommended by the old school of pugilism,
which hath passed away with our earliest years; but
the meanest capacity must perceive, that many constitutions could not bear this kind of treatment, and
acquire strength; several of the men having *trained*

off under its operation, owing to the excitability of
their system of life.   Even when bleeding was resorted to, it was usually carried too far (by all *three
times*), and lowered the subject so much, that he could
not recover in sufficient time for his task; or they
afterwards replenished his blood so rapidly, that the
jugular performed its office too plethorically, and, in
the *actual* contest, he *fell off* his fighting in an *unac-
countable* manner, and went to dorse, or stood up
senselessly to be knocked about.*

Very many are the instances within recollection of
such *fallings off*, that most ring-goers wonder at, but
no man can account for in any more rational manner;
for, truly, the grand error in training all men alike
has been the cause of many strange *losses*, which
seemed like *crosses* of late years.   One man is fat, and
requires reducing by exercise and abstinence, nay,
starvation ; another has too much blood, with heat and
irritation of the whole system, and he must lose a
portion of the *stream of life*, no doubt; but the feverish
(if not inflamed) state of his stomach and intestines are ill calculated to assist in making *better blood*
than that he has lost, and they must be gently emptied of their contents.   If the man's blood be thick,
and move slowly, it must be attenuated (made thin),
and with due exercise and regular living, it shall
move quicker; if he show signs of a scurvical habit,

---

* *Hawbucks*, full of blood, usually fall off in this manner, and
with them is the cause of fatal contests: in *the Ring*, Tom Oliver
is he in whom this effect of mistaken *training* has been exemplified
in more than one, two, or three instances.

viz. much hair, small spots, or the skin having various hues, a course of physic, with sweating and *rubbing-down*, will get rid of a good portion thereof; indeed, as much as is necessary for his *present purpose.* More particular directions how to proceed in either case shall follow at the end..

But it not unfrequently happens, that neither this, that, or the other supposed evil state of the body affects the man to be *trained;* his system of animal life is already too low, probably, to exhibit symptoms of either sort; he requires neither physic or bleeding, is not capable of great exercise, and *hard training*, or training him downwards, by reducing his system; would reduce his strength and animal capabilities, the moral energies would follow on the *hour of trial*, and he would fail to win, for he has (according to technical phrase) " trained off." Such a man requires what we should call " training upwards;" his system of animal life requires *filling up;* the juices that contribute to life and strength must to him be *supplied* instead of being *taken away;* and they may be supplied of such hard materials, or of such hardening qualities as shall render his muscular system hard in texture and strong in action.

Yet do most of our written instructions in training make no sort of distinction whatever in the rules to be observed by this, that, or the other kind of constitution; all are directed to adopt the same plan, though every man is pretty well known to differ in some respect or other from every other man, some totally so. These preliminary remarks were thought highly necessary towards rightly appreciating the celebrated

Treatise on Training, which we now subjoin entire, and which, though coming from the pen of a friend, is well recognized as being of Captain Barclay's dictation, and always bore his name.

Where the captain (or his friend, Mr. Walter Thom) may seem inconclusive or too brief, or their remarks are not sufficiently applicable to Pugilists, the reader will find the discrepancy supplied in the instructions and remarks which follow. Of *medicine,* for the several purposes mentioned, the particulars are there subjoined.

> Ye who would wear a body free of pain,
> Fly the rank city, shun its turbid air,
> And dim mortality. It is not *air*
> That from ten thousand lungs reeks back to thine,
> Sated with exaltations rank and fell,
> The spoil of dunghills, and the putrid thaw
> Of nature; but here floats a nauseous mass
> Of all obscure, corrupt, offensive things.
> Much *moisture* hurts; but here a sordid bath,
> With oily rancour fraught, relaxes more
> The solid frame, than *simple moisture* can.

CAPTAIN BARCLAY'S METHOD

OF

TRAINING THE PEDESTRIAN;

AND, BY NATURAL INFERENCE,

THE PUGILIST ALSO.

OPINIONS AND PRACTICE OF THE ANCIENTS. OB-
JECT. PROCESS OF ABSORPTION AND RENOVATION.
MEDICINE, EXERCISE, REGIMEN; SWEATING, AMUSE-
MENTS, DIET: WIND IMPROVED—CONDUCIVE TO
HEALTH, VIGOUR OF MIND AND LONG LIFE. CRIBB'S
PROCESS—EXERCISES, WALKS, DIET—EFFECTS THERE-
OF; ANECDOTE OF THE CHAMPION.

THE art of training for *athletic exercises* consists in
purifying the body and strengthening its powers, by
certain processes, which thus qualify a person for the
accomplishment of laborious exertions. It was known
to the ancients, who paid much attention to the means
of augmenting corporeal vigour and activity; and
accordingly, among the Greeks and Romans, certain
rules of regimen and exercise were prescribed to the
candidates for gymnastic celebrity.

We are not, however, in possession of any detailed
account of the particular kind of DIET in use among

the Greeks previously to the solemn contest at the
public games; but we are assured, that the strictest
temperance, sobriety, and regularity in living, were
indispensably requisite. The candidates, at the same
time, were subjected to daily exercise in the GYMNA-
.SIUM for ten months, which, with the prescribed
regimen, constituted the preparatory course of training adopted by the ATHLETÆ of ancient Greece.

Among the Romans, the exercises of the PALÆ-
STRA degenerated from the rank of a liberal art, and
became a profession, which was embraced only by the
lowest of mankind. The exhibitions of the GLADIA-
TORS were bloody and ferocious spectacles, which
evinced the barbarous taste of the people. The combatants, however, were regularly trained by proper
exercise, and a strict observance of regimen. In the
more early stages, their diet consisted of dried figs,
new cheese, and boiled grain. But afterwards, animal
food was introduced as a part of the athletic regimen,
and PORK was preferred to any other. GALEN asserts,
that " pork contains more real nutriment than the
flesh of any other animal which is used as food by
man: this fact," he adds, " is decidedly proved by the
example of the Athletæ, who, if they lived but for
one day on any other kind of food, found their vigour
manifestly impaired the next."

The preference given to pork by the ancients does
not correspond with the practice of modern trainers,
who entirely reject it in their regimen: but in the
manner of preparing the food they exactly agree—
ROASTING or BROILING being preferred to BOILING,
by both; and *bread unfermented*, to that prepared by

leaven. A very small quantity of fluid was allowed, and this was principally water. When the daily exercises of the Athletæ were finished, they were refreshed by immersion in a tepid bath, "where the perspiration and *sordes** were carefully removed from the surface of the body by the use of the STRYGIL.† The skin was then diligently rubbed dry, and again anointed with oil. If thirsty, they were permitted to drink a small quantity of *warm water*. They then took their principal repast, after which they used no more exercise that day.‡ They occasionally also went into the cold bath in the morning. They were permitted to sleep as many hours as they chose; and great increase of vigour, as well as of bulk, was supposed to be derived from long-continued and sound repose."§

Previously to entering on this regimen, the Athletæ were subjected to the evacuating process, by means of emetics, which they preferred to purgatives. *The sexual intercourse was strictly prohibited.* "To exercise their patience, and accustom them to bear pain without flinching, they were occasionally flogged on the back with the branches of a kind of *rhododendron*, till the blood flowed pretty plentifully. By diminishing the quantity of the circulating fluid, this rough kind

---

* Scurf, pustules, or filthy adhesions.

† For this instrument, rough coarse cloths are adopted with advantage.

‡ *Plain* water and sleep *after* dinner (as we understand), however, are little adapted to the athletic powers of the present age, or this country.

§ *Little sleep* is now prescribed; but its quantity should depend upon circumstances of fatigue, &c.

of cupping was also considered as salutary, in obviating the tendency to plethora (or redundancy of blood) to which they were peculiarly liable."

Pure and salubrious air was deemed a chief requisite; and accordingly by the principal of schools of the Roman Athletæ were established at CAPUA and RAVENNA, the most healthy places in all Italy. They exercised in the *open air*, and became familiarized, by habit, to every change of the weather, the vicissitudes of which soon ceased to affect them.

The manner of training among the ancients bears some resemblance to that now practised by the moderns. But as their mode of living and general habits were somewhat different from those of the present age, a difference of treatment is now required to produce the same effects.

The great object of training, for *running* or *boxing* matches, is, to increase the muscular strength, and to improve the free action of the lungs, or WIND, of the person subjected to the process, which is done by medicine, may be effected by regimen and exercise. That this object *can* be accomplished. is evident from the nature of the human system. It is well known, (for it has been demonstrated by experiment,) that every part of the firmest bones is successively absorbed and deposited. "The bones and their ligaments, the muscles and their tendons, all the finer and all the more flexible parts of the body, are continually renewed, and as properly a secretion, as the saliva that flows from the mouth, or the moisture that bedews the surface. The health of all the parts, and their soundness of structure, depend on this perpetual absorption and perpetual renovation; and exercise, by promoting at once absorption and secretion, promotes life without hurrying it, renovates all the parts, and preserves them apt and fit for every office."

When the human frame is thus capable of being altered and renovated, it is not surprising that the art of training should be carried to a degree of *perfection* almost *incredible;* and that by certain processes, the BREATH, (or WIND,) strength, and courage of man, should be so greatly improved, as to enable him to perform the most laborious undertakings. That such effects have been produced is unquestionable, being fully exemplified in the astonishing exploits of our most celebrated pedestrians, which are the infallible results of such preparatory discipline.

The skilful *trainer* attends to the state of the *bowels,* the *lungs,* and the *skin;* and he uses such means as will reduce the fat, and, at the same time, invigorate the muscular fibres.* The *patient* is purged by *drastic medicines;* he is sweated by walking under a load of clothes, and by lying between feather-beds. His limbs are roughly rubbed. His *diet* is beef or mutton; his drink, strong ale; and he is gradually inured to *exercise* by repeated trials in walking and running. "By extenuating the fat, emptying the cellular substance,

---

* The application of those principles to pugilists *particularly,* and the distinction between the requisites for the one or the other kind of athletic exercise, will be shown in our further ' Practical Advice on Training, with a particular View to Pugilistic Encounters."

hardening the muscular fibre, and improving the breath,
a man of the ordinary frame may be made to fight for
one hour, with the utmost exertion of strength and
courage," or to go over one hundred miles in twenty-
four hours.

The most effectual process for training is that practised by Capt. Barclay; and the particular method
which he has adopted has not only been SANCTIONED
by professional men, but has met with the unqualified
approbation of amateurs. The following statement,
therefore, contains the most approved rules; and it
is presented to the reader, as the result of much experience, founded on the theoretic principles of the
art.

The pedestrian, who may be supposed in tolerable
condition, enters upon his training with a regular
course of physic, which consists of three doses. Glauber Salts are generally preferred; and from one ounce
and a half to two ounces are taken each time, with
an interval of four days between each dose.* After
having gone through the course of physic, he commences his regular exercise, which is gradually increased as he proceeds in the training. When the
object in view is the accomplishment of a pedestrian

---

* It is not so generally known as it ought to be, that a salt, introduced into medical practice by Dr. George Pearson, of London,
is as excellent a purge as Glauber's salt, and has none of the nauseous
taste which renders that purge so disagreeable to many persons. The
phosphat of soda is very similar to common salt in taste, and may be
given in a basin of gruel or broth, in which it will be scarcely
perceptible to the palate, and will also agree with the most delicate
stoma h.

match, his regular exercise may be from twenty to twenty-four miles a day. He must rise at five in the morning, run half a mile at the top of his speed up-hill, and then walk six miles at a moderate pace, coming in about seven to breakfast, which should consist of beef-steaks or mutton-chops under-done, with stale bread and old beer. After breakfast, he must again walk six miles at a moderate pace, and at twelve lie down in bed without his clothes for half an hour. On getting up, he must walk four miles, and return by four to dinner, which should also be beef-steaks or mutton-chops, with bread and beer as at breakfast. Immediately after dinner, he must resume his exercise, by running half a mile at the top of his speed, and walking six miles at a moderate pace. He takes no more exercise for that day, but retires to bed about eight, and next morning proceeds in the same manner.

After having gone on in this regular course for three or four weeks, the *pedestrian* must take a four-mile SWEAT, which is produced by running four miles, in flannel, at the top of his speed. Immediately on re-turning, a *hot liquor* is prescribed, in order to promote the perspiration, of which he must drink one English-pint. It is termed the SWEATING LIQUOR, and is composed of the following ingredients, viz. one ounce of caraway-seed; half an ounce of coriander-seed; one ounce of root liquorice; and half an ounce of sugar-candy; mixed with two bottles of cider, and boiled down to one-half. He is then put to bed in his flannels, and being covered with six or eight pairs of blankets and a feather-bed, must remain in this state from twenty-five to thirty minutes, when he is taken out and rubbed perfectly dry. Being then well wrapt in his great coat, he walks out gently for two miles, and returns to breakfast, which, on such occasions, should consist of a roasted fowl. He afterwards proceeds with his usual exercise. These sweats are continued WEEKLY, till within a few days of the performance of the match, or, in other words, he must undergo three or four of these operations. If the stomach of the pedestrian be foul, an emetic or two must be given, about a week before the conclusion of the training, and he is now supposed to be in the highest condition.

Besides his usual or regular exercise, a person under training ought to employ himself in the intervals in every kind of exertion, which tends to activity, such as cricket, bowls, throwing quoits, &c. so that, during the whole day, both body and mind may be constantly occupied.

From the above account of Capt. Barclay's method of training, it will be seen, that he commences with the evacuating process, and that three purgative doses are deemed sufficient to clear any man from the impurities which it is requisite to throw off, preparatory to entering on the course of regimen and exercise. And in this stage of the business, the objects to be attained are the purification of the animal system and the promotion of the digestive powers.

The *diet*, or *regimen*, is the next point of consideration, and it is very simple. As the intention of the trainer is to preserve the strength of the pedestrian, he must take care to keep him in good condition by nourishing food. Animal diet alone is prescribed, and beef and mutton are preferred. The lean of fat beef cooked in steaks, with very little salt, is the best, and it should be rather under-done than otherwise. Mutton, being reckoned easy of digestion, may be occasionally given, to vary the diet and gratify the taste. The legs of fowls are highly esteemed. It is preferable to have the meat BROILED, as much of its nutritive qualities is lost by roasting or boiling. De Willich says, "It may serve as a preliminary rule, that *fresh meat* is the most wholesome and nourishing. To preserve these qualities, however, it ought to be *dressed* so as to remain tender and juicy; for it is by this means, it will be easily digested, and afford most nourishment." Biscuit and stale bread are the only preparations of vegetable matter which are permitted to be given; and every thing inducing flatulency must be carefully avoided. Veal and lamb are never allowed, nor pork, which operates as a laxative on some people : and all fat and greasy substances are prohibited, as they induce bile, and consequently injure the stomach. But it has been proved by experience, that the lean of meat contains more nourishment than the fat, and in every case, the most substantial food is preferable to any other kind.

Vegetables, such as turnips, carrots, or potatoes, are never given, as they are watery, and of difficult digestion. On the same principle, fish must be avoided, and, besides, they are not sufficiently nutritious. Neither butter nor cheese is allowed; the one being very indigestible, and the other apt to turn rancid on the stomach. Eggs are also forbidden, excepting the yolk taken raw in the morning. And it must be remarked, that salt, spiceries, and all kinds of seasonings, with the exception of vinegar, are prohibited.

With respect to *liquors*, they must be always taken cold; and *home-brewed beer*, old, but not bottled, is the best. A little red wine, however, may be given to those who are not fond of malt liquor; but never more than half a pint after dinner. Too much liquor swells the abdomen, and of course injures the breath. The quantity of beer, therefore, should not exceed three pints during the whole day, and it must be taken with breakfast and dinner, no supper being allowed. Water is never given alone, and ardent spirits are strictly prohibited, however diluted. It is an established rule to avoid liquids as much as possible, and no more liquor of any kind is allowed to be taken than what is merely requisite to quench the thirst. Milk is never allowed, as it curdles on the stomach. Broths and soups require little digestion; weaken the stomach, and are attended by all the pernicious effects of other warm and relaxing drink. Soups are not used; nor is any thing liquid taken warm, but gruel or broth, to promote the operation of the physic; and the sweating liquor mentioned above. The broth must be cooled in order to take off the fat, hen it may be again warmed; or beef tea may be used in the same manner, with little or no salt. In the days between the purges, the pedestrian must be fed as usual, strictly adhering to the nourishing diet by which he is invigorated.

Profuse sweating is resorted to as an expedient for removing the superfluities of flesh and fat. Three or four sweats are generally requisite, and they may be considered the severest part of the process.

Emetics are only prescribed if the stomach be disordered, which may sometimes happen, when due care is not taken to proportion the quantity of food to the digestive powers. But, in general, the quantity of aliment is not limited by the trainer, but left entirely to the discretion of the pedestrian, whose appetite should regulate him in this respect.

Although the chief parts of the training system depend upon SWEATING, EXERCISE, and FEEDING, yet the object to be obtained, by the pedestrian would be defeated, if these were not adjusted, each to the other, and to his constitution. The skilful trainer will, therefore, constantly study the progress of his *art*, by observing the effect of the processes, separately and in combination.

If a man retains his health and spirits during the process, improves in WIND, and increases in strength, it is certain that the object aimed at will be obtained. But if otherwise, it is to be apprehended that some defect exists, through the unskilfulness or mismanagement of the trainer, which ought instantly to be remedied by such alterations as the circumstances of the case may demand. It is evident, therefore, that, in many instances, the trainer must be guided by his judgment, and that no fixed rules of management can, with absolute certainty, be depended upon, for producing an invariable and determinate result. But, in general, it may be calculated, that the known rules

are adequate to the purpose, if the pedestrian strictly
adheres to them, and the trainer bestows a moderate
degree of attention to his state and condition during
the progress of the training.

It is farther necessary to remark, that the trainer,
before he proceeds to apply his theory, should make
himself acquainted with the constitution and habits of
his patient, that he may be able to judge how far he
can, with safety, carry on the different parts of the
process. The nature of his disposition should also be
known, that every cause of irritation may be avoided ;
for, as it requires great patience and perseverance to
undergo training, every expedient to soothe and en-
courage the mind should be adopted.

It is impossible to fix any precise period for the
completion of the training process, as it depends upon
the previous condition of the pedestrian ; but from
two to three months, in most cases, will be sufficient,
especially if he be in tolerable condition at the commencement, and possessed of sufficient perseverance
and courage to submit cheerfully to the privations
and hardships to which he must unavoidably be subjected.

Training is indispensably necessary to those who are
to engage in corporeal exertions beyond their ordinary powers. Pedestrians, therefore, who are matched
either against others or *against time*, and pugilists,
who engage to fight, must undergo the training process before they contend, as the issue of the contest,
if their powers be nearly equal, will, in a great mea-

sure, depend upon their relative condition at the hour of trial. But the advantages of the training system are not confined to pedestrians and pugilists alone: they extend to every man; and were training generally introduced, instead of medicines, as an expedient for the prevention and cure of diseases, its beneficial consequences would promote happiness and prolong life.

It is well known to physiologists, that both the solids and fluids which compose the human frame are successively absorbed and deposited. Hence a perpetual renovation of the parts ensues, regulated as they are by the nature of our food and general habits.* It, therefore, follows, that our health, vigour, and activity, must depend upon regimen and exercise, or, in other words, upon the observance of those rules which constitute the theory of the training process. The effect has accordingly corresponded with the cause in all instances where training has been adopted; and, although not commonly resorted to as the means of restoring invalids to health, yet is there every reason to believe, that it would prove effectual in curing many obstinate diseases, such as the gout, rheumatism, bilious complaints, &c. &c.

"Training (says Sir J. Sinclair) always appears to improve the state of the lungs. One of the most striking effects is to improve the wind; that is, it enables a man to draw a larger inspiration, and to hold his breath longer." He farther observes,—"By training, the mental faculties are also improved. The

---

* Bell's Anatomy, vol. i. p. 12.

attention is more ready, and the perception more
acute, probably owing to the clearness of the stomach,
and better digestion."*

It has been made a question, whether training produces a *lasting* or only a *temporary* effect on the constitution ? It is undeniable, that if a man be brought
to a better condition, if corpulency and the impurities of his body disappear, and if his *wind* and
strength be improved by any process whatever, his
good state of health will continue, until some derange-
ment of his frame shall take place from accidental or
natural causes. If he will relapse into intemperance,
or neglect the means of preserving his health, either
by omitting to take the necessary exercise, or by in-
dulging in debilitating propensities, he must expect
such encroachments to be made on his constitution as
must soon unhinge his sistem. But if he will observe a different plan, the beneficial effects of the
training process will remain until the gradual decay
of his natural functions shall, in mature old age, intimate the approach of his dissolution.

The ancients entertained this opinion. — "They
were (says Dr. Buchan) by no means unacquainted
with, or inattentive to, these instruments of medicine,
although modern practitioners appear to have no idea
of removing disease, or restoring health, but by pouring drugs into the stomach. HERODICUS is said to
have been the first who applied the exercises and
regimen of the gymnasium to the removal of disease,
or the maintenance of health. Among the Romans,

---

* Code of Health, vol. ii. p. 103.

ASCLEPIADES carried this so far, that he is said by CELSUS almost to have banished the use of internal remedies from his practice. He was the inventor of pensile beds, which were used to induce sleep, and of various other modes of exercise and gestation, and rose to great eminence as a physician in Rome. In his own person he afforded an excellent example of the wisdom of his rules, and the propriety of his regimen. PLINY tells us that, in early life, he made a public profession that he would agree to forfeit all pretensions to the name of a physician, should he ever suffer from sickness, or die but of old age; and, what is more extraordinary, he fulfilled his promise, for he lived upwards of a century, and at last was killed by a fall down stairs.

It may, therefore, be admitted, that the beneficial consequences, both to the body and the mind, arising from training, are not merely temporary, but may be made permanent by proper care and attention. The simplicity of the rules is a great recommendation to those who may be desirous of trying the experiment, and the whole process may be resolved into the following principles: 1st, The *evacuating*, which cleanses the stomach and intestines.—2d, The *sweating*, which takes off the superfluities of flesh and fat.—3d, The *daily course of exercise*, which improves the *wind* and strengthens the muscles;—and, lastly, The *regimen*, which nourishes and invigorates the body.

The criterion by which it may be known whether a man be in good condition, or, what is the same thing, has been properly trained, is the state of the skin, which becomes *smooth, elastic,* and *well-coloured,* or

Transparent.—The flesh is also *firm*, and the person trained feels himself light, and full of spirits. But in the progress of the training, his condition may be ascertained by the effect of the *sweats*, which cease to reduce his weight; and by the manner in which he performs one mile at the top of his speed. It is as difficult to run a mile at the top of one's speed as to walk a hundred, and, therefore, if he performs this short distance well, it may be concluded, that his condition is perfect, or that he has derived all the advantages which can possibly result from the training process.

The manner of training *jockeys* is different from that which is applicable to pedestrians and pugilists. In in regard to jockeys, it is generally *wasting*, with the view to reduce their weight. This is produced by purgatives, emetics, sweats, and starvation. Their bodily strength is of no importance, as they have only to manage the reins of the courser, whose fleetness depends upon the weight he carries; and the muscular power of the rider is of no consequence to the race, provided it be equal to the fatigue of a three or four mile heat.

Training for pugilism is nearly the same as for pedestrianism, the object in both being principally to obtain additional *wind* and strength.—But it will be best illustrated by a detail of the process observed by CRIBB, the champion of England, preparatory to his grand battle with Molineux, which took place on the 29th of September, 1811.

The champion arrived at Ury on the 7th of July of that year. He weighed sixteen stone; and from his mode of living in London, and the confinement of a crowded city, he had become corpulent, big-bellied, full of gross humours, and short-breathed; and it was with difficulty he could walk ten miles. He first went through a course of physic, which consisted of three doses; for two weeks he walked about as he pleased, and generally traversed the woods and plantations with a fowling-piece in his hand. The *reports* of his musket resounded every where through the groves and the hollows of that delightful place, to the great *terror* of the magpies and wood-pigeons.

After amusing himself in this way for about a fort-night, he then commenced his regular walking exercise, which at first was about ten or twelve miles a day. It was soon after increased to eighteen or twenty; and he ran regularly, morning and evening, a quarter of a mile at the top of his speed. In consequence of his physic and exercise, his weight was reduced, in the course of five weeks, from sixteen stone to fourteen and nine pounds. At this period, he commenced his *sweats*, and took three during the month he remained at Ury afterwards; and his weight was gradually reduced to thirteen stone and five pounds, which was ascertained to be his *pitch* of condition, *as he would not reduce farther without weakening*.

During the course of his training, the champion went twice to the Highlands, and took strong exercise. He walked to Mar Lodge, which is about sixty miles distant from Ury, where he arrived to dinner on the second day, being now able to do thirty miles a day with ease, and probably he could have walked twice as far if it had been necessary. He remained in the Highlands about a week each time, and amused himself with shooting. The principal advantage which he derived from these expeditions was the severe exercise he was obliged to undergo in following Captain Barclay. He improved more in his strength and wind by his journies to the Highlands, than by any other part of the training process.

His diet and drink were the same as used in the pedestrian regimen, and in other respects, the rules previously laid down were generally applied to him. That he was brought to his ultimate *pitch* of condition was evident from the high state of health and strength in which he appeared when he mounted the stage to contend with Molineux, who has since confessed, that when he saw his fine condition, he totally despaired of gaining the battle.

Cribb was altogether about eleven weeks under training, but he remained only nine weeks at Ury. Besides his regular exercise, he was occasionally employed in sparring at Stonehaven, where he gave lessons in the pugilistic art. He was not allowed much rest, but was constantly occupied in some active employment. He enjoyed good spirits, being all the time fully convinced that he would beat his antagonist. He was managed, however, with great address, and the result corresponded with the wishes of his friends.

It would be perhaps improper, while speaking of Cribb, to omit mentioning, that, during his residence in the north of Scotland, he conducted himself in all respects with much propriety. He shewed traits of a feeling, humane, and charitable disposition, on various occasions. While walking along Union-street, in Aberdeen, he was accosted by a woman apparently in great distress. Her story affected him, and the emotions of his heart became evident in the muscles of his face. He gave her all the silver he had in his pocket.—" God bless your Honour," said she, " *ye are surely not an ordinary man!*"—This circumstance is mentioned with the more pleasure, as it affords one instance at least, in opposition to the mistaken opinion, that professional pugilists are ferocious, and totally destitute of the better propensities of mankind. The illustrious Mr. Windham entertained juster sentiments of the pugilistic art, as evinced by the picture he presented to Mr. *Jackson* as a mark of his esteem. In one compartment, an *Italian*, darting his stiletto at his victim, is represented; and, in the other, the combat of two *Englishmen* in a ring. For this celebrated genius was always of opinion, that nothing tended more to preserve among the English peasantry those sentiments of good faith and honour which have ever distinguished them from the natives of Italy and Spain, than the frequent practice of fair and open Boxing.

So far Capt. Barclay; the circumstance of *the picture* just alluded to was mentioned, in detail, in a former volume of this Work.

PRACTICAL ADVICE

ON

TRAINING,

WITH A PARTICULAR VIEW TO

PUGILISTIC ENCOUNTERS.

MAIN OBJECTS OF TRAINING—BENEFICIAL IN EVERY
STATE OF SOCIETY. PREVIOUS HABITS OF MEN, HOW
VITIATED AND RECLAIMED: THE TRAINER; QUALIFICA-
TIONS, MANAGEMENT, DIFFICULTIES, FAITHFULNESS.
THE MAN: *his mind, disposition, confidence—passions.
Of the skin, and cleansing it—soap—drastic medicines
improper; habit of body, scorbutic appearances, bright
skin.* SWEATING *precautions, rubbing down, reducing
and bracing up.* Vomiting, *correctional remedies.*
EXERCISES, *incongenial, blown subjects—rubbing and
champooing* (note), *hours, air, and atmosphere; repasts,
meals, runs, breathings, rests, lodgings: Sparring.*
MEDICINES: *Purgatives, salts, aloes; physic-taking,
precautions; emetic tartar, double purpose. Erroneous
applications:* the oils;—*clothing, flannel, cotton.*
REGIMEN, *in particular cases; beer, ale,* home brewed,
*its age, wine; training upwards, tea and coffee, gruel;
meats, bread, and vegetables.* FIGHT AND WIN.

THE three great objects sought to be attained in
TRAINING, are *strength, activity,* and *wind;* or, in

other words, hardness of muscle, with the power to bear up against fatigue; pliability of limbs, and free, deep, and lasting respiration. These inspire a man with confidence, or pluck, and, if they do not *impart courage*, tend mainly to increase it. To be sure, several other desirable qualities accompany the improvement of those indispensable requisites of an accomplished ATHLETIC, that are no less valuable in every other state of society, and in every occupation: these are, 1st, general good health; 2dly, a clear understanding, and quick perception of the points at issue; 3dly, longevity.

Hence would arise a question, very proper to be solved, whether men who are so liable to be called upon to put forth their greatest exertions as pugilists are, had not better carry on, unceasingly, the *practice of training*, in some degree at least. Some men, we know, do observe certain points of good conduct regarding their mode of living, that may be considered a minor species of training, as regular exercise, early hours, abstemiousness as to spirits, the enjoyment of fresh air, &c. &c. Again, some men enjoy these benefits *naturally*, or are compelled to practise self-denial, and to take regular, and even violent exercise, by reason of certain circumstances. *Labour* ever keeps down the humours of the animal system, though a man may live never so grossly; if this be carried on in the open air, he becomes *ruddy*, though fleshless almost; and if he be born and bred up in a detached cottage, or a gipsy encampment, years of irregularity and lodging in close apartments will be required to spoil his wind. By establishing in our minds the course that is hurtful to our natures, we arrive at a knowledge of what is right, or beneficial. Then, let him who is tired of possessing good lungs, a free respiration, and the capacity of sudden exertion *without blowing*, take nice tit-bits for supper, close tightly the window of his chamber, and draw as many curtains as mistaken profusion has hung around his bed, and he shall soon feel a difficulty of breathing, a thick viscid spittle will proceed from his throat of a morning, accompanied by stinking breath, and a fulness about the neck, ears, and temples, such as will soon convince him, that, in pretending to *support nature*, he has been overloading her in the most sensible part.

But in the midst of this, or a much more vitiated course of life, how is such a man to be reclaimed, and brought into the observance of a mode of living, and the adoption of a plan more suited to his *engagements* in the Ring? Surely not of a sudden: the privation *at once* would affect his mind, his feelings, or his love of pleasure; for, if his whole mind does not go along with his bodily endeavours, vain will be the trainer's care: "Gently does it," is the phrase of the most habile of our city horse-breakers at first *going out;* and it applies the more forcibly to *man*, in the ratio that he possesseth more reasoning powers than *the horse.* The greater *its* viciousness, the more gentle be the first steps towards breaking in; if *the man* have given way to abasing debaucheries, his repugnance to training severely, and *at a push*, will be greater, and less likely to answer the end proposed, than if the new course of living here recommended be but a continuation or modification of his former mode of life; the one proceeds cordially hand in hand, as it were, the other meets old habits right in the teeth, and causes a jar. Let *the mind* be consulted from the first minute, let the trainer talk of nothing but how the victory is to be obtained, and *show his man* HOW: lead the soul along, and the body must follow; yet guard him against blind confidence, and tell him of his faults, for I have presumed all pugilists have their errors—mere boxers a great many, and that *the sparring* hath commenced already.

A good portion of judgment, then, in THE TRAINER, in discovering and managing his man's *temper*, is a necessary prelude to conducting the important business aright; and the qualifications of the trainer himself well deserves a moment's previous consideration in this place. That he be intelligent and firm in his manner, divested of prejudices and devoid of vulgar notions on the use (abuse) of medicines; that he be open to instruction, and willingly obedient to the rules laid down for his guidance, with *power* (of person or of *tongue*) to enforce them, are indispensable requisites in *the trainer*, as we term him, *who has the care* of the *expected pugilist*. That he is *faithful*, we presume to hope; the *backer*, or his agents or friends, must bring into play all their arts to discover this vital fact, this leading move upon the board, around which all the subsequent play is to centre—their bets, stakes, the laying on and edging off, all rest upon this main point of faithfulness in the trainer. He may even be tempted by some unknown agent to swerve from his duty, if he is not known to be attached to the well-doing of his man by some motive more binding than mere

payment comes to; indeed, he should be placed above
a bribe, or he himself be so closely watched in his
movements, as to render certain the detection of his
unfaithfulness, should such exist. We blush and feel
sorrow, while we strenuously insist on this vulnerable
point, which might render nugatory all our labours.
Our trainer's post is no *bed of roses;* he will find his
labour cut out by night and by day. He must never
quit his man, nor *show by example* that his precepts are
mere words, " thrown to the desert air," or that " what
is one man's meat is another man's poison:" if he
must *whet,* let him do so *on the sly;* but he shall neither smoke, snuff, nor *quid it,* while so engaged. He
must be careful of the *implements* of training, viz.
gloves, jackets, towels, and stockings in good number.
His *medicines* must be marked plainly, and always kept
locked up: of these more particulars hereafter. His
reports of the progress made to his employers (the
backers,) must be stern facts; if he tell falsehoods on
trivial matters, he is unfit to be trusted with those of
more importance. He must practise *self-denial,* but it
is hardly to be supposed he will carry this so far as *his
man* is compelled to do.

So much for the trainer.

No man engages to fight, unless he himself feels
convinced that he shall win; and, next to this moral
conviction of the event, will be his desire to *train
properly:* I would call it an *anxiety* to train, but for
my unwillingness to instil into his mind (if he have
any,) notions that may give it pain, or load it with
care. *The trainer* must proceed, during the first days
of his labour, to find out if his man be over thought-

ful, wanting of confidence, or despairing of victory;
and remove such obstacles to well training by inspiring
contrary notions.   If the person neglects any of the
rules, sets them at nought, or runs counter to the
plans laid down; if he be peevish at the watchfulness
of his trainer, and would be out of sight more than a
minute at a time, takes ill the severest part of the
sparring, *grunts* in his sleep, *breathes hard*, and with
difficulty, or, worse than all, *groans* in the night—
training will have proceeded but uselessly for such a
man; his *better part* is concerned in each of these indications, and if he does not *train off*, he will at least
show sallow, or with skin of various hues, or one part
more red than others.   He must lose his battle.   The
loins, the ribs, the pit of the stomach, should exhibit
the *same hue*, viz. greater paleness than when he showed
before training, and if with a tint of red, the more
vigour will be found in his system, more *strength*.

Of course the trainer would be the last person to
irritate *his man*, either by *treatment*, or by permitting
improprieties tending that way; he will therefore reduce imperceptibly the quantity of indulgences which
may have been habitual to him.   Spirits, porter, gross
feeding, stimulants, tobacco, onions, pepper, and *the
sexual intercourse*, must vanish, and be no more heard
of within the first week; let a choleric disposition be
smoothed down, suavity be taught, and none but
pleasant thoughts, fine walks, and cheerfulness prevail
during all this time.

Meanwhile, let the skin be well cleansed of its impurities by washing (in doors), in soapy water, *the entire body;* getting rid of the *first water* by repetitions

of that which is clean, since *soap* (or at least the *pot-asse* used in making it) contracts the *membranous* part of the system.* But we can get rid of the long adhering dirt and grease of perspiration by no other means; unless, instead, by the adoption of a clayey, soapy kind of earth, found at the edge of some rivers, and is goodly detersive, but not easily procured, or very desirable on other accounts.

Coarse linen cloths only must be used in rubbing down the body, and used with celerity too, until a glow of warmth is felt, particularly in winter time, and in coolish or damp weather A brisk walk should follow each washing, and a brisk rubbing of the body nearly all over with dry cloths follow each sweating, if produced by *the walk.* Washing of the body and feet is to be sedulously followed every day, though less might do in winter; but the cold bath (in-doors or sheltered) may be employed daily in summer to advantage, taking a *short walk* before going in, and *remaining in* but a short space at any one time. Neither body-washing, bathing, rubbing, nor walking, so as to produce perspiration, however, is to take place the day of taking purgative physic, at least not until its effects are gone completely off.

Physicing requires great attention : it has generally been carried on upon wrong principles, drastic or griping medicines being resorted to, and these repeated to a certain extent upon every man alike.

---

* The *skin* which lies under the outer skin (as seen in the animals killed for food), contracts by the use of soap, and I infer, so does that which pervades the whole system of solids.

Cases *may occur* when no physic whatever may be proper, *that is to say*, when *the man* is already in a *low state*, and requires feeding or training upwards to *begin with ;* as also, when his body is in that open state, or relaxed, that the exhibition of the usual physic (salts) is sure to *train off* such a subject.

In general, however, we find *the men*, when matched for pugilistic encounters, of full habit, flushed countenance, somewhat scorbutic, and a full pulse, sanguine, and usually slow, until nature has received one of those *fillips* which stimulate but to destroy. Sir Thomas Parkyns, an ancient trainer (of wrestlers), said, exultingly, " Give me your man of scurvical habit, before a rheumatic one, who is in general a milksop or tea-drinker ; there we have blood and strength to work upon ;" and he was right in the main, though our system of training at the present day tends principally to subdue every *appearance* of that sort upon the *surface*. So much is this the case, that *the condition* of the men is invariably estimated by the state of the skin on stripping. Indeed, our *men*, for the most part, strip as fair as women ; which is brought about by the system of training here laid down ; the perspiration, and the rubbing, and subdued manner of living, throwing off, or absorbing those numerous little scorbutic eruptions and pustules, in which hair is engendered. This *absorption* and *throwing off* is best brought about by perspiration, procured in the first place by walking exercise, with good rubbing down, emptying the bowels, and keeping them open. If, notwithstanding those reducings of his system, the person retain his *passions* to the full, with quick action of the

D

pulse, this is a sign of irritation— if he feel repugnance
at washing the body, these signs of great excitability
of inflammatory symptoms, tell forcibly he must be
bled and purged well, though he may and ought already to have taken one dose of a brisk cathartic.
Dull heavy eyes, with a great disposition to sleep,
starting in his sleep, or pricking of the skin, demand
that he should be blooded; opening physic should
ever follow bleeding.

Sweating profusely, for two or three days and nights
early in the second week, should be regulated by circumstances of more or less bodily strength, (hardness
of constitution,) by the quantity of loose flesh and inside fat. The latter is ascertained by his being soon
blown at running ; in sparring, the man's loose meat
may be perceived shaking on his sides, breasts, &c. ;
if it lie about the chops, it is seen he is blubber-headed,
and his head must be sweated particularly. As this
course will reduce his strength, he cannot extend his
exercises far while this is going on, without inconvenience, yet is not this circumstance to be considered
a *bad symptom.* Warm clothing and possets procure
these sweats by night, with the help of walking hard
or running by day. He must be ever rubbed down
after the runs, and changed of body-clothes often, in a
close shut up chamber : it is *the trunk* more than the
limbs that require this kind of attention. If he shiver
from within at any time, the *forcing sweats* must be
discontinued ; it is the sign of wanting stamnia, or
that the reducing part of the process has been carried
full far enough. The degree, or quantity, of reduction
a man may bear without harm, may also be ascer-

tained by loss of weight; if he lose 7lbs. the first day, six the second, and five (let us *suppose*) the third day, he should continue this evacuation longer; but if the *ratio* descend rapidly, from 9lbs. to 4lbs. to 2lbs. let it cease; the system of this latter man requires immediate bracing up.

Vomiting is a very proper and easy remedy for foul stomachs, as well as for getting rid of the crudities which do not go off by the use of purgatives. It must be resorted to in all cases where the pugilist feels nausea, hot foetid breath, or shows a white tongue of a morning.

Those are the *cleansings preliminary* to that regular course of living and exercise, which is the best calculated to improve a man's *stamina*, as before hinted at; and though they should cease with the second week or commencement of the third, yet it may be found necessary, *under circumstances*, to have recourse to *opening physic* long afterwards. The necessity for such will be found, if his digestion is obstructed—as may happen from *feeding* too fast, or from any other accidental debauch to which our frailties are liable; even *the port-wine* he may take has the effect of constipating many men, an effect that rather proves the strength of his bowels than otherwise. Such indications must, however, be removed gently; for which purpose the *blue pill* remedy (hereafter recommended) should be administered. At any rate, the person trained should produce one stool per day: if that be *in form*, or shape, and of a yellow tinge, he will have no occasion for physic; a healthful indication, that may be effected, perhaps, by varying the kind of food

(animal, vegetable, or liquid) from day to day—a
regimen which acts alteratively on most constitutions.
If the belly gets hard to the *touch* of his trainer's fists,
or a short cough comes on after running, the *blue pill*
is the remedy.

EXERCISE.—From the moment he is taken in hand,
the trainer should begin his exercises, unless *his man* be
lately come out of a debauch of spirituous liquors, or
is weak from recent disease, privation, or the sexual
intercourse. [Mind this all along.] Should he walk
down to the place of training, or run a hundred yards,
with inconvenience, coughing, or pain in his side, the
hams or back, the trainer seizes this opportunity of
operating upon his understanding, by insisting that
those obstacles shall vanish by a strict attention to his
instructions and example; and, indeed, so important
is this species of inculcation, that in default of his
man's complaining of pain any where, or of being
evidently blown, inquiries should be made on those
points, or the man be exercised hard until he do give
in. That part of his system which is so first affected,
while his body is yet unemptied, may be noted as the
weakest point about him; and that part, wherever
situate, should ever undergo rubbing with *the hand*
of a *morning,* and first receive attention with *the cloths*
whenever the person is rubbed down. This species of
rubbing, or friction, has been found a highly service-
able kind of treatment in all cases of rheumatic affec-
tions, or pains in the limbs ;* and should be followed

---

* In the Edinburgh Hospital, Dr. Hamilton prescribes to his
patients, " pommelling with the fists," very much resembling our

assiduously by the careful trainer, who would show his employers early indication of a fine skin—that just criterion of condition in man and horse. In fact, it is through the skin chiefly that the loose fat is to be evacuated which hangs about the kidneys and intestines, about the ribs, the heart, and the *skirt;* and as he will perspire more copiously when the bowels be full than after they have been emptied (on account of the intimate connection that exists between the bowels and skin), by sweating him, *in the first place,* that grease comes off through the skin, which would otherwise go off by the guts. Hereby the skin will be rendered soft and supple, which is a great advantage in those cases where the *subject trained* has a naturally *dry skin.*

Sweat he must and sweat he shall; and if his nature does not bend and *give out,* before *exercise* and *culinaries,* he must take *tartar emetic* or the *Dovers.*

Powders.—At this place I may not unaptly observe, that the "hot liquor," made of spices, which Captain Barclay recommends for *pedestrians,* hath not got my approbation as regards the pugilist.

Early hours, in respect to *training,* are marked by day-light, and dark-night only—the *dial* having no-

sparring bouts: 'it always afforded relief, he says, and sometimes effected the cure of chronic pains.' Our West-Indian planters employ the black servants in beating a slight *tattoo* of canes all over the body of *massa* and *missee,* until the pampered creatures are lulled asleep by the operation, and the absence of pain it occasions. In India and China, the operator carries still farther his attentions, by pulling and tweaking all the limbs and joints: it is there called *champooing,* and I admire the *champoo* so much, that I have adopted the word into English slang.

thing at all to do with these at any time of the year.
Night-fall should send the trainer and his man *in door,*
and, if it be summer time, *to bed;* dawn of day and
the clarion of chanticleer call him forth, if he be not
already abroad, as he would no doubt *desire to be,* in
case of sultry nights and a clear sky. Damp atmosphere and chilling winds must be guarded against,
and instead of running abroad, let *the pair* sparr at
home, grind the meal, rub down a horse, play at
nine-pins, leap-frog, or any manly exercise other than
riding, swinging, dancing. With these precautions,
the walk to the *bath* may be followed by *a trot* after
it, *i. e.* the extreme pace of *toe and heel* for a mile;
then *a rest,* as long as one might eat a dry biscuit or
stale crust ; and then *a run* home to breakfast, increasing in quickness daily, and perhaps in the length of
the whole excursion also, up to three or four miles.

His *first repast* being finished in ten or fifteen minutes, he will have more time for the rubbing down
which is to *follow* or to *precede* it, according as the
perspiration may subside *a little ; after breakfast,* being
the preferable time for this operation and the change
of linen, by throwing off the night shirt and its load
of impurities. In half an hour, he will be ready for
the morning walk, and *wish* for it, too, provided he
has been *reduced* sufficiently by the *profuse sweats.*
While toddling along, the conversation should be of
the pleasant sort, *viz.* concerning the coming battle,
his former encounters, how battles are won and lost,
and so on. All at once, or by pre-concert, *a mile run*
at nearly top speed is to be knocked up; next day,
two ; and soon after, three miles may be done: *then*

the bare suggestion of the propriety of being at home to meet *the patron*, or see some friend, or to have a lark with Jack, Tom, Dick, or Harry, or any other desirable talk (except of eating) will bring back *the pair* to head-quarters.   As he cools .he will require *suction* of some sort; but if he take too much tell him of it *soon after*, while

SPARRING; when he may be touched *hard* in the bread-basket.   Doubtless, he will *grunt* or belch then, but blame his greedy guts for the unseemly vulgarism. On this topic, though most important, I shall not *enlarge* here, except as an exercise, since it lies beyond my present purpose.

At no time, by day or by *night*, will the trainer omit to *sparr* his man, whenever occasion imposeth on them the task of keeping within-doors, particularly during very bad weather, and of winter-evenings.   On such occasions, and soon after meals, however lightly they may then play with each other, the heaviest combat of the day is to take place about noon, or one o'clock—indeed, at that precise hour when the *actual battle* is appointed to take place; and let the sham fight resemble, in earnestness and duration, the expected encounter.   Combining the peculiar tactiques of his opponent with his mannerism, language, accent, and vulgarism, the trainer is to assimilate the two things together, as near as may be: one hour, at least, should the fray continue, including one bout, or more, after the dinner is announced as *quite ready*. Whichever *gives-in* should be *chalked up* one.

DINNER being ended, *the sitting* should not exceed an hour, nor the whole *rest* above two; but both

occupying less time in winter than in summer; because, in one case, it is desirable that this part of the
day should wane, while *the pair* are sheltered from the
scorching sun; in the other, that they should take
advantage of its presence to conclude the day in
open air.

At night, nothing should be eaten after the last
exercise, and very little drank. The *going to bed*
need not be protracted; it should be gone about pleasantly, and take place in an airy chamber with chim-
ney, but without curtains of any sort; on a hard bed
(so called) with coarse *linen,* and not too much—for
he wants no *forced sweats* at this stage of his training.
Enough clothes, however, should be at hand, to put
on upon an emergency—as change of weather, &c.
When the night is fine and open, the window should,
in like manner, be opened wider than usual; for that
is a vulgar error which maintains the night air is un-
wholesome at any time, the danger lying mostly in
the manner of exposing to its influence the vulnerable
parts of the body—as the throat, chest, &c. But
much of the *management* of his trainer in this respect
must depend upon the former habits of *the man;* if he
has been *stove*-bred in the populous purlieus of a large
town, he may find the rare air of the country over-
power the compass of his lungs, if let in upon him at
once; be he a country-bred one, a cottager, or bush-
cove, the trainer must stand no repairs as to the free
admission of air. On windy nights a different course
should be pursued; and when the winds arise *after the
going to bed,* a contrivance may be adopted, by which
to arouse the party concerned: an ill-hung window,

or flapping casement, are among the most obvious means of accomplishing this end. When the trainer turns out of a morning, as well as at going to bed, he must watch the breathings of *his man:* if the air be confined and the chamber hot, his respiration will seem difficult—each *inspiration* scarcely perceptible, each *expiration* quick and troubled; then let him open the windows to a good extent, and in two or three minutes the beneficial effects thereof, on the sleeping subject, will be visible, in the full inflation of his lungs, in a kind of tasting and smacking of the lips, and a sleepy thankfulness for the boon conferred: he will stretch out his legs and arms, the breathing will now be carried on by the nostrils, and each inspiration and expiration be co-equal. A cold or standing sweat, which might hitherto be felt upon his face, by placing the back of the hand there, will subside, and be replaced by a genial heat. Let him slumber half an hour while inhaling this new supply of health.

Medicines are generally relied upon too much, and administered with a blind zeal that often does harm. For a very young man, simply opening the bowels once is fully sufficient to prepare him for the acquisition of strength, by regularity, air, and exercise. But from the drastic nature of the medicines usually administered by trainers, the body becomes greatly agitated, and recovers slowly the great commotion kicked up in his inside. Aloes and salts is the only *variety* of purgatives employed by them, and these

they prescribe without regard to the temperament of
the person so treated. Doubtless, if a man be of a cool
habit, a couple of Scot's pills, (Inglis's), given at *night,*
will empty the stomach and chief canal of the body;
if he be of a hot and sanguine temperament (and these
kind of customers prevail, three to one), the adminis-
tering an ounce of salts, given in *the morning,* will
achieve the same end—and little fault is to be found
with either kind of the doctor-trainer. But it not
unfrequently happens, that the drastic nature of these
medicines occasions the gut to *protrude,* particularly,
with elderly persons, which if not *repressed* by force, produces the disorder called *piles,* or, at least, a disposition towards contracting that disagreeable affection
during life. Besides the evil just noticed, the *repetition*
of those two medicines *fail to operate as at first.*

To avoid those disadvantages, let the person requiring
simply opening medicine, take, at going to bed, a small
blue pill,* about the size of a grey pea ; this will produce
one stool ; take the pill a little larger and two or more
stools may come, proportioned to the quantity of offensive matter that lurks in the bowels. In those other cases,
where a *thorough cleansing* is required—a *small blue pill,*

---

* The *blue pill* here prescribed is made (according to College Law)
upon the same principle of *strength* every where; but its chiefest
recommendation lying in the *minuteness* and care with which the
particles of mineral are distributed over the *mass,* that excellence
is to be found in the preparation of Apothecary's Hall, where *a
machine* performs the labour of *mixing,* at which kind of toil the
strongest arm will tire too soon. It were best purchased at the
said *hall,* " in the *mass,*" per ounce ; but be careful not to use too
much at any one time.

taken at night, and *half an ounce* of salts in the morning, will effect that end. Let the dose be much diluted, and taken *lukewarm.*

On the day that this medicine is operating, it would be highly improper to run him a heat as usual, though he should *move about,* and the celerity of his move-ments be precisely adverse to the motion of his physic. Neither should he eat of the same kind, or so much solid food as usual, notwithstanding the *access of appetite* which ever follows physic-taking — especi-ally in very strong healthy persons, those above all others whom such a course would harm most. For whatever he now takes is quickly converted into blood (the pure stream of life), and that most rapidly.

> " The blood, the fountain whence the spirits flow,
> The generous stream that waters every part,
> ·And motion, vigour, and warm life conveys
> To every particle that moves or lives."

But principally towards the head, the neck, the jugu-lar, is the *new blood* rapidly conveyed that is so rapidly concocted; and if, in the contest which fol-lows, this particular man is battered about the *upper-works,* he goes off to *dorse,* and loses his battle, blunt, and character.*

Emetic tartar made into small doses will excite to vomiting, and is preferable to *ipecacuhana;* two such doses of the tartar, taken at once, operate *not as an emetic does,* but excite to *sweating,* and may be used

---

* Many are the men who became *deaf to time* latterly on this account. See note to page iv.

instead of the *treacle-posset* or the "hot liquor" before recommended, or alternately therewith, but not both at the same time.

Dover's powders, in the quantity of 10 grains, will sweat a *little one*, 12 for a stronger man, and 15 grains for a *big one*.

Emetic tartar.—From 1 to 3 grains will cause a man to vomit according to the quantity of offensive matter to be ejected; if this be little or none, perspiration will ensue;—6 grains of this incomparable medicine are a sure *sweat*, but no vomit, and will open the bowels, too, when given in a larger dose; which latter course I would not *recommend*.   But

The blue pill, of the size of a pea (as aforesaid), contains above 1½ grains, is the proper and readiest alterative, as it forms also a neat adjunct to salts, &c. rendering a lesser quantity of this drastic medicine fully sufficient for a brisk cathartic.

———

Considerable error prevails among the trainers on several points, besides those before noticed, viz. the use of *the oils* (of the farriers) for stiff-jointed subjects,* and the application of *opodeldoc* to a joint or other part where pain is felt. Both are injurious; the first mentioned *madly so*. Opodeldoc being made of

———

* This horrid mixture, alike incongenial to man and horse, was employed in training Bob Gregson, whose activity was estimated low; at least something like the oil (or with an addition thereto), which stunk the house over, was applied in that particular case of training upon mistaken principles. Whatever difference of opinion may exist regarding opodeldoc, none can doubt as to those oils.

soap, spirits of wine, and camphor, the reader will anticipate that (after what has been said) we could not coincide with the first-mentioned ingredient; and as to the effects of spirits of wine upon the ligaments and tendons, most persons know, perhaps *from expe-rience*, that it greatly contracts those (so called) leaders. No: the remedy for pained limbs or stiff-joints, which arise from over exercise, or local weak-ness, is sweet oil and camphor *well rubbed* over the part. Moreover, the chemists make up an *elegant preparation* hereof, by first dissolving the gum in one-eighth its weight of spirit (its proper *menstruum*, as they say), and then mixing it well with the oil: this may be used to advantage.

To some trainers it may be a recommendation, to know that the mixture just described was that nearly which was used by the ancients; to me, I own, it brings some weight on that account, fond as I am of antiquity in faces, fashions, families, and practices, until either is proved false by demonstration.

"Let us never meet an old friend with a new face."

Another mistaken notion is the clothing in *flannel, next the skin*, men of warm temperament, after they have ceased to reduce their weight; the pores being hereby kept inordinately open, the discharge by this secondary evacuation becomes too much for its powers, for it is thereby relaxed, (as the bowels sometimes are,) and retains not enough of its oily quality to keep the skin supple. A constant disposition to *catch cold* is the consequence of this mistake; and after wearing it awhile, such a man can almost as soon part with

the skin off his back as his flannel waistcoat. It has
become second only to nature; yet it is a very filthy
habit; with many persons it is offensive, and liable to
engender cutaneous diseases in some habits, vermin
in others.

> Give me the presence of a donneken drag,
> Before such a rip drest in dark flannel rag.

Cotton shirts—cotton sheets—cotton napkins, are
equally to be eschewed: I had very nearly included
in the proscription cotton stockings and drawers—but
that our observations apply mostly to *the carcase*,
rather than the *limbs*.

In pursuing the foregoing train of remarks and observations, I have avoided the repetition of whatever
appears applicable to *our purpose* in Captain Barclay's
method, to which the *studious reader* will please to
refer as to other particulars that may be equally applicable to pugilistic as to pedestrian exercises. I might
here add, too, without affecting more appearance of
modesty than belongs to me, that, after all we can say
upon paper, a good deal must yet be left to the trainer's
own judgment and experience, and the particular case
of each individual *man* that may be confided to his
care. Yet will he be thankful, no doubt, for a few
items of information on some minor points connected
with this great and vital (though *preliminary*) part of
the momentous contest.

Then, as to victuals and drink, and the manner and
times of refreshing, no greater variety of opinions and
practices exist on any part of the subject now under
consideration, and each of the argumentators may

have been in the right regarding certain *individuals* who may have been placed under his care; but I deny the *general application* of such doctrines to *all men*: what, because Joe Ward's *men* succeeded after taking his *three threes*, as mentioned above (p. iii), or Dan. Mendoza's protegée, Dutch Sam, trained upon gin, are we, at this improved state of science, to allow of the like insane courses? So true is the adage (and such *saws* are sometimes of service), " What is one man's meat may prove another's poison." All depends upon previous habits, and he who would lead another out of bad into good ones, must go about his work gently, that he may succeed more certainly. A good Spanish proverb has it, " Set out on your journey *softly*, that you may come home *safely*," or *poco poco*.

Beer has been interdicted *in toto* by many trainers, and if the injunction were laid against London-brewed beer (porter and ale), let it stand; the most stimulating seeds and extracts that can be devised by the brewers' druggists (unenviable trade), enter into our *London beverage*. That the *town's* people do not die *in heaps* is no argument for the continuance of deleterious admixtures, for many *do die* in the seasoning, or live with limbs paralyzed, or fall sick and nauseate all things; but, when our ATHLETIC hath been cleansed out of every offensive matter, and the *vessels*—whose office it is to take up the *next coming* food and drink that is to nourish, and succour, and harden the fles'', and give new life and vigour to the blood—lie open, athirst to suck up all that comes, is he, at such a critical time in fit state, to swallow even *suspected nourriture*, because a few thousands have taken it, and happene l to escape with impunity, whilst only a few hundreds fell victims in death, or, by loss of limb and injured stamina, drag out a life of misery? Yet, slow poison though it be, I would not advise that the man, who is just taken into training should be *denied porter altogether*, though he should be cut off to one half his *usual quantity* the first day; and in the course of a fortnight, if he cannot do without, be allowed only a pint a day, taken along with his animal food (at twice), and *always stale*, bottled stout being the next best malt liquor to the kind which alone we would *recommend*. This should be *home-brewed beer*, made of hops, malt, and water, of the strength three bushels to the barrel (or thereabouts), with hops enough to keep it six months at least; *double that age*, however, would answer our purpose better, but in no case should the beer be drank to the ordinary quantity he has been in the habit of taking. Our man may avoid taking the beer of two *different breweries* on the *same day ;* for the *variety* of proportions and kinds of ingredient used, (if nought worse.) will kick up a combustion in his guts. Such were among the occasions when the celebrated *Dick Suet,* of facetious memory, would sing out—

> " My great guts and my small,
>   They cry out, ' one and all,'
>   Hark away ! altogether, my brave boys.
>   Hark, hark away !"

Wine.—In case he gets such malt liquor as is just described, he will require but little *wine*. This should be *port*, drank diluted in water that has been boiled, and got cool again. Port wine is a main assistant in

Training upwards a man who has been too much reduced. If such an one take his dinner of roast or broiled meats, using salt, and drink a glass of wine at two or three sups in the intervals, he will *make blood* (i. e. increase its quantity, and) of a good quality, faster than by any other means we know of. The sick and valetudinary cannot take this method, but as soon as they become *convalescent,* let them adopt it in a smaller degree; but exercise should *precede* and *follow* such a meal—up to the pitch of his strength *before* dinner, *long* but slow *after* dinner. He may then drink tea, by way of diluent; and, as he acquires strength, increase his potion of wine to *two* glasses— no more.

Tea, however, nor *coffee,* are the adjunct liquids I would recommend, though neither is to be debarred *him altogether* who has been habituated to the use of such, particularly after taking a solid and frugal dinner. Instead of those

Catlapperies for the breakfast, let water-gruel be taken; than gruel, well made, there is not, in the whole dispensatory, a better preventive of diseases, or more able assistant in the recovery of patients, or more certain strengthener of man in health. Oatmeal, and water, and salt, are the only ingredients of gruel; put into it *any further thing,* and it ceases to be *gruel.* Smoothness, thinness, and slowness in the preparation, are indispensable requisites for my men; at any hour of the day or night, hot, cold, or lukewarm, at exercise or idling—indeed, *asleep* or *awake*—let no man who seeks health deny himself all-potent *water-gruel*—iron prince of health and strength!

E

Of meats, Captain Barclay's *method* has said enough, as also where he negatived soups and broths; but we may as well observe, that the flesh of *full grown* animals is ever preferable to that of *young ones,* and those which are *naturally* fed—on grass, &c.—to those they pamper with grease and stimulants. All *oily messes,* melted butter, and buttered toast, and gravies, are to be eschewed; the meats taken next, after physicking and purging medicines have laid open the *lacteals,* should be dressed more than ordinary, i. e. until the redness all disappears; it should *then consist of boiled meat,* and mutton, in every case, is the best flesh article a man can line his paunch withal—nutritious and easy of digestion, and less liable to be pampered for *the butcher's knife* than beef; we have ever preferred mutton for those reasons. *Yellow*-flesh meat may be avoided: the *gall* of sadness has run over, and though we taste nought, yet is it present. Of *pork* eat little; *bacon* none. After all is said and done, probably, we may add, that exercise and hard work will digest *any food whatever;* but take this into consideration, at the same time, that such stomachs as can achieve this must have been unused to the debauches of great towns. Dr. Armstrong says,—

> Nothing so foreign but th' *athletic man*
> Can labour into blood: the hungry meal
> Alone he fears, or aliments too thin.
> The languid stomach curses ever the pure
> Delicious fat, and all the race of oil:
> For more the oily aliments relax
> Its already feeble *tone.*

Bread place we the last of *alimentary* substances, to

show that total disregard of the *old saw*, as to its being "the staff of life," which such a vulgar error deserves. The phrase may do very well in Cockneyshire, where the *thorough-breds*, the Cheapside people and Clerkenwellers, deride *the potatoe* (prince of esculents!) but, no aphorism can be more unhappy, as regards London-made bread, the which, instead of being "the *staff* of life," may more appositely be re-baptized "the *club* of death," whereby many a cockney gets *knocked down*. *Alum*, which keeps the loaf together, and *the stuff* which makes it mount up so high in the oven with *slack baking*, have, together, the effect of *contracting* the whole alimentary canal through which the sophistication passes, and no doubt sometimes closeth it up entirely, and terminates life. I know it has occasioned *disease*, causing slow death. Remarks those which are not thrown out in the latitude of general censure, but after a long, and laborious, and painful investigation, in which *this pen* was engaged, and the results whereof are already before the public. ATHLETICS should eat their bread *a day old*, at least, and the trainer should take care to have *dry biscuit* always at hand; a small bit taken as soon as the eyes open in the morning is an excellent absorbent of the accumulated mucus of the mouth, throat, and windpipe. And remember,—

The opening of the eyes,
Is the signal to arise.

The potatoe is that thing which best corrects the evil effects of *London-made bread*, as it doth also absorb the oleaginous parts of the animal food; and whether our TRAINER and his MAN can or cannot procure

country-made bread, they may, in either case, take
good dry mealy potatoes with their meats, or *mashed
potatoes* and milk alone (on *physic* days, &c.) ; nor will
they hereby find inconvenience in the bowels, as to
flatulency, which was so much depreciated by the
trainers of the old school. Take no other *vegetable*,
however, nor of these an inordinate quantity.

Now, SIR, GO, FIGHT YOUR MAN, AND SEE YOU
WIN, OR SEE NOT MY FACE AGAIN.

On this very interesting subject, the ingenious Mr.
Robert Breakwindow, the poetical faunist, having put
a *few lines* into the mouth of Randall's trainer, in the
form of a *chaunt*, I feel no hesitation in giving them a
place here, by way of *finish* :—

THE TRAINER'S RONDO.

UP in the morning, near the pump-handle,
There I stand, Jack, with a heart full of glee;
　　Come, open each peeper,
　　You feather-bed sleeper,
And up in the morning, Jack Randall, with me.
Though in the Fives Court, you can *fib it* and *sparr it*,
　And prove of neat hits both a giver and taker ;
Yet 'tis morn's early rising, and beef steaks, and claret,
　Will string up your nerves, to *wap* Martin, the Baker.
　　　　　Then up in the morning, &c. &c.

Drawn by I.R. Cruikshank.

A SPARRING MATCH AT THE FIVES COURT.

Published April 14th 1821, by George Smeeton, 139, St. Martins Lane.

Etched by G. Cruikshank.

BOXIANA.

An Englishman will take his part,
With courage *prime,* and noble heart;
Either forgive, or resent offence—
And *bang-up* in his own defence.
No sword or dagger—nor deadly list—
And rise or fall but by his *fist!*
The battle's o'er—all made amends,
By shaking hands, becoming friends.

JOHN BULL.

CURSORY REMARKS ON THE ORIGIN, RISE, AND PROGRESS, OF PUGILISM IN ENGLAND.

To whom we are indebted for the first principles of BOXING is completely uncertain, it appearing that few, if any, of our learned Antiquarians, by not possessing a taste for the *Fancy,** have felt themselves more interested in endeavouring to ascertain the authenticity of an old monument or ancient coin than that of investigating into the animated traits of Pugilism; darkness, of course, clouds it origin: and whether our first parent, ADAM, had any pretensions to this art, is also involved in too great obscurity, at this remote period, for us to

---

* As many of our readers may not be *flash* to the above term, it perhaps becomes necessary to state, that it simply means, any person who is fond of a particular amusement, or closely attached to some subject: a *lively* instance fortunately presents itself in illustrating the phrase beyond all doubt—as the old woman observed, when she kissed her cat, that it was—" *her fancy!*"

No. I.   B

penetrate into with any possibility of success. It therefore must remain enveloped—for it would be sheer
gammon indeed, were we to get our readers *into a string*,
by swelling out the half of BOXIANA in striving to
prove, from musty records and mouldy papers, to whom
were entitled the honours of being denominated—ITS
FIRST PROFESSORS. We disdain such subterfuge,
firmness is our motto—and upon a *striking* subject, like
the present, we shall decide for ourselves; perfectly
coinciding in the deliberate opinion lately delivered by
a distinguished law chief, in the most grave and solemn
assembly in the kingdom, that precedents often betray*
ignorance, however great the celebrity their authors
might have acquired.

That precedent, so superior to all others upon every
occasion, we shall refer to in this instance—NATURE!
and to whom a more interesting foundation cannot be
traced, that we owe the trait of BOXING—wounded *feelings* brought manly *resentment* to its aid—and *coolness*,
checking fiery passion and rage, reduced it to a perfect
science. Let hyper-critics " grin a horrid, ghastly
smile!"—let the fastidious sneer and shrug up their
shoulders with contempt—but never let Britons be
ashamed of science;—yes, A SCIENCE that not only
adds generosity to their disposition—humanity to their
conduct—but courage to their national character. A

---

* Friday, July 17, 1812.—When BLACKSTONE, the author of those
celebrated " Commentaries," which have stood the test for so many
years, and decided so many knotty points, has been deemed *ignorant*,
our researches to boast an authority after this assertion would be mere
alum.

country where the stiletto is not known—where trifling quarrels do not produce assassination, and where revenge is not finished by murder. Boxing removes these dreadful calamities; a contest is soon decided, and scarcely ever the frame sustains any material injury.

It is far from our intention, by way of apology, to prove that Pugilism is of an ancient date in reference to the Greeks and Romans, and that it was sanctioned by these distinguished nations, in their public sports, and in the education of youth, to manifest its utility in strengthening the body, dissipating all fear, and infusing a manly courage into the system. The gladiatorial display of the Romans we admire not—nor any public exhibitions tending to degrade mankind; but the manly art of Boxing has infused that true heroic courage, blended with humanity, into the hearts of Britons, which have made them so renowned, terrific, and triumphant, in all parts of the world.

We shall, therefore, view it as a national propensity, independent of every other consideration; and that Pugilism is in perfect unison with the feelings of Englishmen, references to dates, if necessary, will bear us out. Distinction of rank is of little importance when an offence has been given, and in the impulse of the moment, a PRINCE has forgot his royalty, by turning out to box, to prevent the imputation of a coward—a DUKE, his consequence in life—and a BISHOP, the sanctity of his cloth; displaying those strong and *national* traits so congenial to the soil of liberty.

Refinement of character has been the object of many eminent writers—and public stage-fighting has, perhaps, in many instances, received just and merited censure,

under an alarm that our feelings might become callous,
and acts of brutality be viewed with indifference from
the witnessing of those prize combats. We do not
war with these writers for their opinions, trusting they
have been promulgated for the general good—but we
are equally afraid, in turn, that the English character
may get too *refined,* and the *thorough-bred* bull-dog
degenerate into the *whining* puppy. Lord CHESTER-
FIELD, with his superior refinement, graces, and politeness, did more real injury to the cause of morality than
all the public exhibitions of boxing have done, from
the renowned days of *Broughton,* down to the milling
æra of *Cribb!*

The punishing *Coves* may, from their want of education, in some instances, disgust, by bad language and
inebriety of conduct—but this is not generally the case;
for, though they are not *down* to the " Sublime and
Beautiful," or *up* to the " Diversions of Purley," yet
they are not so completely *obscured* as to be destitute of
the common courtesy due to society; and by their intercourse with several of the *Upper-Customers* of the
community, the manners of many of them, from their
experience and observation, have become softened into
the mild and agreeable companion, and only appear
terrible—in battle.

The fastidious writer, who too often from superficial
observation and a pretended delicacy of feeling, in not
visiting the *milling pannies,* where characters are to be
drawn from real life, and human nature is developed in
a variety of shapes, exhibits deformed pictures instead
of faithful likenesses; and, inflated with his vanity, fine
sentiments, and crude opinions, endeavours to impose

upon the world by an assumed knowledge, as a criterion
for mankind to act upon, respecting this manly science;
condemns unseen, traduces unknown, and holds up to
satire, unauthenticated portraits, which, upon examination, betrays the most gross ignorance, and turns into
ridicule, against himself, those satiric efforts, which
otherwise might prove of advantage to the world at
large, in being founded on truth. FIELDING's *Tom
Jones* and SMOLLETT's *Lieutenant Bowling* will never
die, but gain length of years by every fresh perusal;—
the superior traits of GEORGE MORLAND on the canvas
can never be effaced but by the hand of unrelentless
Time ;—nor the exquisite touches of a WILKIE be forgotten, while taste and sound judgement hold their
empire.

No men are subject more to the caprice or changes of
fortune than the pugilists ; *victory* brings them fame,
riches, and patrons; their bruises are not heeded in the
smiles of success; and, basking in the sunshine of prosperity, their lives pass on pleasantly, till *defeat* comes
and reverses the scene : covered with aches and pains,
distressed in mind and body, assailed y poverty,
wretchedness, and misery,—friends forsake them—their
towering fame expired—their characters suspected by
losing—and no longer the " *plaything of fashion !* "*

* The *swell* tinman, HOOPER, was one of those " *playthings* " of the
great ; and, sheltered under the wings of nobility, he became pampered,
insolent, and mischievous. His courage was undoubted, and though his
frame was but small, it contained the heart of a lion; big men struck no
terror to his feelings, and he opposed them with all the hardihood of
an equal competitor, determined to conquer, without reflecting on the
inequality of his own make ; and, at one time, was considered, as to size,

they fly to inebriation for relief, and a premature end puts a period to their misfortunes.

It is one of the greatest failings of human nature, incident to most men in every station of society, that, while in prosperity, and a long run of good luck, few are provident enough to provide against a rainy day ; much more from those who are in a line of life where a great deal depends upon *chance,* and an unlucky throw may reduce them considerably worse than their first outset in life; a memorable instance is to be remarked toward strengthening this argument, respecting the late *Tom Johnson,* of pugilistic celebrity, who, by his extraordinary success in fighting, it is said, had realised the astonishing sum of nearly £5,000 ; and might, after contending for the championship of England, in about

---

one of the best *" bits of stuff "* in the kingdom. The late Lord BARRYMORE, whose eccentricities would fill a volume, was his patron ; and at whose country seat he principally dwelt.—Here poor HOOPER lost himself; the station was too high for his mind, and he fancied himself a great man. His Lordship was fond of *larking,* and whenever he could not *come through the piece* in style, HOOPER appeared as his bully— whose name overawed, and, many time, he has saved his patron a good *milling.* HOOPER's insolence at length became intolerable; and, unfortunately, for a *prime squad of spunging coves,* that stuck to his Lordship like so many leeches, he began to reform, or more properly speaking, he was *bowled out,* and these enviable characters were *turned up!* HOOPER soon afterwards became wretched—disease overtook him, and repeated intoxication brought him to the brink of the grave ; and one evening, a few years since, he was found insensible on the step of a door in St. Giles's, and conveyed to the watch-house; and, on inquiring who he was, he could very faintly articulate, *" Hoop—Hoop ;"* but, being recognized as the miserable remnant of that once powerful pugilistic hero, he was humanely taken to the workhouse, where he immediately expired !

sixteen fights, have retired from the scene of " battles
bravely fought and hardly won," into the vale of ease, become respectable, and have ended his days in peace and
happiness. But by want of conduct he lost his property
and his home; *necessity* compelled him to fight another
battle; and, flattered that the *chance* was still in his favour, whereby he might recruit his exhausted finances,
he entered the field with all the gaiety of an adventurer;
but, alas! capricious Fortune turned her back upon him,
and he, *(Tom Johnson,)* the hero of the tale, who had always been borne off upon the shoulders of his friends,
amid the shouts of victory, was now doomed, O dire reverse! by the desperate conflict he sustained, to GIVE IN
—beat almost lifeless; the laurel torn from his veteran
brow, and death the ultimate consequence, from the
severe blows he had received. *Tom's* reputation being
gone as a pugilist in London, he strolled from race-
grounds to fairs, endeavouring to *pick up a crust* as a
gambler, but that proving a *queer lay,* he resorted to
teaching the art of defence in Ireland, where he made
his grand exit; proving the absolute necessity to men
in such an uncertain way of life, before they are completely *done up,* of " making hay while the sun shines."

   BOXING, at any rate, has been patronized for upwards
of seventy years in England; and among its numerous
leaders several of the Blood Royal have stood conspicuous towards its support, independent of Dukes, Lords,
Honourables, &c. &c. Besides, at one period, having an
amphitheatre established, the *amusements* of which were
publicly advertised whenever they took place, and money paid for admission; under the direction of a regular
manager, a variety of scenes of course were produced,

both of the serious and comic cast; and a number of *striking* situations witnessed from the celebrity of the actors in the drama ; and, if the language did not rise to the sublimity of Shakspeare, or the bards of old, in making an impression upon the finer sympathies of the mind, the auditors, doubtless, were frequently awakened by the ballet of action, to *touches* of the most *feeling* sort. And from the best authorities that can be obtained, it appears that the audiences *then* were not only extremely respectable, but highly delighted with the entertainments catered for them : the theatre, in general, was crowded upon these occasions, and the bill of fare given out for the next performance with all the regularity of the most refined place of amusement.

But what of that! have not our classic theatres, within the last five-and-twenty years, possessing all the advantages of authors the most exalted and refined ; actors the most inimitable and chaste, either to extort the tear or provoke the laugh ; music the most ravishing ; scenes and decorations, in point of magnificence and splendor, unparalleled—invited PUGILISM to their boards, and the names of some of the first-rate boxers enriched their play-bills ; and the audiences (of whom no doubt can attach to their respectability) testified their approbation by loud plaudits, at the liberality of the managers in thus publicly displaying the principles of Pugilism? And it is mentioned upon good authority, that the most fashionable daily newspaper of that period, under the direction of an *amateur* captain, had a rapid increase of sale, in respect to its containing the genuine correspondence between those celebrated heroes of the fist—*Humphries* and *Mendoza.*

In 1791, Pugilism was in such high repute, and so strongly patronised, that *Dan Mendoza* was induced to open the small theatre, at the Lyceum, in the Strand, for the express purpose of public exhibitions of sparring; and, in his managerial capacity, assured the public, by a very neat and appropriate address, that the manly art of boxing would be displayed, divested of all ferocity, rendered equally as neat and elegant as fencing, perfectly as useful, and might be as gracefully acquired. Several imitations would be given of celebrated ancient and modern pugilists; eminent performers were engaged to portray the science; and the whole conducted with the utmost propriety and decorum, that the female part of the creation might attend, without their feelings being infringed upon, or experiencing any unpleasant sensations.

About this period, a similar exhibition was opened, near the Haymarket, under the guidance of a Frenchman, who undertook to prove that *science*, in competition with *strength*, was of no avail; but *John Bull* soon took the *conceit* out of him, as he had done many more of his countrymen, in more formidable contests than that of *sparring*, by exposing his *gasconade*. The Frenchman very soon got *milled*, and, shortly afterwards, *mizzled*; so that the science received but little interruption from *his* lectures on the gymnastic art.

In illustration of *Boxing* being a national and important feature of the English people, we relate the following anecdote of an illustrious personage:—

The late Lord B—— (the firm of that *elegant* family quartette, knowingly styled, Newgate, Hellgate, Cripplegate, and Billingsgate), about the year 1789, was in

Vol. 1.   c

the very zenith of his fun, frolic, and *lark-ery;* and, if
we *can believe* his Lordship's panegyrist,* he was, notwithstanding his volatile propensities, a man of observation and talent; and *correct* in music, if nothing else.
No *milling* match of note his Lordship ever missed, but
he was always conspicuous in the scene; and the lessons
he had received, under the first-rate professors of the art,
rendered him no mean adept in the science. Though he
performed in public on the classic stage, we never
heard that he had ever sported his *Corinthian canvas* as a
pugilist in the open ring; but was fond of kicking up a
row, and not afraid to fight his way out of it. He was a
public character in the extreme at Brighton : and his
eccentricities at that watering-place will not easily be
forgotten. In one of his wild freaks, unfortunately, he
horse-whipped from his phaeton a respectable perfumer,
(a Mr. Donadieu, who was in a gig,) for not getting
out of his way : his Lordship's thorough-bred cattle soon
distanced the *man of scent,* before he could well recover from his surprise; but the next morning, Mr. D.
perceiving Lord B——upon the Steine, in company
with several sporting men, pugilists, &c. went up to
him and remonstrated on the ill-usage he had received
upon the preceding day, when his Lordship, instead of
redressing, set about *milling* him for his insolence ; but
the perfumer being an Englishman, and not feeling dismayed by the superior rank of his antagonist, and having
a good *pluck,* quickly returned the *favour* with interest;
his Lordship soon saw he was on a *wrong scent*; that
not only his *fame* as a pugilist was at stake, but his honour, as a peer, in danger of being wounded, and began

---

* The *disinterested* Anthony Pasquin.

to take an unfair advantage, when the P—— of W——
who had witnessed the whole transaction from a window
at the Pavilion, exclaimed, with all the native characteristic of a Briton, "*Damme, B——, fight like a man!*"

DUELLING—however honourable and proper such a
mode of settling differences may be considered by the
CORINTHIAN PILLARS OF THE STATE, (when the laws
are not applied to for redress,) we confess, that we are
no advocates for such a *genteel* system; notwithstanding
cowardice must be despised, and urge that no man ought
to put up with a gross insult or unprovoked injury pusillanimously. The laws of honour, doubtless, are of so
fine and delicate a texture, that they are not to be
grasped at by every rough hand, nor to be referred to
upon all occasions; but the *ridiculous appeals* which
have been made, in too many instances, to those sa-
cred laws, forcibly bring to recollection, that, in such
cases, it is "a custom more honoured in the breach
than the observance."

MIRABEAU (brother of the great French senator)
was *distinguished* for his numerous debaucheries and
amours, a celebrated duellist, and was denominated a
MAN OF HONOUR! Seducing the wives and daughters
of his friends, and then fighting their fathers and hus-
bands, by way of giving *satisfaction,* as it is termed, was
the peculiar trait of this most *honourable* character! It
has been said of him, that, in the course of his debauched
career, he had fought upwards of one hundred and twenty duels, in which several worthy members of society
were wounded, and some killed at his hands. He was a
systematic dueller, and had acquired such accuracy in
firing at various marks, independent of the great prac-

tice he had had in public life, that his fame over-awed
many from entering the lists with him, and quietly put
up with their injuries, in preference to losing their lives.
What *chance* could the father or husband have, whose
feelings were wounded to the quick, and their minds
agitated with resentment against the destroyer of their
peace—*compared* with a cold-blooded villain, who
could take as deliberate an aim at a human being as if
firing at a mark or stone? With such characters,
human nature becomes degraded in placing itself upon
a *level* with infamy—and the laws only should *meet*
them and decide upon *their* honour!

The memorable instances, but a few years since, in
that of Colonel MACNAMARA's losing his life concerning the very *trifling* circumstance of his dog being
struck, who had annoyed a passenger in the street, and
Lord CAMELFORD's vindication of a fashionable *prosti-
tute*, have been so perfectly ridiculous in their onsets,
and so remarkably serious in their termination, as to
preclude any further comment.

Man, from the imperfections of his nature, is liable
to quarrel, and to give or receive insults in his journey
through life—how necessary, then, does it appear that he
should be able to defend himself—and that in a way
which will bear reflection. The fastidious, we have little
doubt, will smile at the phrase—REFLECTION; but how
much misery and wretchedness might have been spared
by that reflection, of the dreadful consequences likely to
arise from DUELLING—in making their wives premature
and unprovided widows; their children fatherless and
distressed; and themselves snatched away in a moment,
" with all their imperfections on their heads," and re-

conciliation put out of the question. If it were possible to take a peep into the *penetralia* of those persons who decide quarrels after this *genteel* mode, we rather apprehend that, in deciding with truth, something like *fear* might be perceived at the bottom, if all-powerful honour did not prevent its having a resting place!

Where, *then*, is the relative, however high in pride and pomp, on viewing the father, husband, or brother, killed in a duel—but what would rather that they should have had recourse to the manly defence of BOXING, than the deadly weapons of sword and ball; from which a bloody nose, or black eye, might have been the only consequences to themselves and their families, and neither in their feelings or their circumstances been injured; reconciliation with their antagonists—faults mutually acknowledged—and, perhaps, become inseparable friends ever afterwards?

The life of an individual is a loss to the state, from the peer to the peasant; and it becomes the duty of every good citizen to prevent them from being sported with wantonly.

We have long witnessed the good effects of this manly spirit in England, and we trust it will never be extinguished. Prejudice does much in favour of our native soil; but, upon a dispassionate review of those countries where pugilism is unknown, we find that upon the most trifling misunderstanding, the life of the individual is in danger. In Holland, the long knife decides too frequently; scarcely any person in Italy is without the stiletto; and France and Germany are not particular in using stones, sticks, &c. to gratify revenge; but, in England, the FIST only is used, where malice is not suffered to engender and poison the composition, and induce the inhabitants to the commission of deeds which their souls abhor and shudder at—but an immediate appeal to Boxing—the by-standers make a ring, and where no unfair advantages is suffered to be taken of each other. The fight done, the hand is given, in token of peace; resentment vanishes; and the cause generally buried in oblivion. This generous mode of conduct is not owing to any particular rule laid down by education—it is an inherent principle—the impulse of the moment—acted upon by the most ignorant and inferior ranks of the people. Foreigners may sneer at us for our rudeness of customs and barbarity of manners; but, we trust that Englishmen will ever wish to be admired more for their genuine honesty and rough sincerity than for an assumed and affected *politeness.*

It has been attempted by some writers to prove that Boxing did not originate in Great Britain; but in recurring to the times of the immortal Alfred, according to ancient authorities, we shall find, that *wrestling* and *boxing* formed a part of the manual exercise of the soldiers at that distant period. The ancient Britons have always been characterised as a manly, strong, and robust race of people, inured to hardship and fatigue, and, by the exercise of those manly sports, acquired that peculiar *strength of arm,* which rendered them so decisive in their warlike combats.

That athletic exercises have not been performed in foreign countries at various times by particular individuals, it is not our intention to deny; but, in speaking generally, as a national trait, we feel no hesitation in declaring, that it is wholly—British.

And, were it materially necessary, the curious OLD ENGLISH SPORTS might be traced through the succeeding reigns, with every degree of certainty, except in some few instances, where the conquerors introduced *effeminate refinements*, of which Leland and several other historians speak, as tending towards creating a degeneracy of spirit among the natives of the island.

It appears that Richard III. (commonly denominated *crook-backed* Richard) was distinguished for his acquirement of those exercises which invigorated the body and strengthened the arm; and it is recorded of him, " that he was uncommonly expert, either on foot or horseback, in displaying a variety of manly feats,— such as drawing the bow, raising the sling, or throwing the javelin; but particularly distinguished with a *clenched fist*, when opposed to an antagonist, by the extreme potency of his arm." In those days it was expected, that *even* princes should excel in these necessary and manly accomplishments, as much depended on the power of the *arm ;*—and, however *high-colouring* it may give to stage-effect, in witnessing RICHARD fall in the contest with RICHMOND—had that have proved the fact, that the fate of the nation was to have been decided by a single combat, the superiority of RICHARD's prowess, by his being inured to feats of manhood, and the various hardy exploits he had performed, little doubt can be expressed, but RICHMOND would never have assumed the kingly title of Henry VII. Richard's natural courage was of the first order, and, in the words of our immortal bard, finely expressed :—

" I think there be six Richmonds in the field:
" Five have I slain to-day instead of him."

And it is principally owing to a constant exercise of
these manly sports, that men not only lose sight of
their individual size, but place and circumstance;
their bodies capable of enduring hardships, and their
minds fortified by true and invincible courage.

In the celebrated battle of Dettingen, in the late
King's reign, victory was obtained by the *strength of
arm* in wielding the broad-sword so adroitly,—the lines
of the enemy were forced, and literally cut to pieces;
a total discomfiture and defeat took place, to the increased honour of the British soldiery.

Having thus far cursorily expressed our opinions in
favour of this manly art, we shall now proceed to
shew some of its most powerful *knock-down* arguments :—

JACK BROUGHTON, according to the best authorities,
appears to have been considered as the Father of the
English School of Boxing, and by whose superior skill
and ability PUGILISM obtained the rank of a SCIENCE.

Previous to the days of BROUGHTON it was downright
slaughtering,—or, in the modern acceptation, either
gluttony, *strength*, or *bottom*, decided almost every contest. But, after BROUGHTON appeared as a professor of
the gymnastic art, he drew crowds after him to witness
his exhibitions ; there was a *neatness* about his method
completely new and unknown to his auditors—he *stopped* the blows aimed at any part of him by his antagonist
with so much skill, and *hit* his man away with so much
ease, that he astonished and terrified his opponents beyond measure ; and those persons who had the temerity
to enter the lists with BROUGHTON were soon convinced
of his superior knowledge and athletic prowess : and
most of his competitors, who were compelled to *give in*,

from their exhausted and beaten state, had the mortification to behold BROUGHTON scarcely touched, and to
appear with as much cheerfulness and indifference as if
he had never been engaged in a *set-to.*

He was indebted to nature for a good person ; his
countenance was manly and open ; and possessing a
sharp and penetrating eye, that almost looked through
the object before him, gave a fine animation to his face.
His form was athletic and commanding ; there was an
importance about it which denoted uncommon strength,
and which every spectator felt impressed with that be-
held him.   Six feet, wanting an inch, in height ; and
fourteen stone, or thereabouts, in weight.

BROUGHTON became as a *fixed star* in the pugilistic
hemisphere ; his talents as a Boxer gained him many
admirers and patrons ; but his good temper, generosity
of disposition, and gentleness of manners, ensured him
numerous friends.   He was intelligent, communicative,
and not destitute of wit.   The system he laid down was
plain, and easy to be understood ; and, under his instruction, several of his pupils arrived at a pugilistic eminence, and gave distinguished proofs of the acquirements they had gained under so great a master.

Notwithstanding the inferiority of Boxers, previous
to the days of BROUGHTON, it may not be improper,
as far as they can be traced with any degree of accuracy, so as to render the connexion more complete and
strong, to give some short account of their feats.

SOUTHWARK FAIR, during its continuance, was an
uncommon scene of attraction to the inhabitants in and
contiguous to London, from the various sports and pastimes which were exhibited by its versatility of perfor-

VOL. I.   D

mers. Boxing and cudgelling were strong features
among the other amusements : refinement, it appears,
was not so well understood *then* as at the present period;
although several of the most celebrated actors of that
day did not feel *ashamed* to make known their efforts to
amuse the populace. When even the stage was not considered in a degenerate state, and while the irresistible
and loud roars of laughter prevailed outside the booths,
from an intermixture of all ranks of people, the involuntary tear was seen stealing down the cheeks of the
audiences within, at the imaginary sufferings of the
hero or heroine, from the excellent *manner* in which it
was *told*. Genius and talent were often seen, felt, and
acknowledged, under many of those ragged coverings,
however difficult it may be to experience, under more
classic and magnificent domes ; the *mere* hint at such
things, now-a-days, would make our fixed theatrical
star,

> JOHN KEMBLE—
> *Tremble!*

Nor did that Colossus of Literature (Dr. Johnson)
appear shy, in witnessing the eccentricities developed
by human beings at such places of amusement, where
the finest display of NATURE and ART that could be experienced were to be seen *contrasted*, and REAL LIFE, in
all its abundant varieties, portrayed in its native dress.
To a *mind* like that of Dr. Johnson, few circumstances
escaped his notice, whether attracted by the loud laugh
at the rude and noisy fair, or the *self-approving* smile at
the more refined and splendid chateau : in the manly
display of the pugilist, or in appealing eloquence of
the orator, it was appreciated and treasured up, added
to his midnight sallies with the unfortunate and pitia-

ble Savage, united with his intellectual acquirements; and which, doubtless, formed the *stamina* of those works that have tended to add so much literary reputation to this country.

The learned Doctor, in himself, was another *striking* proof of pugilism being a national trait, by having a regular set-to with an athletic brewer's servant, who had insulted him in Fleet-street, and gave the fellow a complete milling in a few minutes.

BOXING and CUDGELLING, it appeared, degenerated into downright ferocity and barbarity at this Fair, from the drunkenness and inequality of the combatants, and the various artifices adopted to get money, which at last became so disgusting, that it was declared a public nuisance, and, in 1749, Southwark Fair was suppressed.

Smithfield and Moorfields also sported booths and rings for the display of boxing and cudgelling; and where many a good bit of stuff has *peeled* with all the courage of a lion, and who has soon been reduced to the meekness of a lamb : here, also, many a *glutton* has received his belly full, and retired perfectly *satisfied;* and many an *ugly customer* has met with his match, and been frightened in his turn; *milling coves* had the pride taken out of them by mere *novices*; and where many *sparring gills* have found out that, in *reality*, they could not *box!* But, alas! for want of a BOXIANA, to record their valorous deeds, Heroes and Tyros of the fist have, unfortunately, been suffered to " steal ingloriously to the grave," and their qualifications buried with them, leaving the pugilistic posterity to mourn in silence the loss of their achievements.

It was from the above scene of frolic and fun, that the inimitable Hogarth drew his celebrated picture of

Southwark Fair, in which life is exhibited in all its
various shapes, from the King to the Beggar; and
among the variety of characters here portrayed, may
be traced the likenesses of the late King, interestedly
gazing upon the rude and comic touches of nature,
and in viewing the merry countenances of his happy
subjects, enjoying the humours and freedom of their
countrymen, so congenial to the soil of liberty; and
the famous Colley Cibber, of theatrical fame, in observing the display of talent, sported by his brethren of
the *sock* and *buskin* to the gaping crowd, to persuade
the populace to fill their booths, that they might
begin immediately; and the heroic Figg, of pugilistic
memory, challenging any of the crowd to enter the
lists with him, either for money, for love, or a belly full!

The latter character, at that period, was a distinguished personage in the history of pugilism, by references being made to him upon all fighting occasions,
and was considered to possess good judgment. He
might be looked upon as the champion of that day.—
Figg was more indebted to strength and courage for
his success in the battles which he gained, than from
the effects of genius: in fact, he was extremely illiterate, and it might be said, that he *boxed* his way through
life. If Figg's method of fighting was subject to the
criticism of the present day, he would be denominated
more of a *slaughterer* than that of a neat, finished pugilist. His antagonists were punished severely in their
conflicts with him, particularly those who stood up
to receive his blows: in making matches, his advice
was always consulted, as he possessed the character of
an honest fellow—and was looked up to as a leading
fighter among the most distinguished of the *fancy.*

F I G G .

B R O U G H T O N .

Published by G. Smeeton, St Martin's Lane, July 25, 1812.

It appears that FIG was more distinguished as a *fencer* and *cudgeller* than as a pugilist ; and, notwithstanding the former acquirements gave him a decidedly superior advantage over the other boxers of that day, by his thorough acquaintance with *time* and *measure*, yet his favourite practices were the SWORD and STICK, and in the use of which he particularly excelled.

His reputation rapidly increasing as a scientific man in those pursuits, he was induced to open an *Academy*, (perhaps better known by FIG's Amphitheatre), for teaching the use of the small and back sword, cudgelling, and pugilism ; and which place soon became of considerable notoriety, by proving a great attraction to the sporting men at that period, in making and settling matches in the various bouts that were displayed.

It was here that the celebrated Captain GODFREY (the *Barclay* of that time) displayed his uncommon skill and elegance in those manly sports, with the most hardy and determined competitors, contending for the palm of victory : and often was the Captain witnessed by royal and noble personages, who, it should seem, became supporters to a science tending to inure the people to bravery and intrepidity.

To Captain GODFREY's *Treatise upon the Useful Science of Defence*, (now extremely scarce,) published in 1747, we are, in some degree, indebted for an account of the characters of the *Fancy* within his time ; which work was dedicated to his Royal Highness the Duke of Cumberland, and was so well received by the public, that it immediately went through two large editions.

The Captain thus speaks of FIG:—"I have purchased my knowledge with many a broken head, and bruises in

every part of me. I chose to go mostly to FIG, and exercise with him ; partly, as I knew him to be the ablest
master, and, partly, as he was of a rugged temper, and
would spare no man, high or low, who took up a stick
against him. I bore his rough treatment with determined
patience, and followed him so long, that FIG, at last,
finding he could not have the beating of me at so cheap
a rate as usual, did not show such fondness for my company. This is well known by gentlemen of distinguished rank, who used to be pleased in setting us together."

FIG's *Academy* was now in high estimation ; and the
encouragement he received from plenty of scholars and
numerous visitors upon all occasions, made him a man
of no little importance among the heroes of the fist,
stick, or sword ; and he turned out some excellent pupils
in all the various branches of the art of self-defence.

It was about this period that the whole boxing hemisphere was *up in arms !* occasioned by the *insolent* threat
of the English laurels being torn from their native soil,
and transplanted to a foreign land !—It was a *Venetian*
gondolier that *threw down the glove*, boasting, at the
same time, that he would break the jaw-bone of any opponent who might have the temerity to fight him. The
Venetian was a man of prodigious strength, with an *arm*
not only very large and muscular, but surprisingly long ;
he had proved a complete terror to his own countrymen,
by the number of *jaw-bones* which he had sent to the surgeon's to be *set* of those persons who had possessed hardihood enough to oppose him. His fame ran before him,
and his impetuosity was described to be irresistible. The
Venetian was considered a good subject for winning, and
a foreigner of distinction and several of his countrymen

backed him for a large sum : —but JOHN BULL was not
thus to be *bounced* out of his *pluck* or his money—and,
in this situation of affairs, FIG was applied to for a customer to *serve him out*, if such a one could be found !
—"Found," exclaimed FIG, laughing heartily, "aye,
my masters, plenty ; but I don't know, d'ye see, as how
that'ere's truth about his breaking so many of his countrymen's jaw-bones with his fist ; howsomdever, that's
no matter, he can't break BOB WHITAKER's jaw-bone,
if he had a sledge-hammer in his hand. And if BOB
must knock under, why, before this here *outlandish*
waterman shall rule the roast, I'll give him a FIG to
chaw, which, perhaps, he'll find some trouble in *swallowing !*" After this luminous display upon the matter,
the match was made, and the day appointed for the
combat to take place at FIG's Amphitheatre.

It may be necessary to say something here about the
qualifications of BOB WHITAKER, who was selected to
punish this *Venetian* for his vain-boasting, that he would
take *the shine out* of Englishmen ! BOB was an awkward
boxer, and an athletic man ; but possessed true *bottom*,
and was celebrated for his throwing, and contriving to
pitch his weighty body on his fallen antagonist.

Among the *milling coves* the day was looked for with
uncommon anxiety, that was to decide this mighty
contest ;

" When Greek meets Greek, then's the tug of war."

The important moment at length arrived, and, according to all report, it was by far the most splendid company and the politest house of the kind that was ever
seen at FIG's Amphitheatre.

'The stage was ordered to be cleared, when an awful
silence prevailed in the anxiety manifested for the *set-to*.
The *Venetian* mounted with smiles of confidence, and
was greeted welcome by loud plaudits from his countrymen and partisans, and instantly began to strip—his
giant-like arm claimed universal astonishment, and his
size in general struck terror; and even Capt. Godfrey
observes, "That his heart yearned for his countryman!"
Bob appeared cool and steady, in a few seconds afterwards, and was cheered with huzzas. He eyed the Gondolier with firmness, and, quite undismayed, threw off his
clothes in an instant, when the attack commenced,—the
Venetian pitched himself forward with his right leg, and
his arm full extended, and, before Whitaker was
aware of his design, he received a blow on the side of
the head, so powerful in its effect as to *capsize* him
over the stage, which was remarkable for its height.
Whitaker's fall was desperate, indeed, as he dashed
completely against the ground; which circumstance
would not have taken place, but for the grandeur of the
audience, whose prices for admission were so high on
that day as to exclude the common people, who generally
sat on the ground, and formed a line round the stage. It
was then all clear, and Bob had nothing to stop him but
the bottom. The bets ran high, and the foreigners vociferated loudly, indeed, in behalf of the *Venetian*, and
flattered themselves that Whitaker would scarcely be
able to *come again*, from the desperate blow and fall
he had received, and sported their cash freely in laying
the odds thick against him; but Bob was not to be *told
out* so soon, and jumped upon the stage, like a game-
cock, to renew the attack. *Sparring* now was all at an

end ; and WHITAKER found out that something must be done to render the *Venetian's long arm* useless, or he must lose the fight; so, without further ceremony, he made a little stoop, ran boldly in beyond the heavy mallet, and, with one *" English peg"* in the stomach, (quite a new thing to foreigners,) brought him on his breech. The tables were then turned, the sporting men laughing heartily, and the foreigners a little chapfallen. The *Venetian* showed symptoms of uneasiness—was quite sick—and, his wind being touched, he was scarcely to his *time.* BOB now *punished* him in fine style, drove the *Venetian* all over the stage, and soon gave him a *leveller.* The odds shifted fast in favour of WHITAKER, and the foreigners displayed some terrible *long faces!* The Gondolier was completely puzzled, and, in the course of a few rounds, the *conceit was so taken out of him,* that he lost all guard of his person, and was compelled to GIVE IN—to the no small chagrin of the foreigners, who were properly *cleaned out* upon this occasion ; but the *Venetian* had the mortification to retire in disgrace, after his vain-boasting, and with a good *milling;* or, as Captain GODFREY concludes, " the blow in the stomach carried too much of the English *rudeness* for him to bear, and finding himself so unmannerly used, he scorned to have any more doings with his slovenly fist."

FIG was so enraptured with the elegance of the audience, and not wishing to let so good an opportunity slip, instantly mounted the stage, and addressed the spectators, nearly to the following purport:—"Gentlemen, perhaps, as how, you may think, that I have picked out the best man in London to beat this here foreigner ; but if you will come this day se'nnight, I'll produce a man that

shall beat Bob Whitaker, by fair hitting, in ten minutes."—It had the desired effect, by the company proving as great and as fine as the week before, and who came
to see whether Fig was not trifling with them; it being
considered a difficult task to beat such a *bottom* man as
Whitaker in so short a space of time. On the day appointed, the Amphitheatre, as before, was crowded at an
early hour, and poor Whitaker's laurels were doomed
to be but of short duration. Nat Peartree was the
man looked out to deprive him of his honours; and who
was considered a most admirable boxer; and had he not
lost a finger in a desperate conflict, it was supposed that
Peartree was a match for any of the pugilists. He
was famous for fighting at the face, and putting in his
blows with great strength; yet felt doubtful in being able
to beat Whitaker by force, as the latter had proved
himself, upon many occasions, a most enormous *glutton*,
and therefore cunningly determined to fight at his eyes.
The event proved Peartree's judgement to be correct,
for, in about six minutes, he had directed his arms so
well, that Whitaker was shut out from day-light, by
both his eyes being closed up. In this *distressed* situation he became an object of pity, by being completely at
the mercy of his antagonist; when poking about awhile
for his man, and finding him not, he wisely gave in,
with these odd words—"Dam'me, I am not beat, but
what signifies when I cannot see my man!"

Tom Pipes, who had long been the Champion of England till Broughton appeared, was but weakly made ;
his appearance bespoke great activity, yet his arm, hand,
and body, were but small. Pipes was distinguished for
a peculiar swing of his arm, his blows were prodigious,

and he was an uncommon quick hitter. He displayed a great deal of neatness in his boxing; and fought at the face most, where he put in blows with excellent time and judgement. PIPES had fought a great number of battles against men of superior strength; and his skill was so superior, that victory attended him: his fame lasted for several years, and it was the opinion of Captain GOD-FREY, " that it was more owing to debauchery than to the merit of those with whom he contended, that he was beat out of the championship !"

One GRETTING was a strong competitor against PIPES, and both having obtained great celebrity by their skill and prowess, felt somewhat jealous of each other's fame, and had several combats together, when they were almost alternate victors, though BROUGHTON beat them both with ease. GRETTING was a stronger made man than PIPES, and an artful boxer, and had the nearest way of going to the stomach (which *then* was denominated the MARK) than any man of his day, besides putting in his blows remarkably straight; but, notwithstanding, PIPES was his superior, by the thorough *bottom* he displayed, and which most excellent requisite for a pugilist GRETTING did not possess sufficiently enough. In his last two battles with PIPES he was severely beaten. Like too many boxers, in the heyday of their prowess, he thought nothing would hurt him, and drank to excess, which rendered him a mere *plaything* among the fighting men; and a very slovenly boxer, called HAMMERSMITH JACK, beat him with ease, as did every other person that fought him afterwards. GRETTING was certainly entitled to the appellation of a great boxer—

and had it not been for repeated inebriety, must have become quite a first-rate pugilist.

The time was at length arrived, when FIG, notwithstanding his celebrated parryings and severe thrusts, was doomed to meet with a superior antagonist—and *Death* gave him his *knock-down blow* in 1740. It was the opinion of this period, that the English nation were more expert than any other, not only in boxing, but in the use of the back-sword ; and it would be a great pity were they not to continue so at the present day. The amphitheatre, boxing, foil-play, and cudgelling schools, were openly advertised, and the amusements made known, like unto any of the regular theatres—the audiences equally as fashionable ; patronised by the noble and great, and not disturbed, but tolerated by the magistrates. Although it was admitted, that those amphitheatrical practices were productive of some ill, as offering a kind of encouragement to idleness and extravagance among the vulgar ; yet there is hardly any useful thing but what leaves an opening for mischief, and which is not liable to abuse. The practices of back-sword fighting and boxing have been thought commendable by the serious legislator, in feeding and keeping up the British spirit. Courage is allowed to be chiefly natural, and probably owing, in a great measure, to the complexion and constitution of our bodies, and flowing in the different texture of the blood and juices ; but, surely, it may be admitted, that it is not only acquired, but strengthened, by use and familiarity with danger. Emulation and the love of glory are true and powerful breeders of it. To what a pitch of daring do we not see them carry men ? And the innumerable proofs of Englishmen in the above instance demonstrates

GEO: TAYLOR.

JAMES BELCHER.

Copied by Permission of M.rs Belcher, (His Widow) from an Original Portrait in Her Possession.

Publish'd Sept.r 5. 1812 by G. Smeeton, 139. St.Martin's Lane.

the truth of the position beyond all controversy.   Is it not observable in miniature among little children, who, almost as soon as they can go alone, put themselves into attitudes and postures of defence—and the boys bear their little bloody noses without complaint, sooner than be stigmatised as cowards?

During FIG's life-time these manly exercises were carried on with great spirit; but for a short period after his decease appeared rather upon the decline.   And it would not be doing justice to the merits of so celebrated a *Fancier*, before we take our leave of him, were we not to give his character in a few words, by one of his impartial biographers:—"FIG was the atlas of the sword, and may he remain the gladiating statue!   In him, strength, resolution, and unparalleled judgement, conspired to form a matchless master.   There was a majesty shone in his countenance, and blazed in all his actions, beyond all I ever saw.   His right leg bold and firm, and his left, which could hardly ever be disturbed, gave him the surprising advantage already proved, and struck his adversary with despair and panic.   He had a peculiar way of *stepping* in a parry.   He knew his arm, and its just time of moving, put a firm faith in that, and never let his adversary escape his parry.   He was just as much a greater MASTER than any other I ever saw, as he was a greater judge of *time* and *measure*."   FIG was a native of Oxfordshire; and the excellent portrait which is given of him in this work was copied, by permission, from an original likeness in the cabinet collection of an amateur, otherwise it would have been extremely difficult to have procured one, on account of its great scarcity.

GEORGE TAYLOR, known by the name of *George the*

No. II.   F

Barber, now sprang rapidly into notice, by beating all
the celebrated pugilists, excepting BROUGHTON. He had
so good an *opinion of himself*, that he attacked the Champion first; but his judgement not proving so sound as his
courage, he was soon laid prostrate by the potent and
well-directed arm of BROUGHTON; and, like many a
brave fellow that had done so before him, was compelled,
reluctantly, to acknowledge that he had got a master.
But, notwithstanding his defeat, his fame was not injured,
when comparisons were made between them, as GEORGE
was not more than twenty, and the Champion in the
very zenith of his age and art. TAYLOR soon distinguished himself among all the first-rate boxers; but it
does not appear that he had ever any notion of *trying it
on* any more with BROUGHTON. He was rated as a
strong, able pugilist, possessing a most extraordinary
skill, and, aided by his knowledge of the small and back
sword, and a remarkable judgement in the cross-buttock-
fall, was considered to be able to contend for victory
with any one. With these pretensions he considered
himself as a proper person to succeed the late FIG in his
Amphitheatre, and lost no time in becoming its proprietor; which circumstance he soon made known by
public advertisements of the performances which were
to take place under his management at the theatre; and
inviting the most celebrated men in the different
branches of self-defence to display their skill. That the
terms were upon the most equitable scale, and the ad-
mission-money should be honourably disposed of according to any agreement that might be made. It was
no uncommon thing for the receipts of the house, at that
time, to produce from one hundred to one hundred and

STEVENSON.

TOM (Otherwise Paddington) JONES.

Publish'd Oct.14.1812 by G.Smeeton, 139 S. Martin's Lane.

fifty pounds. This publication had the desired effect —in not only bringing numerous audiences, but collecting together the most celebrated performers of the gymnastic art, to display their abilities; and among those who appeared at TAYLOR's Amphitheatre, was a man of the name of

BOSWELL, who was possessed of every requisite to constitute a finished boxer—except *courage*. He was noted for putting in a blow with the left hand at the jaw, which has been represented something like the *kick of a horse*. Captain GODFREY, who had often witnessed his efforts, thus speaks of BOSWELL:—" Praise be to his power of fighting, his excellent choice of *time* and *measure*, his superior judgement, despatching forth his executing arm! But fie upon his dastard heart, that mars it all! As I knew that fellow's abilities, and his worm-dread soul, I never saw him beat, but I wished him to be beaten. Though I am charmed with the idea of his power and manner of fighting, I am sick at the thoughts of his nurse-wanting courage. Farewell to him, with this fair acknowledgement, that, if he had a true *English* bottom (the best fighting epithet for a man of spirit) he would carry all before him, and be a match for even BROUGHTON himself!" GEORGE TAYLOR and BOSWELL contended for the honour of victory; but the latter became no difficult conquest to TAYLOR, as the fight was only of short duration. But TAYLOR, although in every other respect was considered a most consummate boxer, was well known to be deficient in *bottom*; and that blows equal to his own strength he could not stand, but quite disconcerted his science.

GEORGE STEVENSON, the *Coachman*, and TOM

SMALLWOOD, stood high upon the list as *bottom* pugilists. The former stood up to BROUGHTON manfully; and it was observed of SMALLWOOD, that he was thorough *game*, with judgement equal to any, and superior to most. He was capable of standing against any man, if he had but possessed weight. SMALLWOOD fought with DIMMOCK, when he was in his infancy of boxing, and but a mere strippling. The latter was a man of great strength and not destitute of skill, and he was near an hour before he gained the victory over SMALLWOOD. It was the opinion of Capt. GODFREY, " that if he was to chuse a boxer for his money, and could but purchase him strength equal to his resolution, SMALLWOOD should be the man."

In the course of a few months after the above period, SMALLWOOD proved himself fully entitled to the high opinion which had been held of him respecting his *science* and *bottom*, in a desperate conflict with one DICK HARRIS, a proper piece of hardihood. It was a most obstinate battle indeed, continuing above an hour, and was considered as *game* a one as had been witnessed for many years. HARRIS knowing that he had got a *trump* to deal with, showed out with all the courage of a hero; and SMALLWOOD, to recover from his former defeat with *Dimmock,* endeavoured to place himself on an eminence with the first-rate pugilists of the day, by the science and intrepidity which he displayed: the fight was *primely* contested, and victory, for a long time, appeared doubtful—but DICK, not being so thoroughly acquainted with the advantages of the art to relieve himself when distressed for wind, was reluctantly compelled to acknowledge the superiority of SMALLWOOD.

Broughton, who witnessed the fight, was much pleased with the *set-to* of Smallwood, and his method all through the contest; and clapping him upon the back, exclaimed, " well done, Tom! such courage and science ought not to go unrewarded!" The battle was for fifty pounds.

Smallwood also fought the *fighting Quaker,* so denominated, but whose name was Bill Willis. His appearance was remarkably plain and formal, and the heroes of the fist were his *voluntary* god-fathers, and thus it appears he was christened the *fighting Quaker.* Whether Bill Willis ever belonged to that respectable sect we have not been able to ascertain; but we learn that he possessed one of its requisites, plenty of *stiffening.* In *setting-to,* he portrayed that he was not unlike the *faithful,* by the *spirit* with which he attacked Smallwood, and contended for victory with no inconsiderable share of manhood: but, in the course of a short time, the *spirit* no longer *moved him*—the *stiffening* was taken out of his carcass—and he was obliged to sing, *Small-*wood I am content. Tom Smallwood fought several other battles, in all of which he proved victorious ; but the combatants were not of sufficient importance to claim particular mention.

Jack James was considered a most charming boxer ; and a complete master of the art. A spring of the arm peculiar to himself, and remarkably delicate in his blows in fighting, his wrist appeared delightful to the lookers on, but terrible to his antagonist. Thorough *bottom,* but not possessing much strength. The above pugilist had a severe encounter with a poulterer, which terminated highly to the honour of James. His *pretty* wrist was

again conspicuous in the fight, but the marks it occasioned upon the face of his antagonist was far from being
considered *handsome*. His opponent was styled *Chicken*
HARRIS; but it appeared that JAMES could beat a
brood of such birds, till they had not a feather to fly!

About this time, the noted BUCKHORSE fought the
clog-maker, HARRY GRAY; when the latter got most
severely *punished* by the former *rum-customer*. For an
account of whose character, we feel much indebted to
the Proprietor of the ECCENTRIC MAGAZINE, (a
work abounding with anecdote and interest,) in permitting us to copy the following extract :—

" BUCKHORSE, one of those singularities of Nature,
and whose real name is said to have been JOHN SMITH,
first saw the light in the house of a *sinner*, in that part
of London known by the name of Lewkener's Lane—a
place notorious in the extreme, for the eccentricity of
characters it contained : *here* the disciples of *Bamfylde
Moore Carew* were to be found in crowds, and where
cadgers of all descriptions resorted to regale themselves
upon the *good things of this life*, laughing at the credulity
of the public in being so easily duped by their impositions;
groups of the frail sisterhood adorned its purlieus, whose
nudicity of appearance and *glibbiosity* of mother-tongue
formed a prominent feature in this conglomeration of
the vicious and depraved, by their coarse amours and
bare-faced pilfering; the juvenile *prig* was soon taught
to become an adept in the profession, by taking out a
handkerchief or a snuff-box, from the pocket of a coat
covered with bells, without ringing any of them—and the
finished thief *roosted* here from the prying eye of society,
and laid plans for his future depredations in the arms of

his unsophisticated charmer : those timber-merchants
who reduced their logs of wood to *matches,* to light the
public, might be observed issuing out in numbers from
this receptacle of *brimstones !* Costermongers in droves
were seen mounting their *neddies,* decorated with ham-
pers, *scorning* the refined use of saddles and bridles ; and
Lewkener's Lane was not only celebrated amongst all its
other attractions, in being the residence of a finisher of
the law (TOM DENNIS), *slangly* denominated JACK
KETCH, but acquired considerable notoriety by giving
birth to the *ugliness* of a BUCKHORSE, and beauty to
Miss——, a female possessing those irresistible charms
that levelled all distinctions of rank before its superior
power, and transplanting her from the rude and dirty
company of the dust-hill, to the downy couch of Royalty ; and who has for many years past been the enviable
and elevated rib of a celebrated four-in-hand Baronet
of the old school of whips, whose feats in driving, and
sporting high-bred cattle, have been considered the
very acme of style ; and acknowledged one of the most
knowing Lads upon the turf, when he led this *fair piece*
of the creation to the Hymeneal altar, who has long
been, and still continues, a *fixed star* in the hemisphere
of fashion."

It appears, then, that few places could boast of more
originality of character than *that* from which BUCK-
HORSE sprang ; and, from the variety of talents here
displayed, there is little doubt he did not remain long
a *novice.* As we have never been troubled with any
account—to what *good natured* personage he owed his
origin, we cannot determine ; but suffice to observe, that
little BUCKHORSE and his mother were turned out upon

the wide world long before he knew its slippery qualities, by the cruel publican, their landlord; which in-
human circumstance took place about the year 1720.

This *freak* of Nature, it should seem, was indebted
to his mother for what little instruction he received,
the principal of which was an extraordinary volubility
of speech; and from his early acquaintance with the
streets, he *picked up* the rest of his qualifications.

Buckhorse's composition, however rude and un-
sightly, was not without *harmony;* and although his FIST
might not appear *musical* to his antagonists by its potent
touch, yet, when applied to his own chin, was capable of
producing a variety of popular tunes, to the astonishment of all those who heard and saw him, and by which
peculiar trait he mostly subsisted, added to selling little
switches for a halfpenny a-piece; his *cry* of which was
so singular, that Shuter, the celebrated Comedian,
among his other imitations, was more than successful
in his attempts of Buckhorse, and which was repeatedly called for a second time.

As a pugilist, Buckhorse ranked high for courage
and strength among the boxers of his day, and displayed
great muscular powers in the battles he had contested;
and, like a number of the sporting *gemmen,* was distinguished for his numerous amours with the *gay
nymphs* of the town, *more* by the potency of his arm
than the *persuasive* powers of his rhetoric, notwithstanding his rapid improvements of the tongue. He
is represented as a most impetuous character, and his
principal features were, Love and Boxing.

An anecdote has been mentioned of Buckhorse,
but we cannot vouch for its authenticity, that he

was the person whom the late Duke of Queensberry selected to ride for him, when the Duke won his celebrated wager against time at Newmarket.

It may, perhaps, be necessary to consider here, (previous to entering into the merits of one, whose scientific knowledge and manly display of Pugilism placed him at the top of the art, renders the character of BROUGHTON worthy of particular attention,) *the necessary requisite which constitute a Boxer ; the superiority and evident advantages of the Science that may be gained over persons ignorant of the Art ; and the nature and effect of particular Blows explained, that have so often terminated battles.* It is principally from the pen of a celebrated amateur captain, who had made it his particular study from practical observation ; and though extremely plain and intelligible, yet perfectly scientific, founded on the true principles of anatomy and the powers of the human system, and cannot be read by any person without advantage and improvement—towards gaining a knowledge of SELF-DEFENCE :—It has ever been the opinion of the scientific, that BOXING is a combat, depending more on strength than the sword ; but art will yet bear down the beam against it. A less degree of art will tell far more than a considerably greater quantity of strength. Strength, most undoubtedly, is what the boxer ought to set out with, but without art he will succeed but poorly. The deficiency of strength may be greatly supplied with art ; but the want of art will have but heavy and unwieldy succour from strength.

The strength of man, it appears, chiefly consists in the power of his muscles, and that power is greatly to be increased by art. The muscles are as springs and

No. II.   G

levers, which execute the different motions of the body;
but by art a man may give additional force to them.

The nearer a man brings his body to the centre of
gravity, the truer line of direction will his muscle act
in, and consequently with more resisting force. If a
man designs to strike a hard blow, let him shut his fist
as firm as possible; the power of his arm will then be
considerably greater than if but slightly closed, and the
velocity of his blow greatly augmented by it. The
muscles which give this additional force to the arm, in
shutting the fist, are the flexors of the fingers, and the
extensors are the opposite muscles, as they open or
expand the same; yet in striking, or using any violent
efforts with your hands, these different orders of the
muscles contribute to the same action. Thus it will appear, that when you close the fist of your left arm, and
clap your right hand upon that arm, you will plainly feel
all the muscles of it to have a reciprocal swelling. From
hence it follows, that muscles, by nature designed for
different offices, mutually depend upon each other in
great efforts. This consideration will be of much advantage in that artificial force in fighting, which beats
much superior strength where art is wanting.

*The position of the body is of the greatest consequence
in fighting.* The centre of gravity ought to be well
considered, for by that the weight of the body being
justly suspended, and the true equilibrium preserved,
the body stands much the firmer against opposing force.
This depends upon the proper distance between the legs,
which is *the first regard a Boxer ought to have,* or all
his manly attempts will prove abortive. In order to form
the true position, the left leg must be presented some

reasonable distance before the right, which brings the left side towards the adversary; this the right-handed man ought to do, that, after having stopped the blow with his left arm, which is a kind of buckler to him, he may have the same readiness and greater power of stepping in with his right hand's returning blow. In this posture he ought to reserve an easy flexion in the left knee, that his advances and retreats may be the quicker. By this proper flexion, his body is brought so far forward as to have a just inclination over the left thigh, insomuch that his face makes a perpendicular, or straight, line with the left knee; whilst the right leg and thigh, in a slanting line, strongly prop up the whole body, as does a large beam an old wall. The body by this means is supported against all violent efforts, and the additional strength acquired by this equilibrium is greatly to the purpose. How much greater weight must not your adversary stand in need of, to beat you back from this forward inclining of the body, than the so much less resisting reclination of it. By this disposed attitude, you find the whole body gently inclining forward with a slanting direction, so that you shall find from the *outside* of the right ancle all the way to the shoulder, a straight line of direction, somewhat inclining, or slanting, upward, which inclination is the strongest position a man can contrive; and it is such as we generally use in forcing doors, resisting strength, or pushing forward any weight with violence, for the muscles of the left side, which bend the body gently forward, bring over the left thigh the gravitating part, which, by this contrivance, augments the force; whereas, if it was held erect or upright, an indifferent blow on the head or breast would overset it. The body, by this position, has the muscles of the right side partly relaxed and partly contracted, whilst those of the left are altogether in a state of contraction; but the reserve made in the muscles of the right side is as springs and levers to let fall the body at discretion.

By delivering up the power to the muscles of the left side, which, in a .very strong contraction, brings the body forward, the motion which is communicated is then so strong, that, if the hand at that time be firmly shut, and the blow at that instant pushed forward, with the contracting muscles, in a straight line with the moving body, the shock given from the stroke will be able to overcome a force, not thus artfully contrived, twenty times as great.

From this it is evident, how it is in our power to give additional force and strength to our bodies, whereby we may make ourselves far superior to men of more strength, not seconded by art.

Let us now examine the most hurtful blows, and such as contribute most to the battle. *This is a most important consideration to pugilists and others, and claims their particular attention.* It is well known, that very few of those who fight, know *why* a blow on such a part has such effects, yet by *experience* they know it HAS; and by these evident effects they are directed to the proper parts; as for instance, hitting under the ear, between the eye-brows, and about the stomach. The blow under the ear is considered to be as dangerous as any that is given, if it light between the angle of the lower jaw, and the neck, because in this part there are two kinds of blood-vessels, considerably large: the one brings the blood immediately from the heart to the head, whilst the other carries it immediately back. If a man receive a blow on these vessels, the blood proceeding from the heart to the head is partly forced back, whilst the other part is pushed forwards vehemently to the head: the same happens in the blood returning from the head to the heart, for part of it is precipitately forced into the latter, whilst the other tumultuously rushes to the head, whereby the blood-vessels are immediately overcharged, and the sinuses of the brain so overloaded and compressed, that the man at once loses all sensation, and the blood often runs from his ears, mouth, and nose, altogether owing to the quantity forced with such impetuosity into the smaller vessels, the coats whereof being too tender to resist so great a charge, instantly break, and cause the effusion of blood through these different parts.

This is not the only consequence, but the heart being overcharged with a regurgitation of blood, (as may be said with respect to that forced back on the succeeding blood coming from its left ventricle,) stops its progress, whilst that part of the blood coming from the head is violently pushed into its right auricle; so that as the heart labours under a violent surcharge of blood, there soon follows a cardiaca, or suffocation, but which goes off as the parts recover themselves, and push the blood forward. The blows given *between the eye-brows* contribute greatly *to the victory:* for this part being contused between two hard bodies, viz. the *fist* and *os frontale,* there ensues a violent echymosis, or extravasation of blood, which falls immediately into the eye-lids; and they being of a lax texture, incapable of resisting this influx of blood, swell almost instantaneously; which violent intri-

mescence soon obstructs the sight. The man thus inde-
cently treated, and artfully hoodwinked, is beat about
at his adversary's discretion.

The blows on the stomach are very hurtful, as the
diaphragm and lungs share in the injury.

It is particularly recommended to those who box,
*never to charge their stomach with too much food on the
day of combat;* for, by observing this precaution, they
will find great service. It will help them to avoid that
extraordinary compression on the *etorta descendens,* and,
in a great measure, preserve their stomachs from the
blows, which they must be the more exposed to, when
distended with victuals. The consequence of which may
be attended with a vomiting of blood, caused by the
eruption of some blood-vessels, from the overcharging
of the stomach : whereas the EMPTY STOMACH, *yielding
to the blow,* is as much less affected by it, as it is more
by its resistance, when expanded with food.

Therefore, it is advisable for a man to take a little cor-
dial water upon an empty stomach, which, it is thought,
cannot fail in proving of great service, by its astringing
the fibres, and contracting it into a smaller compass.

The injury the diaphragm is subject to from blows
which light just under the breast-bone, is very considerable, because the diaphragm is brought into a strong
convulsive state, which produces great pain, and lessens
the cavity of the thorax, whereby the lungs are, in a
great measure, deprived of their liberty, and the quantity of air retained in them from the contraction of the
thorax, through the convulsive state of the diaphragm,
is so forcibly pushed from them, that it causes great
difficulty of respiration, which cannot be overcome till
the convulsive motion of the diaphragm ceases.

The scientific boxer may, in some degree, render the blows less hurtful on this part, by drawing the belly, holding his breath, and bending his thorax over his navel, when the stroke is coming.

Strength and art have both been mentioned as the two principal requisites for a boxer to possess ; but there is another equally as necessary, and without which no pugilist can be termed complete—denominated *bottom*. In establishing *bottom*, there are two things required—*wind* and *spirit*, or *heart*, or wherever you can fix the residence of courage. *Wind* may be obtained by a proper attention to diet and exercise, but it is *spirit* that keeps the boxer upon his legs. Without this substantial requisite both art and strength will avail a man but little.

In tracing thus far, anatomically, the severe *effects* that blows have upon the human frame, and their ultimate consequences in quickly deciding a contest, or of proving seriously dangerous; little doubt can be entertained, but that, by an attentive perusal of the foregoing remarks, persons, in becoming acquainted with those peculiarly *sensitive parts*, may be enabled, whenever occasion requires, to protect themselves from any threatened danger. This is the ground-work of *science*, and which, in the course of this work, the reader will perceive practically illustrated, by viewing the Heroes of the Gymnastic Art, and their valorous exploits.

About the year 1740, and upwards, public challenges of the Pugilists were advertised ; and at the various fairs hand-bills were distributed of their feats to be displayed ; and, endeavouring to make BOXIANA as complete a book of reference as possible, we are induced to insert the following specimens:—

AT

FIG'S GREAT TIL'D BOOTH,

On the Bowling-Green, Southwark,
During the time of the FAIR,
(Which begins on SATURDAY, the 18th of SEPTEMBER,)
The TOWN will be entertained with the
MANLY ARTS OF
Foil-play, Back-sword, Cudgelling, and Boxing,
in which

The noted PARKS, from Coventry, and the celebrated gen-tleman prize-fighter, Mr. MILLAR, will display their skill in a tilting-bout, showing the advantages of *Time* and *Mea-sure.*

ALSO,

Mr. JOHNSON, the great Swordsman, superior to any man in the World for his unrivalled display of the *hanging-guard*, in a grand attack of SELF-DEFENCE, against the all-powerful arm of the renowned SUTTON.

DELFORCE, the finished Cudgeller, will likewise exhibit his uncommon feats with the *single-stick;* and who challenges any man in the kingdom to enter the lists with him for a *broken-head*, or a *belly-full!*

BUCKHORSE, and several other *Pugilists*, will show the Art of Boxing.

To conclude

With a GRAND PARADE by the Valiant FIG, who will exhibit his knowledge in various Combats—with the Foil, Back-sword, Cudgel, and Fist.

To begin each Day at Twelve o'Clock, and close at Ten.

Vivat Rex.

N. B. The Booth is fitted up in a most commodious man-ner, for the better reception of Gentlemen, &c. &c.

" Daily Advertiser, April 26, 1742.

" At the Great Booth, Tottenham-Court, on Wednesday next, the 28th instant, will be a trial of manhood, between the two following champions :

" Whereas I, WILLIAM WILLIS, commonly known by the name of the *fighting* Quaker, have fought Mr. SMALLWOOD about twelve months since, and held him the tightest to it, and bruised and battered him more than any one he ever en-countered, though I had the ill-fortune to be beat by an acci-dental fall; the said SMALLWOOD, flushed with the success blind fortune then gave him, and the weak attempts of a few vain Irishmen and boys, that have of late fought him for a minute or two, makes him think himself unconquerable; to convince him of the falsity of which, I invite him to fight me for ONE HUNDRED POUNDS, at the time and place above-mentioned, when I doubt not but I shall prove the truth of what I have asserted, by pegs, darts, hard blows, falls, and cross-buttocks.

"WILLIAM WILLIS."

" I, *Thomas Smallwood,* known for my intrepid manhood and bravery on and off the stage, accept the challenge of this *puffing quaker,* and will show him that he is led by a false spirit, that means him no other good than that he should be chastised for offering to take upon him the *arm of the flesh.*

"THOMAS SMALLWOOD."

" *Note.* The doors will be opened at ten, and the combatants mount at twelve.

" There will be several by-battles, as usual; and particularly one between *John Divine* and *John Tipping,* for five pounds each."

In this second trial of skill between *Smallwood* and *Willis,* the superiority of the former was again manifested, and the *fighting quaker* retired with a *broken* spirit, and was *shown-up* as a complete *ranter!* *Smallwood* beat him easy; notwithstanding his terrible threats of " pegs, darts, hard blows, and cross-buttocks."

The *calls of honour,* it appears, were numerous to be settled, and little time was suffered to intervene from the following public notice:—

" May 24, 1742, at *George Taylor's* Booth, Tottenham-court-road, there will be a trial of manhood to-morrow, between the following champions, viz.

" Whereas, I, *John Francis,* commonly known by the name of the *Jumping Soldier,* who have always had the reputation of a good fellow, and have fought several bruisers in the street, &c nor am I ashamed to mount the stage when my manhood is called in question by an Irish braggadocio, whom I fought some time ago, in a by-battle, for twelve minutes, and

No. III.   H

though I had not the success due to my courage and ability in the art of boxing, I now invite him to fight me for two guineas, at the time and place above-mentioned, where, I doubt not, I shall give him the truth of a good beating.

"John Francis."

"I, *Patrick Henley,* known to every one for the truth of a good fellow, who never refused any one, on or off the stage, and fight as often for the diversion of gentlemen as money, do accept the challenge of this *Jumping Jack;* and shall, if he don't take care, give him one of my bothering blows, which will convince him of his ignorance in the art of boxing.

"Patrick Henley."

Paddy kept his promise, for he so *bothered the gig* of the *Jumping Soldier,* that he was not able to *move,* much more to *jump,* for some time: *Paddy* gave him a Tipperary *fling,* which so completely *shook* all his recollection out of him, that he never troubled the town afterwards with any more of his *epistolary* challenges!

Several other minor fights and trifling events, which occurred at *Taylor's* Booth, &c. might be introduced, to show that PUGILISM was, at that period, rising fast into notice, and had gained considerable patronage and support; but lest that, in pursuing them further, when more important objects are at hand, it should appear

As in a theatre, the eyes of men,
After a well-grac'd actor leaves the stage,
Are idly bent on him that enters next,
Thinking his prattle to be tedious:—

we shall, *sans cérémonie,* clear the boards, to make room for the entrance of that principal and celebrated first-rate performer in the pugilistic art,—

JACK BROUGHTON:

" Advance, brave BROUGHTON !" exclaims *Captain Godfrey*; " Thee I pronounce Captain of the *boxers*. As far as I can look back, I think I ought to open the characters with him: I know none so fit, so able, to lead up the van. This is giving him the living preference to the rest; but I hope I have not given any cause to say, that there has appeared, in any of my characters, a partial tincture. I have thoroughly consulted nothing but my unbiassed mind, and my heart has known no call but merit. Wherever I have praised, I have no desire of pleasing : wherever decryed, no fear of offending.— BROUGHTON, by his manly merit, has bid the highest, therefore has my heart. I really think all will poll with me, who poll with the same principle. Sure there is some standing reason for this preference : what can be stronger than to say, that, for seventeen or eighteen years, he has fought every able boxer that appeared against him, and has never yet been beat? This being the case we may venture to conclude from it: but not to build alone on this, let us examine farther into his merits. What is it that he wants? Has he not all that others want, and all the best can have ? Strength equal to what is human, skill and judgement equal to what can be acquired, undebauched wind, and a bottom spirit never to pronounce the word *enough*. He fights the stick as well as most men, and understands a good deal of the small-sword. This practice has given him the distinction of *time* and *measure* beyond the rest. He stops as regularly as the swordsman, and carries his blows truly in the line ; he steps not back, distrusting of himself, to stop a blow, and

piddle in the return, with an arm unaided by his body,
producing but a kind of fly-flap blows, such as pastry-
cooks use to beat those insects from their tarts and
cheese-cakes. No; BROUGHTON steps bold and firmly in, bids a welcome to the coming blow; receives it
with his guardian arm; then, with a general summons
of his swelling muscles, and his firm body seconding
his arm, and supplying it with all its weight, pours the
pile-driving force upon his man.

  " That I may not be thought particular in dwelling
long upon BROUGHTON, I leave him with this assertion, that as he, I believe, will scarce trust a battle to
a warning age, I never shall think he is to be beat, till
I see him beat."

  With such a character, and from a patron so distinguished as *Captain Godfrey*, who was no *finicking*
FOP or *empty* SWELL, that ran after PUGILISM, because it was thought *knowing* and *stylish*—but had viewed its effects NATIONALLY, in producing those scenes
of heroism in the field of glory, where he had fought
and bled for his country;—and who, in his leisure moments, had *practised* the science for pleasure and profit
with the above hero, of whom he acknowledges, that
" my head, my arm, and leg, are strong witnesses of
his convincing arm. As I said before, I have tried
with them all, and must confess, my flesh, my bones,
remember him the best."

  It can be a matter of no surprize, after such a display
of the capabilities of BROUGHTON, that he did not want
either friends or money to put him forwards in the
world; and it was hinted to him by the *sporting world*,
that a more eligible place was necessary than *Taylor's*

Booth for their accommodation, and that if BROUGH-
TON would undertake the management of such a house, a
subscription would be entered into to defray the expenses of the same by the nobility and gentry.   Under the
cognizance of so respectable a firm, a building was soon
erected, denominated BROUGHTON's NEW AMPHI-
THEATRE, every way convenient and fit for the purpose,
in what is now called *Hanway-street*, Oxford-street. In its
interior appearance, it was somewhat similar to Astley's
Riding-school, with boxes, pit, and gallery, and a commodious stage for the combatants, and which was opened
on March 10, 1743, with the following public notice:—

AT BROUGHTON'S NEW AMPHITHEATRE,

OXFORD-ROAD,

The back of the late Mr. FIG's,

On TUESDAY next, the 13th instant,

Will be exhibited

THE TRUE ART OF BOXING,

By the *eight famed* following men, viz.

ABRAHAM EVANS,	——— ROGER,
——— SWEEP,	——— ALLEN,
——— BELAS,	ROBERT SPIKES, and
——— GLOVER,	HARRY GRAY, the
	clog-maker.

The above eight men are to be brought on the stage, and to
be matched according to the approbation of the gentlemen who
shall be pleased to honour them with their company.

N.B. There will be a BATTLE ROYAL between the

NOTED BUCKHORSE,

and SEVEN or EIGHT more ; after which there will be several
BY-BATTLES by others.

Gentlemen are therefore desired to come by times.   The
doors will be open at nine; the champions mount at eleven;
and no person is to pay more than A SHILLING.

The appearance of the above public notice operated
like a *death-blow* to the feelings of *George Taylor,*
who immediately saw the impending consequences that
must inevitably result from the importance that BROUGH-
TON possessed with the *sporting men;* and to save complete destruction, circulated, without any hesitation, an
address, nearly to the following purport, all over the town:

To THE PATRONS AND ENCOURAGERS OF THE MANLY
ART OF BOXING.

Whereas, Mr. Broughton, well knowing that I was to fight
Mr. Field, on Tuesday next, the 13th of March, 1743, in order
to injure me, has maliciously advertised to open his Amphitheatre
on that day, and where several battles are then to be fought.
To prevent the public from being deceived, I feel it my duty to
inform them, that the principal part of the persons mentioned
were never made acquainted with such circumstance, and have
no intention of so doing.   Mr. Broughton wishes to make it
appear that he never imposed upon any of the pugilists who had
been concerned with him in any transaction whatever; but his
impositions shall soon be made manifest to the world.   And to
show Mr. Broughton that I have no animosity against him
as a pugilist, or any jealousy concerning his amphitheatre, I am
willing to fight him, as soon as he may think proper, wherever
it may please him, not regarding, as he loudly sets forth, the
strength of his arm.
                                        GEORGE TAYLOR.

BROUGHTON smiled at this *bombastic* attempt to reduce his character as a man, or his fame as a pugilist: it
was like a drowning man catching at a straw. *Taylor*
had already fell beneath the all-conquering arm of
BROUGHTON; and the challenge of the former was
considered nothing more than a *mere threat*, without
any serious intention of putting it into practice.   To

clear up the imposition that TAYLOR alleged against
BROUGHTON, the latter made it appear that he had not
received from the public one hundred pounds, and that
his amphitheatre had cost him upwards of £400, and
acknowledged that he had appropriated a third part of
the door-money for his own individual emolument,
which he trusted was only fair and reasonable: and
that the rest had been shared among the pugilists. This
account proving perfectly satisfactory to the amateurs
and the public, BROUGHTON was now firmly established as a manager; and TAYLOR preceiving that it would
be useless to oppose so powerful an opponent, relinquished his booth, and was engaged as a principal actor
at the amphitheatre, where his performers soon followed him, and BROUGHTON became in possession of a
strong company. Some plan appearing necessary for
their future conduct, the following

RULES

Were produced by MR. BROUGHTON, *for the better regulation
of the Amphitheatre, approved of by the Gentlemen, and agreed
to by the* PUGILISTS, *August* 10, 1743:—

1. THAT a square of a yard be chalked in the middle of the
stage; and every fresh set-to after a fall, or being parted
from the rails, each second is to bring his man to the side
of the square, and place him opposite to the other; and till
they are fairly set-to at the lines, it shall not be lawful for
the one to strike the other.

2. That, in order to prevent any disputes, the time a man lies
after a fall, if the second does not bring his man to the side
of the square, within the space of half a minute, he shall
be deemed a beaten man.

3. That, in every main battle, no person whatever shall be
upon the stage, except the principals and their seconds; the
same rule to be observed in by-battles, except that in the
latter, Mr BROUGHTON is allowed to be upon the stage to

keep decorum, and to assist gentlemen in getting to their places; provided always he does not interfere in the battle; and whoever presumes to infringe these rules, to be turned immediately out of the house. Every body is to quit the stage as soon as the champions are stripped, before they set-to.

4. That no champion be deemed beaten, unless he fails coming up to the line in the limited time; or that his own second declares him beaten. No second is to be allowed to ask his man's adversary any questions, or advise him to give out.

5. That, in by-battles, the winning man to have two thirds of the money given, which shall be publicly divided upon the stage, notwithstanding any private agreements to the contrary.

6. That, to prevent disputes, in every main battle, the principals shall, on the coming on the stage, choose from among the gentlemen present two umpires, who shall absolutely decide all disputes that may arise about the battle; and if the two umpires cannot agree, the said umpires to choose a third, who is to determine it.

7. That no person is to hit his adversary when he is down, or seize him by the ham, the breeches, or any part below the waist: a man on his knees to be reckoned down.

These RULES may be called the *data* of Boxing—and no man, from his experience, was better able to frame such a code than BROUGHTON. It does not appear, that any Pugilist previous to, or since the days of that acknowledged hero, has, generally speaking, ever possessed, either in point of *theory* or *practice*, the SCIENCE in so eminent a degree as BROUGHTON; and this circumstance is observed, very far from any intention of detracting merit from a number of deservedly celebrated pugilists since his time, but with a view of advocating, if necessary, the superior talents and genius of so great a master in the art of Boxing,—intending, at the same time, by way of hint, that no doubt can exist, but there still is room left for considerable improvement in the practice. Most first-rate Pugilists have, independent of their knowledge of the SCIENCE, a peculiar mode of their own in fighting, and which cannot be *exactly* communicated to their pupils, from the want of studious application, which every SCIENCE so essentially requires, before any professor can be rated as a *finished* master. BROUGHTON, from the study and attention that he paid to it *theoretically*, added to the great practice he had, not only in *sparring*, (with whom the first use of gloves originated,) but in his numerous public contests : that he became so thoroughly acquainted with every *minutiæ* of the art, as to be peculiarly happy in communicating it to his scholars ; a memorable instance of which will be hereafter shown, from one of his pupils, who, weighing only *nine* stone, fought a man of *seventeen*, and beat him in the course of ten minutes !

Unfortunately, most HEROES OF THE FIST are too apt to forget the numerous *knock-down* blows and dreadful bruises which they have received in climbing up to the *daring height* of CHAMPION ! and that one fatal blow can hurl them from the high precipice—level them with the ground—and wrest that *hard-earned* title from their brows ! Let them also bear in mind, that in becoming the mighty CHAMPION OF ENGLAND (enviable sound!) they appear as a *public mark* to hit at, and whoever *throws down* the glove, whether in possession of youth in opposition to their age, superior strength, or science, THEY *must pick it up;* and, if they mean to continue in their elevated seat, *wear it.*

Few, very few Pugilists, have died in possession of the Championship ; and however desperate and chequered No. III. I

the road may be to procure that title—the DIFFICULTY
rests in keeping it.   The smiles of *victory* have often
blinded and ruined many, by plunging them into excess
and gaiety—instead of being tremblingly alive to their
future fame. SOBRIETY will prove their best friend, and
they should endeavour never to turn their back upon so
invaluable a monitor ; and that in gaining fresh acquaintance, which their success will naturally occasion,
they will find no better one than in *investigating the*
SCIENCE again and again, whereby they may discover
some NEW stop or hit that was unknown to them before ;
but above all, let them endeavour to become *acquainted*
with THEMSELVES, study their defects, and improve
them ;—if *passionate* in their nature, learn to suppress
that overwhelming quality so dangerous to pugilists, for
if they cannot view the attacks of their antagonist with
coolness—conquest, *then*, is more indebted to *chance* than
judgement ! Here it was that BROUGHTON proved himself so much master of the SCIENCE—and so superior to
all his competitors—as his mind was continually at work
to improve his knowledge in giving blows with more ease
and effect to himself, and in warding off those powerful
attacks aimed at his destruction from his adversary ;
while, on the contrary, *they* were too generally spending
their time in drinking and other pastimes, instead of improving themselves and becoming adepts in the art, leaving every other consideration to strength and chance.

BROUGHTON, like all great masters, generally exhibited something NEW in every performance ; and those
pugilists who had witnessed his contests, and afterwards
entered the lists with him, expecting to find that he
would fight upon the *old suit*, were most terribly de-

ceived ; as, contrary to most other boxers, he did not depend upon any *particular* blow, although he was distinguished for giving some remarkable hits, which were
scarcely ever *forgotten*.   BROUGHTON, when necessary
in the conflict, by putting in HIS *stomach-blow*, has often
decided the battle ; and his lunge under the EAR generally produced terrible consequences to his opponent—
the *eye* of BROUGHTON was most lively and acute, soon
perceiving the weakness of any adversary ; and his *arm*,
keeping pace with that valuable assistant, protected him
from the most destructive blows : and his quick pene-
tration made him always aware of any direct intent pursued by his adversary, as immediately to render it futile
and unavailing.   His guard was considered so complete,
that his frame appeared as well secured as if in a fence :
uncommon strength and *bottom* often fell before him ;
and his expertness in the cross-buttock was great.   His
various attitudes in the fight were fine and impressive,
and his countenance always animated and cheerful.

Pipes and *Gretting* were both distinguished pugilists—the former of whom nobly maintained the rank
of Champion for a number of years ;—but they appeared *nothing* in the hands of BROUGHTON, who gave
them several chances to recover their lost laurels—
which proved severe beatings to them, and only tended
to increase his growing fame.

George Taylor, of whom honourable mention has
been made, was an easy conquest to BROUGHTON.

George Stevenson, the *coachman*, stood up for
the length of forty minutes in a most heroic style to
BROUGHTON.   It was a hasty match, and although
BROUGHTON was extremely unwell, sooner than make

any excuse, he agreed to fight *Stevenson* without having that *regard for his preparation,* as he afterwards FOUND *he ought to have had.* But here his *true bottom* was proved, and his conduct shone and admired. The battle was fought in one of the fair-booths at Tottenham-court-road, railed at the end towards the Pit. After a most desperate conflict of thirty-five minutes, being both against the rails, and the Coachman endeavouring to get the *whip-hand* of BROUGHTON; the latter, by his superior genius, got such a lock upon *Stevenson,* as no mathematician could have have devised a better. There he held him by this artificial lock, depriving him of all power of rising or falling, till resting his head for about three or four minutes upon his back, he found himself recovering, then loosed his hold; by this manœuvre, BROUGHTON became as a new man—and, on *setting-to* again, he gave the Coachman a most tremendous blow, as hard as any he had given him in the whole battle, that he could no longer stand, and his brave contending heart, though with reluctance, was forced to yield. *Coachee* was a beautiful hitter; he put in his blows faster than BROUGHTON, but then one of the latter's told for three of the former's. *Stevenson* had a most daring *spirit,* but his *strength* could not keep pace with it. BROUGHTON expressed a very high opinion of *Stevenson* as a pugilist.

Jack James, a dashing boxer, and who ranked high in the annals of pugilism, and a *thorough-bred* man, was compelled to acknowledge that he had found out his master in BROUGHTON. *James's wrist,* which in other contests had been considered so remarkably *handsome,* lost all its attraction when in contact with the *beautiful* athletic arm of BROUGHTON.

It would be occupying too much space, as well as time, to enumerate all the battles that BROUGHTON had gained in eighteen years, during which long period he reigned the CHAMPION OF ENGLAND ; but immediately proceed to that contest, wherein his proud and deserved title was unluckily torn from his veteran head —his fame eclipsed—and his future prospects ruined !

We cannot vouch for the authenticity of the following statement, but it is reported, that at Hounslow Races, a butcher of the name of *Slack*, and known as a good pugilist, had behaved in an improper manner towards BROUGHTON, when the latter having a whip in his hand, threatened to horsewhip him for his insolent conduct—*Slack's* pride felt hurt at this indignant mode of treatment to *a man of his blood*, and instantly challenged BROUGHTON, which was immediately accepted.

BROUGHTON, it should seem, viewed this challenge of *Slack's* in rather too trifling a light, and felt persuaded that the contest would prove so easy to him, although he had not fought for a long time, that there was no necessity for *training*. This fatal confidence proved his downfall—the error was discovered too late—and he was left to regret not following the good old maxim, that a skilful general should be armed at all points.

On the evening previous to the battle (Tuesday, April 10, 1750) taking place, BROUGHTON, who had invited his patrons and numerous friends to witness the combat, was rather apprehensive that *Slack* would not fight, and, for fear any disappointment should take place, made the latter a present of ten guineas, not to break his engagement.

The time of fighting at length commenced, when

BROUGHTON's superiority over *Slack* was so evident,
for the first two minutes, that the odds were ten to one
in his favour. *Slack*, recovering himself a little from
the violent effects of his antagonist's blows, made a sudden and unexpected jump, and put in a desperate hit
between BROUGHTON's eyes, which immediately closed
them up; BROUGHTON now appeared like one stupid,
and it was two or three minutes before this circumstance
was discovered by the spectators, whose attentions were
attracted by the strange and unusual manner in which
BROUGHTON appeared to *feel* for, instead of boldly facing and attacking his man : at length his patron, the
Duke of Cumberland, earnestly exclaimed, "WHAT
ARE YOU ABOUT, BROUGHTON—YOU CAN'T FIGHT!
—YOU'RE BEAT!" To which question BROUGHTON instantly replied—" *I can't see my man, your Highness—I
am blind, but not* BEAT; *only let me be placed before my
antagonist, and he shall not gain the day yet.*"—BROUGH-
TON's situation was truly distressing—the audience were
disgusted—and *Slack*, following up this singular advantage, obtained a victory in *fourteen minutes!*—The *faces*,
in the Amphitheatre, upon this occasion, are better imagined than described; but suffice to say, they were of
all manner of *colours* and *lengths*—TEN to *one* had been
laid pretty thick, and the favourite had lost. The above
Royal Duke lost several thousands, and the *knowing ones*
were completely *done up.* The door-money produced near
£150 besides a great number of tickets at a guinea and a
half each; and as the conqueror was to have the produce
of the house, it is supposed that *Slack* got near £600.

Thus, in the short space of *fourteen minutes,* alas !
was the FATHER OF BOXING, BROUGHTON, de-

BROUGHTON AND SLACK.

In the memorable battle, at the Amphitheatre, on Tuesday, April 10; 1750.

Copied by Pennylvion from the Original Painting in the possession of Mr Thomas Belcher.

prived of all his laurels! Hear it ye CHAMPIONS!
Weep for the veteran's downfall! and profit by his loss
—BE NOT TOO CONFIDENT—and *remember*, that it was
occasioned by *one* fatal error—neglect of *training* ! ! !
Notwithstanding this unfortunate defeat, according to
the opinions of the best informed of that period, *Slack*
was in every respect, as a pugilist, inferior to BROUGH-
TON, and that it was more owing to accident than design, that *Slack* gained the victory. It was well
known among the *sporting men*, that *Slack* was not the
slightest object of envy to BROUGHTON ; as the former
had been beaten by *Taylor*, and who was an easy conquest to BROUGHTON. However, it proved his complete
overthrow — the Duke of Cumberland, his stanch
supporter upon all occasions, never could speak of this
transaction with any degree of temper, declaring, that
he had been sold, and nothing could persuade him to the
contrary, being so firmly persuaded that BROUGHTON
was every way so superior to *Slack*. His Royal Highness instantly turned his back upon him, and, by the interference of the Legislature, his Amphitheatre was shut
up. BROUGHTON never fought again. Previous to this
battle, he had grown considerably into flesh, and was
of a plethoric habit, by which his frame was rendered
much softer than heretofore, that the blows made him
bleed at the touch, and his flesh swelled amazingly.

BROUGHTON, after such a sudden reverse of fortune,
retired into private life quite disconcerted and unhappy
—occasioned, it is said, from his *Royal Patron* entertaining so *unjust* an opinion of him, and became, in
consequence, much dejected.—We cannot take leave
of so distinguished a HERO without remarking, that he

deserved a better fate ; and that the *veteran* might exclaim in the words of the poet :

> " So farewell to the little good you bear me ;
> Farewell, a long farewell to all my greatness !
> This is the state of man ; to day he puts forth
> The tender leaves of hope, to-morrow blossoms,
> And bears his blushing honours thick upon him ;
> The third day comes a frost, a killing frost,
> And when he thinks, good easy man, full surely
> His greatness is a ripening, nips his root,
> *And then* HE FALLS AS I DO !"

JACK SLACK,

Rendered a pugilist of some prominency, by his victory over *Broughton,* and in being elevated to the
rank of CHAMPION !—He was a man of considerable
strength and bottom : firmly made ; in height about five
feet eight inches and a half, and in weight nearly as
heavy as *Broughton,* but not quite fourteen stone.
SLACK was very little indebted to *science,* and trusted to
a method almost exclusively his own : his blows were
generally well put in, and given with a most dreadful
force. His attitudes were by no means impressive : there
was a want of elegance in his positions to attract the
attention of the spectators, and he appeared as a most
determined fighter, scarcely giving time to his adversary
to breathe, and bent upon nothing else but *victory.* He
stood remarkably upright, guarding his stomach with his
right hand, and as if protecting his mouth with his left.
Whenever *Slack* meditated giving a blow upon any
particular part of his antagonist, he rushed in furiously

SLACK.

From the Bust in the Possession of Mr. Thos. Belcher.

BERKS.

Published Sept. 30, 1812, by G. Smeeton, 139, St. Martin's Lane.

regardless of the consequences of a *knock-down* blow in the attempt. It is but justice to say of him, that he disputed every battle manfully; was above shifting; and his *bottom* was of the first quality. SLACK was noted for a back-handed blow, which often operated most powerfully upon the face of his opponent : and it was observed, that being so used to *chopping* in his business as a butcher, that, in fighting, the CHOPPER proved of no little service to him in producing victory.

SLACK's first battle of note was with *George Taylor*, in 1750; but the superior science of *George* rendered his ferocity unavailing; and SLACK, after a severe contest for near thirty minutes, was obliged to acknowledge that he had got ENOUGH. It was a battle spoken highly of by the sporting men of that day, for a prime display of *science* and *bottom*.

After *Broughton's* defeat—PUGILISM in the Metropolis was *done up ;* and a period of upwards of four years elapsed before a battle of any consequence took place, and then it was fought in the country, between one *Pettit*, a Frenchman, and SLACK, at *Harleston*, in *Norfolk*, in 1754.

This battle proved as singular a conflict as ever took place in the annals of pugilism : *Monsieur*, on the first *set-to*, darted with uncommon fury at SLACK, and seized him by the throat, and, for half a minute, held him tight against the rails, till SLACK was nearly choked and black in the face; and it was with some difficulty that SLACK released himself from this unpleasant situation.—The next ten minutes the *Frenchman* appeared like a blacksmith *hammering* away at SLACK, and driving him all over the stage with uncommon im-

No. III.　　　　　　　　　　　　K

petuosity, till at length SLACK closed upon *Pettit,* and
gave him three desperate falls; but during which period
he canted SLACK twice off the stage.—*Monsieur* began
to appear shy of SLACK's method of throwing, and ran
in upon the latter and seized him by the hams—and
tumbled him down, by which means SLACK fell easy. A
Guinea to a *Shilling* was the odds against SLACK after
they had been fighting eighteen minutes, when at the
commencement of the fight it was four to one in his
favour. SLACK now changed his method of attack, and
followed the *Frenchman* up so close, that he had no opportunity of running in at him, but was compelled to
stand up and fight; when SLACK closed one of his eyes,
and disfigured his face in a shocking manner. *Pettit's*
wind began now to fail him, and SLACK was recovering
his strength fast, when the odds were shifting rapidly on
his side. *Pettit* once more got a little advantage and
threw SLACK over the rails—but, in going over, SLACK
put in a desperate blow under the ribs of the *Frenchman,*
that made him cry *peccavi.* SLACK was not long in
mounting the stage; but *Monsieur* was so *panic struck,*
that he *brushed* off with all the haste imaginable, never
stopping to look back after his opponent. It was the
opinion of the spectators, that *Pettit* was full strong
when he *bolted.* The battle lasted twenty-five minutes,
perfectly ridiculous at times, and equally dreadful by
turns. The *Frenchman* not returning to finish the contest, SLACK was declared the conqueror, and drew the
first ten guineas out of the box.

About a twelvemonth after this fight, one *Cornelius
Harris,* a collier, from Bristol, cha llenged SLACK for
one hundred guineas. *Harris* proved himself a good

bit of stuff, teazed the CHAMPION a great deal, and disputed the ground manfully ;—but SLACK's experience was too much for him, and, after a severe *set-to* for twenty minutes, *Harris gave in.*

SLACK now laid by in peace for upwards of four years, till one *Morton*, of Acton-Wells, had the temerity to call the Champion out to the field of honour, for fifty pounds. SLACK accepted the challenge with alacrity, and the moment of decision arrived, when *Morton* showed himself a good *bottomed* man, and kept the *game alive* for thirty-five minutes, in a style of great excellence. SLACK had *his work* to do; but ultimately was declared the victor.

Ten years had now elapsed since SLACK had vanquished the renowned *Broughton,* and held the title of CHAMPION—but the honour was dazzling, and another hero put in his claim for the towering prize. SLACK's fame was well established; and here Royalty was once more busy in the pugilistic scene, by *Broughton's* old patron, the Duke of Cumberland, stepping forward, and backing him for one hundred pounds against one *Bill Stevens*, a *nailer,* whom the Duke of York took under his patronage. The Haymarket was the scene of action, and a stage was erected in the Tennis-court, James-street. SLACK entered the field with all the confidence of a veteran, and was acknowledged to have the advantage in the first part of the battle ; but the *Nailer,* with an arm like iron, received the ponderous blows of his antagonist on his left with ease, while with his right arm he so punished the CHAMPION's *nob,* that he knocked off the title—picked it up, and wore it !—Thus fell the hitherto mighty SLACK ! .

SLACK now returned to his business as a butcher,
and opened a shop near Covent-garden; and, being
a *public man*, the curiosity of the people in going
to see a great fighter, brought him considerable custom.
SLACK had a number of accidental skirmishes in his visits
to fairs and other places of amusement, and was fond of
what he termed—"*giving the natives a small* TASTE;" but
at a country fair, affronting (what now is styled) a *Johnny
Raw*, who, on the impulse of the moment, gave the
CHAMPION, for his bit of fun, a prime *lick on the smel-
lers*, which rather disconcerted SLACK, who, thinking he
had got a mere *plaything*, immediately put in one of his
best hits as a *finisher*; but he was mistaken, and a regular *set-to* commenced. *Johnny Raw*, being a fine athletic
young man, and plenty of *pluck*, fell upon SLACK as if
he had been *threshing corn*, and positively would have
soon *served out* the CHAMPION—but SLACK, now perceiving that he had picked up a *troublesome customer*, resorted to the following manœuvre, by way of intimidating
Johnny, cried out, with some degree of emphasis,
" What! a *chaw bacon* attempt to beat JACK SLACK!"
This stratagem had the desired effect upon the nerves of
the unsuspecting countryman, who simply thought it impossible that he should be able to conquer so renowned
a hero, exclaimed—" Dang it, what have I been fiten
with that noted mon, SLACK—no, no, I moant have
no more to do with he!" and instantly gave up the contest; though, in all probability, SLACK would have
been drubbed most soundly!

The above anecdote reminds us of a number of similar circumstances (which have induced us to offer the
following remarks, with the most friendly intention,

trusting they may operate as a useful *hint* in future) that have taken place at various times, occasioned by wanton, foolish young men, who, being in possession of considerable *strength*, and knowing how to *fight a little*, (and even *some* celebrated PUGILISTS, who ought to known better,) have been guilty of taking up liquor in strange company, and drinking of it that has not belonged to them, merely, as it is termed, for a *lark;* and which upon being resented as a most gross affront, by the persons who have been thus insulted, from their not being able to contend with such powerful opponents have frequently got *beaten* in the bargain. Such acts are most grievous indeed, and, consequently, brings PUGILISM into disgrace; but, surely, men who are gifted with only a trifling share of common sense must be well aware that such conduct is truly despicable; and if they have the smallest intention of being respected in society, they will never take such unwarrantable liberties, in sporting with the feelings of the harmless and unoffending stranger. No Englishman will PASSIVELY put up with such treatment—so derogatory to the character of a Briton !

> " O 'tis excellent
> To have a giant's strength; but it is *tyrannous*
> *To use it like* A GIANT !"

GEORGE TAYLOR,

Although defeated by the Champion *Broughton*, yet he stood high upon the list as a *prime article*, in vanquishing the mighty *Slack* and other Pugilists of note;

and rendering himself popular in succeeding FIG as
master of the Amphitheatre—that we cannot pass over
his last *set-to* without respectful mention; and by placing
him in a proper situation after those renowned heroes.—
The noted *Tom Faulkener*, celebrated for his knowledge
of cricket and pugilism, and who had been twice *milled*
by GEORGE, yet still thought there was another *chance*
left, and, therefore, challenged TAYLOR for two hundred guineas and the door-money. TAYLOR, who had
grown old in the service, and now kept the Fountain
Tavern, Deptford, where he lived in peace and quietness,
serving his customers, smoking his pipe, and recounting
o'er his battles—yet the *pluck* still remained, and he accepted the challenge without hesitation. It was to be
decided near St. Alban's, in Hertfordshire. *Faulkener*,
although the odds were much against him, *sported* all
he possessed, and felt confident of winning. The combatants knew each other, and that no time should be
lost upon either side, it was a complete HAMMERING
set-to. For the first twelve or thirteen rounds *Faulkener*
was *punished* most dreadfully, and *floored* several times,
without knocking down his antagonist. The fourteenth
round proved a proper trial of skill and strength ; at
length, *Faulkener* levelled TAYLOR, when the odds
began to drop a little, and *Faulkener* was getting into
favour. GEORGE, finding that his man gained upon
him, began to shift, and fell now and then without a
blow, which occasioned considerable murmuring, and
the friends of *Faulkener* insisted that he had won the
battle : but *Faulkener* was above taking any advantage
and wished to fight it out. The combatants *set-to*
more furious than ever—and the *knowing ones* were

puzzled how to *sport* their cash with any degree of certainty, the *chances* were so various, and the conquest so *doubtful*. TAYLOR, inspired with the thoughts of his former victories, and his fame, fought like a HERO thirsting after more glory; and *Faulkener*, recollecting that it must either *make* or *break* him, stood up like a LION, without a particle of fear. The spectators were astonished at the intrepidity displayed. After a most terrible conflict of an hour and seventeen minutes, the veteran GEORGE TAYLOR *blushed* to acknowledge that he was conquered. Greater courage and skill could not be displayed; and it was entertained by the *sporting men*, that had not TAYLOR laboured under the manifest disadvantage of an eye, (which he had been blind of for some years,) *Faulkener* could never have beat him; as the contest was only put an end to by TAYLOR's having the other eye closed from a dreadful blow given by *Faulkener* upon it. Neither of the combatants were able to walk off the ground. TAYLOR died in three months after this *set-to*.

EDWARD HUNT,

The celebrated pupil of *Broughton*, (whom we have alluded to in a former part of this work,) was a most distinguished pugilist; and, like his great master, a first-rate scientific artist. *Thorough-bred* in bottom, and well acquainted with the *arcana* of boxing, he acquired great reputation in conquering men twice his weight. HUNT was of a size that must be considered little for a boxer, being scarcely five feet five inches in height, and his weight not above eight stone and a half. He had no competitors of his own size, and, consequently, was generally overmatched—his rich display of the art with one *Hawksley*, a life-guardsman, in 1746, completely established his fame. HUNT, on the *set-to* with the guardsman, (who weighed *seventeen* stone,) appeared like a boy to *Hawksley's* weight and height, that the odds were ten to one against him.; but HUNT was not the least intimidated by the disparagement between him and his lofty opponent, and stood up to *Hawksley* as prime as a *game-cock;* for the idea of *shifting* he spurned, and never fell without a *knock-down* blow. He so confused *Hawksley* by the various attitudes he assumed during the fight, that he *punished* the guardsman in the most effectual manner, and soon changed the odds in his favour. HUNT's knowledge of the SCIENCE was so manifest, that he *stopped* the heavy blows aimed at his head or body, by his powerful antagonist, with apparent ease, and returned instantly a desperate hit. The guardsman could do nothing with him; and after a severe beating, which he got in the short space of ten minutes, *Hawksley* left HUNT in possession of the field. It was supposed, if HUNT had weighed about twelve or thirteen stone, no pugilist at that period would have stood any chance with him.

In the course of a twelvemonth after this time, a match was made for one hundred and fifty guineas between HUNT and *Tom Smallwood* of great pugilistic notoriety. Such a battle had not been seen for some time—here was *science* against *science*, and bottom *against* bottom. The sporting world expected much from this meeting, and, in the event of it, were not deceived, knowing both the articles to be thorough *game !* The scene of action was upon a stage erected at Hounslow, and for the first half hour the spectators did not know how to lay their money,—it was *diamond cut diamond!* NED's strength began now to be on the decline, and *Smallwood*, being the heaviest man, threw HUNT very often; but still the *game* was not to be taken out of him easily, and HUNT continued the fight for near an hour before *Smallwood* was declared the conqueror.

Notwithstanding NED experienced a defeat, his character was not in the least tarnished as a finished pugilist—his SCIENCE was universally admired, and his friends were only sorry that his frame was not strong enough to operate as a second to so much spirit and art.

HUNT distinguished himself considerably in all the battles he fought, and particularly in those where victory was against him; feeling anxiously to establish a good character as a Boxer. He had a most desperate conflict, for upwards of an hour, with one *Dick Mills*, but was compelled to GIVE IN. Considerable sums were lost upon HUNT in this battle.

BILL STEVENS—*the Nailer.*

A most tremendous Boxer, and, at one period of his life, beat all before him—who also conquered the famous *Slack*; and, from his skill and uncommon strength, might, in all probability, have retained the title of Champion till he had made his grand exit off the stage, or, at least, for a considerable number of years; but want of *principle* blighted his prospects, and ruined his

No. IV. L

character as a Pugilist. His conquests, at one time, it is said, were so numerous, that he sat down, like the great ALEXANDER, *weeping that he had no more heroes to overcome !* But gold, powerful gold, seduced him from his honesty; and ever afterwards, as he most justly deserved to be, was without a friend or patron to back him. However, notwithstanding all his failings, STEVENS was considered a most desperate *punisher;* and whenever inclination prompted him so to do, he could *serve it out* in the first style of finished excellence ! His *Championship* was but of short duration, owing to his treachery.

STEVENS fought a terrible battle in 1760, against one *Jacob Taplin,* a *coal-heaver,* in Mary-le-bone-Fields. The spectators were exceedingly numerous from the *bottom* characters of the combatants. At the commencement of the fight, the *Coal-heaver* gave STEVENS repeatedly knock-down blows, which raised the odds upon *Taplin;* but STEVENS, recovering from the powerful blows of his antagonist, and finding he had not much time to lose, put in a most desperate body-blow, which brought *Taplin* down, and followed it up by several other violent hits. The odds now changed five to one upon the *Nailer,* and the contest was soon decided in his favour. This battle raised his fame, and it was but a few months after this time, when he fought *Slack,* the Champion—and added more laurels to his brow.

In less than twelve months, after his name had become almost a terror to Pugilists, by his beating the Champion, he entered the lists with *George Meggs,* a Bristol collier, for 200 guineas, at the Tennis-court, James-street. STEVENS scarcely knew *how* to make a fight of it—and let *Meggs* drive him about as he pleased ; and after seventeen minutes in *humbugging* the spectators— STEVENS gave in. The *sporting men* were properly swindled upon this occasion; and the *Nailer* had the impudence to acknowledge soon after, that he was *tipped* handsomely to lose the battle, and that he had gained more by so doing—exclaiming, at the same time, " that he was as good a man as ever !" The *Nailers* and *Black-smiths* of the Metropolis were finely *spoke to* by the loss of this battle, as they had backed the *man of iron*, from his former stanch character, for considerable sums. It is said, that a celebrated engraving, now extant, of a blacksmith's shop where the *Nailer* had worked, the men of which had sported their *little cash* upon his head, was taken from their hearing he had lost the battle !

> " I saw a smith stand with his hammer, thus,
> The whilst his iron did on the anvil cool,
> With open mouth, swallowing a tailor's news ;
> Who, with his sheers and measure in his hand,
> Standing on slippers, which his *nimble haste*
> Had falsely thrust upon contrary feet."

The fights of the *Nailer*, after the above circumstance, cannot prove interesting, as he had grossly forfeited all pretensions to *honour :*—STEVENS beat an Irish pugilist of the name of *M'Guire*, behind Montague-house; and was defeated in a battle with one *Turner*. The *Nailer's* last battle of any consequence was with the noted *Sellers*, (the conqueror of *Peter Corcoran*, of pugilistic celebrity,) in which STEVENS stood no chance with *Sellers* ; eighteen years having elapsed since he fought *Slack*, his powers, of course, were considerably on the decline, as a pugilist.

MISCELLANEOUS PUGILISM.

From the year 1761 to 1783, a period of twenty-two years, the CHAMPIONSHIP was in a very unsettled state, and *knocked* about quickly from one *nob* to another; as there were few heads that could be found whom the CONQUEROR'S CAP would *fit* for any length of time:—GEORGE MEGGS, who *bought* the title from the *Nailer*, had it soon wrested from him by MILSOM, the *baker;* TOM JUCHAU soon *milled* it out of MILSOM; and the renowned BILL DARTS *punished* all pretensions toward the elevated prize from TOM JUCHAU—when BILL, experiencing the vicissitudes of fortune, although contending for the honour of wearing it for nearly five years, lost it in a desperate struggle with LYONS, the *waterman—here the* CHAMPIONSHIP *was at a stand-still for a short time*—when DARTS had once more an opportunity of gaining it with PETER CORCORAN; but PETER grasped it so hard and fast, that it was *seven long years* before they could get it out of his hands; at length one HARRY SELLERS got possession of the TITLE, but, if report speaks true, he *paid* for it; and who knew its value so very little, as to let FEARNS, an Irish boatswain, carry it off in less than *five minutes!* Thus was the CHAMPIONSHIP *badgered* about — till TOM JOHNSON appeared, and put in his claim to support it with true courage and dignity. TOM soon *tried on* the CAP OF HONOUR, and it appeared to *fit* him so tight and well, that many a brave fellow, for a long time, endeavoured to *knock* it off—but without effect!

In order to prevent any chasm in the History of Pugilism, although many of the battles may be of inferior note, yet still we deem it perfectly necessary to insert trifling accounts of them.

TOM FAULKENER,

Who beat the veteran *George Taylor*, fought with *Joe Eames* (brother to Jack James, celebrated at Broughton's School,) at Putney, in Surrey, upon a stage erected in a field. The odds at *setting-to* were considerably in favour of *James*, and continued to increase during the fight. FAULKENER appeared to stand no chance with *Joe*, as the latter *floored* him every round. FAULKENER at length brought down his antagonist, when *James* immediately gave in, to the great indignation of the spectators. The battle was for one hundred pounds, and the *sporting world* considered it to be little short of a CROSS !

GEORGE MEGGS,

Of no particular note as a Pugilist, except beating the *Nailer*. He received instruction from *Slack*, and fought with *Milsom*, the *baker*, at Calne, in Wiltshire, for forty minutes, which was well contested, but *Milsom* was declared the conqueror. MEGGS was not satisfied, and demanded another trial, when *Milsom* beat him easy the second time.

PARSITT MEGGS, brother to the above Pugilist, also *tried it on* with *Milsom*, but, in the event, got a severe beating.

TOM JUCHAU—*the Paviour*,

A most excellent bit of flesh, and a *glutton* of the first *mould*, was matched against *Charles Coant*, a *butcher*, for a considerable sum; the battle was decided at Guildford, in Surrey, and, on the *set-to*, the odds were high upon the *Butcher*, who kept increasing them for the first half hour, that JUCHAU could scarcely put in a blow to do any harm to his antagonist. The *Butcher* kept getting on in such superior style, that they were all *betters* and no *takers*. A fair opportunity now offering, JUCHAU put in a desperate body-blow, which levelled this *prime cove*, when the odds began to move directly, and the next round JUCHAU followed up his advantage so quickly, that the bets became even. JUCHAU now *showed off* in such a spirited manner, putting in his blows right and left, that *Coant*, in a few rounds more, was compelled to cry stop, and JUCHAU pronounced Conqueror; the fight lasted near fifty minutes.

Milsom, who had beat the *temporary* Champion *Meggs*, now entered the field with JUCHAU, near St. Alban's. *Milsom* by no means disgraced himself in the contest; but was under the necessity of allowing JUCHAU to be his master. The *Paviour* was now considered a first-rate man, and soon matched himself against some of the most distinguished Pugilists.

BILL DARTS—*the Dyer*,

Of no mean rank as a Boxer, and considered one of the most desperate hitters of his time—plenty of strength, good *pluck,* and not destitute of science, was backed to fight *Tom Juchau,* at Guildford, for *one thousand guineas!* The *Paviour* had been tried, and not found wanting; and DARTS was known to be thorough GAME. The *sporting men* anticipated a fine display of the art, and, in the event, were not disappointed. *One thousand guineas* were dazzling indeed—and they both entered the field with uncommon gaiety, determined upon victory. The contest was long and doubtful—the odds continually varying—and, after a most dreadful struggle, DARTS came off victorious.

A West-country Bargeman, celebrated for strength, challenged BILL DARTS, after his successful contest with *Juchau,* for one hundred pounds. *Dogget* was the hero of the country, and, from his great prowess, flattered himself he could make an easy conquest of DARTS ;—but, in the field of battle, he experienced so many severe *darts* from his antagonist, that he was quickly slain. *Dogget* acknowledged that he was the *worst customer* he had ever met with.

A *butcher,* who felt rather anxiously for *a taste* of DARTS' quality, called him out to the plains of honour ; but *Swansey,* the butcher, was soon *cut up.*

BILL DARTS now went on *swimmingly,* and kind Fortune had smiled upon him in all his adventures; but BILL was envied, and a *Waterman* was determined to try if he could not *row* in the same lucky boat with him. *Lyons,* therefore, sent him a challenge, to fight at Kingston-upon-Thames, which BILL, upon receiving, was too *gay* to refuse. The time was appointed, and the *set-to* commenced. For the first twenty-five minutes the Waterman's *scull* was knocked about as if it did not belong to him, and the odds were ten to one upon DARTS; but the *tide* soon turning, the *Waterman* pulled up at every *stroke*, and, in the course of twenty minutes afterwards, DARTS was completely distanced. This battle afforded considerable amusement to the amateurs; and both the Pugilists got great praise; but it does not appear that *Lyons* fought much after this contest—giving DARTS an opportunity of regaining his laurels.

Notwithstanding that BILL DARTS was defeated by this able *Waterman,* he soon had the temerity to enter the lists with a more terrible opponent—*Death!* (so denominated for his singularly pale face when fighting, a Pugilist of great renown, and one of *Broughton's* principal favourites). It was supposed that *Death* had fought more battles than any boxer in England; was a neat, tight-made man, weighing about twelve stone, possessing uncommon agility, but not much strength; thorough *bottom,* and never nice in being overmatched. He was considered the best *sparrer* of his time, and had made the SCIENCE his study. *Steven Oliver* (for that was his real name) was no trifling antagonist for DARTS to contend with; but then *Oliver* was going fast down hill, and twenty years had elapsed since his patron *Broughton* had left the field. It was a well-contested battle; and it was supposed by the *sporting world,* that there was never more strength, science, and *bottom,* shown in any *set-to* than that between DARTS and *Death!* *Oliver,* tough as bell-wire, struggled hard to hear the pleasing sound of victory once more grace his listening ear, but in vain—DARTS put in such tremendous blows, that *Oliver* was compelled to GIVE IN —thus, for once, was *Death* defeated!

BATTLES

(Contested at various Times, although not very important, yet necessary to render the Connexion complete to the Time when TOM JOHNSON *commenced Champion)*

IN WHICH

THE FOLLOWING PUGILISTS WERE ENGAGED :

JACK SHEPHERD,	GEORGE RING,
JOHN WHITE,	JACK WARREN,
DENNIS KELLYHORN,	ABRAHAM DA COSTA,
OLIVER, ALIAS DEATH,	ISAAC MOUSHA,
PHILIP JUCHAU,	JEMMY, *the Postman,*
HARRY PAYNE,	WILLIAM SMALL,
JACK LAMB,	PETER EDWARDS,
JOHN PEARCE,	TOM NICHOLS,
CHARLES COANT,	BILL JOYCE, &c.

In commencing this EPITOME OF PUGILISM, towards completing the above period, the valorous deeds of JACK LAMB, the *plasterer*, stand most prominent :—his name was far from indicating his character, as MEEKNESS was not in his composition. JACK was a good second-rate pugilist, and was not afraid of his *canvas.*—PAYNE, the *carpenter,* challenged LAMB for twenty pounds ; when the battle was decided in (a celebrated place for minor pugilists) Islington-Hollow. The fight was well-contested, and the odds were in favour of PAYNE ; but in the event of the conflict Master *Chip* was defeated.

JEMMY, the *postman,* well known for a *bit of blood* in the fighting world, entered the field with LAMB. Considerable sums were sported on the issue of this contest, and Moorfields were half filled with spectators. It was a complete *mill* on both sides, and, after a *hammering* of near fifty minutes, they both agreed to *sheer* off !

No. IV.

M

LAMB was getting rather an object of jealousy among the inferior *milling coves,* and challenges came in upon him thick :—SIMPSON, a *carman,* who felt a little pride in the pugilistic way, fought LAMB upon Bethnal-green; but the *Knight of the Whip* soon acknowledged that the *Lamb* was too tough for him. ISAAC MOUSHA, at Stepney, and ABRAHAM DA COSTA, in Moorfields, two of the tribe of Israel, wished to take *the conceit out* of JACK; but they were most terribly disappointed in not finding the LAMB quite so *tender* as they imagined, by his proving, what they did not like—a PRIME *piece of pork!*

But LAMB had now got quite unruly, and began to challenge in his turn, and offered *fifty pounds* to *thirty* to beat a SHEPHERD of some experience. The LAMB was the favourite, and the odds were sported high upon his head; but the SHEPHERD, who knew how to manage a flock, in the event chastised the LAMB for his daring temerity, in forty minutes, so as not to be able to run away any more from the SHEPHERD. LAMB was carried out of SAMPSON's Riding-school, Islington, nearly lifeless!

CHARLES COANT and the above JACK SHEPHERD had a most desperate *set-to,* at Barnet, for upwards of thirty minutes; when SHEPHERD proved the conqueror.

An Hibernian pugilist, of the name of JOYCE, fought a battle at Mill-hill, near Hendon, with NICHOLS, a *butcher;* the latter was but a small-made man, and JOYCE possessing considerable strength and fame, the odds were very high in his favour. But bets are very deceiving frequently, and so they proved in this instance; for in the first round NICHOLS put in such a desperate blow on the face of his antagonist, as to break JOYCE's

jaw—the fight was soon over after this circumstance, and
the *sweaters* and *trainers* were completely in the *basket!*

Two *Sons of St. Crispin*, JACK PEARCE and JACK
WHITE, who felt some thirst for pugilistic honours, had
a *set-to* for twenty pounds, at the Riding-school, Islington. The *Heroes of the Last* were showing off in *prime
style*—several *knock-down* blows were the consequence
of their efforts, and PEARCE was going on fast for victory, when an unmannerly fellow, with a staff in his
hand, put an end to the contest, by showing his authority, to the no small disappointment of the spectators,
and the chagrin of PEARCE. However, they chose a
more favourable opportunity to settle this honourable
reckoning, at a town in ESSEX, when WHITE, unexpectedly, was the conqueror.

A most obstinate battle was contested opposite
Bethlehem-gates, Moorfields, between JACK WARREN,
a *butcher*, and the *coachman*, PHILIP JUCHAU, for ten
pounds, which terminated most fatally to the latter!
The success was alternate, and great *bottom* displayed,
when, unfortunately, WARREN gave JUCHAU a *cross-
buttock*, by which throw he came down upon his head,
and died immediately.

BILL SMALL, a *butcher*, had the temerity to enter
the lists with the noted OLIVER, better known by the
appellation of DEATH, for twenty pounds. This contest was decided at Barnet; but DEATH very soon
proved too much for SMALL.

GEORGE RING, a *baker*, and who had distinguished
himself as a pugilist at Bath, fought one EDWARDS, a
butcher, at Kilburn-wells. T ere was no *bottom* wanting on either side, and a great number of *knock-down*

blows were given in the course of the fight, which lasted upwards of an hour and twenty minutes. EDWARDS was the favourite; but the *Baker* proved the conqueror.

SAM PETERS—*a Birmingham Hero!*

Well known, in that part of the country, as a Pugilist of some eminence, and who now wished to try his skill with a few of the first-rate *millers* in the metropolis :— SAM was not long in meeting with a *customer* to answer the purpose, and, upon Epping-forest, an Irishman, of the name of *Trainer*, fought with PETERS for £30. The Birmingham lad was *game*, and not easily daunted ; but *Trainer* was too powerful, and was declared the conqueror in thirty-eight minutes.

PETERS was not so soon *satisfied*, and shortly afterwards fought with another *Paddy*, called *Rossemus Gregory*, upon the same Forest, but PETERS, considering himself unfairly used, declined fighting any longer then ; however, it was but a little after this period, when PETERS had a *set-to* with *Gregory*, at Islington, in the Riding-school, when he *served* the latter *out* in good *twig*, in less than half an hour.

JOE HOOD—*the Weaver,*

A Pugilist of considerable celebrity, fought several battles with some of the first-rate heroes, and in many of which he had proved victorious. JOE entered the lists with *Jem Parrot*, in White-conduit-fields, Islington, who was looked up to as a prime *bit of stuff*, for twenty pounds. The contest was carried on with great spirit for nearly forty minutes, when *Parrot*, on the account of a foul blow, left the ring; but it was decided in favour of HOOD.

Dennis Kellyhorn, an Irish boxer of note, fought with HOOD, at Chinkford-batch, in Essex, for fifty pounds, when HOOD was again victorious.

JOE received a challenge from a *sawyer*, of the name of *Macdonald*, to fight for ten pounds; it was accepted without hesitation, and a most dreadful *set-to* commenced. HOOD had no *flat* to deal with, and it was upwards of fifty minutes before the *Sawyer* could be persuaded he had got *enough*, which was not till his jaw was broken, and both his eyes were closed.

Higgins, a celebrated Pugilist from Birmingham, who was the conqueror in fifteen battles, now called out JOE to decide which was the best man. HOOD was not to be frightened by his great character, but instantly matched himself. *Higgins* was a bottom man, but not able to contend against the science of HOOD. The Birmingham hero took a decent *milling* before he GAVE-IN.

Peter Bath, from Bristol, fought HOOD at Maidenhead, during the races, for fifty pounds. JOE having pleased the *sporting gentry* in several of his battles, they backed him two to one, although HOOD was not in good health. The fight soon changed in favour of the Bristol lad, who was in good condition, and proved too strong for JOE, who, after a *set-to* of twenty-three minutes, GAVE-IN.

JOE HOOD had also been *milled* by a neat, light boxer, of the name of *Bill Day*, in Smithfield.

PETER CORCORAN,

A most celebrated Pugilist from the Sister Country, was born at Athoye, in the county of Carlow, who took the lead for some years as a boxer in England, and might be said to be the *best man* of his time ; was five feet eleven inches in height, well-proportioned limbs, and of prodigious strength. PETER, from a boy, was distinguished for his uncommon intrepidity; and was looked upon in the vicinity of his father's MUD EDIFICE as the *cock of the walk !* He left Ireland a mere stripling, and in his peregrinations to the metropolis—Birmingham *chanced* to fall in his way ; in which place, through an accidental skirmish, his fame rose so high as a pugilist, that it was not long in reaching London. CORCORAN was accompanied from the *sod* by another tight boy, and they being somewhat fatigued with their journey ; or, as an Irish or English poet, no matter which, most sublimely and *poetically* observes :

" They who have money can ride in Post-chaises—
But HONIES that have none, *must walk*, by JASUS !"

and so it fell out with PETER and his friend, for money was the *lightest* thing they had about them—but, notwithstanding this scarcity of the *rhino*, hunger will very often intrude where there are no pockets at all—and a *beautiful* little shoulder of mutton, hanging at a butcher's shop, so *fastened* on the longing imagination of hungry PETER, that he could not pass it, and instantly went in to know the price. Some difference occurring respecting the terms, *Master Steel,* without any hesitation, threatened to knock the shoulder about poor

PADDY's *nob !* It appeared that this Butcher was a bit
of a *hit-a-body,* and well known in Birmingham as a
pugilist, and distinguished for his insolence, and who
flattered himself that he should have a little sport with
these *haymakers,* as he termed them ; but, in the sequel,
it turned out somewhat different. PETER, who had not
only felt himself baulked of his *beautiful little joint,* but
insulted also, exclaimed, with all the fervour of the
brogue, " By Jasus, Mr. *Butcher,* but you have too
much prate—and for half a pin, but I'd *bate* the mutton
out of your greasy carcase!" PADDY had scarcely uttered the words, when the *Butcher* showed fight, and a
regular *set-to* commenced—a concourse of people soon
collected, and PETER, with his clumsy thumps, *served
out* the *Knight of the Cleaver* in the presence of his
neighbours, and *knocked down* his consequence as a fighting man, in the course of a few minutes ; and shortly
afterwards enjoyed his mutton with as keen an appetite
as if nothing had happened ; and the next day pursued
his journey to London.

CORCORAN, upon his arrival in the Metropolis, commenced coal-heaver ; but which calling he soon left for
that of chairman ; and, owing to some trifling dispute,
it was not long afterwards when he went to sea, where
the rough elements gave additional vigour to his athletic
frame ; and, from the frequent specimens he at times
had displayed, was considered, for a *mill,* the first man
in the fleet, and was patronised by Captain *Perceval.*
When at Portsmouth, he performed a number of feats
of strength ; and one, among the number, was beating
a whole press-gang, and breaking the Lieutenant's
sword over his head. PETER, on leaving the navy,

came to London, and took the *Black Horse,* in Dyot-
street, St. Giles's, where his disposition was experienced
to be generous, truly good-natured, and remarkably ten-
der-hearted. As a pugilist—he was a first-rate ARTICLE,
possessing *bottom,* which could not be excelled, as he
did not know how to *shift,* and scorned to fall without
a *knock-down* blow ! PETER was denominated a straight
fighter ; put in his blows with uncommon force ; and
possessed great confidence in his own powers : his attitude was considered too erect, his arms not sufficiently
extended, by which means his guard was incomplete.
But CORCORAN was distinguished for the use of both
his hands with equal facility ; his aim was generally
correct, and he scarcely ever missed the object in view
—and was peculiarly successful in taking advantage of
any trifling neglect in his adversary ; and likewise
celebrated for an extraordinary jumper. PETER had
several scholars, among whom was *Big Pitt,* well-
known for many years as one of the turnkeys of Newgate, a man of uncommon size and strength ; and
being one night at *Joyce's* house, a pugilist, in the Haymarket, *brim-full* of conceit, surrounded by fighting
men, foolishly exclaimed, " that some of the *milling
coves* had taught their pupils so well, that many of them
were able to beat their masters !" Upon which PETER
instantly got up, and addressing himself to *Pitt,*
" What's that you say, you *spalpeen !* come, come out !"
Pitt stood up, but received such a *leveller* upon the
head, as completely knocked all recollection out of him,
for a few minutes, of what he had been *throwing-off*
about ! and, upon recovering himself acknowledged he
had been most wofully deceived.

PETER beat one *Turner*, who fought him for twenty pounds; and, although the latter had beaten the *Nailer*, yet, in the hands of CORCORAN, he was soon disposed of.

In the Long-fields, behind the British Museum, PETER had a good battle with one *Dalton*, an Irishman; and also with *Jack Davis;* they were both beaten dreadfully.

A desperate contest took place in Moorfields, between *Smiler*, the *brickmaker*, and CORCORAN; when PETER was again victorious.

The famous *Bill Darts* now mounted the stage with CORCORAN, for two hundred pounds, to give additional sport to Epsom races. The *set-to* commenced with cautious sparring upon the part of *Darts*, who soon discovered that he could not win; and in a short time *gave in!* A singular report crept into circulation, accounting for *Darts* losing the battle—that Colonel *O'Kelly* (one of the most celebrated sportsmen upon the turf, and who, undoubtedly, was *awake* to every manœuvre in gambling that could be *tried on* with any degree of certainty, either on the Turf or at the Table—Play or Pay—Cockpit or Racquets) backed his countryman for a large amount; but to make his bets dead sure, on the night previous to the fight, he presented *Darts* with one hundred pounds not even to try to win the battle, but *positively* to lose it. Surely, no *thorough-bred* sportsman could commit such a bare-faced robbery! And, upon the best information, we are assured, that *Darts*, in his *prime*, was never half man enough for CORCORAN!

Sam Peters, who fought PETER at Waltham-Abbey, in Essex, was the best man, according to CORCORAN's

No. IV.   N

own account, that ever *set-to* with him.   It was a comple *hammering* fight; and, at the expiration of ten minutes, *Peters* declared he was *satisfied*; and CORCORAN's body for several days afterwards was entirely black, the bruises being extremely severe.

CORCORAN, who had hitherto beat all the men which had been brought against him, and whose powers appeared not in the least diminished, was now doomed to sink fast into obscurity, from his memorable contest with *Sellers*, a west-countryman.   There is a considerable mystery hanging over that transaction; and it was, most undoubtedly, at the period when they fought, October 16, 1776, the general opinion of the SPORTING WORLD, that it was a complete DO!   It being well understood, that *Sellers* was deficient in *science* and *bottom* when placed in competition with PETER.   The battle was for one hundred guineas, and decided at Staines. On the *set-to,* PETER (who had always fought for victory previous to this combat) began, as usual, and drove *Sellers* about the stage like a shuttle-cock, and put in a blow, so powerful in its effect, as to knock down *Sellers*, who fell at a considerable distance from him. The odds were considerably high on PETER.; who, as if *recollecting* that he had done too much, immediately *suffered* himself, so as to make it have the appearance of a fight, to be beat about the stage for ten minutes, when he *gave-in!* This *contest*, if it can be so called, took twenty-three minutes.—The *knowing ones* were completely *dished,* at least, those who were not in the *secret;* and the poor *Paddies* were literally ruined, as many of them had *backed* their *darling boy* with every farthing they possessed.   St. Giles's was in a complete uproar, with mutterings and disapprobation at PETER's conduct.

Previous to the fight, *Peter's* house was almost destitute of any liquor, and he had been threatened with an execution for rent, &c.; but in a day or two after the *set-to*, the house was flowing with all sorts of spirits, &c. graced with plenty of new pots; the inside and out painted, and every thing got up in a superior style to what it ever had been witnessed before : and the very next morning after the *mill*, PETER CORCORAN was playing at skittles at the *Blakeney's Head*, St. Giles's, with all the activity and cheerfulness of a man who had never been engaged at all in pugilism. He shortly afterwards sunk into beggary and contempt, and was as much despised as he had been before respected; and was so miserably poor at his decease, that his remains were interred by subscription !—reminding us, that—

> " Honour and shame from no condition rise,
>   Act well your part—THERE all the honour lies !"

HARRY SELLERS

Was brought into notice by his conquest over *Peter Corcoran.* SELLERS was a west-countryman, possessing some *science,* and not deficient in strength ; but he was not generally considered as a pugilist of stanch *bottom,* although he had gained several battles in the country parts of England. Whenever the fight proved too hot for him, SELLERS had recourse to dropping on his knees, and striking his adversary as he fell, by which manœuvre he saved himself many a *leveller*, and was able to protract the combat. He never ranked as a *thorough-bred* Boxer, nor was looked up to as a *first-rate* Pugilist.

Joe *Hood* fought with SELLERS, at Ascot-heath races, for fifty pounds; but was compelled to *give-in*; yet *Joe*, in a short time afterwards, flattered himself that he could beat him, and insisted upon another trial with SELLERS; which was agreed to upon the part of the latter, and another *set-to* commenced: the battle was well contested, and *Joe* made use of all his judgement and *bottom*; but SELLERS, as before, proved victorious.

HARRY also beat the *Nailer*.

An Irish Boatswain, *Jack Fearns*, had a *set-to* with SELLERS for fifty pounds, and disposed of him in a *few minutes!* The amateurs were so taken by surprise, that their money was lost before they had scarcely time to recover from their *astonishment*, and much grumbling ensued! The odds had been betted upon SELLERS.

HARRY, after his victory over *Corcoran*, was continually insulting the *Paddies;* and being, one *St. Patrick's* evening, at the Black Dog, Holloway-mount, a Mr. *Harvey*, a lamp-black-maker, was among the company, who had a Shamrock in his hat, in honour of that *Saint!* SELLERS (who, it appears, was unknown) began sneering and laughing at *Harvey*, and observed, " that he ought to take that thing from his hat, as the *conceit* had been completely taken out of the *Paddies* since their Cham_ pion *Peter* had been defeated!" In consequence of this insult, words arose, and *Harvey*, feeling warmly for the honour of his countrymen, talked about resenting such conduct; when SELLERS immediately offered

to fight him NINE guineas to *four*, which was accepted
by *Paddy*; the stakes were instantly made good; and it
was agreed the contest should be decided, the next morning, in the most convenient field near the house. *Harvey* was a tall, well-made man, but a total stranger to
the science; yet possessing that manly courage which
would not let him put up with a gross affront pusillanimously. *Harvey* was there at the time appointed, contrary to SELLERS' expectation, who vainly imagined,
that if his antagonist had found out WHO *he* was, that
he would forfeit the money rather than enter the lists
with so *great a man!*—but viewing *Harvey* so cool and
collected about the business, SELLERS did not half like
him; and, by way of terrifying *Harvey*, said, " my
name is SELLERS—I don't want to hurt you, and will let
you off for a *leg of mutton and trimmings!*"—" By de
powers of *Moll Kelly*," replied *Paddy*, " if a single
potate would buy me off, I'll not give it you, Honey!
and Devil may care whether you're SELLERS or any
other big blackguard; but I *mane* to give you a good
bating for your impertinence !" Words were now useless,
and SELLERS finding his fame at stake, the combatants
entered the ring, and the *set-to* commenced—when the
anticipated fears of SELLERS were too soon realized,
and he found that *Harvey* was not to be trifled with.
SELLERS tried all the manœuvres of the art to puzzle
and exhaust his antagonist—but *Harvey's* true courage
rose superior to all the attacks of his adversary, and
straight forward completely *punished* SELLERS in a
quarter of an hour. SELLERS, thus deservedly disgraced and beaten, soon fell into disrepute and oblivion.

TOM JOHNSON

(THE ONCE CELEBRATED CHAMPION OF ENGLAND)

Was a pugilist of singularly distinguished abilities in
the gymnastic art ; and *if* TOM was not equal, at least,
he came the nearest to *Broughton* of any Boxer since
the days of that renowned veteran.   In the pugilistic
annals, JOHNSON was a hero among heroes, possessing all those requisites for pugilism, which rarely falls
to the lot of an individual.   NATURE had given him a
form almost of Herculean strength, which rendered him
either capable of resisting with ease, or in attacking
with the utmost impetuosity ; and he had improved
these natural qualifications by a most minute attention
to ART.   His courage was of the finest order, well
versed in the science, and possessed of a native coolness
of disposition, that infused into his composition a superior degree of firmness over most of his competitors :
and, added to these great capabilities, JOHNSON had
learned to subdue his passions—that, like the unrivalled
Broughton, when he mounted the stage, he was complete in his part, and proved himself a first-rate actor.

JOHNSON (whose real name, it is said, was *Jackling*)
was a native of Yorkshire, born in the same year that his
great prototype in the science was defeated by *Slack,*
and who, at a very early age, came to London, where he
followed the vocation of a corn-porter for nearly twenty
years, upon the several wharfs leading to Thames-street.
His surprising strength was first discovered from an act
of benevolence, highly worthy of recital—JOHNSON's
fellow-porter was taken ill, and having a wife and large

family entirely depending upon his labour for support, were likely to be reduced to want, had not JOHNSON immediately undertook (unknown to them) to do his fellow-porter's work, united with his own. The warehouses where the corn was deposited were situated at some trifling distance from the wharf, upon a hill, denominated, from its steepness, " *Labour-in-vain-hill,*" and to which place TOM carried every journey two sacks of corn instead of one, and gave the money to his family, till the porter was able to return to his work. It was no uncommon thing for JOHNSON, by way of evincing his strength, to take up a sack of corn in one hand, and twirl it round his head; which circumstance he once did within an hour after fighting a celebrated pugilist, to show how little he had suffered in the conflict. JOHNSON had fought with all the *picked* men of England, and who were reluctantly compelled to acknowledge his vast superiority. His appearance indicated, when stripped, more of strength than beauty of form; and he was in height nearly five feet nine inches, and about fourteen stone in weight; a remarkably round-made man, with very fine chest and shoulders, and displaying those strong loins that few human frames could boast such. JOHNSON was by no means a showy fighter, and his guard was generally considered as inelegant; his attitudes appeared more upon the defensive than otherwise; in the fight he was peculiarly steady, watching every movement of his antagonist with a coolness unequalled; receiving the attack unappalled; and scarcely ever failing in the *return* of planting a most desperate hit. The head was his favourite object, and if his adversary did not possess considerable science, he was in extreme danger of being put

in the *dark*. JOHNSON worked round his antagonist in
a way peculiar to himself, that so puzzled his adversary
to find out his intent, that he was frequently thrown off
his guard, by which manœuvring JOHNSON often gained the most important advantages: TOM was thorough
game, and showed the utmost contempt for *retreating;*
at the same time careful to avoid exposing his person
too much to the attacks of his antagonist.

JOHNSON's first *set-to*, in 1783, was with a fighting
Carman, of the name of *Jarvis ;* and though TOM was
looked upon as a mere *novice* in the art, yet he displayed
so much superiority over the *Carman*, that his fame was
soon made known. *Jarvis* had *milled* a few good men
himself—but in the hands of JOHNSON he got so
dreadfully beaten, that he was scarcely able to walk out
of Lock's Fields, where the contest was decided.

The *Croydon Drover*, a man of pugilistic notoriety,
now fought JOHNSON upon Kennington-common; but
JOHNSON *finished* him in a very short period.

Steevy Oliver, the noted *Death*, although growing
old fast, and who had been fighting ever since the days
of BROUGHTON, entered the lists with TOM JOHNSON,
and proved himself a good *bit of stuff*—but his day was
gone by—and JOHNSON was not long in getting the
victory. Some thousands of spectators were upon
Blackheath to witness this display of science.

Bill Love, a *butcher*, challenged JOHNSON for fifty
guineas, which was decided at Barnet; but the *Knight
of the Cleaver* was, in a few minutes, so completely *cut
up*, as to leave JOHNSON in possession of the ground.

Jack Towers, who had overcome *Death*, thought he
had little more to fear, and therefore, without hesitation,

agreed to fight JOHNSON at the above place ; but TOM had likewise got the better of *Death*, and, in a very short time, *Towers* was completely *satisfied* that he stood no *chance* with JOHNSON, and so *gave in !*

A man of the name of *Fry* offered to fight JOHNSON for fifty guineas, at Kingston, in June, 1786, which TOM cheerfully agreed to ; but, in less than half an hour, *Fry* got so much *broiled*, as to be very glad to put an end to the contest; and TOM walked off the ground not even *pinked !*

JOHNSON, about this period, (1787,) beat every one that was opposed to him, when it was deemed necessary by the *sporting world* to look out for a *customer* who might be able to stand something like a chance with him. As the metropolis could produce no such character, *Bristol* was searched, (the hot-bed for pugilists,) when *Bill Warr* was selected as an *article* that could be depended upon ; and he was backed to fight JOHNSON for two hundred guineas, upon a stage, at Oakhampton, in Berkshire, on January 18, 1787. In the first round *Warr* found out that he had got a *trump* to deal with, by receiving nearly a *doubler* from JOHNSON, and he immediately acted upon the defensive. In fact, it was scarcely worthy of being called a fight, and the amateurs were not only disappointed but much displeased. *Warr* was convinced that he could not beat JOHNSON by standing up to him, and therefore determined to try whether he could not *tire him out* ; and, generally, when TOM attempted to put in a good blow, *Warr* was down on his knees. This *humbugging* lasted for nearly an hour and a half, JOHNSON's intentions being continually frustrated by

No. V.   o

Warr's dropping on his knees ; at length a prime blow
made him cry out " *foul!*" and he instantly *bolted*,
notwithstanding the remonstrances of his second to
come back and finish the fight. JOHNSON was now
firmly established as the Champion ; his fame ran before him, and it was some months before any person
could be found hardy enough to dispute his well-earned
title : at length a brave Hibernian chief, who, like
TOM JOHNSON, had *milled* all his opponents, came
forward, and was instantly backed, when they were
soon *pitted*, like two *game cocks!*

Ryan's well-known skill and *bottom* stood so high
with the *Swells of the Fancy* that the odds were six to
four before the fight, which took place at Wradisbury,
in Buckinghamshire, on December 19, 1787. The
seconds were chosen from the first-rate pugilists, *Humphries* for JOHNSON, and *Dunn* for *Ryan ;* and even
the bottle-holders were of equal rank, in *Tring* for the
latter, and *Mendoza* for the former. The spectators
were numerous ; many of whom were distinguished
for great classical ability. The late celebrated *Mr.
Wyndham* and *General Fitzpatrick*, &c. &c. were more
than *gazers* on this occasion.

The *set-to* was grand : fear was out of the question,
and science was pre-eminent. It was like unto *Pompey*
and *Cæsar*, attended by their best generals to give advice upon the least disorder, in contending for the high
honour of the *purple*. True courage was never finer
displayed, and perfect heroism was seen upon both
sides. The contest was doubtful in the extreme, though,
at the commencement, the odds were in favour of
Ryan. After the fight had continued for nearly twenty
minutes, and at the close of a most tremendous round,

Ryan put in a dreadful blow upon JOHNSON's temple, which so completely stunned him that his arms fell down as useless by his side, and was following up this advantage with another *hit*, which must have decided the contest, when *Humphries* ran in to save JOHNSON, and caught *Ryan* in his arms. The cries of "*foul! foul!*" now resounded from all parts of the spectators, and the friends of *Ryan* instantly demanded the money, by observing that, as long as JOHNSON had not fallen, it was perfectly fair on the part of *Ryan* to strike him, and that the latter had won the battle. Here a general clamour took place, during which *Ryan*, with the warmth peculiar to his country, indignantly told his second, *Dunn*, that he had not done his duty by him as a man, in suffering such conduct to take place without resenting it, and, had he not been prevented, would have *milled Dunn* upon the spot, his rage was so great. Considerable time having now elapsed, JOHNSON was perfectly recovered, and challenged *Ryan* to renew the combat: the latter, like a man, notwithstanding it was considered there was no necessity for so doing, agreed to it, thinking he could beat JOHNSON. The battle was at length renewed; but it was soon perceived that *Ryan's* strength was exhausted by passion, and he now, in about ten minutes, became an easy conquest to JOHNSON, by giving away the *chance*. *Ryan's* conduct in the battle was so noble, and his manly courage and science so truly apparent, that the amateurs were still left in doubt to decide accurately WHICH *was the best man!*

In consequence of this opinion, a second battle was determined upon, and fought upon a stage near Rickmansworth, in a gentleman's park, for six hundred guineas, on February 11, 1789. It was a contest of great

anxiety, and the whole of the bruising world were
there, from the *Corinthian pillar* to the *costermonger!*
JOHNSON, with his second, *Humphries,* and *Jackson*
as his bottle-holder, mounted the stage at three o'clock,
and were immediately followed by *Ryan,* who was seconded by a *Mr. Rolfe,* a baker, and *Nowlan* as bottle-
holder. The *set-to* was one of the finest ever witnessed
in the annals of pugilism ; the science was displayed
in all its perfection, and the parryings and feints were
as well executed as if they had been fencing-masters
of the first reputation ; the silence and axiety were so
great among the spectators, that a pin almost might
have been heard to fall. At length *Ryan* put in a
severe blow upon JOHNSON's chest, that brought
him to the ground. The second round, which continued about two minutes, was terrible beyond description—science seemed forgotten—and they appeared
like two blacksmiths at an anvil, when *Ryan* received
a *knock-down* blow. The battle was well sustained on
both sides for some time ; but *Ryan's* passion getting
the better of him, and which was much increased by
the irritation of JOHNSON's second, in reflecting upon
his country, that he began to lose ground. *Ryan's* head
and eyes made a most dreadful appearance, and JOHN-
SON was severely *punished.* The contest lasted for
thirty-three minutes, when *Ryan gave in.* A hat, or-
namented with blue ribbons, was placed upon the conqueror's head ; and JOHNSON gained a considerable
sum of money, independent of twenty pounds per
annum, which was settled upon him by his master, who
won some thousands in backing TOM. The door-
money, amounting to a considerable sum, was divided
between the combatants.

Brain, denominated *Big Ben,* was now considered the only man capable of meeting JOHNSON, and a match was made for *one thousand pounds;* but *Ben,* being taken ill at the appointed time, forfeited his deposit, which was one hundred pounds.

JOHNSON's fame was now so considerably heightened that he was challenged, in a few months afterwards, by *Isaac Perrins,* of Birmingham, one of the strongest men in the kingdom, and who had lifted into a wagon upwards of eight hundred weight of iron without difficulty. Few men ever stood up to him more than five minutes, and he had beaten all the heroes of Warwickshire, Worcestershire, Staffordshire, &c. He had won numerous battles with ease, was not destitute of *science,* and for *bottom* unequalled. He had " *crept into favour with himself* " a little, by sending forth a public advertisement, challenging all England for five hundred guineas. *Perrins* was six feet two inches high without his shoes, and weighed close upon seventeen stone, which was *three* heavier than JOHNSON, extremely active, cheerful, and good tempered. The odds were considerably in his favour, and many of his Birmingham friends sported TWO to *one* against JOHNSON. The battle took place at Banbury, in Oxfordshire, upon a turf-stage, twenty-four feet square, railed in, and raised about five feet from the ground, on October 22, 1789. *Bill* and *Joe Ward* were the assistants to JOHNSON, and his umpire *Colonel Tarleton : Perrins* was seconded by *Pickard,* and his brother officiated as bottle-holder, and *Mr. Meadows,* of Birmingham, as his umpire. The combat commenced at one o'clock.

On stripping, *Perrins* looked, in comparison, like a

Hercules, and JOHNSON, who, in other fights, appeared
as a big man, by the side of *Perrins* now looked as a
boy ; the spectators were struck with the difference,
and even JOHNSON's friends began to *shake*. The awful
set-to at length commenced, and anxiety was upon the
utmost stretch, JOHNSON steadfastly viewing his mighty
opponent, and considerable skill was manifested by both
the combatants for nearly five minutes ; *Perrins* then
made a blow, which, in all probability, had he not
missed his aim, must have decided the contest, and
JOHNSON been killed, from its dreadful force, but TOM
was *awake* to the intent and eluded it, and in return put
in a *hit*, which could be of no trifling nature to *knock a
man down of seventeen stone!* [Great applause, " *Bravo,
Tom, well done,* TOM !"] JOHNSON followed up this
advantage for three more rounds with success, and his
science was of great service in puzzling his antagonist.
Perrins now went into JOHNSON, regardless of all danger, and knocked him down without ceremony, and
continued *punishing* him for several more rounds. TOM,
finding he was over-matched, was obliged, for the first
time in his life, to have recourse to *shifting* to prevent
his being beat straight forward ; which conduct occasioned some murmuring from the spectators, and *Perrins* begin to treat him with contempt, by exclaiming,
" *Why, what have you brought me here! this is not the
valiant* JOHNSON, *the Champion of England! you have
imposed upon me with a mere boy.*" TOM's manly heart
felt most bitterly this keen sarcasm, and bursting with
indignation, instantly cried out, " By G—d ! you shall
soon know that TOM JOHNSON *is* here !" and directly
made a *spring* at *Perrins,* and put in a lunge over the

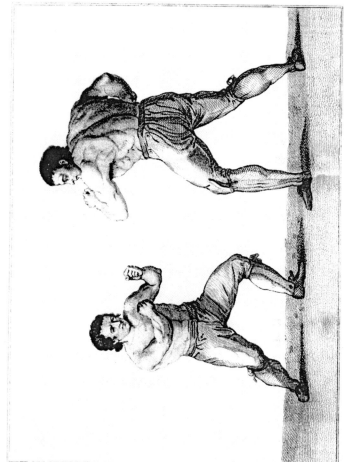

JOHNSON & PERRINS.

Published Aug.st 27 1812. by G. Smeeton, 17 Martin's Lane.

left eye that closed it up in a twinkling, and his wind likewise getting bad, JOHNSON's friends took the *hint* and began to sport their money upon the *Champion's* head. *Perrins,* like a brilliant of the first water, appeared not the least dull or dismayed by this loss, but rallied in fine style, and went into JOHNSON and closed his right eye in return. The odds began to waver immediately, and the Birmingham men offered to lay it on thick. Forty rounds and upwards had now taken place, and the combatants still *game.* JOHNSON began to be extremely careful, and to make the best use of his one eye, finding that it was still *up-hill work,* and gave *Perrins* a desperate blow upon the nose, which slit it down so completely as to have the appearance of being done with a knife : odds, TEN to *one* upon TOM. The manly fortitude of *Perrins* astonished all present ; his *bottom* was still sound, and undismayed he went in to JOHNSON, and endeavoured, by a terrible *hit,* to close his other eye. *Perrins's* friends began to revive, and in a few more rounds claimed the victory, as JOHNSON fell without a blow ; but the umpires allowed it fair, as the articles of agreement did not mention falling. *Perrins's* frame now began to fail him, but his mind was still cool and collected, and he had recourse to another method of attacking his antagonist, and which proved rather successful, till TOM became *down* to it. JOHNSON's knowledge of the science was here displayed in fine style in warding-off the chopper and back-handed strokes of his adversary, by which means TOM recruited his strength. Every round now *Perrins* appeared much the worse for, and fell repeatedly from his exhausted state. JOHNSON had it nearly his own way, *hit* where he liked, and put in several tremendous *facers*, that *Perrins's* head had scarcely the traces left of a human being! Still his courage never forsook him, and, had not his friends interfered and prevented him from fighting any longer, it was the general opinion that *Perrins* would have continued the contest till he had died! *Perrins* positively refused to *give out*, and was literally forced from the stage. *Sixty-two* such rounds of fighting, for an hour and a quarter, were scarcely, if ever, before witnessed in the annals of pugilism. The disparagement was spoken of as much too great between the combatants; and, notwithstanding JOHNSON performed prodigies of valour, by beating so uncommonly large a man, and was entitled to every praise, yet still there were parts of the fight that the amateur could not approve of and the spectators disliked. It was reported among the sporting men that *Mr. Bullock* made JOHNSON a present of *one thousand pounds*, and that he had gained, by the vast odds he had betted upon TOM, £20,000. The door-money amounted to nearly £800, out of which JOHNSON received £533. TOM called upon *Perrins* and left a guinea to drink *Isaac's* health, previous to his quitting Banbury.

A match was at length made between *Big Ben* and JOHNSON for five hundred guineas. The former was under the patronage of the *Duke of Hamilton*. This battle, which had long been expected, excited considerable interest in the *sporting world*, and bets to the amount of several thousands were laid upon its decision. The characters of the combatants stood high; JOHNSON, from *what* he had done, was surrounded by friends, and the odds were seven to four in his favour. *Ben* was also well known for thorough *game*: a most powerful hitter, and both hands of equal use to him; he had also given ample proofs in town and country that he might be depended upon, and was not without a host of supporters. At Wrotham, in Kent, upon a stage twenty feet square, was the Championship of England once more to be decided, on Jan. 17, 1791. JOHNSON, attended by *Joe Ward* for his second, and his bottle-holder, *Mendoza*, mounted the stage at one o'clock, with firm and decent composure; and almost at the same instant *Ben* followed, with a cheerful countenance, accompanied by *Bill Warr* and *Humphries*, as his second and bottle-holder. The *set-to* was more furious than usual upon these occasions, and JOHNSON, from a desperate blow on the face, fell upon his nose, which completely stupified him. The effects appeared evident in the second round, when *Ben* put in another *leveller.* JOHNSON *plucked* up, and in the next *set-to*, laid *Ben* upon his back. Well as these pugilists knew the *science*, they now appeared to lay it aside; and *ferocity* was the order of the day. The blows were dreadful in the extreme, and given and taken reciprocally; at length JOHNSON, in missing his aim at *Ben*, struck the stage with his hand, and broke his middle finger. TOM soon afterwards became desperate, and with the agonizing idea that his proud fame was fast expiring, completely lost himself, and caught hold of the hair of *Ben's* head several times, shifted, and had recourse to those manœuvres so unlike his former conduct, that disapprobation was publicly expressed by the spectators. *Ben*, after *milling* away for twenty minutes, decided the battle, by putting in a most tremendous *hit* upon JOHNSON's ribs, and by another, cutting his lip nearly in halves. Thus was the valiant

No. V. P

and truly renowned TOM JOHNSON deprived of the
Championship, which he had so nobly maintained for
several years unsullied!

The conduct of JOHNSON throughout this fight astonished his friends very much indeed; that coolness of
temper, which shone so conspicuously in all his other
battles, here seemed totally eradicated, and his mind irritated to excess. Whether JOHNSON was impressed
with the superiority of his antagonist, or his courage
depressed from his heavy losses at gambling, has not
been ascertained; but there was a miserable *falling-off*
in him altogether! JOHNSON never fought afterwards,
but took the Grapes, in Duke-street, Lincoln's-Inn-
fields. The customers proving too *flash,* the license
was taken away, and JOHNSON once more adrift. He
was also routed, by the magistrates, from Copper-alley,
Dublin, from his house not proving so consonant to the
principles of propriety as was wished. He died at
Cork, Jan. 21, 1797, aged forty-seven years. JOHN-
SON complained of the blows which he received from
Big Ben, and attributed his death to that fight.
As a pugilist he was of the highest order; and, in all
probability, many years may elapse before a second
TOM JOHNSON is seen in the prize-ring. He was,
however, imprudent, and the latter part of his life was
marked by dejection and want!

RICHARD HUMPHRIES,
THE GENTLEMAN BOXER!

So denominated from his genteel appearance and behaviour. RICHARD was a remarkably graceful boxer,
and his attitudes were of the most elegant and impres-

HUMPHRIES

GULLEY

sive nature. He was about the middle size, strong, and well-limbed; and had studied the science with great advantage. His blows were very powerful, and the stomach, and under the ear, were the principal objects of his aim: in general, he struck with his right, and stopped with his left; but did not make use of both hands with equal facility. His *game* was unquestionable; and HUMPHRIES was considered a most distinguished pugilist: he was so attractive as to revive PUGILISM, which had been on the decline for some time; and on its being publicly announced, that he was to fight *Martin*, the *Bath butcher*, on a stage, at Newmarket, May 3, 1786, the whole of the amateurs rallied, and the *set-to* was witnessed by their Royal Highnesses *the Prince of Wales*, the *Duke of York*, the *Duke of Orleans*, and most of the French nobility then in England. A guinea was the price of admission, and some hundreds cheerfully paid it; which collection was to go to the winner. Between *thirty* and *forty* thousand pounds were sported upon the occasion, bets were so flush. *Martin* was a boxer of some repute, but shorter than HUMPHRIES, yet a well-made man, and who had seen some service in the pugilistic field of honour. The *set-to* was distinguished for science, and HUMPHRIES parried off his adversary's attacks with great adroitness, and stood up to *Martin* manfully. The latter was deficient in *distance*, and sometimes fell, which rendered his hits rather feeble. HUMPHRIES was the favourite. *Martin*, finding that his *distance* was wrong, went boldly in to HUMPHRIES; the contest was now *prime*, and betting equal. However, HUMPHRIES soon appeared the *fancy* man, by giving his opponent a most tremendous *leveller,* and varied the odds in his favour. *Martin,* notwithstanding, appeared *game* and fought well, contesting every inch of ground; and not till after a complete *mill* for three quarters of an hour, and receiving a blow from HUMPHRIES which nearly *rolled him up,* did *Martin* signify that he had had ENOUGH. The amateurs were highly gratified, and both the pugilists established their fame, but more particularly HUMPHRIES.

Numerous *sporting men* rallied round PUGILISM, and the professors of the science were not without high and noble patrons. Royalty frequently witnessed the displays of the art, accompanied by Dukes, Earls, Honourables, &c. and men of the first distinction felt not *ashamed* of being seen in the *ring,* or in acting as *umpires* at a boxing match.

The science, courage, and gentleman-like conduct of HUMPHRIES had secured him many friends, and, with a mind by no means destitute of intelligence, he became a real *fancy article*—that when *sported* upon any occasion, he did not fail in claiming admiration and respect. But deservedly distinguished as HUMPHRIES stood in the boxing hemisphere, a *competitor* had lately risen up to share his fame and glory; if not, *even* to aspire to superiority. He was not only a daring, but a most formidable rival, as his pretensions to pugilistic excellence were known to be sound; he had been proved, and his specimens of skill, in the trying conflict, had made a deep impression upon the amateurs, and it was judged expedient, by the men of note, that *Mendoza* should enter the lists with their favourite HUMPHRIES.

Negotiations were commenced, and the preliminaries being agreed to; Odiham, in Hampshire, for 400 guineas, upon a raised twenty-four feet stage, in a paddock, and the door-money divided between the combatants, were the terms and place where this memorable contest was to be decided. The day (Jan. 9, 1788) being known, description falls short in portraying the anxiety which prevailed upon the decision of this grand *set-to*, both in town and country. The first-rate *fanciers* were off in thorough-bred style; and no sporting *kid* that could muster the *blunt* was absent; distance was out of the question, and weather was no object, HUMPHRIES and *Mendoza* were to fight, and that was the *only* consideration. From the towns and villages near the scene of action, the country people seemed equally *interested*; and numerous pedestrians were seen in all directions moving towards the fight; so that, within an hour previous to the battle, the assemblage, collected together in one spot, was truly astonishing and irresistible. To prevent the combatants from being *bilked* out of the door-money, (which was half-a-guinea for each person's admission,) the most athletic of the *milling* race were selected for the protection of the entrance, and the potent arms of *Dunn*, *Ryan*, and *Tring*, with *little bits* of *shillelahs* in their fists flourishing about, assisted by other powerful pugilists, kept for some time the saucy intruders at bay; but, as the time drew near for the combatants to mount the stage, *John Bull's* anxiety increased beyond every other thought, and with one desperate effort, like a mighty flood, swept all before it, that the door-keepers were soon lost by the violence of the torrent, and thousands never gave themselves any trouble as to the *expense* of admission. All was noise, uproar, and confusion, for some minutes, occasioned by this sudden interruption; but, upon the appearance of hostilities commencing, their attention was so completely rivetted, that an awful silence, as if by one impulse, instantly prevailed.

HUMPHRIES, upon ascending the stage, was received with loud and repeated cheers, which he gratefully acknowledged by his genteel deportment, when *Tom Johnson* appeared as his second, the athletic *Tring* as his bottle-holder, and Mr. *Allen* as umpire. *Mendoza,* almost instantly following, was greeted with the most flattering marks of attention and respect from the surrounding spectators; a Mr. *Moravia* acted as his umpire, *David Benjamin* was his second, and *Jacobs* his bottle-holder, and the whole of them were Jews. HUMPHRIES' appearance when stripped for the fight was peculiarly attractive, and his fine manly form was seen to great advantage; he had on a pair of fine flannel drawers, white silk stockings, the clocks of which were spangled with gold, and pumps tied with ribbon. The dress of *Mendoza* was plain and neat. About twenty minutes after one, every thing being ready, the usual salutations took place, when the display of the science was infinitely fine; much was expected from two such skilful artists, and the *feints* made by each party were elegant and scientific. *Mendoza* felt no terrors from the proud fame of his antagonist, and HUMPHRIES viewed the admirable skill displayed by his opponet with firmness and composure; the parryings were long and various, and the amateurs experienced one of the richest treats ever exhibited in this noble and manly art: at length, *Mendoza* put in the first blow, and recoiling from its effects slipped and fell upon his back, in consequence of the stage being slippery from the rain which had fell previous to the battle; yet it was of no material effect against HUMPHRIES, as he warded it off and retreated. In the second round *Mendoza*, full of vigour, went in to his antagonist and knocked him down: and in closing, in the next, the Jew threw HUMPHRIES. The odds, which had been much in favour of HUMPHRIES, were now changing rapidly upon *Mendoza*. The Jew, flushed with his success, found his *game* all alive, and *showed* himself off to the best advantage, with all the heroism of a most experienced pugilist. HUMPHRIES appeared to make no way against *Mendoza*, who had now knocked DICK down six times in succession. The Jews sported their cash freely, as the Christian, it was supposed, must soon be vanquished; but the friends of HUMPHRIES were not to be dismayed, and took the odds greedily. At one time the contest was nearly coming to a premature termination, from the cry of " *Foul, foul!*" by the friends of *Mendoza*, who, in the early part of the fight, had driven HUMPHRIES upon the rail of the stage, and while the latter was upon the balance, aimed a blow at his ribs which must have finished the battle, but *Johnson* caught it. The umpires considered it a knock-down blow, and that *Johnson* was correct. The stage was so slippery that HUMPHRIES could scarcely stand upon his legs, and soon discharged the *finery* from them, for the more substantial service of worsted hose. DICK now felt his feet, went in with his usual confidence, and the bets became even. HUMPHRIES was now himself, and fast recovering in wind and strength, the amateurs were delighted with his undaunted courage and neatness of execution. *Mendoza* was thrown, and in falling pitched upon his face; his forehead was dreadfully cut just above the right eye, and his nose assumed a different shape : but the Jew's *pluck* was good, and in the next round he gave HUMPHRIES a prime *facer*, so that the bets were still alive. HUMPHRIES was gaining ground fast, and soon put in a *doubler* upon the loins of *Mendoza*, one of the Jew's most vulnerable parts, which was followed up by one in the neck: the Jew reeling fell with his leg under him, sprained his ancle, and was reluctantly compelled to acknowledge the superiority of the Christian. *Mendoza* almost immediately afterwards fainted, and was taken from the stage. Thus ended this truly celebrated contest, in twenty-eight minutes, fifty-four seconds, in which, perhaps, there never was so much skill and dexterity ever witnessed; nor more money depending upon its termination. The Jews were severe sufferers; but, although *Mendoza* was defeated, his fame and character as a pugilist were considerably increased; his style of fighting was highly spoken of by the scientific amateur; and in close fighting, and as a quick hitter, he was evidently superior to his antagonist. The advantage was also upon the side of *Mendoza* in point of strength of arm, and, when struggling to obtain the throw, he *punished* his adversary considerably by keeping down his head. His guard was excellent, and displayed a thorough knowledge of the art, by keeping it closer to his body than that of his adversary, by which means his blows were given with more force when he hit out; and with respect to stopping, he was not deficient to HUMPHRIES; but for elegance of position, cool and prompt judgement, fortitude of manner, and force of blow, he was materially inferior. He wanted also that personal courage, which was so apparent in HUMPHRIES, and whose confidence rendered him so indifferent of himself; but in point of throwing, Mendoza, though not expected, had the complete advantage, and the activity he displayed throughout the fight was considerable. *Mendoza* contended for victory with all the style and valour of a true hero.

HUMPHRIES displayed all those superior requisites of the *science*, that it is difficult to point out any thing like an equal to him: his attitudes were of the most manly and tasteful description, and even in the most trying moments of the fight, his postures were considered graceful. His intellectual capacity had rendered him more acquainted with the properties of the human frame than pugilists in general; and his habits of life had tended to make him more conversant and attractive in society, than fighting men, perhaps, think essentially necessary. His manners were also conciliating; and he endeavoured through life to portray the gentleman. His friends were not diminished, but materially increased, by such conduct.

It was extremely difficult to appreciate which was the neatest pugilist in the fight; so much activity, science, elegance, and bottom, were displayed upon both sides, yet extremely different as to character and manner: but it appeared that HUMPHRIES, in the defensive position, though he kept his adversary at a distance by extending his arms, yet he lost that celerity and power which his *hits* must otherwise have effected had they have been nearer his body.

Mr. Bradyl, well known in the annals of pugilism, was the patron of HUMPHRIES, and prevented from attending the battle by business of a private nature; but who felt so anxiously for the issue of the contest, that

No. V.   O

his servant was ordered to witness the conflict, and
convey to him the earliest intelligence. HUMPHRIES,
immediately after the fight, like the heroes of old,
wrote the following laconic epistle to Mr. Bradyl.

" SIR,

" I have *done* the *Jew* and am in good health.

                    " RICHARD HUMPHRIES."

HUMPHRIES lived several years after the above conflict, in the capacity of a coal-merchant, in good repute,
and much respected.

The above battle brought BOXING into general notice;
and the abilities of the two pugilists occasioned considerable conversation at that period, both in the BIG and
Little world. The newspapers teemed with anecdotes
concerning them; pamphlets were published in favour of
pugilism; and scarcely a print-shop in the Metropolis
but what displayed the *set-to* in glowing colours, and
portraits of those distinguished heroes of the fist. HUM-
PHRIES and *Mendoza* were the rage: the modern co-
medies glanced at their exploits, and the *sporting hemisphere* was quite charged with it. Two such pugilists had
not been seen since the days of the renowned *Broughton* and *Slack,* and they rose up like a NEW FEATURE
of the TIMES! Boxing became fashionable, followed, patronized, and encouraged. Sparring matches took place
at the Theatres and Royal Circus. Schools were established for the promulgation of the art; and the *Science*
of SELF-DEFENCE considered as a necessary requisite for
all Englishmen. Among its numerous splendid patrons
and supporters were to be seen His Royal Highness the
Prince of Wales, Dukes of York and Clarence, Duke
of Hamilton, Lord Barrymore, Alderman Combe, &c.

BRISTOL HEROES.

" *What's* in a name? that which we call a rose,
By any other name would smell as sweet :"

Most assuredly it would, and we cordially acquiesce
in the justness of the Poet's remark; being well aware
that valiant men are to be found in all countries, and
that true courage is not confined to any particular place,
colour, or station. Cowardice has often been experienced
in men of six feet high; and heroism has shone resplendent in men of the most diminutive stature. Impartiality should be the peculiar feature of all Biographers,
in recording the deeds of the brave, and a love of truth
superior to every other consideration manifested; that
no wrong bias may prejudice the mind of the reader,
and posterity receive an account which may be depended
upon. BRISTOL or *Baltimore* are but sounds to the man
of liberality; and when an Englishman holds the scales
of justice, we trust he will be *blind* to every other balance but that of—HONESTY. Characters may then be
fairly appreciated—actions not too highly coloured from
gross adulation or ill-timed friendship; nor deeds of
valour suffer from malignity, or the baleful spirit of
envy: and like the faithful mirror that reflects the true
likeness, neither adding nor diminishing the portrait,
but always keeping in view,—" nothing to extenuate,
or set down aught in malice!"

BRISTOL has, for the last twenty years, been rendered
conspicuous from the production of its numerous race of

celebrated Pugilists—the *skill* of whom, generally speaking, have proved pre-eminent; and whose thorough *bottom* rarely equalled, but never excelled. The CHAMPIONSHIP OF ENGLAND has, at various times, graced the heads of several of the NATIVES of *Bristol*; and two of its most prime Boxers have carried that distinguished appellation with them (a circumstance which happens to so few) to their graves! ANOTHER, whose pugilistic career will long be remembered by the amateurs, possessed it for a considerable length of time, with the most honourable and enviable reputation; and, it might be observed, only transferred its dignity when his *stamina* was on the decline, and his frame had experienced the material loss of ONE of its most principal organs:—and, at the present moment, (June 5, 1819,) it is still in the *unsullied* keeping of a NATIVE of the above ancient city.

This, it appears, from such noble specimens of valour, hardihood, and science, is the principal reason which we can account for that kind of partiality, which has arisen, by not only giving importance, but frequently a preference, to the sound of—" HE's A BRISTOL MAN!"

BENJAMIN BRAIN,
otherwise BIG BEN,
(who remained CHAMPION *till his death!)*

Rendered truly memorable in wresting the laurels from the hardy and scientific *Tom Johnson.* BEN was a most powerful pugilist—a remarkably straight and tremendous hitter—and dealt out *punishment* with equal severity from both his hands. His adversaries found great difficulty in opposing his impetuosity; and BEN's particular aim was to prevent any of his opponents recovering themselves, when at fault, till the round was completed.

BRAIN was of an athletic make, but not particularly so as to merit the appellation of *Big!* scarcely exceeding the size of *Johnson.* He was born in 1753, and in the early part of his life was employed as a collier in his native place: it was here that BEN first distinguished himself, as a pugilist, with *Clayton,* the Shropshire man, by the science and game that was observed in the fight. A good battle also took place between BEN and a collier belonging to Kingswood, of the name of *Harris.* They were both compelled to acknowledge the superiority of BEN's pugilistic powers. He arrived in the metropolis, in 1774; where, at the Adelphi wharf, he was employed many years as a coal-porter. He was a good-looking man, and when out of his business always appeared clean and respectable; mild and sociable in his demeanour, and never ridiculously presumed upon his qualities as a boxer.

BEN's first *set-to* in London was with the *fighting Grenadier,* in the Long-fields, on October 31, 1786, in which, had it not been for the assistance of a medical man, who witnessed the contest, BEN must have been defeated. The Soldier was a first-rate *punisher,* and BEN's eyes were so swelled up, from the heavy blows he received, that he could not see out of them; when just at this juncture the ring was broken: during which circumstance the swellings were skilfully lanced by a surgeon, and BEN restored to perfect sight. A fresh ring was made, and the combat renewed;

No. VI.   R

but in the course of a few minutes the *Grenadier* gave *in*.

Corbally, an *Irish chairman*, fought BEN, upon a stage, twenty-five feet square, at Knavestock, in Essex, on December 31, 1788. Notwithstanding the weather was extremely severe, the combatants stripped with the most perfect indifference, and the fight was carried on with determined courage on both sides; but *Corbally,* at length, was compelled to *give in*.

BEN fought a most desperate battle with *Tring*, at Dartford, in Kent. The latter was defeated in nineteen minutes. See page 298.

BEN, in 1789, forfeited one hundred pounds to *Johnson*, which sum was deposited in part of one thousand pounds stakes, BRAIN being in a bad state of health.

BEN received a challenge from *Jacombs*, a *Birmingham pugilist*, which he accepted, and the battle took place at Banbury, in Oxfordshire, upon a twenty-four feet square stage, railed in, on October 23, 1789. *Jacombs* was a stout-made man, plenty of *pluck*, and not without some science. On the *set-to Jacombs* portrayed his determined resolution, and went in to BRAIN in fine style; but whether BEN felt any doubt about the fight, he did not conduct himself after the accustomed method of boxing, but was on the retreat, *shifting* often, to avoid *Jacombs'* blows, and fell frequently without a touch. *Jacombs*, on the contrary, received BEN's attacks undaunted. Considerable disapprobation being expressed by the spectators, particularly the Warwickshire men, who were getting outrageous at BEN's manœuvring, BRAIN at length stood up to his adversary, and showed what he was capable of performing, by putting in a tremendous *leveller*, and soon convinced the spectators that he was a *prime bit of stuff*. The contest was now worth looking at, and heroism was displayed upon both sides; when, after a most dreadful battle of one hour and twenty-six minutes, the brave *Jacombs* was conquered. The Birmingham men lost considerable sums upon *Jacombs*.

Hooper, the *tinman*, was now backed to fight BEN; but a more ridiculous match never took place in the annals of pugilism: a fight it could not be called; and, in fact, it was little more than making fun of pugilism. *Hooper* was over-matched, and BEN treated him with the most sovereign contempt. The first round was well-contested; but BEN put in such a *doubler*, that *Hooper* could never be induced to put it in his power to do so again. *Hooper* fell every round without a blow, ran all over the stage, squirted water in BEN's face, and called him by the most opprobrious epithets, thinking that by such acts BEN might be provoked, and put off his guard, and fall an easy prey to his disgusting manœuvres. BEN received several severe *facers* from the activity of *Hooper*; and had no means of returning a blow, as his antagonist, after striking, was upon the ground. However, BEN adopted a plan that all the stratagems of the *tinman* could not divert him from. BRAIN stood up like a rock in the middle of the stage, and there waited till *Hooper* thought proper to come up to him. This piece of *diversion* took place upon August the 30th, 1790, at Chapel-row-revel, near Newbury, in Berkshire, and continued for *three hours and a half*: the night coming on fast, several of the amateurs asked BEN if he should be able to finish the battle that day? when BRAIN jocularly replied; "That it entirely depended upon his antagonist; and, laughing, observed, "they had better begin the next morning at six o'clock, and have the whole day before them." The *fancy* in general were completely disgusted at such treatment. After what was *termed* one hundred and eighty rounds having taken place, and it being nearly dark, it was declared *a drawn battle!* and BEN walked off without receiving any particular hurt.

BEN's next *set-to* was altogether as different; for, in the contest with *Johnson*, the blows from that hero told so severely upon his frame, that his constitution was materially injured; and, we are credibly informed, that he attributed his death to that fight. Though BEN did not appear to be visibly hurt at the time, yet he was never in sound health afterwards: and excellent as both the above pugilists were versed in the *science*, after the third round, it was downright FEROCITY, and nothing but death-like blows heard. It was truly a most slaughtering conflict.

A match was made in January, 1794, between BRAIN and *Will Wood*, the *coachman*, a pugilist of considerable celebrity; but death interfering, prevented the conflict from taking place: and, on the 8th of April, in the above year, he received his last *knockdown* blow! Upon his body being opened, it was found that his liver was considerably injured, in consequence of the many desperate battles which he had fought. On the 11th, his funeral was conducted with decent solemnity, and *Tom Johnson*, forgetting all past differences, was foremost among the mourners, to show his respect to the deceased; *Warr, Wood,* &c. &c. attended to see the remains of the Champion respectably interred in St. Sepulchre's church-yard.

WILLIAM WARR, (generally called WARD,)

A pugilist of considerable eminence, and expressly brought to London to fight *Tom Johnson*; possessing uncommon agility, and a thorough knowledge of the *science*. But much as his talents were respected, it has been the expressed opinion of several amateurs, that in many of his battles he appeared somewhat *too scientific*; and that so much *shifting* appeared more like a deficiency in *bottom*, and less calculated to please, than such *fine* displays of the art. A manliness of style in fighting is a sure criterion of *game*, it prevents any imputation of *fear*, and is always hailed with respect. WARR's activity in battle was truly conspicuous, and his adversary has often been looking from whence the blow came, he has been so soon at a great distance after striking his opponent. Extremely well formed in the breast and arms; and about five feet nine inches in height; strongly made; his general appearance robust, and well calculated for a pugilist. As a teacher of the *science*, he possessed considerable merit; and some of his pupils have proved themselves first-rate articles. As a *second* he was equally good, and few fights of any note have taken place, but BILL WARR has played a prominent character in them.

Captain *Robinson* having a *fancy* coachman, that, besides *driving* in style, could *box* a little, matched him against WARR, to fight at Knavestock, in Essex, upon a stage, on Dec. 31, 1788. It snowed incessantly during the combat, and the pugilists were only affected from its slippery qualities upon the boards, occasioning more falls than otherwise might have happened. *Wood*

No. VI.   s being but little better than a *novice*, trusted more to impetuosity than judgement; but displayed *bottom* of the richest kind. WARR's *science* was manifest, and he opposed the violent attacks of his adversary with much adroitness; but the *shifting* was thought to be too prominent. Notwithstanding, it is but justice to remark, that the battle was carried on with great spirit on both sides for twenty minutes; *Wood's* eye was soon closed after this period, yet he fought in *prime* style for ten minutes longer, when, becoming blind, he was obliged to *give in!*

BILL WARR and *Watson*, in their journey to witness the fight between *Humphries* and *Mendoza*, at Stilton, met with an unfortunate circumstance, at the Black Horse, Enfield Highway, where they had accidentally put up to take some refreshment. The company in the parlour were warmly engaged upon the ensuing fight; and a respectable blacksmith, of the name of *Swain*, speaking highly of *Mendoza*, which was not relished, and immediately opposed by WARR; high words took place, and a regular *set-to* instantly commenced. WARR was in danger of receiving a good *milling*, as he had no room to retreat, and *Swain* was *serving it out* in good style, when BILL proposed an adjournment to a field, where *Swain* had a severe blow upon his stomach, that, unhappily, killed him. WARR was confined three months in Newgate, being found guilty of manslaughter.

WARR fought *Mendoza*; but the superiority of the *Jew* was manifested in twenty-three rounds.

A match was made by the amateurs between *Stanyard*, a pugilist of celebrity from Birmingham, and BILL WARR, for 100 guineas, which took place at Colnbrook. This proved a well-contested battle for thirteen minutes, and WARR convinced his friends that he was not without *game*, and stood up most heroically. The *set-to* was good, and some excellent sparring took place; but WARR was *levelled*. *Stanyard* soon repeated the action ; but, in the third round, BILL put in one of the severest blows ever heard, which completely broke *Stanyard's* jaw at the angle ; yet still the latter possessed so much *bottom* as never to complain of the circumstance, and knocked WARR down; and, in the next round, followed it up with equal success. In the sixth *set-to*, *Stanyard* excited considerable astonishment, in holding up WARR by main strength, *punishing* him dreadfully, and dashing him upon the stage with great violence. In the seventh, eighth, and ninth rounds, WARR experienced tremendous *levellers.* In the tenth and last, a complete *milling* took place on both sides— WARR put in several terrible *hits* upon his opponent's broken jaw; and, in struggling for the throw, both fell down. It was by far the best round, and *Stanyard gave in.* WARR received much praise for this valiant display of the art, and, in the weakness of the moment, challenged *Tom Johnson* to fight, who had performed the office of second to *Stanyard ;* but *Tom* only smiled at this *insignificant* threat. This battle was fought on Saturday, October 27, 1792.

WARR again contended for victory with *Dan Mendoza ;* and it should seem that BILL entertained an idea that there was a *chance* left of taking the *shine* out of the *Jew;* but a quarter of an hour sufficiently satisfied him it was *grounded* in error !

BILL WARR died of a consumption ; and his remains were interred in St. James's burying-ground, Pancras.

JEM BELCHER,

(One of the most heroic CHAMPIONS OF ENGLAND,)

Descended from the mighty *Slack*, of pugilistic celebrity, and grandson of that renowned boxer. The
family of the BELCHERS have long been distinguished
for their prowess—and the three brothers, JEM, TOM,
and NED, in their various trials of skill, have, in no degree, *sullied* the *milling* fame of their ancestor. In
tracing the valorous deeds of BELCHER, candour alone
dictates us to observe, that, in finding scarcely any thing
to condemn, we are almost overwhelmed with circumstances to applaud.   To him MODERN BOXING is principally indebted for that extensive patronage and support which it has experienced from the *higher flights* of
the FANCY! Upon JEM's first appearance as a pugilist,
he was considered a perfect phenomenon in the gymnastic art—*a mere boy*, scarcely twenty years of age, putting
all the celebrated heroes of the *Old School* at defiance—
their scientific efforts, when placed in competition with
his peculiar mode of fighting, were not only completely
baffled, but rendered unavailing. BELCHER had a prepossessing appearance, genteel, and remarkably placid in
his behaviour. There was nothing about his person that
indicated superior bodily strength; yet, when stripped,
his form was muscular and elegant. The *science* that he
was master of, appeared exclusively his own—and his
antagonists were not aware of the singular advantages
that it gave him over those who studied and fought upon
the accustomed principles of pugilism; it was completely intuitive; practice had rendered its effects pow-

erful, and in confusing his antagonists he gained considerable time *to* improve this native advantage with promptitude and decision. The quickness of his *hits* were unparalleled; they were severely *felt*, but scarcely *seen*: and in springing backwards and forwards, his celerity was truly astonishing—and, in this particular respect, it might be justly said that JEM was without an equal! BELCHER's style was original; the amateur was struck with its excellence; his antagonists terrified from the gaiety and decision it produced; and the fighting men, in general, were confounded with his *sang froid* and intrepidity. It appears that BELCHER made his appearance under the auspices of *Bill Warr;* and it is but justice to observe that the talents of so *finished* a pupil reflected great credit upon that experienced veteran in the gymnastic art.

In his social hours JEM was good-natured in the extreme, and modest and unassuming to a degree almost bordering upon bashfulness. In the character of a publican no man entertained a better sense of propriety and decorum than BELCHER did; and the stranger, in casually mixing with the *Fancy* in his house, to behold *Nature* in her *primest* moments of recreation, never felt any danger of being affronted, from the attentive conduct of the landlord. Good order reigned predominant, and frequently very animated criticisms have taken place concerning the merits of the *stage;* and the various talents of most of the first-rate performers, who *sported* their *figures* upon the boards, have given rise to considerable discussion, in which the high and dignified legislator has been heard to *argufy the topic* in the most earnest manner, to convince his *plebeian* opponent (whose situation in life was, perhaps, not more elevated than that of a *coal-porter* or a *coster-monger*) of the superior abilities of some particular actor, whose *action* has proved more *convincing* in a few minutes than all the words contained in *Johnson's* folio dictionary could effect; and, in turn, those *composites* of the state have been listening with the most minute attention to the flowing harangue of some *dusty cove*, *blowing a cloud* over his porter, and lavish with his *slum* on the beauties possessed by some *distinguished* pugilist, whose talents for *serving it out* were elegant and *striking*. And also where *flash* has been *pattered* in all that native purity of style and richness of eloquence that would have startled a *high toby gloque* and put a *jigger screw* upon the alert to find so many *down;* and, even among the heterogeneous crowd have been found ad-mirers of *Hermes*, who have retired well persuaded that ALL *were not barren !*

> " Yet more; the diff'rence is as great between
> The optics seeing, as the object seen.
> All manners take a tincture from our own,
> Or come discolour'd, through our passions shown,
> Or Fancy's beam enlarges, multiplies,
> Contracts, inverts, and gives ten thousand dyes."

BELCHER's *bottom*, judgement, and activity, have never been surpassed—in his battle with *Paddington Jones*, a pugilist extremely well versed in the *science*, and of good *bottom*, who had also distinguished him-self in several fights, and was considered by the ama-teurs a man that might be depended upon, and one that was not *easily* disposed of, was compelled, in a short conflict, to yield to BELCHER. *Jack Bartholo-*

mew (a thorough-bred and sound pugilist) was defeated by JEM; when the latter performed such prodigies of valour that he astonished the most scientific professors. *Gamble,* who had *milled* all the *primest coves* in the kingdom for some years, *lost,* in a few minutes, all his *consequence,* from the dexterity of BELCHER. In his various fights with *Burke,* either prepared or taken *unawares,* he *hit* away, and gave that most inordinate *glutton* several hearty meals, with all the ease and facility of an experienced *caterer. Fearby,* (the *young Ruffian,)* who had distinguished himself so manfully in several excellent matches, and who had obtained the appellation of a first-rate pugilist, both for *science* and *bottom,* from the best judges among the amateurs, yet, when in competition with BELCHER, his abilities were so reduced as to appear more like that of a third or fourth rate boxer, and was *punished* most dreadfully by JEM, while BELCHER scarcely appeared touched : such, most undoubtedly, was the superiority of BELCHER's talents in all the above battles.

It was warmly, if not perhaps ill-naturedly expressed, by one of the most scientific pugilists in the whole circle of boxers, in giving his opinion respecting the battle between the *Game Chicken* and BELCHER, *" That had* JEM *been in possession of* FOUR EYES, *he was never able to beat Pearce."* Here it was, for the first time in his life, that his judgement proved defective as a pugilist; and, in acting from the envious impulse of the moment, JEM BELCHER only portrayed the infirmities of human nature and the want of stability in man. His character was established, and never did any pugilist's fame stand upon a more elevated and stronger basis; he

had retired into private life, respected by his friends,
and supported and admired by the *Fancy* in general, who
were no strangers to his integrity and private worth,
—*there* he should have remained, where his days might
have glided happily along, without regret, and his
life, in all probability, been lengthened from the placid
scene—but his rest was unhappily disturbed, and poor
JEM, like the greatest part of mankind, had not *fortitude* enough to rise superior to the baleful attacks of

> "————————— malicious ENVIE rode
>   Upon a ravenous wolf, and still did chaw
>   Between his cankred teeth a venomous toad,
>   That all the poyson run about his jaw;
>   But inwardly he chawed his own maw,
>   At neighbour's wealth, that made him ever sad,
>   For death it was, when any good he saw,
>   And WEPT, *that cause of weeping* NONE HE HAD!"

In constitution BELCHER had materially declined,
independent of the loss of an eye, and the serious
effects which his frame sustained upon that afflicting
accident had endangered the safety of his life. Upwards of two years had elapsed in retirement, when
BELCHER came forward to meet an opponent more
formidable than any one he had hitherto met with,
and who possessed, in a superior degree, every requisite to constitute a first-rate pugilist, and who, likewise, had improved under his tuition, and might be
said *a* CHICKEN *of his own rearing!* BELCHER, unfortunately, could not be persuaded of the difficulties he
would have to encounter from the loss of an eye, and
that the *chance* of success was against him, TILL *it was
too late!* and then the error was too glaring to be re-

trieved. But how did he fight? How HE *did fight*
will be long remembered by those who witnessed the
grievous, yet truly honourable combat; a combat in
which more unaffected courage was never seen, and
where humanity was more conspicuously displayed and
gratefully applauded. ANIMOSITY appeared to have
no resting-place, and it was proud HONOUR, only, struggling for victory. BELCHER fought in his accustomed
style, and planted his favourite *hits* with his usual adroitness; but he lost his distance, and became an easy victim
to his own incredulity. In the course of the fight, as JEM
afterwards acknowledged, his sight became so defective,
from the *hits* which he received over his good eye,
(the peculiar object of his antagonist's aim,) that the
blows he gave his adversary were merely accidental,
his aim was lost in confusion, and certainly was out
of the question. BELCHER, with the most undaunted
heroism, endeavoured to make up the deficiency of sight
by a display of *bottom* and gaiety, astonishing and unequalled. The skill upon both sides claimed universal
respect: yet, notwithstanding the spectators perceived
a deficiency in BELCHER's fighting in several parts, from
his not being able to guard off the attacks as heretofore, and the severe *punishment* which his head and face
had sustained in the combat; his afflicting situation
made a deep impression, not only upon his friends, but
the company in general, and the involuntary tear was
seen silently stealing down the iron cheek of many present, for the loss of departing greatness in their favourite
hero. JEM's spirits never forsook him; and, in surrendering his laurels, HONOUR consoled him, that he had
transferred them *unsullied;* and appeared only affected,

No. VI.   T

by declaring, " that his sorrow was more occasioned
from the recollection of the severe loss of a particular
friend, who, in fact, had sported every thing which he
possessed upon his head, and also one of his most
stanch backers and supporters through life, than as to
any particular consideration respecting himself!" Notwithstanding the excellence evinced by the *Chicken*
in science, wind, strength, and bottom, and, by no
means, feeling the slightest wish to detract from the
merits of so respected and deservedly distinguished a
pugilist—yet, if we may be allowed the supposition,
that had the above contest had taken place when JEM
BELCHER possessed his eye-sight in full perfection, we
hesitate not in observing, that *its* TERMINATION might
have been very *doubtful!*

Respecting BELCHER's two battles with *Cribb*, when
the circumstances of the case are duly appreciated;
when it is recollected that his spirits must have been
somewhat damped in descending from his elevated eminence, to rank only with men of minor talents, who,
when in the plenitude of his health and strength, dared
not to have thus presumed; but JEM was down, and
down with him, as is too generally the case with the unfortunate, and his powers well known to be on the decay, previous to his *set-to* with the *Chicken*, and which
were by no means improved from that circumstance;
yet still his heroism and *science* shone resplendent, and
he left his opponents at a vast distance.

In the first fight with *Cribb*, as may be traced, JEM's
superiority was evidently manifest. The former was
severely *punished;* and not until BELCHER had received
a most violent *hit* over his good eye, and sprained his

right hand, did *Cribb* appear to have much *chance*. In the seventeenth round, the odds were TWO to *one* on BELCHER, and in the eighteenth, FIVE to *one!* when *Cribb* was so much beaten, that considerable doubts were entertained whether he would be able to come again: and even at the conclusion of the battle, *Cribb* was in a very exhausted state. The amateurs were delighted with the uncommon skill BELCHER displayed upon this occasion, and were completely astonished at his gaiety and vigour; and, till he had lost his *distance*, from his confused sight, victory appeared to hover round him.

In the last battle that ever BELCHER fought, his *bottom* was good in the extreme, and he by no means proved an easy conquest to *Cribb*. Since the loss of his eye, it was the positive wish of his best friends that he would fight no more; but he was not to be deterred, unfortunately neglected good advice, and seemed not aware of the decline of his physical powers. In this last *set-to* the disadvantages he had to contend against were great indeed: his antagonist had made a rapid improvement in the science, was in full vigour, and a GLUTTON that was not to be *satisfied* in a commom way; yet still JEM portrayed that the *science* was left in him, but the *strength* had departed; his hands had become enfeebled, and could not execute their accustomed task, and were so dreadfully lacerated for several of the last rounds, that the flesh had separated from the nails. *Death* was almost as agreeable to his feelings as to utter those unwelcome sounds to the courageous mind, an acknowledgement of *defeat*. Never was it given with more reluctance, and his friends positively forced it from him, after a contest of FORTY MINUTES!

BELCHER's display with *Tom* (better known by the

name of *Paddington) Jones,* convinced the amateurs of
his peculiar *science, spirit,* and *bottom:* and after a
desperate conflict, in which considerable judgement took
place upon both sides, BELCHER was declared the conqueror.   He soon rose rapidly into fame, and was
matched against the most distinguished pugilists.

The *sporting world* were now all upon the alert, with
a match which had long excited considerable attention,
between *Jack Bartholomew,* a pugilist of high repute, and JEM BELCHER.   The former was a great favourite among the *fancy,* and had attained the age of
thirty-seven ; while the latter had not reached his
twentieth year.   The battle was for 300 guineas, and
fought upon a stage, on Finchley-common, on Thursday, May 15, 1800.

About half-past one the combatants appeared, and the
set-to immediately commenced :—sparring was out of
the question, and ferocity the leading feature ; but
BELCHER showed himself off in such good style, and
convinced the spectators that the advantage was upon
his side, that the odds were now laid upon him.   *Bartholomew,* not in the least dismayed, went in boldly,
and gave BELCHER a *leveller.*   The friends of *Bartholomew* were weak enough, upon this circumstance,
to send a pigeon to London with the intelligence,
making up their minds that the battle was a *dead
thing* in their favour ; but they soon had to repent of
their temerity, for in the fourth round BELCHER with
great agility threw *Bartholomew* upon his head,
the shock of which was so violent as nearly to deprive him of his senses, and materially to effect his
eye-sight.   *Bartholomew,* still *prime,* fought in good
style, and contested the battle with great firmness,

and dealt out some most tremendous blows, until the close of the seventeenth round, wherein he received a desperate hit in the stomach from BELCHER, that made him vomit great quantities of blood, when he acknowledged he had had *enough*. The battle, for the time it continued, twenty minutes, was very desperate; and considered as obstinate a contest as had been for some years. *Bartholomew* entertained an idea that there was a *chance* left, and ventured a second trial; but he became an easy conquest, and in considerably less time.

Gamble, having been successful in EIGHTEEN battles, and his knowledge of the *science* being undisputed, it now became the wish of the amateurs, that he should enter the lists with JEM BELCHER, who had given such early proofs of excellence, and that it should be decided, whether the honour of the *Championship* was to remain with England or Ireland. Accordingly, a match was agreed upon for one hundred guineas, to be decided in the hollow, near the gibbet of that extraordinary character, *Jerry Abbershaw,* upon Wimbledon-common, on Monday, December 22, 1800. It would be impossible to describe the roads to Wimbledon; the numerous vehicles of all descriptions, and the pedestrians who were flocking to witness this combat. It seemed as if all the inhabitants of London were upon the alert; and the *swells* of the FANCY were unusually prominent! besides the heroes of the pugilistic art, as *Mr. Jackson, Bill Gibbons, Brown, Back, Paddington Jones, &c.*

BELCHER entered the ring about twelve o'clock, accompanied by his second, *Joe Ward,* and *Bill Gibbons* as his bottle-holder; and *Tom Tring* as an assistant. *Mendoza* was the second to *Gamble;* his bottle-holder *Coady,* and *Crabbe* as deputy. Messrs. *Cullington, Mountain,* and *Lee,* were the umpires. *Cullington,* the publican, held the stakes.

Notwithstanding *Gamble* had beat *James* the Cheshire man, a pugilist that had been successful in seventeen pitched battles, and whose *bottom* was said to be superior to any man in the kingdom; yet still the bets from the first making of the match were *seven* to five in favour of BELCHER; and *Bill Warr,* before the combatants stripped, offered *twenty-five* guineas to twenty. However, upon stripping, *Gamble* appeared much the heaviest man, and his friends and countrymen sported *three* to two upon him; but that was by no means the general opinion A few minutes before one o'clock the fight commenced :—

First round.—The *set-to* was good, and Gamble put in the first *hit,* which was neatly warded off by Belcher, and who with a celerity unequalled, planted in return three severe blows in different parts of Gamble's face : they soon closed, and Belcher, being well aware of the superiority of his opponent's strength, dropped. The *paddies,* in their eagerness to support their countryman, offered five to four.

Second.—Belcher, full of spirit, advanced towards Gamble, who retreated. Jem made a feint with his right hand, and with his left struck Gamble so dreadfully over his right eye, as not only to close it immediately, but knocked him down with uncommon violence. Two to one on Belcher.

Third.—Gamble began to retreat, but put in several severe blows in the body of his antagonist. Belcher, by a sharp hit, made the *claret* fly copiously from his opponent; but Gamble, notwithstanding, threw Belcher with considerable violence, and fell upon him cross-ways. The odds rose four to one upon Jem.

Fourth.—Belcher, full of coolness and recollection, showed himself possessed of excellent science. His blows were well directed and severely felt, particularly one in the neck, which brought Gamble down. Twenty to one Belcher was the winner.

Fifth and last round.—Gamble received two such blows that struck him all of a *heap*—one on the stomach, that nearly deprived him of breath; and the other on the kidneys, which instantly swelled as big as a twopenny loaf. Gamble, completely exhausted, *gave in.*

It is reported that not less than *twenty thousand pounds* were sported upon this occasion. The Irish were completely *dished,* and full of murmurings at *Gamble's* conduct, who was beaten in five rounds, and in the short space of *nine minutes* and *three quarters!* *Gamble* fought very badly; and from his former excellence much was expected: but he appeared frightened at his opponent's activity. BELCHER laughed at him throughout the fight, and treated his knowledge of the art with the most sovereign contempt. BELCHER was carried upon the shoulders of his friends round the ring, in triumph, after the battle was over.

The following conversation immediately afterwards took place between *Mendoza* and BELCHER. A match had been in agitation for some time past between the above celebrated pugilists, for a considerable sum; and, to prevent any injury arising to *Mendoza,* in his capacity as a publican, or the possibility of an interruption to the contest, it was agreed that it should be decided in Scotland; but the match *was off,* and JEM felt rather displeased at the circumstance:—

Belcher. Dan Mendoza!

Mendoza. Well, what do you want?

Belcher. I say, these were the shoes I bought to give you a thrashing in Scotland.

Mendoza. Well, the time may come.

Belcher. I wish you'd do it now.

The parties becoming rather irritated with each other; an immediate *set-to* was nearly the consequence; but their friends stepped in, and prevented it.

Belcher, witnessing a battle, between *Elias*, a Jew, and one *Jones*, which took place upon Wimbledon-common, on Monday, July 13, 1801, a man of the name of *Burke*, a butcher, who had behaved himself improperly in the outer ring, and who had been *milled* out of it twice by some of the professed pugilists, called out for Belcher, the Champion. Upon Jem's mildly asking him what he wanted, the latter received a blow in return for his civility. A dreadful *set-to* instantly commenced—in which *Burke* displayed so much *bottom* and strength, although intoxicated, that the spectators scarcely knew what to think about the termination of the contest. An opinion also prevailed, that had not Belcher possessed a thorough knowledge of the *science*, there was a great probability of his falling a sacrifice to this outrageous *knight of the cleaver*.

Burke having showed so much *game* under such evident disadvantages, *Lord Camelford* was induced to back him, for a second combat in a more *regular* manner, for one hundred pounds. He was accordingly put out to *nurse*; a *teacher* appointed to initiate him into the mysteries of the *science*; and it was reported of *Burke* that he was a *promising child*—took his food regularly, minded what his master said to him, and, for the short time that *he* had taken to *study*, great improvement was visible. *Burke* ultimately turned out one of the most *troublesome* customers, and the hardest to be disposed of, that ever entered the lists with BELCHER.

After some time having elapsed, occasioned by the interruption of magistrates, a stage was erected at Hurley-bottom, a few miles distant from Maidenhead, on November 25, 1801. *Joe Ward* and a *Bristol lad* filled the usual offices for BELCHER—and *Harry Lee* attended as *Burke's* second, and *Rhodes* as his bottle-holder. The odds were nearly two to one, on *setting-to,* upon BELCHER.

First round.—Burke did not give much signs of *improvement* from his tuition—several blows were exchanged, Burke gave Belcher a terrible blow under his right eye that made him reel. They closed, and fell.

Second, third, and fourth.—Blows were the leading features in these rounds. *Science* was not displayed by either of the combatants.

Fifth.—Burke had his nose laid open, by a severe *hit* from Belcher, and *floored.*—TEN to *one* on Jem—no takers.

Sixth.—Shyness was prominent; but Belcher put in a low upon Burke's forehead; the blood now issued copiously from all parts of his head, that his second found it a difficult task to keep him clean.

Seventh, eighth, and ninth.—The former two were of little consequence; but in the latter Belcher was thrown with considerable violence.

Thirteenth.—*Milling* was the signal, and this round displayed a fine specimen of their talents for *hammering.* The best round in the fight.

Sixteenth.—Burke completely *done up*—yet too much pride to confess he was beat; and his second declared that the fight was over.

Since the days of *Johnson* and *Ben,* it was the opinion of the amateurs, so desperate a battle had not

No. VI.   u taken place. Twenty-five minutes of hard fighting. *Burke* was heavier than BELCHER, and greatly superior in point of stature ; JEM appeared little the worse for the conflict, declaring that he had scarcely felt a blow in the fight : and, in the gaiety of the moment, challenged *Mendoza* to fight in less than a month for three hundred against two hundred guineas : but *Dan* was not to be had, and observed, he had done with pugilism.

Warrants were now issued for the apprehension of BECLHER, *Burke,* and their seconds, *Harry Lee* and *Joe Ward,* " for unlawfully assembling, and publicly fighting, at Hurley, in Berkshire." But this proved to be nothing more than a *reprimand* when brought into court, on their pomising not to break the peace again.

Burke was not yet *satisfied;* and another trial of skill was granted, Captain *Fletcher* backing him ; and *Fletcher Reid,* Esq. on the part of BELCHER, for fourteen hundred and fifty guineas a-side, which were made good. The combatants appeared upon the stage, which was erected in a bye-place, at a village called Grewelthorpe, about nineteen miles from Middleham, in Yorkshire. A dispute taking place about *Burke's* second, BELCHER offered to fight him a few rounds for *love;* but as *Burke* would neither fight *for* LOVE nor *money,* the consequence was, that the *Fancy* were got into a complete *string!* JEM received fifty pounds for his trouble from Mr. *Reid,* who also allowed him five pounds for travelling expenses.

Burke now endeavoured to justify himself through the medium of the Oracle newspaper, in a long letter to the editor : but it was looked upon as *gammon!*

At Camberwell fair, these heroes met for the first time after the *bubble* in Yorkshire. *Burke* was rather *lushy*, and entertained the *swells* round him, how *he* would *serve it out* to JEM if he was present. BELCHER was nearer than he imagined, and overheard this *bouncing* of *Burke*, and invited him to another *taste;* which the latter readily accepted, and on the bowling-green, at the Golden Lion, they *set-to.* *Burke* commenced so furiously, that he attacked BELCHER before he was undressed; but JEM, on being prepared for the fray, put in his blows so hard and fast, that *Burke* had one of his front teeth knocked out, and a prime *leveller* into the bargain. BELCHER was somewhat indisposed, and *Burke,* now coming a little more to his *recollection* —their friends interfered—and they mutually agreed to postpone the fight till the next day. They met according to appointment, (August 20, 1802;) and in a field behind St. George's Chapel, near Tyburn turnpike, a most extensive ring was prepared, and though the circumstance was so sudden, and kept very private, yet the spectators were immense. Mr. *Fletcher Reid* and Mr. *Cook* being the only two of the principal amateurs present. A purse of thirty guineas was subscribed for the winner, and five for the loser. *Joe Ward* seconded BELCHER, and *Bill Gibbons* was his bottle-holder; *Burke* had *Owen* for a second, and *Yokel,* a Jew, as bottle-holder. *Burke* expressed a wish that three quarters of a minute might be allowed instead of half, which was resisted.

First round.—Burke was determined to avail himself of his uncommon strength, and ran in upon Belcher, and endeavoured to throw him, but failed in the attempt. Belcher, taking advantage of his mistake, soon had him down by his dexterity. Several blows exchanged, but no *corks* were drawn.

Second.—Burke still upon the same suit, but received a *throttler* for his attempt, that made the *claret* fly. They closed, and Burke found himself upon the *ground*.

Third.—Burke, full of spirit, ran in and put home a fierce blow on the right cheek-bone with his left hand; and another between the shoulder and breast, which was of no effect. They closed, and Burke was down.

Fourth.—Burke, still *prime*, rushed upon his opponent, but, missing his blow, fell. Some murmurs, and calling out " Burke's at his old tricks;" but he soon showed the charge was false.

Fifth.—Burke, with the most determined resolution, ran in and caught Belcher by the hams, doubled him up, and gave him a cross-buttock. The spectators were in fear that Belcher's neck was broken, as Jem pitched upon his head with great violence. " Foul, foul! was shouted; but Belcher rose with uncommon gaiety, and said, " No, no—never mind!!"

Sixth.—The best round that had been fought. As usual, Burke ran in full of spirit, and severe blows were exchanged. Belcher put in several severe hits on the head, neck, and throat. They closed, and considerable skill was manifested on both sides in wrestling; but they both fell without any advantage.

Seventh.—Burke on the decline; his strength was leaving him, but his spirit was good. Closed, and Burke thrown.

Eighth.—Burke wished now to convince the spectators that he was not destitute of *science*, and fought upon the defensive; but Belcher smiled at the attempt, gave him several severe blows, and ultimately had Burke upon the floor.

Ninth.—Twenty to one on Jem, who was as sprightly as if he had not been fighting—laughing and talking to his antagonist, but not forgetting to put in severe hits. Burke down again.

Tenth.—Burke, full of *pluck*, set-to with great spirit, and close fighting ensued. Belcher, losing no time, cut Burke under the left eye; under the right; and another blow so dreadful in its effects between the throat and chin, as to hoist Burke off his feet, and he came down head foremost. Belcher also fell from the force with which he gave it. Both on the floor, when Bourke squirted some blood out of his mouth over Belcher: Jem threatened that in the next round he should have it for such conduct—but Bourke declared it was accidental.

Eleventh.—Bourke's face was now one amss of blood, and he was completely beaten. But still he stood up; few blows were exchanged—they closed, and Bourke was thrown; when Jem, very honourably, fell upon his hands, with an intent not to hurt Bourke any more by falling upon him, which practice is not unusual, and consistent with fair fighting.

Twelfth.—Bourke's weakness was now too evident to be disguised; his second could scarcely get him from the floor.

Thirteenth.—Bourke came again, but Belcher did as he pleased with him; closed and threw Bourke. The latter now was convinced there was no *chance*, and wished to give it in; but his seconds persuaded him to proceed.

Fourteenth.—Bourke was *game*, but it was useless and only rendered his situation worse; he was knocked about like a feather, and not the least shadow of success remained for him. Belcher closed, and Bourke was thrown upon his chest, he could not come in time, and gave IT IN.

Thus was this *desperate customer* disposed of AT LAST. His face was so disfigured, that scarcely any traces of a human being were left; while, on the contrary, BELCHER was without any visible marks of the contest, excepting a bruise upon his cheek. BELCHER's rapidity of action in this battle claimed universal attention and astonishment—and his judgement was equally sure and good. *Bourke* was too strong for him, and he never closed but when necessity compelled him. BELCHER walked round the field several times after the fight, displaying feats of agility.

The *sporting men* were now satisfied of JEM's superiority; and the whole of the immense bets depending

No. VII.   x

upon the Yorkshire contest was decided by the above battle.

Notwithstanding *Bourke* suffered so severely from the effects of this battle, his recovery and strength surprised every one—for in three days after, at a pugilistic dinner, given by *Mr. Fletcher Reid,* at the One Tun public-house, St. James's Market, *Bourke* dined there —shook hands with BELCHER, and acknowledged *Jem* the best man : a match was made for one hundred yards for the best runner, to be decided immediately. *Bourke,* to the astonishment of all present, beat *Jack Ward* (son to the veteran) by five yards.

BELCHER, soon after the above battle, was taken into custody for not keeping his promise to keep the peace, and bound over for £200, and two sureties in £100 each.

Jack Fearby, better known by the appellation of the Young Ruffian, who had acquired great fame as a pugilist, was now matched with BELCHER for one hundred guineas. The contest was to have been decided at Newmarket; but the magistrates interfering, they travelled out of the county, and halted at a spot of ground, about half a mile beyond Linton, and fifteen from Newmarket, and made a ring. The combatants then agreed that the winner should have ninety guineas, and the loser ten. On Tuesday, April 12, 1803, at a quarter past nine, the *set-to* commenced.

First round.—Great anxiety prevailed for the first blow— sparring took place for some seconds, when Fearby put in a blow at Belcher's head, which Jem parried, and returned two blows right and left; no mischief done: they closed, and Belcher fell underneath. Offers to take two to one that Fearby would win—Betters shy.

Second.—Fearby received a severe blow in the mouth, the blood from which issued most copiously; and Jem followed it up by a desperate right-handed hit upon the Ruffian's side, that brought him down. Three to one Belcher was the conqueror.

Third.—Much science displayed on both sides—blows reciprocally given and stopped—when Belcher fighting half-armed, and followed up his adversary close, the Ruffian fell.

Fourth.—A good rally, and several severe blows exchanged. They closed, Belcher fell upon his knee, and in that situation received a blow from Fearby. "Foul! foul!" was the cry, and Belcher wished the point to be decided, but had no desire to take advantage of the circumstance. A constable, followed by a clergyman, now made their appearance; but the clamour was so great that the *exhortations* of the reverend divine could not be heard, and the

Fifth round commenced.—Fearby seemed rather shy of his opponent; his eye now appeared black, and he vomited a great deal of blood—Belcher smiled and beckoned the *Ruffian* to come forward. Fearby made a blow, but it was too slow, and which Belcher avoided by bobbing his head aside; and Jem, in aiming to put in a desperate blow on Fearby's ribs, fell. The Ruffian appeared distressed.

Sixth.—The best round in the fight—Belcher quite gay, but Fearby on the decline. The Ruffian, irritated, made several blows at his antagonist, but they were all thrown away. Belcher taunted him, and with the most apparent ease put in a severe hit upon the stomach; and, in closing, Fearby received a violent cross-buttock.

Seventh.—*Milling* on both sides. Ten to one on Belcher.

Eighth.—Fearby rallied with a good spirit, and made a hit at Belcher, which he parried with great neatness: and, in return, cut the Ruffian's lips severely. Fearby, still *game*, gave Jem a sharp touch, but did not fetch the *claret*. Odds reduced five to one.

Ninth.—Belcher, full of gaiety, and without ceremony, put in a desperate hit over his adversary's right eye, and with all the coolness imaginable, put himself in a defensive posture, and sarcastically asked, " How do you like that, Johnny?" This was too much for Fearby, who was not quite so placid as to pass it over without some notice, and immediately endeavoured to answer the question by a severe blow, but overreached himself in so doing, and fell upon the ground. Belcher smiled, and pointed at him very ironically.

Eleventh.—Belcher now tried to put an end to the fight, by following Fearby round the ring, and putting in several blows, which the Ruffian tried to parry off, but not sufficiently. Belcher, at length, put in a *leveller*, when Fearby's friends made him decline the contest.

The amateurs were much disappointed in this battle, in not witnessing that excellent display of the science so much expected. *Fearby* had no *chance* whatever, and appeared like a different man—his former excellence seemed *frightened* away. It was over in twenty minutes.

The above extraordinary Pugilist was born at his father's house, in *St. James's Church-yard*, Bristol, on the 15th of April, 1781. JEM lived some years with a butcher of that place, but was never apprenticed to the trade; and, when quite a boy, he signalized himself for his pugilistic prowess, and at Lansdown Fair his feats soon rendered him conspicuous. He was about five feet eleven inches and a half in height. On his coming to London, *Bill Ward* invited BELCHER to his house, and a private sparring-match (with the gloves on) took place in *Ward's* dining-room, when the veteran was so astonished at JEM's superior knowledge of the art, that he exclaimed, in falling over a table from one of BELCHER's *touches*—" By G—d ! JEM, I am perfectly satisfied that you can beat any man in the kingdom." In conversation with *Ward*, after dinner, BELCHER observed, " *I could have done a great deal better, Sir, but I was afraid I might hit you too hard, and you should be affronted.*" — " Come along, my boy," replied the Veteran, " we'll have no gloves on now, and you shall do your best; I am not, nor ever was afraid of a blow!" The *set-to* instantly commenced, when the GUEST (out of pure friendship) *levelled* his HOST several times. *Ward* wanted no further *convincing* proofs of his talents. They sat down, and spent the remainder of the evening very harmoniously, and *Ward* immediately offered to back JEM against any man in the country.

After the unfortunate circumstance of losing his eye, on July 24, 1803, in playing at Racquets, in company with Mr. *Stuart*, in St. Martin's Street—JEM declined in health; his spirits were not so good as heretofore; and, at times, he felt much depressed from this afflicting loss. Soon after the above accident he took the *Jolly Brewer*, in Wardour-street, Soho, which house was well attended. In losing the battle with the *Chicken*, (which, we are credibly informed, was principally occasioned by a quarrel between *Pearce* and a brother of JEM's since dead,) his brave heart was almost bursting with grief. The loss of his eye now preyed upon him so much, that his temper became very irritable; and so confident of success was BELCHER, in his last contest with *Cribb*, that, after betting all his money, he sported his gold watch, worth thirty pounds. After this fight, he began to droop, and fretted considerably. His confinement in Horsemonger-lane for twenty-eight days, also having to pay a considerable sum for breaking the peace by that battle; added to a cold he caught in the above prison, hastened his death. It was, however, an expressed opinion, that he died more from a family complaint than from the blows he had received as a pugilist. His circumstances at one time after his defeats were much injured, and he was considerably reduced. The *Fancy* ought not to have let such a man as JEM BELCHER (at any period of his life) felt loss from his pugilistic efforts —for more honour, integrity, and affection never resided

in the human heart. In his latter moments, he displayed much sense, penitence, and resignation, and
endeavoured to atone for those errors which he had
committed, with all the firmness and piety of a good
Christian. He suffered a great deal from expectora-
tion, having an ulcer upon his liver. A short
period previous to his death, he made his will.

On Tuesday, July 30, 1811, died, at the sign of the
Coach and Horses, Frith-street, Soho, (of which he
was the landlord,) the renowned JAMES BELCHER, in
the 31st year of his age; and on Sunday, August 4, he
was buried in Mary-le-bone ground. The concourse
of people eager to witness the last of their once-dis-
tinguished Champion was immense. His funeral was
of the most respectable kind :

THE HEARSE
Preceded by a Man carrying a Plume of Feathers.
In the first Mourning Coach,
Mrs. BELCHER (his Widow), Mrs. PHILPOT, and TOM
BELCHER, &c.
Second Ditto,
Mr. Harmer (his Nephew), Mrs. Harmer, Messrs. Gregson,
Richmond, Bitton, &c.
In the Third,
Mr. Sumner (an Attorney), Mr. Shabner, Mr. Hawkins, &c.
And in a Glass Coach following,
Bill Wood, Powers, and several Amateur Friends.

As they moved along in solemn procession, the
numbers of people were so great in joining it, that, upon
their arrival at the church-yard, which was already nearly
filled, the mourners could scarcely reach the grave.
Wood and *Jack Powers* staid to pay the last respects to
their departed friend, and dropped a tear to his memory.

A more general sympathy was never witnessed among spectators, (principally sporting persons,) in shedding a profusion of tears; as did most of his pugilistic brethren, at the loss of so great a hero!

In visiting the ground where his remains are deposited, we should think BOXIANA wanting in respect, if not incomplete, were we to omit the words upon his tombstone :—

In Memory of

JAMES BELCHER,

Late of St. Anne's Parish, Soho,

who died

The 30th of July, 1811,

AGED 30,

Universally regretted by all who knew him.

With patience to the last he did submit,
And murmur'd not at what the Lord thought fit;
HE with a Christian courage did resign
His soul to God at his appointed time!

On July 2, 1811, a benefit was given for him, at the Fives Court, St. Martin's Street. BELCHER, in consequence of some improper information being given to the Police, on April 6, 1802, at his benefit, at the Pea-hen, Gray's-inn-Lane, he and his fistic brethren were conveyed to the watch-house, but liberated the next morning. At another period, when JEM intended to have given *John Bull* a treat of sparring, at Sadler's Wells, with the concurrence of the Manager,

the *Lord Chamberlain* prevented the amusement, and
poor JEM was again deprived of making a benefit.
Previous to this circumstance, in a *set-to* at the above
Theatre, BELCHER's display of the art was universally admired, and his efforts to please were crowned
with reiterated plaudits. It was from this favourable
reception, that his friends persuaded him to make the
attempt; and it was agreed by the Manager that JEM
should have *half* the receipts of the night.

Lord *Camelford* was a great patron of BELCHER;
and, previous to his death, gave him his celebrated dog,
Trusty, observing, that the two conquerors ought to
reside together; and that he could not have a better
servant than *Trusty*, who had proved victorious in
upwards of fifty battles. *Trusty* was in the possession
of Captain *Barclay* when he died.

We feel much indebted to the politeness and liberality
of Mrs. BELCHER (his widow), of the Coach and
Horses, Frith-street, Soho, in granting permission to
copy the likeness of the late JAMES BELCHER, from
the original picture in her possession. The great similarity of the above portrait to a most distinguished
Hero on the Continent is truly curious, and might
be almost said to be a *fac simile* of that warlike character, excepting the difference of the eyes.

In taking leave of this late distinguished pugilist,
we cannot do better than conclude with the words of
the poet :—

> " Yet e'en these bones from insult to protect,
>   Some frail memorial still erected nigh,
> With uncouth rhymes and shapeless sculpture deck'd,
>   *Implores the passing tribute of a* SIGH !"

PEARCE.

MENDOZA.

Published August 12, 1812, by G. Smeeton, St Martin's Lane

HENRY PEARCE,

Scientifically denominated the GAME CHICKEN !

(THE BROUGHTON OF HIS TIME,)

And one of the most heroic and humane CHAMPIONS OF ENGLAND, *who not only added fresh laurels to the title, but never lost that distinguished appellation, till it was wrested from him, by that Conqueror of Conquerors—Death !*

" There is a kind of *character* in *thy* LIFE,
That, to the observer, doth thy history
Fully unfold : thyself and thy belongings
Are not thine own so proper, as to waste
Thyself upon thy virtues, they on thee.
Heav'n doth with us as we with torches do,
Not light them for themselves: for if our virtues
Did not go forth of us, 'twere all alike
As if we had them not. Spirits are not finely touch'd
But to fine issues : nor NATURE never lends
The smallest sample of her excellence,
But, like a thrifty Goddess, she determines
Herself the glory of a creditor,
Both thanks and use."

NATURE—to some of her favourites has been peculiarly bountiful in the distribution of her favours ; uniting health, strength, and symmetry of form to grace the person of one individual ; and also in adding those fine requisites to render the system complete in all its parts, that have made her works so transcendently beautiful and towering, over all the attempts of ART. To HER Man is indebted for those sensibilities, which outvalue mines of wealth, and likewise for

No. VII.   Y the performance of those heroic actions which stamp him—GREAT.

NATURE too, sportive in her mood, has rendered the peasant, in obeying her dictates, content and happy upon his bed of straw; while the mighty and powerful monarch, enjoying all the meretricious blandishments of ART, has been seen restless and uneasy upon his downy couch. And also in giving feeling and understanding to the most obscure individuals has rendered them prominent and interesting members of society; in spite of those *soi-disant* refined critics, who have in vain attempted to oppose the law of NATURE.

It might be said of the GAME CHICKEN, that he was not only a favourite, but a pupil of the above Deity— and who, in giving him a fine athletic form, strength, wind, and agility, had finely tempered those rare requisites with the most manly courage and sublime feeling. *If* ever greatness of soul raised the character of man, or humanity shone resplendent in the breast of a human being—a purer claim to those inestimable qualities was never witnessed, than that of—HENRY PEARCE.

His pretensions as a PUGILIST stand upon a proud eminence, that few, indeed, can ever expect to attain. In possessing a thorough knowledge of the *science* he was equal, if not superior, to all his competitors; and supported with *strength,* almost Herculean, that enabled him either to receive the attacks of his adversary with the most steady composure, or put in his *hits* with giant-like force. His *wind* so truly excellent, that in all his battles he was scarcely ever seen much distressed; and for *game* or *bottom* unquestionably unrivalled, that his noble and daring spirit never drooped to cry ENOUGH; He had fought with men who ranked high as pugilistic heroes—and whose superior strength, *gluttony*, and experience, had rendered them truly formidable in the boxing list of candidates for fame. *Bourke*, whose *ferocity* and inordinate *gluttony* were not *satisfied* with FOUR desperate *millings* from the potent arm of the renowned *Jem Belcher*, entered the lists with the CHICKEN, and in two dreadful combats, was completely *served-out* by the all-conquering PEARCE, and carried away almost lifeless from the scene of action. *Elias Spray,* the *coppersmith*, whose reputation stood high as an experienced and *bottom* pugilist, and who was a most powerful man, and had gained several good battles; yet, when in competition with the CHICKEN, was rendered truly *insignificant*. *Cart*, of Birmingham, (a second *Perrins,*) who had vanquished several *prime milling coves*, was in the hands of PEARCE a mere plaything; and while the CHICKEN showed scarcely any traces of the conflict, *Cart* miserably portrayed his want of judgement, and exhibited severe *punishment*. By the above victories PEARCE had arrived at the very *acmé* of perfection as a pugilist—his *science* was generally acknowledged as pre-eminent, and he now took the elevated seat, surrounded with glory, as the brave and noble CHAMPION OF ENGLAND. But he had not yet done enough to *satisfy* the *sporting world* that his CLAIM to that proud title was *indisputable*—and he had again to enter the ring to evince further greatness, and more *strongly* to consolidate his fame and honour.

It is true that PEARCE had completely disposed of

Bourke, Spray, and *Cart*—but now, a Hero of no common stamp presented himself as a candidate for the dazzling prize—his townsmen and his friend. But in the thirst for glory all distinctions are banished. In throwing down the gauntlet, his pretensions to pugilism were considered so excellent, that any eulogium here is perfectly unnecessary. On these boxers meeting, as might be expected, finer skill, greater courage, thorough bottom, and more general manliness, were never exhibited; and the Champion, in receiving an additional *brilliant* to grace his cap, did not overlook his brave but fallen competitor, by generously acknowledging—" that he was the only man who had ever stood up to him, and that it was with some difficulty he now stood upon his legs." *Gulley,* although in defeat, had exalted his fame; and the Champion, in again ascending the chair, added additional dignity and lustre to the seat. But now, (not altogether unlike JULIUS CÆSAR, in receiving the unkind stab from his beloved BRUTUS,)—arriving at the very pinnacle of his greatness, flattering himself with peace and tranquillity, his mind was disturbed by his dearest friend, his patron, and his tutor, who had drawn him from obscurity. One who had also been endeavouring to promote and establish his greatness in public life. But, it is said, growing jealous of his pupil's excellence and distinguished reputation, and not being content at enjoying his well and hard-earned laurels in peace and retirement, *Jem,* in an irritable moment, when envy triumphed over reason, dared his pupil to the combat. This might be termed not only an unkind but an *unnatural* challenge. Two sworn and almost inseparable friends. The CHICKEN received the invitation with serious concern. *Fear* never entered his noble heart: and though a professed pugilist, yet he was not insensible to the afflicting circumstance of *beating* the man to whom he stood indebted for his eminence, his reputation, and every thing he possessed in life. His manly nature grieved at being thus situated. Reflection only made it worse ; yet the calls of honour now rose superior to every other consideration, and nothing, but to support his darling fame, could have induced him to commence this forced *set-to*.

> " Oh heaven ! were man
> But constant, he were perfect ; that one error
> Fills him with faults."

The battle was truly desperate ; and the display of *science* unprecedented in the annals of pugilism. If ever there was a contest in which nobleness of soul and generosity of disposition were exemplified, the GAME CHICKEN manifested it before thousands, in the twelfth round. When PEARCE threw *Belcher* upon the rope, and while his body was balancing in that unprotected, yet fair situation, the CHICKEN had an opportunity of ending the fight, by one of his tremendous blows, but his generous mind spurned the committal of a deed that would have grieved his soul, and putting himself in an attitude to convince the spectators of the obvious *chance* that presented itself, and looking round the ring, pathetically exclaimed—" *I'll take no advantage of thee, Jem ; I'll not hit thee, no,* LEST I HURT THINE OTHER EYE!" In the sixteenth round, to his memory be it also recorded, he pursued the same magnanimous line of conduct. The audience

were lost in admiration—and my UNCLE TOBY never
uttered a finer sentiment, or performed a nobler act
more worthy of registering. While the sensibilities
of our nature are awakened, by those delicate touches
of the art, to respect and veneration for an *imaginary
personage*—never let it be said, by *that* mind who has
strength enough to admire heroism and virtue wherever it comes across him, that REALITY shall be passed
over with silent neglect; or, that the deeds even of a
Pugilist, when they are praiseworthy and laudable of
imitation, shall not have justice done to them. *Men of
honour,* here is a circumstance worthy of your notice
—*Sentimentalists,* improve upon it if ye can, and place
it in a more conspicuous point of view—but *Pugilists,*
never let it be forgotten, even when the fight rages
desperate, and an advantage should present itself
(like the above), recollect that the brightest gem in
your character, is *humanity,*—THEN will ye remember
HENRY PEARCE.

The CHICKEN had now proved himself a *thorough-
bred* GAME COCK, and the walk might fairly be said *all
his own !*—But a keeper of *game,* who had been dazzled
with the superior qualities of this CHICKEN, felt a wish
to become his master—but could not *af*-FORD to produce the ingredients to get him into his possession. It,
perhaps, was a fortunate circumstance for him, that he
could not post the *blunt,* as there is but little doubt,
he would have soon proved *blind* to his own interest.

HARRY PEARCE, unhappily, like too many of his
predecessors of pugilistic notoriety, foundered upon the
same rock of destruction upon which they had split.
Examples, advice, or lessons, it should seem, all lose

their effect upon persons when in the bloom of youth, health, and vigour, and who laugh at the idea of incurring any serious consequences from intemperance, till they *feelingly* find it out themselves, and then it is generally too late to be remedied. The CHICKEN, it appears, during his residence in the Metropolis, had made rather too free with his constitution; yet we have authority for observing, that it originated more from circumstances and place, than sheer inclination. In company with *sporting men* frequently, he poured down copious libations at the shrine of Bacchus, added to the fond caresses of the softer sex, among whom he was a most distinguished favourite. His health became impaired, and he retired to his native place, to enjoy peace and the comforts of domesticated life; and by the advice of his friends, immediately relinquished the profession of a pugilist for that of a victualler.

We are now arrived at that part of his life, when description must fall short, and the pen of the most brilliant writer fail in doing justice to the merits of the case, in which PEARCE proved himself almost more than mortal. In the month of November, 1807, a fire broke out at Mrs. *Denzill's,* a silk-mercer, in Thomas-street, Bristol, and the flames had made such rapid progress, that the servant of the house, a poor girl, who had retired to rest in the attic story, was nearly enveloped in flames before she awoke to behold her dreadful situation. Frantic with despair, she presents herself at the window imploring help—her screams pierce the hearts of the spectators, who appear rivetted with agony to the spot, expecting every moment her threatened destruction. But none move; all are petrified with fear and horror.

At length, PEARCE appears in the crowd; he saw the
life of a human being in danger, and felt the necessity
of an immediate rescue, or all must be lost.   As if inspired with a god-like spirit, by the aid of the adjoining
house, he reaches the parapet, and hanging over it, firmly
grasps the wrists of the wretched girl—the multitude
are lost in astonishment, and never did a more, if *such*
an interesting moment present itself—hope, fear, and
all the finer sensations of the mind are upon the utmost
stretch in beholding the intrepidity of a man valuing no
other consideration but that of delivering the object
from its danger.   The additional weight, added to the
height from the parapet, is almost too much for the
nearly exhausted exertions of PEARCE, his mind agitated with not being able to keep his equilibrium, but

> " Cowards die many times before their deaths,
>   The valiant never taste of death but once."

And so it proved :—his brave heart leaped within him,
and with a noble effort (as if an instrument in the hands
of Providence) he draws his trembling charge from the
window, places her safe upon the parapet, and in an
instant she is out of all danger!—Universal joy prevailed.   The delighted and astonished multitudes were
lost in the ecstasy of the plaudits—and the almost lifeless
sufferer clinging round the knees of her deliverer, invok-
ing blessings on his name.   This was the happiest moment of PEARCE's life.   The shouts of victory, and
the flattering praises that had so often attended him in
the field of honour, were mere *shadows* to this feeling—
compared with that of an approving conscience!—Yet,
this was the act of a *Pugilist!*—and one who had entered
the field to obtain a purse of gold as a prize-fighter.   Yet,

in all those engagements, he had a choice left in leaving that ring whenever danger pointed out the necessity of withdrawing from it. *But here was no* GOLD to tempt him to risk his life, which was placed in the most imminent peril and with scarcely a chance of success. The smallest deviation of balance must have precipitated him headlong to destruction, and no opportunity of retreating from the consequences. The gallant soldier in mounting the *forlorn hope*, and the hardy tar in boarding the ships of the enemy, are stimulated by a thirst of glory and love of country, that prompts them to those deeds of heroism ; but PEARCE was actuated by no other motive than that of *feeling*. Never did human nature appear with so much real grandeur and unaffected dignity—and that " *recording angel* " who dropped a tear and blotted out for ever an *intemperate* expression we sincerely trust may be affected by the same sort of sympathy in obliterating the *past deeds* of A MAN, that when the book is opened the name of PEARCE shall stand free from imputation.

To the honour of the *sporting world* be it spoken, an immediate subscription was entered into to reward such unparalleled heroism ; and soon afterwards the following effusion appeared in a Magazine peculiarly dedicated to that part of society :—

" In Bristol city, while a house in flames
　　Fills the beholders with amazement dire,
　A damsel at an upper window claims
　　Their utmost pity, for th'approaching fire—
　Which every moment seems to gather near,
　Nor hope of rescue does there aught appear.

No. VII.   z

" At length upon the neighb'ring house-top seen,
    A gallant youth now hastens to her aid,
And o'er the fearful parapet does lean,
    With spirit dauntless, to assist the maid ;
Endow'd by Heaven with more than common might,
He grasps her arms, and draws her to the height.

" Oh! glorious act ! Oh ! courage well applied !
    Oh! strength exerted in its proper cause !
Thy NAME, O PEARCE ! be sounded far and wide,
    Live, ever honour'd, midst the world's applause ;
Be this thy triumph ! know, ONE creature saved
Is greater glory than the world enslav'd."

It was but a very short period after the above noble
deed, that the GAME CHICKEN again distinguished himself in rescuing one of the fair sex from insult and
danger.   In his way over Clifton-downs, near Bristol,
PEARCE perceived a young woman, suffering much from
the brutal attacks of three athletic men, game-keepers.
The CHICKEN, regardless of the consequences, immediately remonstrated with them upon their unmanly conduct, when they instantly all fell upon him with the
utmost fury ; but the courage and science of PEARCE
soon made them severely repent of their temerity. The
CHICKEN received the violence of his assailants with
coolness and intrepidity, by rendering their attempts unavailing ; but, in return, he so successfully planted his
death-like *hits* upon their frames, that one of them,
of the name of *Hood*, was so *satisfied*, in seven minutes, that he *bolted*, and left his two companions to
the care of PEARCE. In a quarter of an hour, the CHICK-
EN so *served out Morris* and *Francis*, the other two,

that he left them prostrate on the earth, begging for mercy. Thus was the CHICKEN once more successful, in proving himself a Champion for the fair sex. *Morris,* while PEARCE was defending himself against *Francis* and *Hood,* gave the CHICKEN a most violent blow on his head, that produced a severe contusion.

Bourke, after the retirement of *Belcher,* considered himself, or rather assumed the appellation of Champion: and, in justice to him, it might be observed, that, however deficient in *science,* his *bottom* was of the most unquestionable nature; and upon the whole he could be considered as no mean rival to contend with for victory. Upon the arrival of the CHICKEN in London, his pugilistic fame at Bristol rendered him an object of envy to *Bourke ;* and after enjoying a day's sport, in the old English manner, in the vicinity of Shooter's Hill, these two rivals first met, not under the most favourable impression towards each other. The amateurs, upon *their* return to town in the evening, having expressed an anxious desire to have an immediate appeal to the fist between the above heroes—the CHICKEN was called up out of bed, (at his lodgings, in Wardour-street, Soho,) and upon being made acquainted with the circumstance, agreed to it without the smallest hesitation ! A room was selected for the occasion, well-lighted, and notice sent round to the amateurs that a trial of skill was to take place, between the new Bristol Youth and the celebrated *glutton, Bourke.* Numbers soon assembled, and, between the hours of eleven and twelve, the battle commenced. *Bourke's* inferiority was soon discovered. His slow and round method of fighting failed in doing any execution, when opposed to the rapid *hits* of his

adversary; and his *bottom* only served him to receive
uncommon *punishment*. The CHICKEN, aware of the
gluttony of his opponent, lost no time in displaying the
graces of the *science,* but put in his blows so hard and
fast, that *Bourke* soon exhibited signs of weakness.
During a desperate contest of twenty minutes, in which
fifteen rounds of tremendous *milling* took place, *Bourke*
evinced great courage, and endeavoured to show some
little *science,* by parrying off the blows of the CHICKEN,
but the latter followed him up so straight-forward, that
it was impossible for *Bourke* to resist the consequences ;
and he was *levelled* twice by the CHICKEN, from such
tremendous hits, that he lay apparently dead. The
two blows were allowed, by all present, to have been
the most terrible that ever had been given. *Bourke*
was so dreadfully *milled*, that he could scarcely articulate ; but yet had the candour to acknowledge, that he
had never before experienced so *prime a taste* in all
his life.

The amateurs were anxious for a second combat, and
Bourke flattering himself that a *chance* was still left,
one hundred pounds was staked, and it was agreed that
the winner should have ninety pounds and the loser ten.
On Wimbledon-common, Monday, January 23, 1804,
a ring was formed, and the battle fought. *Bourke*
was seconded by *Owen,* and *Paddington Jones* was his
bottle-holder. PEARCE had for his second *Bill Gibbons* and *Caleb Baldwin* as his bottle-holder. On stripping, in point of appearance *Bourke* appeared the tallest.
The odds were considerably in favour of the CHICKEN.

First round. — Considerable caution displayed upon both
sides, Pearce fully aware of the impropriety of exposing himself too openly to superior strength—and Bourke's recollec-

tion of his former *milling* had taught him not to be too precipitate : they closed before any blows were exchanged, and both fell. Two to one the Chicken wins.

Second.—Bourke upon his mettle, *game to the back-bone,*—he showed he was not to be disposed of easily, and fought like a hero ; but the Chicken, awake to his intent, put in a *stopper* upon his forehead, that made him reel again, when the Chicken caught him staggering and threw him.

Third.—Bourke, although bleeding profusely, stood up well to his man, and a good display of hits were seen upon both sides, when Bourke was thrown.

Sixth.—Chicken put in a blow, which Bourke returned so well as to bring down Pearce on his knee.

Seventh to Eleventh.—Bourke exceedingly shy of his opponent, always waiting for the hit of his antagonist—and suffered much from the repetition of his blows. From this to the

Fifteenth, the Chicken wasso much the favourite, that the odds were four to one upon him. It was manifest that Bourke was not a match for his man : his style of fighting was considerably inferior to that of his opponent's, and he began to appear much *distressed.* The severe blows he received from the Chicken made him unruly and intemperate, and he was becoming fast an easy conquest to the

Twentieth. — Bourke's passion was now exhausting his strength—his nose bleeding considerably — and irritated in mind, that no chance offered of proving successful, he ran in furiously upon his opponent. His intemperance rendered him a complete object for *punishment,* and the Chicken *milled* him in every direction. Twenty to one the winner named ; and even bets that Bourke don't come again.

Twenty-first.—Passion uppermost, and Bourke desperate in the extreme, and by running in headlong, missed putting in a hit, and fell ; Pearce smiling at his want of prudence ; and holding up both his hands in triumph.

Twenty-second.—A good rally, but Bourke received a most tremendous leveller.

Twenty-fourth and last..—Bourke, still insensible to propriety, received a severe *milling,* when he gave IT IN.

Bourke, as usual, displayed uncommon resolution, and, notwithstanding the persuasion of his friends, obstinately contested the battle for several rounds, when there was not the smallest degree of *chance*.   He was compelled at last, after an hour and seventeen minutes, reluctantly to acknowledge that he was done.   His aspect was truly woeful.   The CHICKEN was as gay the last round as when he entered the ring, and challenged *Bitton* for two hundred guineas.

Elias Spray, the *coppersmith,* who had distinguished himself as a pugilist in Bristol, now entered the lists with the CHICKEN.   *Spray* had a good character, and a considerable display of *science* was expected by the amateurs.   The day appointed for the meeting to take place was on Monday, March 11, 1805, at Hampton-court, but, fearing something like an interruption, they agreed to cross the water, and decide the contest upon Molesworth-meadow.   Considerable confusion took place in finding vehicles to convey the numerous followers across the river, where several not only experienced a good ducking, but some narrowly escaped drowning, in their eagerness to reach the destined spot.   At length every thing being completed, PEARCE, attended by *Maddox* and *Hall,* as his second and bottle-holder, entered the ring, 20 feet square, when he threw up his hat in defiance.   *Spray* soon made his appearance, followed by *Wood* as his second, and *Mountain* as bottle-holder.   The bettors were on the alert, and offered seven to four on PEARCE; and even bets were sported that the contest did not continue 25 minutes; and also that the CHICKEN was not vanquished in thirty.

First round.—Several feints took place, but Spray not minding his *distance,* hit short; when the Chicken, taking advantage of the fault, put in a severe blow, and Spray was *levelled.*

Second.—Several good hits exchanged—Spray gave the Chicken a severe blow upon his breast; Pearce rallied, and in the event, Spray received a knock-down blow. Nine to four upon the Chicken.

Third.—A good round, Spray full of courage, and stood up heroically. Closed and both fell.

Fourth.—Spray too hasty, and out of *distance* again; his blows all thrown away. The Chicken gave Spray a cross-buttock.

Fifth.—Spray distressed already—the Chicken *bang up*, flourishing with all the graces of the *science*, and showing himself off to *prime* advantage, went in and knocked the Coppersmith down, and smiled at his weakness.

Sixth.—Both well engaged, and several good blows passed —Spray put in a desperate hit upon the Chicken's stomach : the Chicken rallied, and threw his man very neatly.

Seventh.—The Chicken was considerably affected by Spray's stomacher, made a hit, but failed in the attempt. Odds fell some little.

Eleventh. — Nothing material occurred in the last four rounds, but the Chicken had the advantage.

Twelfth.—Spray went in with spirit, and put in some severe blows, but his *distance* was incorrect; however, he brought the Chicken down by a terrible hit on the nose.

Thirteenth.—The Chicken covered with blood - Spray much distressed, and, in making a hit, fell.

Fourteenth.—Pearce, full of *game*, put in a most severe blow upon his antagonist's jaw, that fears were entertained he had broken it; Spray fell in consequence of its severity! Ten to one on Pearce.

Fifteenth.—Spray stood up to his man boldly, and received a *leveller* from the Chicken.

Sixteenth. —Courage manifested well on both sides; and Spray put in some well-directed hits. In closing, Pearce gave him a cross buttock.

Seventeenth.—Spray on the decline; attempted to rally; but received a most desperate blow upon his temple, that nearly deprived him of his recollection, and which spoilt him for the remainder of the fight. The last five rounds upon the part of Spray were little better than stupidity.

Twenty-third.—All in favour of the Chicken. Twenty to one, but no takers.

Twenty-fourth.—Spray again showed himself, but his efforts

were feeble indeed.   The Chicken smiled at his weakness ;
yet, the Coppersmith showed considerable skill ; and continued it to the

Twenty-seventh.—But no fighting—Spray *levelled* as soon
as he appeared.

Twenty-eighth.—Spray could scarcely stand, but wished to
have another chance, and endeavoured to face his opponent.
It was *all up* with the Coppersmith, the Chicken hit him in any
part that he liked, and knocked him off his legs.

Twenty-ninth and last.—Spray stood up, but only to be
ridiculed.   The Chicken pointed at him in derision, and put
in another leveller—when Spray gave *it in.*

The contest lasted 35 minutes, when the CHICKEN,
full of gaiety, jumped over the ropes,—and accepted of
a challenge from *Cart*, a Birmingham pugilist, of some
notoriety, for fifty guineas.   The stakes were instantly
made good, and they agreed to fight within six weeks.
The CHICKEN laid upon the ground for a few minutes,
and then started for town, full of spirits.

On Saturday, the 27th of April, 1805, the day appointed for *Cart* to enter the lists with the CHICKEN, the
parties met at Shepperton-common, near Chertsey, in
Surrey. The superiority of the CHICKEN was so manifest,
that *Cart* had not the least chance whatever, although
six feet three and a half inches in height ; and it would
only be a waste of time and paper to give the rounds in
detail. Suffice it to observe, that after a contest of thirty-
five minutes, in which twenty-five rounds took place,
Cart, from his ignorance of the art, received a most
terrible *milling ;* while, on the contrary, the *science* of
the CHICKEN protected him so securely from the attacks
of his adversary, that he scarcely had a mark visible.

The above pugilistic rivals were *mere* TYROS, compared with one who now came forward to contend for the

laurels—and it appears, that *Gulley* was so great a favourite with several of the amateurs, that it was agreed he should be immediately liberated from *durance vile*, and his debts discharged, that he might fight the CHICKEN. This was accordingly put into practice by Mr. Fletcher Reid, and *Gulley* was sent into training at Virginia-water, about two miles beyond Egham. It appears that *Gulley* was scarcely known in the Metropolis, having never appeared or distinguished himself as a pugilist ; and that he was excited to a trial of skill from a casual friendly sparring match with the CHICKEN, in which he planted some severe *hits*, from which circumstance, his ambition prompted him to think that he could beat PEARCE. Notwithstanding the great reputation of the CHICKEN, who, for COURAGE, SCIENCE, and BOTTOM, stood unrivalled, *Gulley* flattered himself with the thoughts of victory.

The friends of the CHICKEN, who had upon all occasions found him *game*, readily came forward, and backed him for six hundred guineas to four hundred, to fight on Saturday, the 20th of July, 1805. Various rumours were now afloat among the FANCY, and the *sporting world* were somewhat divided as to the issue of the contest. Virginia water was the appointed rendezvous, and thither the company repaired ; but it being understood, that the fight would take place at Chobham, about three miles further, the company was off in all directions, to obtain good places. A ring was made at Chobham, and nothing wanted but the combatants to enter it to gratify the longing eyes of the spectators. But JOHN BULL had more disappointments to contend against : some talked of a *cross*—

No. VIII.   A a

others that it was a *mixed-up* concern—and several of
the *would-be* intelligent, prognosticated that no fight
would take place that day. While this parley was going
on, it was buzzed about that the magistrates had got
scent, and it became necessary to *broom* towards Blackwater, a few miles beyond Bagshot. This step determined on, the whole cavalcade were *off* like a shot—but
upon their arrivel at Blackwater, the *gammon* was again
pitched about a *cross*; and Mr. Fletcher Reid, being assured that most of the bets were off, determined there
should be no *mill.* But to prove the fallacy of such
assertions, Berkeley Craven and Mr. Mellish publicly
offered to support the CHICKEN to any amount; and said
they should feel no hesitation in permitting PEARCE to
fight six hundred guineas to FIVE only, they felt so
much impressed with his integrity and courage. This
balk increased the anxiety of the *Fancy* in general, and
stories out of number were in circulation; but the bets
kept in favour of the CHICKEN, and the odds given
upon his side. At length the important day arrived
(Tuesday, October 8, 1805), which had kept the *sporting men* so much upon the alert for some time past—
and all the admirers of the pugilistic art that could quit
the Metropolis set off for Hailsham, a small village,
situate between Brighton and Lewes, in Sussex. The
spectators were immense, and the Downs literally covered with equestrians and pedestrians, in eager pursuit
from the above fashionable watering place, to witness the
mighty conflict. On a green adjoining the above village, a twenty-four feet rope ring was made, and, at
one o'clock, *Gulley* entered, with *Tom Jones* for his
second, and *Dick Whale* as his bottle-holder; immediately followed by the GAME CHICKEN, attended

by *Clarke* as his second, and *Joe Ward* as his bottle-holder.

First round.—The *Fancy* were never more attentive, or anxiously interested, than upon the present occasion, and every look of the combatants was turned to account.—Gulley had come well recommended, and he was gazed upon with more than ordinary degree of concern; when, after some little manœuvring, he made a tremendous *hit* at the Chicken, but lost his *distance.*—Pearce, always prepared, knocked Gulley down.—The Chicken three to one.

Second.—Gulley, upon the alert, gave the first *hit*, which the Chicken sharply returned, and Gulley fell.

Third.—The Chicken aimed a blow at his opponent's head, but it fell short.—Gulley made a *hit* and dropped.

Fourth.—Pearce stood up heroically, and a smile of confidence was seen upon his gallant brow: several good blows given and well stopped; but Gulley fell.

Fifth.—The Chicken put in a tremendous blow in the neck, and *levelled* his opponent.

Sixth.—Pearce made play right and left—planted good hits, and brought his man down again.—The Chicken ten to two.

Seventh.—Pearce, immediately on his opponent's facing him, knocked him down.

Eighth.—Considerable science displayed on both sides: the Chicken put in a blow, but Gulley, in the most finished style, stopped it, when they closed and fell.

Ninth.—The Chicken, rather touched, went in and *levelled* Gulley, and smiled at his success.

Tenth.—Gulley rose in good spirits, and made a hit at his adversary; but Pearce neatly warded off its effect, and with a tremendous thump upon the breast brought Gulley down.

Eleventh.—Gulley, full of gaiety, made an excellent hit; but the round finished in favour of the Chicken, who completely knocked Gulley off his legs.

Twelfth.—Gulley put in a most tremendous blow on the mouth of the Chicken, which he sharply returned; and in closing they fell.

Thirteenth.—Gulley distinguished himself in this round for most excellent courage and *science*; and put in some good blows, but fell from their force.

Fourteenth.—Gulley rose quickly, and met his man; but Pearce immediately *levelled* him.

Fifteenth.—The Chicken made a good *hit*, which Gulley returned in good style. Gulley made another blow, but fell.

Sixteenth.—Rather shyness upon the part of Gulley, who fell without a blow.

Seventeenth.—The amateurs were uncommonly interested by the reciprocal manliness displayed in this round—and it was the general opinion that a better one was never contested by any pugilists; it was, most certainly, the best fought round in the battle. Pearce, full of gaiety and confidence, nobly opposed his adversary; while Gulley, with an equal degree of valour and firmness, rallied, and made several excellent *hits*, which were instantly returned by Pearce. Gulley put in two severe *hits* on the Chicken's left eye. Gulley reduced the odds considerably—six to four on the Chicken.

Eighteenth.—Torrents of blood flowing from Pearce—no fighting—and Gulley slipped in making play.

Nineteenth. — Gulley, full of spirit, rallied; which the Chicken quickly returned—several good blows were exchanged, when they closed and fell.

Twentieth.—One of the Chicken's eyes so much swelled that he could scarcely see out of it; and the blood flowing from him copiously; his appearance shy and retreating, which Gulley improving upon, followed the Chicken round the ring, several blows exchanged, when they closed and fell.

Twenty-first.—The Chicken particularly cautious of his adversary; when Gulley, in making a *hit*, fell.

Twenty-second. — Several sharp blows upon both sides, when Gulley fell, and, while in the act of falling, the Chicken put in a desperate blow on the side of Gulley's head, which made him vomit considerably.

Twenty-fourth.—The Chicken, in making a *hit*, lost his *distance*, when Gulley returned a severe blow over Pearce's right eye, and fell upon his knees;—the Chicken, in giving the return quickly, struck Gulley in that situation. Trifling cries of "*foul!*" but not considered of consequence enough to impede the fight.

Twenty-fifth.—The Chicken not so confident as heretofore, when Gulley, with determined resolution, followed him over the ring—good blows given and returned.—Gulley once more fell.

Twenty-ninth.—The Chicken improving every round.

Thirtieth.—Gulley made a tremendous *hit*, and fell. The Chicken, much irritated at this conduct, stood over him with an indignant countenance.

Thirty-first.—Several feints made, each trying for the advantage, when the Chicken, in putting in a blow, lost his *distance.* Gulley, with great agility, struck over his guard, and nearly closed his right eye.

Thirty-third.—Pearce on the look-out, acting on the defensive; when Gulley, in the most manly manner, followed him round the ring; but in the event received a terrible blow in the throat, the severity of which brought him down.

Thirty-sixth.—Gulley now betrayed symptoms of weakness, but endeavoured to put in a blow at the Chicken's head, which he parried, and returned a slight *hit.* Gulley, not dismayed, made a severe blow, which the Chicken caught with his left, and knocked down his adversary with his right hand.

Thirty-seventh to forty-third.—In the last six rounds the Chicken displayed a manifest superiority: their figures were bloody in the extreme; but Gulley was literally covered from the torrents which flowed down from his ear, and who now began to appear somewhat shy—his head was truly terrific, and had a giant-like appearance, from being so terribly swelled, and the effect was most singular, for scarcely could his eyes be seen.

Forty-fourth.—The Chicken, with considerable *science* and force, planted his favourite hit in Gulley's throat, when he fell like a log of wood. The fortitude which Gulley had displayed in this most trying conflict had raised him considerably, not only in the estimation of his friends, but the *sporting men* in general. He had been so severely *punished*, that he was not able to face his man with his former resolution and propriety—his brave heart was reluctant to acknowledge superiority, and he endeavoured now and then to put in a *hit*, and falling, until the

Fifty-ninth.—When his friends interfered, and positively insisted that he should fight no longer, as the *chance* was against him; and, at length, he complied with their request—by surrendering victory to the Game Chicken. The contest lasted ONE HOUR AND TEN MINUTES!

In conquering such a formidable antagonist as *Gulley*—(a man, whose determined resolution and *science,*

had gained universal praise, and who bid fair to be a
most distinguished pugilist)—the CHICKEN, if possible,
by his fine display of judgement and bottom in the
above battle, had raised himself higher in the estimation of his friends, and the *sporting world* in general.

PEARCE now received a challenge from his friend,
Belcher, for five hundred guineas, to fight within two
months, play or pay ; which was accepted by the
CHICKEN. The amateurs were considerably divided in
their opinions respecting the event of this contest—the
combatants were men of such sound prowess, *science*,
and *bottom*, that the most KNOWING were somewhat
puzzled to come to any thing decisive upon the subject. The CHICKEN had performed such prodigies of
valour; and *Belcher* had accomplished all that his
most sanguine friends had wished, that it could not but
unsettle the minds of the FANCY—and much better it
might have proved had they never met—

    " But who can rule the uncertain chance of war !"

Supporters were not wanting upon either side, and Mr.
Fletcher Reid, firm to the cause, and true to the HAD
BEEN, backed his old favourite, *Jem Belcher*, for five
hundred guineas; and Captain *Halliday*, with great
liberality, covered the above sum on the part of the
CHICKEN ; and promised, in the event proving successful, that PEARCE should receive two hundred and fifty
pounds. That no disappointment should take place, by
the interference of the police, it was determined that
the battle should be decided at least one hundred and
fifty miles from the Metropolis ; and the particular place
to be settled by a toss up between the combatants, when
Belcher, proving the winner, decided for a common,

within a short distance from Captain *Mellish's* seat,
named Blythe, situated three miles from Barnby-moor,
nine from Doncaster, and one hundred and fifty from London, upon Friday, December 6, 1805. A roped ring was
formed twenty feet square, within another of forty feet:
and every precaution taken to prevent any inconvenience
being felt from the pressure of the spectators. The partizans of each of the heroes sported their favourite
chief's colour:—the *yellow man*, which had so long been
the boast and pride of the circle, and in fact which was
known, nearly over the kingdom, after the name of
Belcher, were to be seen in great numbers; while the
blue silk bird's eye graced the appearance of the backers
of the CHICKEN. *Bill Ward* and *Gibbons* were the attendants upon PEARCE; *Belcher* had for his second
Joe Ward, and for his bottle-holder *Dick Whale*. *Belcher*, upon stripping, did not appear so well as he had
formerly done upon these occasions; but his spirits were
good, and he seemed to feel his usual confidence. The
CHICKEN looked evidently in better condition, and the
strongest man. The combatants shook hands, and the
battle commenced. *Five* to *four* upon PEARCE.

First round. — The *set-to* was masterly, and every manœuvre
of the *science* was displayed upon both sides to obtain the advantage, when Belcher put in a severe *hit* over the Chicken's
guard upon his eye, that made the blood flow in torrents; to
which Pearce gave but a feeble return: they then closed and
Belcher was thrown.

Second. — Belcher, upon the alert, made some feints, which
the Chicken guarded, and put in a *hit*, although he could
scarcely see for blood. Jem, full of spirit, gave the Chicken
two severe blows on his body, when they closed, but soon separated. Pearce endeavoured to put in a tremendous blow;
but Belcher, with considerable neatness and agility, stopped it:
a rally took place, in which the Chicken struck twice with some

effect, and Jem was thrown again.   The Chicken wins, *twenty* to *twelve.*

Third.—A well contested round, in which considerable skill was displayed, but Pearce had the best of it.   The Chicken rallied, and several good hits were exchanged.   They closed and Jem was thrown upon the ropes.

Fourth.—The Chicken lost his distance, and his blows were useless ; when Belcher rallied, and obtained some advantage; but in the event was thrown.

Fifth.—Pearce, full of confidence, although bleeding very much, went in full of *pluck*, and rallied, but Jem threw him.

Sixth.—Belcher exhibited some of the finest specimens of the art ; but did not appear to meet his adversary as *prime* as heretofore ; yet, notwithstanding he rallied, and some excellent hits were given and taken, during which they closed and fell, the Chicken uppermost.

Seventh.—Pearce made a blow, which Jem parried very neatly with his left hand, and with his right gave the Chicken a desperate *facer :* a rally ensued, when the advantage appeared on the side of Belcher ; but, in closing, Pearce got Jem's head under his left arm, and *punished* him severely with his right, when, in struggling, both went down.

Eighth.—Belcher, with the most determined courage, went in and rallied—and never did he display a finer knowledge of the art : his superiority in this round was manifest, by putting in several hits with his right, and warding the Chicken's blows off with his left hand ; and at length threw Pearce out of the ring.   The bets became level.

Ninth.—Belcher gave the Chicken a severe *facer,* which marked him strongly.   Both appeared in good spirits, and several sharp hits passed, when they closed and fell.

Tenth.—Jem exhibited symptoms of becoming rather exhausted ; and the Chicken appeared to have the best of the round.

Eleventh.—Pearce, by endeavouring to put in a good *hit,* lost his *distance* considerably, when they closed.—Jem neatly disengaged himself, and gave the Chicken a blow, but ultimately was thrown.

Twelfth.—The character of a pugilist was never seen to greater advantage than in this round—the Chicken rallied most furiously, and Belcher was losing his strength fast—they closed, and Pearce threw Jem upon the rope, (and might, most undoubtedly, have put an end to the fight, had not his HUMA-NITY rose superior to every other consideration). Belcher was balancing on his back, and in a most pitiable and defence-less state; but the Chicken, like a man, was above taking so cruel an advantage of his friend, and putting himself in an offensive posture, to show that Belcher was in his power, ex-claimed, most feelingly, " I'LL TAKE NO ADVANTAGE OF THEE, JEM—I'LL NOT HIT THEE, NO, LEST I HURT THINE OTHER EYE !" Such a circumstance ought never to be forgotten—the spectators felt it at the time, by their universal plaudits—and it will live long in Humanity's memory.

Thirteenth.—Belcher's *hits* were scarcely of any effect, and Pearce made a determined rally, when they closed ; but, not-withstanding Belcher's weakness, he gave the Chicken a severe cross-buttock.

Fourteenth.—More sparring than necessary ; Belcher, who was bleeding most terribly from the effects of the last round, wishing to gain time, and somewhat shy of his man. Pearce fol-lowed him over the ring, and put in, through his guard, a se-vere blow under the eye that was dark, and threw Jem easily.

Fifteenth.—It now became as a *forlorn hope* to poor Jem, who, too late, experienced the loss of his eye, and who also found out that his constitution was not so good as heretofore. This round decided the bets concerning the first *knock-down* blow.

Sixteenth.—The Chicken received a blow in the face ; but Belcher was now too feeble to do much execution. Pearce rallied him, and, as in the twelfth round, got him again on the ropes, but was too honourable to take any advantage of his unfortunate position, and walked away. It was feared that one of Belcher's ribs was broken, by his being thrown upon one of the stakes to which the rope was fastened. The odds were ten to one, but no takers.

Seventeenth.—Jem, full of courage, was determined to make another stand, and endeavoured to put in a good hit—his mind was good, but his strength was gone, and the Chicken had it all his own way, by following him to the ropes, and throwing him.

Eighteenth.—Belcher stood up ; but it was only to display his exhausted state, as his left arm was entirely useless, and he could not move it from his side ; and Jem now, for the *first time in his life*, declared he could fight no longer !—The

No. VIII. B b

Chicken, elated with the sound of victory, and particularly
from the hitherto invincible Belcher, to show his activity,
leaped in and out of the ring, and threw a somerset.

PEARCE displayed throughout the above combat
great *science* and courage : and, in point of strength, he
was much superior to *Belcher*, by the tremendous falls
which JEM experienced whenever they closed. The advantages were all on the side of the CHICKEN, excepting
the *science*, and *Belcher's* defective sight rendered even
that of less importance every round. It was the serious opinion of PEARCE, that twice in the fight he
could have killed his adversary, he was so much exhausted and defenceless. The CHICKEN, now *sported*
the *blue spotted silk handkerchief*, as the *Champion's* colour ; and " that handkerchief," which had so long
been the fashion *(à la Belcher)* in gracing the bosoms
of some of our most elevated and beautiful country-
women, and which had likewise so often formed a part
of the dress of the successful partizans, in compliment
to their favourite hero, was at length placed in a secondary point of view ; but, in losing its situation, let it
never be forgotten, that, in adhering to strict justice,
its colour remained unsullied.

It appears, that however PEARCE might deservedly
have been crowned with honour, gratified by the enviable
title of CHAMPION, and admired by his friends in general, and have retired from the busy scenes of life, to
enjoy the comforts of domestic society, and rendered
cheerful amidst the circle of his acquaintance and
townsmen—yet still he was not happy. That source of
true felicity and real consolation, upon almost every occasion, where a man flies to, either to unbosom his

griefs, or to participate in his hard-earned honours—his
HOME :—

> " The fountain from the which my current runs,
>   Or else dries up, to be discarded thence—"

was unhappily polluted, and *incontinence* had rendered
him so miserable, that he left his native place, never
more to return !

PEARCE now went to different country towns exhibiting sparring, and teaching the art of self-defence ; and
at most of the places he was much patronised. The
CHICKEN was in the neighbourhood of Oxford when
Jem Belcher and *Cribb* fought the last time, and felt so
anxiously upon the issue of the combat, that he set off
in a post-chaise to witness the fight. On *Cribb's* proving victorious, he exclaimed, with great earnestness,
" *that he hoped he should get well, that he might* TEACH
Cribb HOW *to fight !*"

The CHICKEN, unfortunately, was very illiterate ;
but good-natured and generous to an excess. Had
his mind experienced the good effects of cultivation,
there is little doubt, from what has been witnessed of
his actions, originating from the impulse of Nature,
that, if united and embellished by art, he might have
become equally sensible as he had proved courageous
and humane.

A benefit took place, for PEARCE, at the Fives Court,
on February 9, 1809, and several good sparring matches
were exhibited. Every interest was exerted to render him
support. PEARCE was now the miserable victim of a consumption, and in the last stage of that afflicting disease,
and scarcely able to walk to the Court to thank his

friends.   But, notwithstanding all their efforts, he was
considerably reduced, and must have experienced want,
had it not been for the humane disposition and kindness
of Mr. *Neale*, of the Coach and Horses, St. Martin's
Lane.   This worthy publican administered those comforts and necessaries to him on his sick-bed which
otherwise he must have received from a place of cha-
rity ! and never forsook him till he was most respectably interred; and, it is said, at his own expense.

In point of form, the appearance of the CHICKEN was
athletic, and in height about five feet nine inches ; and
the roundness of his chest and limbs denoted considerable strength, and not altogether unlike the manly look
of the late *Tom Johnson*. During the time that PEARCE
enjoyed sound health, his excellence as a pugilist was
admitted by all parties ; and he was considered to stand
on a very lofty eminence above all his competitors. In
uniting the courage of a lion with all the softer sensibilities of human nature, it has been observed, that the
CHICKEN was unequalled. He was a most tremendous
hard *hitter,* and in striking with his left hand under the
ear, his favourite aim, his blow was so terrible in its effects, that his opponents have been seen in a complete
state of stupor for several seconds, and have never recovered the proper use of their senses during the fight.

As a proof that he was not fond of vainly courting the
popularity of the multitude, or in making a show of himself, by *cutting a swell* upon the box of some first-rate
Fancier's barouche, in being brought to town in triumph,
with all the honours attending conquest—immediately
upon getting his clothes on, after his memorable fight

with *Bourke*, upon Wimbledon-common, in the bustle of the scene, he stole away unobserved; and being missed, a general inquiry took place among his friends, to know what had become of him. After considerable time being lost in search of the CHICKEN, some person recollected that he saw a man like PEARCE run and jump up behind a coach; upon which information, his second, *Bill Gibbons*, endeavoured to trace him along the road, and, at length, observed the CHICKEN in a public house at Chelsea, cooking himself mutton-chops at the fire, with the most perfect indifference, as if he had never been fighting, when PEARCE immediately invited *Gibbons* to partake of them, without alluding to his singularity of leaving the ground.

Notwithstanding the superiority on the part of PEARCE, in his battle with *Elias Spray*, the copper-smith, the CHICKEN remarked, that he considered *Spray* one of the hardest hitters in the kingdom.

In becoming the panegyrist of any pugilist, we are fully aware of incurring the sneers of the *fastidious,* who are too frequently hurried along from a theoretic opinion, that Boxers in general are men devoid of sensibility, and, indeed, view them as little more than mere brutes. However, in meeting the eyes of men, conversant in the various walks of life, and who can appreciate the superiority of *practice* over that of THEORY, we feel confident, not only in a candid examination into such eulogiums, but an honourable acquittal from any thing like an attempt to mislead the senses, by the high colouring of sentences, or in substituting *ophistry* instead of NATURE—acting only upon the

enlightened principles of one of our most distinguished poets—that

> " Worth makes the man, and want cf it the fellow,
>   *The rest* is all but leather and prunella."

It was at the house of Mr. *Neale,* on Sunday, April
30, 1809, that the GAME CHICKEN departed this life.
His fortitude never forsook him, and, in the most afflicting moments, he displayed calmness and resignation ;
he experienced no terrors from his approaching end, but
expressed a wish to die in friendship with all mankind.
His habits of life had rendered him unacquainted with
the different systems of religion ; but he was strongly
impressed that there was " another and a better world !"
and, in his probation to it, he trusted in the consolation of the sincere Christian, that " God would be
merciful to him as a sinner !"

He expressed a strong desire that he might be buried
by the side of *Bill Warr,* in St. James's burying-ground,
Pancras, and entertained an idea, that " ultimately they
might be able to converse together in another place."
His wish was complied with respecting his interment.

PEARCE was nearly thirty-two years of age.

> " Srength too ; thou surly, and less gentle boast
>   Of those that laugh loud at the village ring ;
>   A fit of common sickness pulls thee down
>   With greater ease than e'er thou didst the stripling
>   That rashly dar'd thee to th' unequal fight.
>   ————————————How his great heart
>   Beats thick ! his roomy chest by far too scant
>   To give the lungs full play.   What now avail
>   The strong-built sinewy limbs, and well-spread shoulders ?"

JOHN GULLEY,

(After the secession of PEARCE, *considered as the*
CHAMPION OF ENGLAND,)

A PUGILIST of distinguished reputation, and brought
into notice by his *first* and memorable contest with the
Game Chicken—and, unlike most other boxers, acquired
renown even in *defeat*. GULLEY's ambition was of the
highest order; second-rate pugilists, it should seem,
were beneath his aim; and spurning the general mode
of acquiring greatness *step* by *step*, HIS daring spirit
prompted him to the temerity of raising himself to the
dignity of a Hero at one stride, by attacking the above
justly renowned and mighty Chief of England. It is
true that he *fell;* but it is equally true, that he rose a
greater man by the attempt than ever. GULLEY convinced the amateurs that he was able to contend with
honour, and even with a considerable chance of success, with the above celebrated pugilistic character;
whose generosity of disposition would not permit him
to quit his vanquished adversary, without complimenting him upon his uncommon bravery and fortitude.

GULLEY, by the *science* and thorough *bottom* he displayed in the above contest, ranked high as a pugilist
and became a distinguished favourite with the *Fancy* in
general. His knowledge of the art of boxing was considered complete, and his courage proved an able second
to his judgement. His supporters were numerous, and
his fame stood so prominent, that upwards of two years
had elapsed, since his battle with the *Chicken*, before he

was called upon to defend his title to the Championship, when, at length, he had to enter the lists with a boxer, of the name of *Gregson*, from Lancashire, a man whose size was considerably in his favour, being nearly six feet two inches high, of prodigious strength, and who had signalized himself in several pugilistic contests in that part of the country, with great success; but, notwithstanding such powerful requisites, his pretensions were considered more on the side of strength than that of *science*. *Gregson's bottom* was so unquestionable, and the amateurs, wishing to see him enter the lists with so distinguished a boxer as GULLEY, a subscription-purse was immediately entered into for that purpose.

On the 14th of October, 1807, this contest, which had been most anxiously looked for, took place in a valley denominated Six-mile-bottom, on the Newmarket-road, and for miles round this part of the country the bustle commenced at an early hour, with groups of people in all directions, eager to witness the battle. Between nine and ten GULLEY and *Gregson* entered the ring, both in excellent spirits and good condition. The former was seconded by *Cribb*, and *Cropley* acted as bottle-holder. *Richmond* was second to *Gregson*, and *Harry Lee* was his bottle-holder. On *setting-to* the odds were considerably in favour of GULLEY.

First round.—The spectators were much attracted by the Herculean appearance of Gregson, who looked formidable in the extreme, and considerable anxiety was felt from his prodigious strength. A good deal of sparring took place, when, a favourable opportunity offering, Gulley put in a desperate *facer*, which Gregson immediately returned, by giving his adversary a severe blow on the side of the head, that made it sound again—they now closed and fell.

Second.—Gregson's strength was manifest to his opponent,

who endeavoured to ward off its potent effects by his thorough
knowledge of the *science,* and Gulley put in another dreadful
facer, which made the *claret* fly in all directions, when Gregson fell. The odds rose twenty to one.

Third, fourth, fifth, and sixth.—In all these rounds a number of good blows were exchanged ; but the advantage, at
times, appeared to be reciprocal.

Seventh.—Gregson, with some dexterity, broke through his
opponent's guard, and put in a desperate blow on Gulley's
right eye, that drew blood, when he fell from its powerful
effects, and lay quite senseless for nearly four seconds. His
eye swelled up so instantaneously, that he could scarcely see
out of it. The friends of Gulley were now under considerable
alarm in witnessing the superiority of strength manifested by
Gregson ; and the odds fell.

Eighth.—Gregson gained considerable confidence from the
success of the last round, and displayed all his *science* and
strength, and went in boldly to his man ; Gulley rallied, and
put in several good blows, and both the combatants stopped
with great adroitness. Gregson, by dint of strength, suddenly
caught Gulley up in his arms, and dashed him violently upon
the ground—and, with the greatest generosity, declined falling
upon him, as he might have done, from the advantage that he
had obtained, and for which noble conduct he was unanimously
applauded from all parts of the ring. It was the opinion of the
Fancy in general, that a better round had neverbeen contested ;
and Gulley's friends now rested their hopes upon his superior
science, in being able to overcome so powerful a man as Gregson. The odds now changed upon Gregson.

Ninth.—Gulley stood up, and gave his antagonist a severe
facer, who slipped upon his hands and knees. This, for the
instant, produced rather an unfavourable sensation, from its
being considered more from design than accident ; but his
manly conduct throughout every round soon chased away any
suspicions that might have been entertained of a contrary
nature.

Eleventh.—Gulley put in a good *hit ;* but Gregson closed,
and Gulley went to the ground.

Twelfth.—Gregson in the best condition, and Gulley manifested considerable weakness. Gulley put in some blows ; but
they were too feeble to do any execution : Gregson gave
his adversary a dreadful blow upon the forehead that knocked
him down. The odds upon Gregson.

No. VIII.   c c

Thirteenth.—Gulley, notwithstanding his weak state, was enabled, by his knowledge of the *science*, to gain the superiority in this round; but his blows were still feeble.

Fourteenth.—Gregson, right and left, *punished* the face of his opponent; when a severe rally ensued, and Gregson, apparently, through weakness, fell on his knees.

Fifteenth.—A few blows were exchanged, when Gregson gave Gulley a *knock-down* blow.

Sixteenth.—Gulley's face exhibited the desperate marks of his opponent's strength, and his right eye was completely closed; a rally took place, when Gregson was knocked off his legs.

Eighteenth.—A good *set-to*, and the advantage completely on the side of Gulley; but who, notwithstanding, received a desperate fall.

Twentieth.—Gregson, in endeavouring to plant his favourite straight-forward blow, lost his *distance*, and, while in the act of falling, Gulley caught him with a *hit ;* a small altercation took place, as to the fairness of the blow, but, as Gregson was not down, it was considered correct, according to the rules of the art.

Twenty-third.—A desperate rally between both the combatants; Gulley full of spirit, but still his weakness was evident, and the strength of Gregson was leaving him very fast. Gulley's *bottom* was known to be of the first quality, that the odds were considerably in his favour.

Twenty-fifth.—The spectators were full of anxiety respecting the decision of the combat; and the backers upon each side were puzzled to know which of the combatants was the most beaten and exhausted; their faces were shockingly disfigured, and they both severely felt the want of time to recruit their wind and strength, and were scarcely able to quit their seconds' knees.

Thirty-sixth and last.—For the last ten rounds it could scarcely be called fighting. Nature was completely exhausted in both their frames, and it was the desperate efforts of the mind seen struggling for victory; their brave hearts endeavouring to protract the scene, reluctant to pronounce the word ENOUGH. In strict honour and justice, it might now fairly be observed, that VICTORY hung upon mere *chance*, more than to any other cause: from the helpless state of the combatants, the betting became even. *Knocking down* seemed out of the question for the last seven or eight rounds, and they fell

continually together, from their feebleness. It has been remarked, that it is impossible to witness any battle, however
perfect strangers the combatants may be, but that the spectator
naturally feels a sort of preference for one more than another
of the pugilists; and here, in this state of the contest, putting
interest out of the question, it would have been impossible to
have made *choice* from any thing like superiority; but, if there
was a favourite, Gulley, perhaps, had the balance. At meeting, in this last round, no drunken men staggered more, or appeared incapable to stand steady than both the combatants did;
at length, Gulley rallied all his strength and spirits, and,
though feeble the attempt, it was of sufficient consequence to
knock down Gregson, and to prevent him rising to his time.
It was a proud moment for Gulley, who, like a tired horse
that is worn out from a long journey, on finding that he is near
home, sets off in a trot; so it operated with Gulley, who endeavoured to make a jump of it, to show how much he valued
the victory. Gregson suffered most terribly indeed, and lay
on the ground for some minutes, totally incapable of moving
or speaking.

It has been the expressed opinion, by all those persons who witnessed the above combat, to be one, if not
positively the most dreadful, in its nature, that ever was
contested. It was scarcely possible to decide which of
the combatants was the most beaten, their figures were
so completely altered. The *bottom* displayed on both
sides excited universal astonishment. *Johnson* had been
terrific in his time; and *Big Ben* tremendous; *George*
the Brewer had shown a hardihood and firmness almost
beyond human nature to sustain; and *Jackson* had
sported *game* of the richest quality; but this was such
a complete system of *milling*, that it might be said to
" *out-Herod Herod !*"

GULLEY exhibited considerable improvement in
SCIENCE since his fight with *Pearce;* but, notwithstanding, the *strength* of his opponent was often nearly too
much for him to overcome, and he had to contend against

a considerable disadvantage in being compelled to wait
for *Gregson's* making a *hit*; *Gregson's* left arm
was considerably stronger and longer than GULLEY'S,
and, in sparring, he always had it completely extended.
Gregson hits tremendously with his right hand, and
so giant-like in its effects, that it is almost impossible
to resist its powerful progress. It was owing to this
circumstance, that GULLEY displayed such a miserable
spectacle, and got his left arm so materially injured at
the commencement of the battle, and which has never
since been perfectly recovered.

Gregson, although so severely beaten in the above
contest, yet flattered himself, that, in the event of another trial with GULLEY, he should prove victorious ;
and his friends coinciding with that opinion, he challenged GULLEY for £200 a-side, which was immediately
accepted by the latter ; and the arrangements were
made by Major *Morgan* and Mr. *Shelton*, who supported *Gregson* ; and by Mr. *Jackson* on the part of
GULLEY. The principal article of which arrangement
was, "neither to fall without a *knock-down* blow, subject to the decision of the umpires." The important
day being appointed, it was soon blazoned abroad, that
the scene of action would be contiguous to Bedfordshire and Buckinghamshire, and the Marquis of Buckingham, upon hearing of the circumstance, and
having no great predilection for pugilism, issued
the following formal notice, in the County Chro-
nicle :—

"*Buckingham House, London, May* 8.
"Information having been transmitted to me, his Majesty's
Custos Rotulorum in and for the County of Bucks, of an intended riotous assembly, aiding and assisting in a breach of the
peace, by a boxing match within that part of the county of

Bucks which touches or joins on the counties of Bedford and Herts, near the town of Dunstable; and that the said illegal and riotous assembly will take place on Tuesday, the 10th instant, notice is hereby given, that proper steps have been taken for the detection and punishment of all persons acting as aforesaid, in breach of the peace, by the attendance of the magistrates, high-constables, petty-constables, and other peace officers, entrusted with the execution of the law within the said county.

"NUGENT BUCKINGHAM,
Custos Rotulorum of Bucks."

The anxiety manifested by the *Sporting men,* and the *Fancy* in general, was so great to witness this second combat, that numbers left London on the Monday, to prevent meeting with any disappointment, in order to be in readiness to follow the cavalcade, should any interruption take place. The magistracy, from the above formal notice, were all upon the alert, and the Dunstable volunteers were called out to secure the peace, and were under arms by seven o'clock on Tuesday morning, May 10, 1808. (The impositions practised upon this occasion by the landlords of the various inns in the country towns near the scene of action, were of the most gross nature. *Two guineas* was the price demanded for a bed, not only the night previous to the fight, but the same sum extorted in the evening when the battle was over.) After considerable bustle and confusion taking place, as to the propriety where the fight should take place, it was judged expedient, to prevent disappointment, that the contest should be decided in Sir John Sebright's Park, Hertfordshire. Notwithstanding it was several miles from the spot first intended for the *set-to,* thither the multitude repaired, without murmuring, in the quickest and best manner they were able.

No. IX.

D d

The string of carriages, and persons upon horseback, travelling in haste to arrive at the destined spot, beggared all description, from the splendid barouche to the jolting taxed-cart, all were seen in rapid motion. Upon their arrival in the park belonging to the above Baronet, a good piece of ground was selected for the purpose, and a forty feet ring soon formed, which was well secured by pedestrians and horsemen.

The weather was rather unpropitious for fighting, and, although the rain had poured down in torrents, the numerous spectators valued no other consideration but witnessing the fight, and the annoyance of *wet clothes* was completely out of the question. Every thing being ready for the contest, the combatants made their appearance in the ring, attended by a numerous assemblage of pugilistic heroes, and were greeted with reiterated plaudits from the anxious spectators.

Gregson was seconded by *Harry Lee*, and *Joe Ward* acted as second to GULLEY, and *Bill Gibbons* was his bottle-holder. Captain *Barclay* undertook the important situation of umpire. Both the combatants fought in white breeches and silk stockings; and, owing, it is said, to *Gregson* having spikes in his shoes, they contested the battle without them.

First round.—After the accustomed salutation, the combatants placed themselves in erect postures, and, minutely observing each other's intent, they continued sparring for five minutes, during which time Gulley retreated round to the exact part of the ring where he first entered ; the greatest anxiety now prevailed for his safety, and so much alarmed were his attendants, that Bill Gibbons and Joe Ward put their hands over the stakes of the ring, apprehensive, from the strength of Gregson, that Gulley might be drove upon one of them, which inevitably must have broken his ribs. Gregson having made a feint with his left hand, Gulley hit out most tremendously upon the left temple of his antagonist, who was instantly *levelled* from its severity. An uncommon silence prevailed throughout this round; when the odds instantly rose upon Gulley.

Second.—Gregson's powerful arm broke through Gulley's guard, and put in a most tremendous blow upon his breast, which sounded like a loud stroke upon a drum; upon which Gulley rallied, and hit Gregson down—a few cries of " *Foul, foul !*"

Third.—Both the combatants cautious, and resorted to sparring for nearly five minutes, without any blows being exchanged; at length Gregson endeavoured to put in a most tremendous hit, which Gulley stopped with his left arm, and fell. It was from this blow, it is supposed, that Gulley's arm has never been properly well since.

Fourth.—A severe rally commenced on both sides—dreadful blows given and taken—when Gulley, in stopping, fell.

Fifth.—In this round the combatants were *milling* away against the ropes, when Gulley, on going in, was knocked down.

Sixth.—Some severe blows passed, when Gregson rushed in and caught Gulley by his thighs, lifted him from the ground, threw him down, and fell upon him, nearly knocking the breath out of his body.

Seventh.—Both upon their mettle, and every exertion made upon both sides for the advantage, when Gulley, by several severe hits, beat Gregson out of the ring, and both fell.

Eighth.—Gulley's superiority began now to appear, not only respecting his knowledge of the science, but as to the termination of the fight; his antagonist's head displayed considerable punishment, and, finally, Gregson was *levelled*.

Ninth.—Some blows were exchanged, when they closed and fell.

Tenth.—This was a truly bloody round—the hits were tremendous in the extreme—Gregson's head was frightful, literally covered with blood, and his left eye nearly useless; quite confused, and fighting rather after the Lancashire method, without any pretensions to science—and, notwithstanding Gulley went down, it was evidently in his favour.

Eleventh.—Gregson, not destitute of *bottom*, rallied, but without doing much execution; and ultimately was knocked down. Gregson appeared considerably on the decline.

Twelfth.—Gregson stood up, and put in a good blow on Gulley's chest, who immediately returned a tremendous hit that knocked him down, and planted another while he was falling—a cry of " *Foul!*"

Fourteenth.—Gregson, nearly blind, appeared much confused, and was more an object of *punishment* now than to act in an offensive manner.—Gulley put in three terrible hits without receiving, and Gregson, as before, was *levelled.*

Fifteenth.—Gregson attempted to rally ; but Gulley, aware of his intention, knocked him down.

Sixteenth.—Gregson, endeavouring to make use of what little strength remained, ran in ; but it proved of no other advantage to him than in closing they both fell.

Seventeenth.—Gregson, in this round, let his temper get the better of his judgement, and he was most miserably *punished* for his temerity. He ran in almost headlong upon Gulley, who, cool and collected, viewing the advantage which presented itself, hit Gregson where he pleased, and stopped his opponent's blows with the most apparent ease. Gregson, almost insensible from this repeated *punishment*, turned his back upon his adversary, and, as if panic struck, made for the ropes—Gulley following him, and changing his position, *fibbed* him, till he was nearly exhausted, and then let him fall.

Eighteenth.—Gulley completely master of the field ; Gregson *punished* in all directions, and ultimately was knocked down.

Nineteenth.—A few blows were exchanged, when Gulley fell.

Twentieth to twenty-second.—It was all up with Gregson —Gulley was every thing in all these rounds, and beat his opponent terribly ; still Gregson closed with him in all of them, and they both fell. Twenty to one against Gregson.

Twenty-third and twenty-fourth.—Gregson's *bottom* made him stand up; but it was completely useless, and his debility was manifest to all the spectators.—Gulley put in a tremendous *hit* under his opponent's ear, which put an end to the contest, by Gregson's being so *finished,* as not to be ready to his time.

The superiority in the above battle was evidently upon

the part of GULLEY; and, during the continuance of
the fight, for FIFTY-EIGHT MINUTES, there was no
comparison whatever between the gaiety of the combatants. Several of the fighting men, and many good
judges of pugilism, had great doubts as to the event of
the battle, from the determined manner in which the
former contest had been decided between these two
heroes; and, who entertained a strong opinion, under
an idea that *Gregson*, in being able to add considerably
more *science* to his great strength, from the practice and
improvement which he had evinced in *sparring*, that
the *chance* was much increased in his favour. GULLEY
possessed so much confidence in his own abilities, that,
a few minutes before entering the ring, he offered to
back himself for fifty pounds (in addition to what he
had already betted) that he was the winner.

GULLEY, it appeared, had signified an intention of
quitting the profession of the pugilistic art, some time
previous to this last contest with *Gregson*, but conceiving himself bound in honour to accept the challenge of
the latter was the principal reason that he had now
given him the opportunity of a second trial, and of his
coming forward in a public manner.—GULLEY informed the *sporting world*, it was his decided intention
never to fight any more; and that, in the above battle,
he had fought under considerable disadvantages, owing
to his left arm being injured. He now took his leave
of them, to follow his profession, as an inn-keeper, at
the sign of the Plough, in Carey-street, Lincoln's-inn-
Fields; to which place he was conveyed, with all the
honours accompanying victory, in the barouche belonging to a nobleman of sporting celebrity.

GULLEY, as a pugilist, will long be remembered by
the amateurs of pugilism, as peculiarly entitled to their
respect and consideration ; and if his battles were not
so numerous as many other celebrated professors have
been, they were contested with a decision, *science,* and
bottom, rarely equalled, and, perhaps, never excelled,
and justly entitled to the most honourable mention in
the records of boxing.   His practice in the art, it was
well known, had been very confined, and his theoretic
knowledge of the *science* could not have been very extensive, from the short period he had entered the lists
as a boxer ; but his genius soared above these difficulties,—and, with a fortitude equal to any man, he
entered the ring a most consummate pugilist.   In point
of appearance, if his frame does not boast of that elegance of shape from which an artist might model to
attain perfect symmetry—yet, nevertheless, it is athletic
and prepossessing.   GULLEY is about six feet in height.

In concluding this trifling sketch of GULLEY, we
should be wanting in truth and candour, if we omitted
to state, that, with a knowledge of the world, he unites
the manners of a well-bred man.   Unassuming and intelligent upon all occasions ; this conduct has gained him
respect and attention in the circles in which he moves ;
and which are by no means of an inferior class.   Thus
proving, in himself, a lively instance, that ALL *pugilists*
are not excluded from polished society ; and that,
without disparagement, he is an object well worthy of
imitation by the professors of the gymnastic science.

Mr. GULLEY was a master butcher of respectability, previous to his pugilistic encounters.   In consequence of his declining the honours of the CHAM-

pionship, it descended to the honourable keeping of the renowned *Tom Cribb*.

Mr. Gulley now (1821) resides at Newmarket, and is a most distinguished sportsman on the turf.

BILL HOOPER, *the Tinman,*

Otherwise denominated " Bully Hooper,*" the "* Lion-hearted Hooper.*"*

Bristol, among all her pugilistic heroes, in point of courage, never turned out a more determined boxer than Bill Hooper, or one so *thorough-bred*. Fear, it should seem, never formed any part of his composition. In all his contests he appeared confident of victory. Respecting the size or strength of his opponents, his feelings never suffered any sort of depression, from a consideration of that nature. Hooper was truly valiant, and his small stature, put in comparison with most of the other pugilists of his time, he stood unequalled. In possessing an excellent acquaintance with the *science*, and supported by a *bottom* that even outlived his nature, he distinguished himself in most of his fights as a first-rate boxer. The patronage of the late Earl of *Barrymore* unfortunately proved his complete destruction. Participating in the festivities of Wargrave; also in *supporting* the eccentricities of that volatile nobleman, in forming one of the appendages to his numerous suite of singular characters, he became so *self-important* from thus being noticed by his Lordship, and by a number of the *higher flights* of the

FANCY, the companions of that sprig of nobility, as to render himself, in most companies, not only insolent and disgusting, but to stamp completely his character as a pugilist with disgrace. His mind was not strong enough to sustain the sudden transition from obscurity to a more prominent situation in life—and ultimately poor HOOPER, from the dissipation and violent excesses he had committed in the sunshine of his prosperity, became, some time before his melancholy end, the miserable victim of disease and wretchedness. In reference to which, see pages 5 and 6 of this work.

HOOPER's first *set-to* in the Metropolis was with *Bill Clarke*, the plasterer, in the fields, near Tottenham-court-Road, (in which latter place HOOPER followed his business as a *tinman)* ; the battle was well contested, and the conflict for some time doubtful ; but the *science* and *bottom* of HOOPER, at length, developing itself in so superior a manner, he, soon afterwards, rose rapidly into fame as a first-rate pugilistic hero.

HOOPER fought a number of good battles, and generally proved victorious. On September 5, 1789, he had a desperate contest, on Barnet-common, with one *Cotterell,* for ten guineas a-side; which continued above half an hour, when HOOPER proved the conqueror.

In a battle with *Wright*, a *carpenter*, who was backed by Lord *Faulkland*, which contest took place at Wargrave, December 3, 1789, the seat of Lord *Barrymore*, who commenced his patron, HOOPER distinguished himself considerably as a pugilist.— *Wright*, who was looked upon as a good boxer, was most severely *punished* in twenty minutes, and his head so terribly swelled, and his face so much disfigured, from the severe blows of HOOPER, as scarcely to be known.

HOOPER was now called upon to enter the list at Langley-close, near Salt-hill, Feb. 17, 1790, with a pugilist of the name of *Watson*, of good *pluck* and great activity, and nearly as equal a match as could be made. The contest proved extremely long, and the advantages, at different times in the fight, were varying and doubtful. Considerable altercations took place as to the propriety of blows, that the two chosen umpires were compelled to call in a third, to make a final decision. The odds, generally speaking, were in favour of HOOPER, who *levelled* his antagonist several times during the contest; but *Watson* evinced considerable *game* throughout the battle, which continued for two hours and thirty minutes, and the amazing number of one hundred rounds; when it was decided in favour of HOOPER, from the unfair *hits* of his adversary.

HOOPER, after the above period, *attempted* to fight that tremendous pugilist *Big Ben;* but it proved a complete *mockery* of boxing, and was declared a drawn battle.

HOOPER was next challenged by one *Bunner*, for 50 guineas, which was decided upon a stage 18 feet square, at Bentley, a few miles from Colchester, on Sept. 4, 1792. *Bunner* possessed considerable strength, and, in the early part of the fight, the odds were, upon that account, in his favour; but the *science* of the *Tinman* soon rendered it unavailing, and *Bunner* proved an easy conquest, from having his arm broken by a fall in the sixth round.

George Maddox, a boxer of great notoriety, now

No. IX.   E e

entered the ring on Sydenham-common, Kent, on Feb. 10, 1794, with the TINMAN, for £25 a-side. *George* had proved himself, upon most occasions, a *game* man ; and considerable expectations were raised from the well-known abilities of HOOPER. Numerous amateurs attended to witness the contest, anticipating a most excellent display of the art, among whom was to be seen the late Duke of *Hamilton*. *Maddox* was the favourite, and the odds, upon *setting-to*, were 5 to 4 that *George* was the conqueror. *Joe Ward* was the second to *Maddox*, and *Bill Gibbons* his bottle-holder ; and *Tom Johnson* and *Jack Butcher* were the attendants upon HOOPER. *Maddox* took the lead for some time, and showed himself to be well acquainted with the principles of pugilism, and endeavoured to *convince* HOOPER that he must surrender all hopes of victory to his *game* and experience ; but the TINMAN, full of *pluck*, and confident of success, contested the battle most heroically for nearly an hour, when *Maddox*, with considerable reluctance, acknowledged that HOOPER was the conqueror.

HOOPER, immediately after the above contest, rose so much into fame, that he was matched to fight *Mendoza*, upon a 24 feet stage, for 50 guineas, within a month. It appeared that *Mendoza* preferred forfeiting his deposit of £20 to having any thing to do in the pugilistic way with the renowned TINMAN.

HOOPER had now to encounter that determined pugilist, *Wood*, the *coachman*, who had distinguished himself in several good fights. The scene of action was upon Hounslow-heath, on June 22, 1795 ; and it proved one of the most desperate conflicts in which HOOPER had been as yet engaged. In a contest of nearly 50 minutes, various turns of success appeared, and the bets were continually changing. *Wood* fought with his usual vehemence and resolution, and appeared almost certain of victory : but the TINMAN's terrible hard *hits* at times completely stunned him, and, in planting his favourite blow under the left ear, reduced *Wood* to a complete state of stupor. The *bottom* of *Wood* proved so *prime*, that he contended for the *chance* for several rounds afterwards; when, finding that success was against him, and that he was little more than an object of *punishment*, he GAVE IN. The TINMAN, in conquering *Wood*, increased his reputation as a pugilist considerably. In no battle whatever did the odds vary more rapidly than in the above contest. Previous to the *set-to, Wood* was the favourite ; and, for the first part of the fight, his superiority was so prominent, that 20 to 1 was laid he would prove the winner; but the courageous spirit of HOOPER, and his knowledge of the science, not only reduced the bets to a level, but, before the fight was half over, 20 to 1 was laid that the TINMAN proved the conqueror.

HOOPER was at length doomed to experience the reverse of that good fortune which had so often cheered him with the sound of victory in his numerous contests ; and HE who had beaten several distinguished professors of the *science,* was now defeated by a boxer almost a stranger to the Prize Ring. *Tom Owen,* who did not want for strength, and who also possessed some knowledge of the science, challenged HOOPER. The fight took place at Harrow ; and *Owen* turned out a much better boxer than had been anticipated. After fighting above an hour, during which time 50 rounds had been contested in a very superior manner, HOOPER dislocated his shoulder. The event might have still proved doubtful; but after this accident HOOPER *gave in*. HOOPER, was scarcely ever able to beat down his antagonist's guard, and deprived of planting a *hit*, till *Owen* had first made a blow. *Owen's* right hand was tremendous.

HOOPER, in point of appearance, was by no means formidable, scarcely exceeding the middle stature of men. His height was about 5 feet 7 inches and a half, and neatly made; but his courage was truly astonishing; and it is only justice to remark of him, that he was a first rate boxer. It is said of HOOPER, that he fought more battles than any pugilist of his time; and, generally speaking, eminently successful in most of them. Previous to his obtaining the patronage of the late Lord *Barrymore*, and, at the time of his entering the lists with *Clarke*, the plasterer, (the first battle that he fought in London,) he followed his business as a tinman, in Tottenham-court-road, and possessed the character of a civil, well-behaved, smart young man. It proved too much for him in being transplanted from making *saucepans* to the elevated situation of a nobleman's country seat. The advantages of mixing with some of the first characters of rank in the country, instead of appreciating the improvement that he might have derived from only a slight intercourse with such superior company, who, amid all their foibles and eccentricities, it should never be forgotten, manifest the behaviour of gentlemen, and who, upon any occasion derogatory to good manners, are the very first to resent improper conduct; but, unfortunately, poor HOOPER could not turn this singular alteration in his life to good account. With no inconsiderable share of pride; much attached to dress; and rather illiterate, his vanity was too conspicuous, and, not bearing in mind the real character in which he stood as a *dependant,* he considered himself of equal importance with his *principal*—who had caressed and noticed him *merely* from his intrepidity and knowledge as a scientific pugilist; this source, from whence all his notoriety sprung, entirely escaped his notice. HOOPER, from not having any friendly monitor to warn him of his want of prudence and discernment; his patron, (notwithstanding his extreme levity and good-nature,) at length, became completely surfeited with his arrogance and presumption.   Also, in the middle ranks of society, in casually mixing with company, his actions were frequently outrageous, and he endeavoured to support them upon his pretensions as a pugilist.

In dwelling upon circumstances like the above, we are only actuated by those motives which ought to characterize the labours of all biographers—an anxiety to promulgate the truth with accuracy and fidelity, as far as can be ascertained consistent with our researches. And in throwing out a hint to those whom it may most concern, by operating as a line of conduct upon any future occasion, we have endeavoured to tread as light as possible on the ashes of the dead, in order that the living may be benefited by obtaining the best of knowledge, in valuing that admirable line of the poet's, so often quoted, but so little followed, that

" The proper study of mankind is man."

HOOPER was a prominent feature in several of the mad freaks committed by the late Lord *Barrymore,* at Brighton; and, unfortunately for his character, he was viewed in no better point of view by the inhabitants of

that fashionable watering place, than that of performing the part of a *bully* to his Lordship—thereby completely reducing his pretensions as a valiant pugilist.
The Earl, from his great popensity to *larking*, kicked
up innumerable *rows* (among which, the *coffin* scene
will long be remembered), and his Lordship not unfrequently left the *Tinman* to settle the difference. It
was thus that HOOPER, poor fellow, rendered himself odious, in acting under a mistaken bias, imagining
that he could do no less than *support* his patron, *right*
or *wrong !* In such instances as the above, he was to
be pitied ; and we can only exclaim—" Alas, poor
Human Nature !"

BOB WATSON,
OF THE BRISTOL NURSERY,

A MOST spirited and active pugilist, and who also
ranked as a *sparrer* of the first reputation. A few years
since, he exhibited a display of the *science* of self-
defence against the late *Bill Warr,* with considerable
applause, in a pantomime at the Theatre Royal, in Covent-Garden. One evening the audience were nearly
experiencing a real *set-to* between those celebrated pugilists—*Warr,* in the impetuosity of the attack, though
undesignedly, knocked out one of WATSON's teeth,
which touched the feelings of the latter rather acutely,
who, forgetting the actual situation in which he stood
(being before an elegant audience), and being full of
vigour and spirit, was for demanding instant satisfaction; but it was passed over, upon his being assured
it was accidental. WATSON is related by marriage
to the family of the *Belchers,* of pugilistic notoriety

and fame. Bob has, for some years past, relinquished all pretensions in the gymnastic profession, to follow in peace his occupation as a respectable master butcher, at Bristol. Watson, in height does not exceed five feet five inches; but, however deficient in point of size, it is well known, that respecting *bottom* and *science* he was not wanting. In the various battles in which Watson had been engaged, he conducted himself with such spirit as to merit the appellation of a good pugilist. His activity and method of fighting resembled, in a great degree, the late *Bill Warr.*

Watson entered the lists with *Elisha Crabb*, a Jew, who had rendered himself somewhat conspicuous in beating the celebrated *Oliver*, (better known by the name of *Death!*) The above contest was remarkably well contested, on June 9, 1788. Watson had not long arrived from Bristol, and was seconded by *Bill Warr*; and *Stephen* was attended by *Ryan*. The fight lasted nearly 46 minutes, during which time Watson's activity and *science* soon brought him into notice as a skilful pugilist, and he was proclaimed the conqueror.

On the race-ground at Brighthelmstone, upon a stage erected for the purpose, Watson fought with *Tom Jones,* August 6, 1788. The combatants both distinguished themselves for spirit and *science*; and, after a very manly contest for near twenty minutes, during which a number of sharp *hits* were exchanged, *Jones,* perceiving that the *chance* was against him, surrendered the palm of victory to Watson.

At Langley-broom, near Colnbrook, on April 25, 1789, Watson entered the lists with *Anderson;* who was soon *disposed of.*

A match was made between Watson and a butcher

from Bristol, of the name of *Davies*, which was decided at Coal-harbour, in Gloucestershire. Previous to
the *set-to* WATSON was the favourite, and the odds were
laid strongly that he would win. But after the first ten
minutes the odds rose rapidly, owing to the superior
strength of *Davies*, and who was by no means destitute
of a good knowledge of the *science*. WATSON, notwithstanding the advantages were so much against him,
continued to dispute every inch of ground with the most
heroic firmness, for upwards of three quarters of an
hour, and continued to fight, deaf to the remonstrances
of his second *(Bill Warr)*, till he could no longer stand.
The amateurs were much pleased with his stanch *bottom ;*
and his character, instead of being diminished, was
considerably raised, although in *defeat*.

WATSON is still living (1821), and frequently fills the
situation of a second in the neighbourhood of Bristol.

GEORGE NICHOLLS,
OF BRISTOL,
(Rendered conspicuous by conquering TOM CRIBB,)

A BOXER who, in all probability, from the two specimens of excellence that he displayed in the Metropolis,
had he continued in the practice of pugilism, might
have reached the very summit of glory—but who can
now only be remembered as a meteor in the pugilistic
hemisphere, whose dazzling qualities caused a momentary blaze, then disappeared, and all its brilliancy has
been since lost in oblivion. However, we were glad to
find, that the Temple of Fame is not so completely
filled with heroes, but that a small niche has been preserved to do justice to the memory of NICHOLLS. In

proving the conqueror of such a hero as Tom Cribb, that circumstance is sufficient to exalt his character, even admitting that it was only during Cribb's novitiate; but then the latter had beaten that renowned pugilistic veteran of the old school, George Maddox; also Tom Blake, a determined boxer; and Ikey Pig, a man of considerable strength; and all of them men of notoriety in the tribe of pugilists. The success of these contests had rendered Cribb somewhat conspicuous, who was rising fast into eminence and fame, when he entered the lists with NICHOLLS, for a subscription purse of £25, at Blackwater, 32 miles from London, on Saturday, July 20, 1805, made up by the amateurs, to compensate them for their loss of time, in being deprived of witnessing the intended fight between the Game Chicken and Gulley. Tom Jones seconded NICHOLLS; and Dick Hall was the second to Cribb. The odds upon setting-to were greatly on the side of Cribb, who was the favourite; but NICHOLLS was aware of Cribb's method of fighting, and fought him after the style of Big Ben, in his contest with Tom Johnson. NICHOLLS, like a skilful general, armed at all points, was not to be deluded by the feints of the enemy—the system of milling on the retreat, which Cribb had hitherto practised with so much success, in this instance failed; the coolness and good temper of NICHOLLS appeared so predominant throughout the fight, that not only his fortitude was preserved, but added vigour to his judgement, which rendered him, either in the attack or in defending his position, a steady and decisive fighter. Cribb became rather puzzled and perplexed from his tactics being thus foiled—the advantages that he had

derived in former contests, by drawing his opponents
after him, and then *punishing* and irritating them in
their pursuit, so as to have the effect of making their
distances incorrect, (consequently their blows were frequently thrown away, and generally too feeble to do
any execution, from his ingenious mode of fighting,)
with NICHOLLS was rendered unavailing. GEORGE
would not suffer *Cribb* to play round him, whereby his
operations might become confused, but, with a guard
like *Ben's*, firm in the extreme, his appearance was
towering and impregnable. NICHOLLS was never induced to quit his position without putting in a tremendous *hit*, waiting with the utmost skill, for the temerity of his opponent, and then giving the *return* with
a *severity* almost unparalleled. GEORGE scarcely ever
failed in breaking through the defence of his adversary,
and ultimately concluding the round with a *knock down
blow*. NICHOLLS was a tremendous hard hitter; and
his *one, two*, rendered him truly formidable. The *science*
and ability displayed by NICHOLLS, in this contest,
completely astonished the Sporting World; many of
whom, in obtaining such knowledge, found out that
they had not procured it at a very *trifling* expense.

The odds were considerably in favour of *Cribb* at
setting-to, from the *gluttony* he had displayed in the
above-mentioned battles; and NICHOLLS having fought
but once before, with *Paddington Jones*, which contest
was considered nothing more than a *drawn battle*, and
who did not stand so high in the opinion of the amateurs
as his opponent; though notwithstanding his character
was admitted *thorough bred*. The first round was well
contested, and good specimens of the art were manifested upon both sides; but NICHOLLS, with a tremen-

dous *hit*, knocked down *Cribb*. In the second and third the advantages might be termed reciprocal; but, in the fourth round, *Cribb* put in a terrible blow under NI-CHOLLS's right eye, that made it twinkle again; yet it by no means disturbed his method of fighting, and he kept his temper wonderfully. The following rounds to the eighteenth were well contested, and though one of *Cribb*'s eyes was nearly closed up, the amateurs were not fickle in their opinions, and still looked upon him as an object that might be betted on with success. In the various rounds after this period, till about the forty-second, the *science* and adroitness of *Cribb* were excellent, and his rallies most courageous and formidable. NICHOLLS now became the hero of the scene, and showed himself off in good style, by exhibiting gaiety and confidence, and putting in his *one, two,* with considerable effect. *Cribb,* at this period of the fight, became much distressed, and endeavoured to recover his wind and strength, with his usual ingenuity—fought very *shy,* and had recourse to shifting; but as he was dead beaten, his *distances* became incorrect, and he fell several times, from endeavouring to make his blows tell: but still his *game* was prime, and he protracted the fight while a *single* chance remained, and the amateurs still *fancied* him, and sported upon his head with firmness; but all the manœuvres of *Cribb* were unavailing, and, in the fifty-second round, he was compelled to utter the reluctant sound—ENOUGH!

However, let it be recollected, that *Cribb* lost this battle during his novitiate; at a time when he was considered little more than a *bottom* man, and a promising young fighter; and that even his most sanguine friends at that period, had not a distant idea of his possessing

that greatness of pugilistic talent which has since been
promulgated, and so eminently placed him as the
proud and enviable Champion of England : but it is
the opinion of the best informed pugilists, that if
NICHOLLS were now to enter the lists with the Champion, the *chance* would be materially against him.

NICHOLLS, we understand, soon after the above fight,
left London, to follow his business as a butcher, in the
neighbourhood of Bristol, where he at present resides.

In doing justice to the merits of the BRISTOL HE-
ROES, of whom, for the present, we must take leave,
till our materials are more digested and matured, in
order that we may be enabled to resume the deeds of
that brave class of men, with spirit, accuracy, and impartiality, we feel it, at the same time, essential to state,
that we cannot remain unmindful of those days when
A RACE OF PUGILISTS appeared, who, for soundness of
bottom, excellence of science, and superior *strength*,
have not since been *equalled* in the aggregate. We
have, however, no hesitation in affirming, that a star has,
now and then for a short period, appeared in the pugilistic hemisphere with uncommon brilliancy; but
whose light has soon faded, and all its resplendency
sunk into a mere glimmering, if not ultimately become
eclipsed. It has been observed, that *Fortune* does
much for some men, who by improving upon propitious events, and aided by high patronage, have
risen rapidly into notice, and become objects of
considerable fame; while others, who have astonished, and have even claimed attention from
their *greatness* in defeat, have obtained but little

more than admiration for their courage; and too many
have been suffered almost to sink into oblivion, whose
deeds of valour were once the general theme of that
period in which they severally exhibited their excel
lences; but, owing to that great love of novelty, so
predominant a feature in the human mind, they now
are nearly forgotten. Be it then the task of BOXIANA
to rescue those heroes from unmerited obscurity, and
place them in that point of view where they may be
recognised with pride, and their abilities acknowledged and judged of according to their respective merits.

DISTINGUISHED HEROES,

Of the SECOND *or intermediate* SCHOOLS

Tracing those periods of pugilistic heroism, **and**
the valorous achievements obtained by

GEORGE MADDOX,	TOM TRING
(*Paddington*) TOM JONES,	DOYLE,
ISAAC PERRINS,	TOM TYNE,
CALEB STEVEN RAMS-	GEORGE, *(the Brewer)*
BOTTOM, (*otherwise Ca-*	ELISHA CRABBE,
leb Baldwin)	SYMONDS, *(the Ruffian)*
MICHAEL RYAN,	DUNN,
DAN MENDOZA,	ANDREW GAMBLE,
JOHN JACKSON,	BILL WOOD, &c. &c.

It has been the expressed opinion of several **of the**
best informed of the FANCY, that, at the present time,
(Oct. 1, 1821,) as a general observation, ancient spirit and nobleness of pugilism, which were wont **to**
prevail, have much degenerated; and the **combatants**

VOL. 1.

do not appear to possess such fine stamina, which so conspicuously marked the days of the above-mentioned pugilists. We are well aware that most minds labour under a kind of fascination in their respect towards antiquity, and the times previous to their existence; in too many instances, we readily admit that it obtains an undue preference, to the manifest injury and even neglect of modern achievements; but, in appealing to those persons who have made the art of self-defence their study, and have traced its rise, progress, and the material changes which it has experienced at various times, (excepting two or three instances within the last four years,) our opinions will be found tolerably correct, in observing, that PUGILISM, generally, *is rather in a degenerate state!*

GEORGE MADDOX,

(A Pugilist of the first quality, and a renowned Veteran in the Field of Glory.)

" Praising what is lost,
Makes the remembrance dear."

IF ever true valour lodged in the human breast— and if the *fastidious* can think it possible that a cos-TERMONGER could have any pretensions to those feelings—courage and humanity,—which enlighten and give importance to the character of a MAN, without being *conversant* with the CLASSICS—the veteran GEORGE MADDOX may be brought forward as a *striking* instance of the fact. He was one of NATURE's roughest gems—his exterior (when divested of the *paraphernalia* of the apparel furnisher) was manly and imposing—but his *penetralia* contained those hidden keys, that when any sympathetic notes were touched upon, the instrument was in perfect tune, and produced most eloquent music. But then, GEORGE was illiterate—he was the creature of the moment, and wanton in those impulses which so unaccountably operate upon the human frame; his language was uttered without the ornaments of *study*, and his voluble effusions were not of the most elegant description; but, notwithstanding this deficiency of *scholastic* advantages, it is equally true, a variety of phrases escaped from his lips, whose point and brilliancy enlivened the *circles* in which they were uttered, and would have completely puzzled the late erudite author of the "Diversions of Purley" to have obtained their immediate signification, independent of tracing their etymology, however elaborate the researches of that very learned man. The refined critic, in all probability, from his *perspective* view of GEORGE MADDOX, (the too general distance of many criticisms,) might have pronounced the *veteran* a fighting blackguard; but the man of the world, in his endeavours to appreciate the advantages of life, upon a nearer approach to GEORGE, and who did not feel contaminated in the company of a *costermonger*, but with a liberality of sentiment acknowledge merit, even in rags, whenever it was portrayed, and not blind to sensibility, although it emanated from a pugilist, experienced in MADDOX good nature and civil conduct, which proclaimed him a MAN. If not a *wit* equal to *that* DUSTMAN, whose spontaneous brilliant compliment to one of the most lovely, enlightened, and dignified females of this country, which *bon bouche* so fastened upon the feelings of that celebrated character, as completely to *distance* all pretenders ever afterwards upon similar occasions—MADDOX was full of those pleasantries and little characteristic touches, that rendered him pleasing and inoffensive. Without one drop of resentment in his whole composition, he fought more battles than any of his competitors, and contested them with a spirit and hardihood, that, in many instances, called forth considerable admiration; while in others, his determined *bottom* and resolution excited universal terror for the safety of himself and his opponents. In particular, his memorable contest with *Symonds* (the Ruffian) was so truly desperate, that the spectators were in one general state of alarm, and loud cries resounded from all parts of the ring, "*Part them, take them away, or else murder will be committed!*" which circumstance of parting them actually took place; but not till TWO HOURS of the most desperate *milling* had transpired that was ever witnessed. It took the renowned *Hooper*, whose *hits* were tremendous indeed, ONE HOUR before he could satisfy the *gluttony* of MADDOX! With *Bitton*, his *game* astonished all the *sporting men*. After ONE HOUR AND TEN MINUTES, notwithstanding the superior strength of the *Jew*, whose arm is by no means impotent in the act of *punishing*, it ended in a *drawn* battle! In his *set-to* with *Seabrook*, he *served it out* in such fine style, in the short space of three rounds, that the *Dustman* was panic-struck, and, to put an end to the contest, *gammoned* that his arm was broken! On the same day, *Richmond*, the man of colour, had a *turn-up* with GEORGE MADDOX, who, likewise, received such a *taste* of the veteran's quality, as perfectly to convince him that he stood no *chance*, and *gave in*, exclaiming, " *O, my eye!*" from a tremendous *hit* that was put in under one of his *sparklers*, after only contesting three rounds. And, let it not be forgotten, that MADDOX, in the *fiftieth year* of his age, entered the lists with the valiant *Tom Cribb*, who was in the prime of his youth, full of strength and wind, and had, as yet, scarcely been *pinked*. After fighting nearly one hour and a half, the odds were four to one in favour of MADDOX; and it was not until seventy-six rounds had been meritoriously contested upon both sides, protracting the period for TWO HOURS AND TEN MINUTES, before the veteran cried— ENOUGH! In his fight with *Coady* he also distinguished himself in a most courageous manner: after half an hour's *milling*, *Coady* took advantage of the ring's being broken, and could not be induced to return, when a new one had been formed, to meet the determined rallies of MADDOX! In his *fifty-fifth* year he was called out once more with *Richmond;* and, notwithstanding Nature was on the decline, the *bottom* he displayed truly astonished all the beholders of the fight. MADDOX protracted the battle nearly an hour, and, although defeated, was loudly cheered for his manly exertions, and rewarded by a purse, to alleviate his bruises.

Though MADDOX never arrived at the towering eminence of CHAMPION, yet few men ever deserved that honour more, either considered as a pugilist or as a man; contented with his *neddy* and his *tumbler*, his mind was never disturbed by restless ambition; and in *peeling* to meet his man, a degree of cheerfulness was observed about him, which reminded the observer, that GEORGE

was only contending for glory. He was a true veteran
in the gymnastic art; *shifting* was not in his creed, and
his peculiar *forte* was manliness. A better-natured man
could not exist; and, if we may be allowed the comparison, MADDOX was in the pugilistic world what the late
enlightened *Charles Fox* observed of the Austrian general *Clairfayt*, an officer uncommonly brave, but seldom
victorious, "that he was like a drum, never heard of but
when he was beaten!" MADDOX, it is true, was known
as a good pugilist; but it is equally certain, that, after
any memorable achievement, he again sunk into his
former obscurity: during the fight he was an object of
attraction, but no longer; and, having no first-rate
Fancier for a patron, he jogged on through life as an
honest, industrious *costermonger*. Although not holding the *belt*, or being in possession of the *cup*, no
boxer ever reflected more nobleness upon pugilism
than did the veteran—GEORGE MADDOX.

BOXIANA, with all his anxiety and research to do
even common justice to his merits as a pugilist, is, from
candour, compelled to declare that he is incompetent
to relate one half of his numerous battles—which
were so nobly contested during the long period of upwards of thirty-five years.

In 1776, he was engaged in a most desperate conflict
in Tothill-fields, and, in the event, MADDOX proved
the conqueror. To render this battle of more notoriety with the sporting world, it is necessary to state
that GEORGE was seconded by his sister, *Grace Maddox*,
and who, upon its conclusion, tossed up her hat in defiance, and offered to fight any man present. GEORGE
has often declared since, that he never had a better

SECOND, and GRACE has been frequently heard to exclaim, whenever her brother had been defeated, "that she was *sartain sure*, if she had had the handling of him, it would not have happened so unfortunately!" This battle gave rise to the following *crambonian* effusion, which was handed about at that period :—

> " MADDOX, the pride of the *milling* race,
>   Secured his conquest *with* a GRACE:
>   But once neglected, changed the case,—
>   GEORGE ne'er had lost, had he said—GRACE!"

At *Datchet*, in Berkshire, on Saturday, December 4, 1792, a battle took place between MADDOX and *Symonds*, which, for desperation and determined resolution, stands unparalleled in the annals of pugilism. It should seem as if the courage of the combatants had increased from their disappointment, in consequence of the magistrates having received previous notice of the circumstance, and who interfered, and prevented the fight taking place at Langley-broom, the spot first intended. It was the opinion of the amateurs present, that such a battle, take it altogether, had never before been witnessed; and it had hitherto been thought physically impossible that the human frame could sustain so dreadful a conflict. *Symonds* (the Ruffian) forcibly portrayed what a man could perform, when the resolution is strong, and the *bottom* sound; his dauntless manhood was truly astonishing, and, for a long time, he received the tremendous *hits* of his antagonist with the most perfect *sang froid*. MADDOX, a true bit of good stuff, determined not to be behind his opponent in appearance, and never suffered his noble spirit to droop, but *hit* away, and *rallied* all through the piece, with the greatest alacrity. It was impossible to decide which possessed the most fortitude;—it was perfect heroism on both sides. Art was out of the question, and the combatants seemed above resorting to any scientific efforts. *Milling* was the prominent feature, and if ever *punishment* was exhibited with all its terrible accompaniments, MADDOX and *Symonds* were truly entitled to be denominated complete professors. To attempt to recount the alternate advantages, the *knockdown* blows, the *rallies*, or the *gluttony* of these determined pugilists, would require pages to give any thing like a faithful portraiture of this tremendous fight. The *Ruffian* was nearly two stone heavier than his antagonist, and appeared to have been beaten the most, and both his eyes were completely closed up when he was carried off the stage. MADDOX was not quite in so desperate a condition as his opponent, he having in general the best of the rallies, and putting in nearly two blows to the *Ruffian's* one, throughout the fight. Had they not have been parted, it is supposed that death to one of the parties must have been the inevitable consequence.

GEORGE entered the ring with *Hooper*, the *tinman*, with considerable success; and his *science* and *bottom* convinced the *Tinman* that there was a great deal of up-hill work to be got over, before his journey could be considered safe.

A match was made between *Bitton* (the Jew) and MADDOX, for twenty guineas a-side, and was decided on Monday, December 13, 1802. The magistrates, being put in possession where the intended fight was to take place, sent out their officers to prevent it, which sudden and unexpected intrusion occasioned considerable delay and confusion, before a proper spot could be selected for this trial of skill; at length, all difficulties being overcome, a ring was formed on Wimbledon Common, when MADDOX entered it, followed by *Joe Ward*, as his second; and the *Jew* was attended by *Lyons*. Upon *setting-to*, *Bitton* endeavoured to convince his adversary of his superior strength by *levelling* him in the first three rounds; but MADDOX, who was not soon terrified, and no stranger to *knock-down* blows, rallied with his usual spirit, and, putting in tremendous *hits*, changed the odds considerably in his favour. *Milling* was the order of the day, and *science* was but little resorted to; both the combatants seemed to prefer making use of their strength. *Bitton*, in the latter respect seemed to have the advantage. MADDOX's body and face exhibited terrible specimens of *punishment;* but his appetite was not easily satisfied, and his *gluttony* so great, upon most occasions of this kind, that very few were to be found who would undertake to give him a *bellyfull!* Both the combatants displayed good *bottom* through the long and trying conflict of seventy-four rounds; when, either from accident or design, the ring was broken, and it was considered a *drawn battle!*

On Monday, January 23, 1804, *Seabrook*, a dustman. (who flattered himself that he had some pretensions to pugilism,) was prevailed upon to enter the ring with GEORGE MADDOX, after those brave heroes of the fist, *Burke* and the *Game Chicken*, had left it. *Seabrook* had no existence before MADDOX, and was so completely frightened out of all his *conceit* in three rounds that he almost *bolted* from the spot.

VOL. I.   2 E

Bill Richmond, the man of colour, who had some little
notion, at this period, of *serving it out*, wished to put
his ideas into practice; and seeing how the *Dustman*
had been disposed of, and imagining that he could not
appear worse than *Seabrook* did, consented to try his
fortune with MADDOX, and a trifle was made up
for the victor.   GEORGE was completely *cleaned out;*
and having no *Neddy* or *Tumbler* to assist him in re-
cruiting the deranged state of his finances, declared he
should be the happiest man living, if he could realise
seven pounds, to put him once more into business.
Having obtained two or three pounds by conquering
the *Dustman*, MADDOX *set-to*, with determined spirit,
laughing at his opponent, and, in terms not the most
refined, telling him what he might expect. *Richmond*,
like *Seabrook*, stood but three rounds, and received a
blow under one of his eyes, which was so tremendous
that it stupified him, and he could no longer continue
the fight.

GEORGE MADDOX, never afraid, and always ready,
entered the lists with *Tom Cribb*, vulgarly called the
" *Black Diamond*," on Wood Green, near Highgate, on
Monday, January 7, 1805, for a subscription-purse of
twenty-five guineas—twenty for the winner, and five
for the loser.   The disparity of years was considerable
between the combatants; and *Cribb*, besides possessing
the advantages of youth, was too inches taller than
MADDOX, and, consequently, rather the favourite.
Paddington Jones was the second of MADDOX, and
Black Sam attended *Cribb* in the same capacity.
GEORGE fought like a hero, and performed prodigies
of valour; and it was with great reluctance that he con-

sented to GIVE IN. In the above contest it was *glutton* against *glutton*, and *bottom* against *bottom ;—Cribb* contending with all the fire of youth, and a stamina pure and untouched, trying hard for the honour of victory; while MADDOX, with all the experience of a veteran pugilist, anxious to preserve his well-earned reputation in not being overcome by a *novice*, contested every inch of ground for two hours and ten minutes, with a perseverance and resolution almost beyond the power of human nature. MADDOX fell gloriously; and *Cribb*, by this conquest, soon acquired a pugilistic fame, hitherto obscured and unknown.

Coady, a boxer of some repute, was matched against MADDOX, and the battle took place on Monday, June 5, 1806, at Padnal Corner, on Epping Forest. At *setting-to* the odds were rather against GEORGE; but MADDOX, by his powerful rallies, and quick hitting, soon brought himself into favour with the amateurs; and, in all probability, would have proved the conqueror, had it not been for the intrusion of the military, and a magistrate desiring them to desist from breaking the peace.

The parties, in compliance with the laws, retired; and, upon a ring being formed in the course of an hour afterwards, *Coady* positively refused again to meet his opponent; in consequence of which refusal, it was declared a *drawn battle!* *Coady* had been so severely *punished* about the *nob*, that his eyes were nearly closed.

Richmond, from constant practice, had considerably improved himself in the pugilistic art, and having entered the lists with some distinguished boxers during the five years which had elapsed since his fight with GEORGE MADDOX, thought that he might recover his reputation in another *set-to* with the veteran, and he was in consequence matched against GEORGE for one hundred guineas. This fight, in a twenty-seven feet roped ring, took place on the coast between Margate and the Reculvers, on Friday, August 9, 1809. The *veteran* had for his second *Gulley*, and *Bill Gibbons* attended as his bottle-holder; and *Bob Clarke* and *Jack Ward* performed the above offices for *Richmond*. At the commencement of the fight, notwithstanding MADDOX was in the fifty-fourth year of his age, the odds were six to four in his favour.

First round.—Maddox, never deficient in *pluck*, went in with his accustomed resolution, and endeavoured to *punish* the man of colour for his temerity, in thus daring him again to the combat; but the *science* and improvement of Richmond were soon made manifest, by his stopping the blows of his adversary remarkably clean, and in giving the *return* with so much sharpness and severity as to *level* the veteran.

Second.—George, not in the least dismayed, rallied—and, in the event of the round, threw Richmond over the ropes.

Third.—Both in good spirits, and no shyness witnessed—a number of good blows exchanged; but Richmond had materially the advantage, and displayed some fine specimens of the *science ;* and, in throwing Maddox desperately, evinced greater strength.

Fourth, Fifth, and Sixth.—Maddox never displayed finer courage than throughout these rounds; but Richmond's superiority was evident.

Fifteenth.—The spectators could not but admire the *bottom* and resolution of Maddox, in bravely contending against numerous disadvantages; and, in the forty-fourth round, his exertions completely astonished all present. Both his eyes were quite closed up, and, being on his knees, by a sudden spring he darted up, and caught hold of Richmond, and continued *punishing* him, till he was so exhausted, that he fell from his own efforts: yet so reluctant was he to acknowledge Richmond the conqueror, that he protracted the battle till the fifty-second round before he *gave in.*

In all the numerous contests in which MADDOX had

Deen engaged his courage was pre-eminent. As a pugilist he was conspicuous for determined *rallying* and quick *hitting;* and, though extremely well acquainted with the *science*, he relied more on his true *game* than in strictly following the principles of the art. It is but justice to his memory to state, according to the best information upon the subject, that PUGILISM was never disgraced by any of his public attempts, nor his character ever stained in making a CROSS.

A short time previous to his death, a benefit was made for him, at the Fives' Court, which was tolerably well attended; and several of the first-rate pugilists exhibited some excellent specimens of self-defence: among whom several of his old opponents, out of respect to his services, were not backward in assisting him by their efforts, as *Cribb, Bitton, Richmond, &c. &c.*

The above brave *veteran* lost his life through an accident. The pipes which convey the water through the streets were repairing, near the Borough Market, and the opening not being properly secured, MADDOX fell to the bottom, and broke his thigh in a most dangerous manner, which brought on a high fever, and ultimately closed his career. GEORGE was in height about five feet eight inches; a pleasant, cheerful looking man; and, by "*the heart that can feel for another*," lived respected and died pitied, although following the humble occupation of a *costermonger*.

BILL WOOD, *the Coachman,*

Was a pugilist of considerable celebrity, and truly entitled to most honourable mention in the annals of boxing; and, although his battles were not very numerous, it is but justice to state, that WOOD contended with the bravest of the brave! In his contests with *Warr*, *George* the brewer, *Hooper*, *Bartholomew*, and *Bitton*, he proved himself entitled to the appellation of a *thorough-bred* boxer, by his display of considerable *science*, and evincing a *bottom* of the richest quality. He possessed an undaunted spirit; was in height about five feet eleven inches; and considered an impetuous fighter. He was a hard *hitter*, and could *punish* with both hands with equal facility.

In his first attempt with *Bill Warr*, at Knavestock, in Essex, though he was looked upon as a *novice* in the pugilistic art, it required all the skill of that scientific boxer to become the conqueror.

WOOD next entered the lists with *George*, (the brewer,) a proper stand-up fighter, at Hornchurch, in Essex, for one hundred guineas, upon a stage twenty-four feet square, on Thursday, February 13, 1793. WOOD was seconded by *Joe Ward;* and *Mendoza* performed the above office for *George*. It was an uncommon desperate conflict; and the *set-to* commenced with unusual violence, the combatants being well aware of each other's *bottom*. WOOD put in a tremendous *hit*, which brought down his antagonist with considerable force. *George*, irritated to excess, attacked WOOD with the utmost impetuosity, was completely *abroad* with passion, and became the victim to his intemperance : the latter took advantage of this opening, and put in a dreadful blow on his opponent's jaw, which produced so loud a crash, that the spectators immediately perceived it was broken. The anxiety at this moment was

great in the extreme, and an opinion was entertained
that *George* would not be able to come again, from
so alarming a fracture, but, to their astonishment, tne
Brewer renewed the attack with increased *game*. *George*
put in so terrible a *thump* upon WOOD's *nob*, that he
was quite *abroad*, and the odds rose two to one against
the *Coachman*. Several excellent rounds were contested after these changes of success; and if ever *milling*
was witnessed in any battle, or first-rate *punishment* exhibited in style, *George* and WOOD might be considered most accomplished artists. The head of the
Brewer was truly terrific from its increased size; and his
body displayed the severity of his antagonist's fist; and
WOOD's appearance was nearly as bad, but at this period he possessed the most strength. The contest lasted
twenty-five minutes; when *George* cried out—ENOUGH.
The *Brewer* was not expected to survive, from the severe beating which he had received.

Bottom, most assuredly, is an important requisite to a
pugilist—in fact, eminence cannot be obtained without
so essential an article; but *impetuosity,* when occasioned
by *irritation,* not only defeats its original intent, but
ultimately produces consequences so diametrically opposite, that any person, viewing it attentively, must be
convinced of its weakness and absurdity. *Coolness* should
be the leading feature of every boxer : it is then
the manifest advantages of the *science* are to be witnessed over the impotent efforts of blind fury and head-
strong passion; and it is also, where FORTITUDE proves
so admirable a *second* to judgment, in sustaining the
heat of the conflict, without losing that equanimity of
temper, which, in *nine* cases out of *ten*, produces VIC-

TORY. The above fight proved a strong instance of the disadvantages of an irritated state of mind.

WOOD, although beaten in his contest with *Hooper*, distinguished himself considerably.

A match was made between WOOD and *Jack Bartholomew*, a pugilist of great notoriety; and which was decided upon a stage erected for that purpose, between Ealing and Harrow, on June 30, 1797. The amateurs were much disappointed upon this occasion, as a good battle was anticipated, from the celebrity of the combatants, but, owing to some foul blows being attributed to *Bartholomew*, the contest was decided in about sixteen minutes in favour of WOOD.

WOOD was now matched against *Bitton*, the Jew, for a purse of fifty guineas, which battle took place on Wilsden Green, on Monday, July 16, 1804. A considerable number of amateurs were present, and a good ring being formed, the combatants entered it in high spirits.

First round.—Wood soon began to manifest his strength, and with his impetuosity broke through his opponent's guard, and put in some *hits*. Bitton returned sharply, and several good blows were exchanged; but Wood took the lead, and drove Bitton against the ropes, the *Coachman* hitting away tremendously, when Bitton fell.

Second.—Wood, full of gaiety, put in the first blow—when Bitton rallied with good spirit, but fell.

Third.—Bitton had the best of the round, and Wood fell

Fourth.—Wood rallied in good style—but Bitton was on the look-out, and planted some good blows; yet, notwithstanding, the *Coachman's* strength was too much for him, and drove him over the ring, when Bitton fell.

Fifth.—Both resorted to science, and showed they were not deficient in possessing a tolerably good knowledge of the art—some tremendous blows were given and taken; and Wood exhibited signs of severe *pinking*, yet rallied Bitton with such severity as to get him against the ropes, where he threw him. Bitton notwithstanding was rather the favourite.

Sixth.—The rays of the sun had a visible effect upon Bitton's face; and, in endeavouring to get the advantage of his opponent in this respect, Wood with impetuosity ran in and threw him

Seventh.—Wood, knowing the value of the shade, was not to be deluded from it, and Bitton received some severe blows from his opponent without being able to stop them, whose exertions were so forcing as to drive the Jew once more to the ropes, where he again fell. Wood rather betrayed symptoms of exhaustion.

Eighth.—Wood still tried on what his strength would do, and ran in with considerable violence, closed, and threw Bitton, and pointed at him, by way of triumph.

Ninth.—This sort of derision was too much for the temper of the Jew, and he rose in a great passion, and began to attack Wood with considerable fury, but completely lost his ground from his irritated state, that the *Coachman* gave him a tremendous left-handed hit, which proved a *leveller.* Wood was loudly cheered for the neatness with which he put in this blow.

Tenth.—Bitton was brought to his recollection, and became somewhat temperate—he rallied with good judgment, and made his blows tell. Wood slipped, and Bitton caught him with a severe blow on the body: the *Coachman* fell from its severity. Odds six to four on Bitton.

Eleventh.—Wood, somewhat shy of Bitton's fist, pursued his old method of running in and throwing his antagonist.

Twelfth, thirteenth, and fourteenth.—Several good blows were given and taken in these rounds, and Bitton displayed some excellent specimens of the science, particularly in stopping very clean, and returning very sharply.

Fifteenth.—Bitton, in a rally, gained considerable advantage by putting in a tremendous stomacher, which not only *levelled* Wood, but so nearly deprived him of all his wind that he could not return *exactly* to his time, (half a minute,) and, from a supposition that the *Coachman* had got his dose, the ring became rather disordered, and some confusion ensued, during which *buz* Wood perfectly recovered, and commenced the

Sixteenth.—Which proved of no material consequence.

Seventeenth.—Bitton full of gaiety; but Wood nearly exhausted; and it was thought he was almost done up.

Eighteenth.—Contrary to expectation, the *Coachman* revived, and went boldly to his man, and had the best of the round.

Twenty-fifth.—Wood, in all the last rounds, convinced the spectators that he possessed a most determined resolution, and a thorough *bottom*, although his blows did not appear to do much execution.

Twenty-sixth.—The ring was now broken; and considerable confusion ensued, when Bitton's party declared it was done designedly, on purpose to deprive him of the fair advantages which he had obtained; and, ultimately, with an intention that he should lose the battle; but, after considerable difficulty, another ring was formed, although extremely irregular, and to the

Thirty-second—It was all bustle and pushing each other about, to keep proper room for the combatants. whose successes were alternate. Bitton was here getting into a weak state and fell often, though now and then making a good hit. A little more regularity began to prevail, till the

Thirty-sixth.—When Wood showed his game to be truly excellent, and stood up like a hero; Bitton, however, had the advantage of vigour, and just lasted long enough to hear his antagonist had *given in*.

Wood always maintained the reputation of a scientific, courageous pugilist. but has left the practice for some years, and now follows the occupation of a *Hackney* Coachman.

TOM TYNE, *the Tailor,*

Was a pugilist of considerable activity and *science,* and, it is said, that Tom was equally as expert in using his fist in the ring, as he had been in throwing about the *steel bar* upon the shop-board; and in himself a contradiction to the old sentiment, that *nine tailors make a man.* Tyne was not destitute of *pluck;* but at times was considered somewhat too *scientific,* in showing that he knew how to shift, and was not an entire stranger to *dropping*, when it answered his purpose: yet, notwith-standing, he fought some good battles; and it is but candid to observe, that he was looked upon by no means as an inferior pugilist. TYNE was in height about five feet seven inches; a left-handed hitter, but could use his right extremely well; and, in several of his contests, exhibited some very good specimens of the art.

TYNE was matched against one *Jones*, a strong athletic man, for fifty guineas, which contest was decided at Croydon, on July 1, 1788. *Tom Johnson* seconded TYNE upon this occasion. It was remarked, that, however TYNE might show the most science, *Jones* portrayed the most manhood. TYNE had re-course to all the worst parts of the ART: *i. e.* fighting *shy*, *shifting*, and *dropping*, trying to WIN the battle by manœuvring, *instead* of fighting it!—while *Jones*, on the contrary, full of fire, seconded by good *bottom*, displayed one of the first principles of pugilism— firmness, and would have *milled* his antagonist in good style, had he given him any *chance*; but, when-ever *Jones* endeavoured to put in a good *hit*, TYNE fell, defeating his exertions, and, ultimately, was the occasion of his losing the battle. *Jones*, in the spirit of the moment, following up his antagonist, put in a blow rather too low, which was declared foul, and TYNE proclaimed the victor; when he obtained the money, but lost the credit of the fight.

TYNE next entered the lists with *Earl*, upon a stage, erected near the stand on the Brighton race-ground, on August 6, 1788. Never were more fashionables assem-bled at a boxing-match than the above. The town of

Brighthelmstone was literally drained of its company, and the race-stand was crowded to excess with nobility and gentry; among whom was his Royal Highness the Prince of Wales. *Earl* was a tall, strong man, and, in point of appearance, the favourite, and was actually becoming so from his exertions, when TYNE put in a blow upon his temple, that made him reel against the rail of the stage, and he instantly dropped down dead; which unfortunate circumstance produced a most afflicting scene; and the Prince declared he would never witness another battle. His Royal Highness, with great humanity and consideration, settled an annuity on Mrs. Earl and family. It appeared, by the evidence before the Coroner's jury, that *Earl* had been for some time previous to the battle engaged in an election contest at Covent-garden, and had been in one continued state of inebriety during the whole of it. It was the opinion of the professional men, that the vessels being so overcharged with blood was the immediate cause of his death.

Elisha Crabbe, the Jew, entered the field of glory with TOM TYNE, contiguous to a place called Horton-Moor, on Monday, March 24, 1790. *Tom Johnson* seconded TYNE, and *James* was his bottle-holder; and *Lee* and *Joe Ward* performed the above offices for *Crabbe*. Upon *setting-to* the odds were in favour of TYNE.

First round.--Both cautious, and the spectators experienced a good display of the *science*, when Crabbe produced an overflow of *claret* from Tyne's nose, and, in closing, the Jew fell.

Eighth.—For the last six rounds no material advantage appeared on either side; but Crabbe now put in a tremendous blow, that *levelled* Tyne, and fell with all his weight upon his body.

Fourteenth.—The *Tailor* was again *levelled*.

Sixteenth.—Several good blows were exchanged; and Tyne put in right and left upon the Jew's *frontispiece* two such severe blows, that Crabbe's countenance underwent a trifling change; but the Jew returned the compliment with a *knock-down* blow.

Eighteenth.—Tyne, not much admiring the Jew's dexterity in so often *levelling* him, *dropped* from his own inclination, which occasioned some murmurings, and cries of " foul!" but the battle went on till the

Twenty-second.—This was the most attractive, if not the best contested round in the fight; and the combatants endeavoured to sound each other's *bottom*. The *Jew* showed off some neat specimens of the *Mendoza* school; and Tyne convinced him that he was no mean adept in the science—giving and taking was the order of the round, and they were not sparing in marking the canvass. The advantages were nearly reciprocal, till the

Thirty-second.—After several blows were exchanged, Tyne put in a tremendous blow on one of Crabbe's eyes, which knocked him down.

Thirty-third.—Tyne in manœuvring fell, and Crabbe, by endeavouring to make one of his blows tell, so completely lost his equilibrium that he went right over his antagonist, and fell on his face against the stage, from which he received considerable injury.

Thirty-ninth,—and last.—The five preceding rounds were more of show than effect, and the combatants seemed pretty well tired of the scene—Crabbe, at length, put in a trifling blow, which caused Tyne to fall; but the *Jew* was so much exhausted, that he was compelled to *give in*.

Upon the whole, the above contest was tolerably well spoken of by the amateurs; and it was considered that very little trifling had taken place during the thirty-five minutes which it continued. The *Jew* proved the most showy fighter; but TYNE did the most execution.

TYNE was challenged by one *Fearby*, a pugilist of more promise than practice; and the trial of skill was decided in the ring in Hyde Park, on Friday, December

31, 1793. The conflict was long and doubtful, and
TYNE endeavoured to avail himself of every minutiæ of
the art, but without effect; as, in the event, he was
obliged to acknowledge himself—" *the Tailor done
over!*"

GEORGE INGLESTON, *the Brewer*:

A truly manly pugilist, and a pupil of the late celebrated *Tom Johnson.* GEORGE was rather a heavy, but
strong-made man, and upwards of six feet in height.
He was brought into notice under the patronage of his
distinguished tutor; and who, like him, was averse to all
shifting. In the proper acceptation of the term, INGLE-
STON was a *stand-up* fighter, and never *bobbed* his head,
or *shifted* his feet, to avoid a blow; but received the *hit*
with heroic firmness, and his *return* was ponderous
indeed. He could not boast of much agility, and
rather slow in his movements, yet his aim, in general,
was tolerably sure. INGLESTON had no pretensions as
a scientific pugilist, but rested all his claims to attention
upon his undaunted resolution and sound *bottom.*

His battles were not numerous; but, nevertheless,
they were conspicuous; and his opponents were of the
first order of pugilists. GEORGE, in proving the
conqueror with *Jackson,* (if such an expression can
be allowed) was entirely owing to accident; in fact,
it would prove more correct, if it was observed, that
the battle was *put off,* as will be seen in the detail of
the fight. On the day after the memorable contest of

Johnson and *Perrins*, GEORGE's battle with *Pickard* will long be remembered by the amateurs, for the manliness, fortitude, and *game* displayed by him and his brave antagonist; and, it must be acknowledged, it exceeded by far the valiant achievements of *Big Ben* and *Tom Johnson*, who preceded them in the field of glory.

At Ingatstone, in Essex, on March 12, 1789, for fifty guineas a-side, a match was decided between GEORGE INGLESTON and *Jackson;* the former was seconded by *Tring*, and the latter by *Big Ben*. Upon *setting-to* the bets were even ; but the superior knowledge of the art was soon manifested by *Jackson*, and, in the event of the round, *Jackson levelled* the *Brewer*. In the second and third, several good blows were exchanged ; but the *science* of *Jackson* made so strong an impression upon the spectators, that the odds were fast moving in his favour. In the fourth round, it was nearly two to one the *Brewer* was defeated, but, unfortunately for *Jackson*, owing to the slippery state of the stage, from the rain that had fallen upon it, he fell down, dislocated his ankle, and the small bone of his leg was also broken. In consequence of this accident, there was no alternative left for him but to *give in*, it being impossible for a man to continue the fight, who could not stand. In other respects, *Jackson* was in full vigour to have carried on the battle ; but, if our information is correct, the report of that day states, that, to prevent disappointment to the numerous spectators, *Jackson*, in order to show his true *game*, and not to be dismayed by the accident, offered to be *fastened down in a chair*, (somewhat similar to the sailors, who are nailed down to their chests, in any pugilistic contest,) if INGLESTON would adopt the like manner, and to fight it out—but we understand the *Brewer* positively refused.

On the 23d of October, 1789, GEORGE fought with *Pickard*, upon a twenty-four feet stage, at Banbury, in Oxfordshire. This was a most desperate *stand-up* fight, and the Birmingham hero, whose character for bravery could not be exceeded, acknowledged, after contending above half an hour, that he was perfectly *satisfied*, and GEORGE was declared the conqueror.

In his contest with *Wood*, the coachman, his true courage will not easily be forgotten.

MICHAEL RYAN

WAS a native of that country whose peculiar warmth of disposition has often subjected its inhabitants to numerous unpleasant situations and serious consequences, frequently defeating their best intentions, and, in too many instances, overpowering their lively discernment. RYAN was an Irishman, and he loved the place that gave him birth with marked sincerity; but the slightest reproach insinuated against *Paddy's* land rendered him impetuous and untractable. He was communicative and good-natured; and if he could not enliven the table with those brilliant sallies of wit, which have so often distinguished numbers of his enlightened countrymen, his drollery and pleasantries, in relating anecdotes belonging to the *sod*, never failed in producing considerable laughter among his companions.

RYAN ranked as a most accomplished pugilist—and

after beating a number of heroes in his own country, he came to England in quest of more glory and conquests. His knowledge of the art was considerable, and in uniting a good theoret'c inquiry with a tolerably extensive practice, he became not only one of the most scientific, but truly formidable boxers. The attitudes of RYAN were firm and elegant; and his neatness in *sparring* was equal to *Mendoza's*, (in the best attempts of that celebrated pugilist, when displaying the advantages of the *science*,)—and, in a *set-to* together, the amateurs experienced a rich and explanatory treat of the offensive and defensive method of pugilism, conducted with as much regularity and precision as the style of fencing. RYAN was a left-handed man, and considered one of the hardest hitters in the kingdom. One of his peculiar traits as a boxer was, in generally giving the first *knock-down* blow; yet he was not wanting in any other respect, had he possessed a cool and steady temper. In those battles wherein he sustained the loss of victory, it might be urged, he was an accessary to his own defeat, from being soon irritated in the fight, which produced a premature exhaustion. He was partial in using the *chopper*, and many of his opponents suffered dreadfully from its operation. His courage kept pace with his *science*, however excellent; and he had all the requisites which constitute (what he really was) a first-rate pugilist. RYAN was an object of considerable attraction among the amateurs; his appearance was manly and athletic; and in height about five feet eleven inches.

RYAN was well aware of his *failing* respecting the irritation of his temper, and endeavoured to conquer it, but without effect. While his mind remained serene in the fight, his guard was admirable, and he appeared as if armed at all points. In his second memorable contest with *Tom Johnson*, at Rickmansworth, during the short period he was in possession of himself, his abilities as a pugilist were conspicuously prominent. In the opinion of those amateurs who had witnessed the various displays of this boxer, little doubt remained, if RYAN could have obtained the *mastery* of his passions, (from the union of such rare qualities in one person, as *strength, science, activity,* and *bottom,* and all of them in a very eminent degree,) the title of CHAMPION must have graced his character; and few men could have been produced who would have stood a *chance* with so celebrated a pugilist. He had paid great attention to the study of pugilism, and, in point of excellence, as a scientific artist, if RYAN was not so easily finished as *Mendoza,* yet it was almost impossible to discover any thing like inferiority. RYAN taught the *science* with considerable facility; and several of his pupils reflected credit, from the rapid improvement they made under the tuition of so distinguished an instructor.

In his contest with *Dunn* he evinced great powers; and no man thought more highly, or expressed himself with greater liberality, in extolling his character as a *thorough-bred* pugilist, than the late *Tom Johnson.* Such pugilists as RYAN are but seldom seen; and his battles were more numerous in *Paddy's land* than in England.

As a publican he conducted himself with discretion and civility—and his house, in St. Giles's, at one period was much resorted to, not only by the sporting men, but it overflowed with his countrymen; and where the "lovers of life" derived much information from the *passing scene!*

SYMONDS, *the old Ruffian.*

Of all the appellations that have been made use of to *designate* the various pugilists, there is no question but that of RUFFIAN is the most uncouth and forbidding. The bare idea is terrific, and its common acceptation is understood, generally, to apply to the worst of characters, and more especially as to appearance—but, in the above instance, SYMONDS was a good-looking man, remarkably well-made, and in height about five feet nine inches. Then, in understanding the phrase in its proper signification, if we are not misinformed, it amounts simply to this, that SYMONDS was a *ruffianlike* fighter! who, disdaining to follow the systematic principles of the art, preferred desperate *rallies* and determined resolution, as the more sure methods to obtain victory than by any scientific displays of judgment; not unlike the sportsman, who dauntless leaps over hedges and ditches, indifferent to the consequences, while the *game* is in view, so that he may be in at the death. This was the plan of SYMONDS—in all his battles the utmost desperation prevailed, and his *gluttony* was of the most inordinate kind. In detailing his contests, one monotonous plan of *milling* was his *forte,* which was so evidently portrayed in his encounters with *Drake, Maddox,* &c. as to render any further observations unnecessary, in the conclusion of his character, than merely to state that SYMONDS was a truly *bottom* pugilist.

TOM (otherwise *Paddington*) JONES,

The first Competitor of the late JEM BELCHER, *in the Metropolis.*

> " As we do turn our backs
> From our companion, thrown into his grave,
> So his familiars from his buried fortunes
> Slink all away; leave their false vows with him,
> Like empty purses pick'd: and his poor self,
> A dedicated beggar to the air,
> With his disease of all-shunned poverty,
> Walks, like contempt, alone."

Rescuing the brave from unmerited obscurity is one of the most pleasing tasks of the impartial biographer ––the great *Belisarius* begged for bread through the towns he once had conquered; and it has been the fate of a number of great men, who, at one period of their lives have been much caressed, and the very idol of popular opinion, in the course of a few fleeting years, completely to lose all their ascendancy, and sink into considerable obscurity, if not to be totally forgotten; such is the inconstancy of mankind!

It appears that *Paddington* JONES has fought more battles than any other pugilist now in existence, excepting *Caleb Baldwin*, and for seven years VICTORY crowned all his attempts. The *Ring* in Hyde Park was the principal spot where he contended for glory, and in which we are informed that he sported his figure no less than NINETEEN times, independent of entering the lists in various other parts of the country with several distinguished pugilists.

PADDINGTON gave birth to this hero, (where he at

present resides,) and from which place, in the pugilistic world, he derives his title. Tom commenced boxer when quite a youth, and, from the intuitive *science* which he displayed at that early period, attracted the notice of the veteran *Tom Johnson*, who pronounced him to be a promising pugilist. The trifling *skirmishes* of this hero are too numerous to be noticed, and we shall commence with his efforts when *stakes* were deposited for the victor.

Tom's first regular contest was about the year 1785, with one *Ned Holmes*, in the fields of Paddington, for the important sum of *half-a-crown;* and, by those persons who witnessed the battle, it appears, it was as well contested as if one hundred pounds had been the stakes—but Jones being a mere novice, and quite a stripling, and *Holmes* a full-grown man, the latter proved the conqueror.

Tom, endeavouring to recover the mortification of defeat, in the course of a few months afterwards, challenged *Holmes* out a second time, upon the regular principles of pugilism, (half-minute time,) for a guinea and a half, when Jones obtained an easy conquest.

One of the Life-Guards, who had been vaunting of his great deeds of pugilistic note at *Tom Johnson's* house, near Lincoln's Inn Fields, was told by *Joe Ward*, in answer to his boast, that he would produce a boy that should soon take the *conceit* out of him: accordingly, a match was made for two guineas against a watch, and *Paddington* Jones was brought forward as the *neat article* to *serve out* the *Lobster*. It was to have been decided in the street, in the first instance, but was removed to Harley-fields. Upon stripping, the *Guards-*

man smiled with contempt at his boy-like antagonist, and with his long arms, had the advantage for the first part of the battle, and dealt out some severe *punishment*, but the *science* and *bottom* of Tom soon stopped his career. After a most desperate conflict, which was witnessed by most of the celebrated pugilists of that day, who were astonished at the intrepidity displayed by Jones, in *milling* his opponent in about fifteen minutes. *Joe Ward* seconded Tom.

Shortly after the above circumstance, in the same fields, Jones fought one *Jack Blackwell*, a lime-burner, for ten shillings; and, although he showed off complete *ruffianism* in the battle, was easily disposed of by Tom. *Tom Burley*, a companion of *Blackwell*, thought he could *now* vanquish Jones, and had the temerity to enter the ring, immediately on the fight being over, and gave him a challenge for the like sum; which Tom instantly accepted. *Burley* was also a complete *ruffian*, and tried what downright force could effect; but Jones so completely warded off his attacks, and put in his blows with so much *science* and execution, that *Burley* requested Tom to leave off, as he was perfectly *satisfied*. The above contests were rendered somewhat conspicuous, from the celebrated Major *Hanger* and his black servant performing the offices to Jones throughout the conflict which all pugilists stand so much in need of.

A match was made between a *one-eyed Sailor*, a most determined boxer, and Tom Jones, for ten guineas a-side, about the year 1786, which was decided in the Ring, in Hyde Park. The contest proved a most desperate one indeed, and the *Sailor* was considered as *ugly* a customer as ever stood up for a *mill;* but, in the event, JONES was declared the victor. This hardy son of Neptune was not *satisfied* with the first broadside, and soon afterwards entered the lists for another ten guineas, when he was again vanquished—yet, like a perfect TRUE BLUE, he was valiant enough to endure a third engagement, in which he was also beaten. The *Sailor* displayed great *bottom,* and was *punished* most severely before he gave in.

JONES, in company with *Pardo Wilson,* anxious to witness the fight between *Hooper* and *Bunner,* at Bentley-green, walked down to Colchester, and was extremely stiff from the effects of his journey. On the next day, a man of the name of *Abraham Chalice,* standing six feet high, and weighing fourteen stone, (a perfect terror to the inhabitants of that part of the country, and who had committed several excesses, from his great strength,) observing TOM JONES upon the race-ground and to show his dexterity, out of mere wantonness, endeavoured to *trip-up* JONES by the heels, he otherwise insulted him, and also threatened to give him a good *hiding.* TOM, notwithstanding the great disparity between them, and the giant-like appearance of *Chalice,* was not to be insulted with impunity, and, perhaps, with more *pluck* than *prudence,* instantly showed fight, by endeavouring to resent the unmanly conduct of this overgrown *ruffian,* who valued himself upon no other consideration but that of his uncommon strength, in being able to conquer most men. *Chalice* laughed at him with the most sovereign contempt, bidding him get along for a boy, or else he would kick his breech for his impudence. The spectators were alarmed at the youthful appearance of JONES, who weighed but ten stone five pounds, and begged of him to desist, as the consequences might prove of the most serious nature; but Tom was not to be deterred, and soon pulled off his clothes. Upon SETTING-TO, *Chalice* had the advantage from his superior strength, and kept it for three rounds; but in the fourth, JONES put in a *hit* under *Chalice's* ear, that knocked him down, when *Tom Johnson* offered to back JONES for one hundred pounds. *Chalice*, on standing up, appeared much confused, and TOM *served* him out in the same style, and continued *punishing* him every round, till he could scarcely move, and who soon acknowledged he had never received such a complete *milling* before. The farmers, and others, who witnessed the contest, were so pleased that this insolent fellow, who had rendered himself so disgusting about that neighbourhood, had received a good threshing, immediately made a subscription purse, which soon amounted to *thirty guineas*, and presented it to JONES for his bravery.

On the next day after the above contest, a countryman, well known in the neighbourhood of Bentley Green under the name of "*Leather Jacket*," mounted the stage, and, with considerable vaunting, publicly challenged any *Londoner* to enter the lists with him : the words had scarcely escaped from his lips, when up jumped TOM, without any consideration for his hands, which were dreadfully bruised and enfeebled, from the effects of the severe *punishment* he had bestowed upon the *nob* of *Abraham Chalice* the preceding day, and instantly began to prepare for action. The *Countryman* seemed almost thunderstruck with astonishment, and with faltering speech exclaimed, "*Na! Na! you be the man that beat Ab. Chalice yesterday—I mean any one but you!"* and made a hasty retreat from the stage, amid the laughter and sneers of the spectators at *Leather Jacket's* vain boasting; thus depriving, in all probability, Tom Jones of adding another laurel to his well-earned fame.

On May 14, 1792, immediately after the fight of *Mendoza* and *Ward*, in Smitham Bottom, near Croydon, upon the same stage, Jones fought *Caleb Baldwin.* The battle was for a purse of twenty pounds, but a dispute arising between the parties, although *Caleb* claimed the victory, it was by the amateurs viewed in no other light than that of a *drawn battle!*

In Paddington Fields, near the cut, a good battle took place between one *Jack Aldridge* and Tom Jones, for six guineas aside; when *Aldridge* was severely beaten.

Soon after the above contest, Jones entered the Ring in Hyde Park, with *Dick Horton,* a baker, for 20 guineas. The latter was considered to have some pretensions to pugilism; but Jones dealt out his hits so hard and fast, that the *baker* was glad to cry out ENOUGH!

Jones fought *Lyons,* the Jew, upon a stage at Hounslow, for twenty guineas. *Tom Johnson* was second to Jones; it was a well-contested battle, in which much *science* and *bottom* were displayed on both sides; but, in the event, Jones proved the conqueror.

Lyons, in a second attempt, upon Blackheath, with Jones, was severely beaten. He was a *bottom* pugilist, and a boxer above mediocrity.

Simpson, a pupil of the late *Tom Johnson,* upon whom considerable expectations had been raised, was matched against Jones, for ten guineas a-side, which

battle was decided on the Green, near Putney. It was
termed a good fight; and Tom proved the conqueror.

Jones was matched in London to fight *George
Nicholls* (since the conqueror of *Cribb*) a man whom he
had never seen. *Mendoza* and *Johnson* took Tom down
to Landsdown, near Bath, for that purpose: but upon
the combatants stripping, and just as they were about
commencing the *set-to*, the following singular circumstance occurred:—*Nicholls* cried out, "*stop!*" and observing that Jones was above his height, declared he
would not fight him, and *sans cérémonie*, immediately
left the ring, to the great astonishment and disappointment of the spectators. After some years had
elapsed, upon *Nicholls* arriving in London, a match
was made for twenty guineas, and they. tried their
skill at Norwood. Three rounds were well contested,
and considerable *science* was displayed; but, in the
fourth, *Nicholls* ran furiously in, and getting his head
between Jones's legs, and catching fast hold of both
his ankles, threw Tom with considerable violence—
this was deemed an infringement upon the articles,
and completely deviating from the rules of pugilism,
by the friends of Jones—a considerable interruption
was the consequence, and the fight was at an end.
The stakes were demanded on the part of Jones; but
Bill Warr, who seconded *Nicholls,* would not suffer them
to be given up. Respecting which was the best man,
it was impossible to form any thing like a decision.
Jones, in his road home, had a *turn-up* with a man
of the name of *Carter*, who had insulted him about
the battle with *Simpson*. Tom, who was not much
hurt from the above contest, *set-to* with good *pluck*,

and so soon convinced *Carter* he was in the wrong,
that he *sheered off* accordingly.

TOM JONES fought *Yokel*, the Jew, at Hounslow,
for ten guineas a-side. This was one of the most terrible conflicts in which TOM had been engaged. *Yokel*
was a desperate *punisher*, and JONES suffered severely
in the fight; but, notwithstanding, *Yokel gave in.*

George Stringer challenged JONES for five guineas
a-side; and which battle was decided in Paddington
Fields. *Stringer* contended hard to obtain the victory;
but he fell, like many others, beneath the potent arm
of JONES.

A man of the name of *Jem Smith*, a carpenter, and
who was not unacquainted with the principles of pugilism, fought JONES for twelve guineas, at Lisson Green,
Paddington. But poor *Chip* was so *milled*, that he was
scarcely able to leave the ground; yet, nevertheless,
Smith was a boxer of no mean pretensions; and displayed not only good *science*, but sound *bottom.*

On the renowned *Jem Belcher's* appearance in the
Metropolis as a pugilist, TOM JONES was the man selected to have the first *set-to* with him, which took
place at Old Oak Common, Wormwood Scrubs, on
April 12, 1799.

Belcher was seconded by *Bill Warr*, and *Bill Gibbons*
acted as his bottle-holder; and JONES had for his attendants, *Joe Ward* and *Dick Hall*. *Belcher* was, at this
period, only nineteen years of age. The odds were, upon
setting-to, six to four upon *Jem*. The spectators were
much interested upon the commencement of the battle,
from the very high character which had been promulgated by *Bill Warr*, upon the astonishing abilities that
his pupil possessed, and the feats which he had achieved

at Bristol. The first round considerable *science* was
displayed upon both sides—the experience and skill of
JONES were well portrayed; and the dexterity and
new mode of fighting, so exclusively *Belcher's* own,
was soon exhibited; but on the termination of the round
Belcher was knocked down. The advantages in the
second and third rounds were perfectly reciprocal; but
in the fourth and fifth JONES was *levelled*. In the sixth
and seventh rounds JONES showed off in most excellent
style—and the amateurs experienced some of the finest
displays of the art; he saw, what always should appear
prominent in trials of skill, manliness and fortitude,
no *shifting*, nothing *shy*, *hugging* out of the question,
and *hauling* not resorted to: it was a clean fight
throughout, *stopping* and *hitting* were the order of the
day, and it might be deemed a *model* for pugilists in
general to follow. *Belcher*, with all the gaiety and confidence of youth, portrayed a *new feature* as a boxer,
and the spectators seemed not to be aware of its consequences. The odds had changed five to four on
JONES. The eighth and ninth were spiritedly contested; but, in the tenth round, *Belcher* put in some
tremendous *hits*, with the rapidity of lightning. This
immediately altered the appearance of things, *Jem* was
looked upon as the favourite, and the odds were laid
upon him accordingly. Yet JONES nobly contested
for victory for the space of *thirty-three* minutes, before he *gave in*. *Jem* weighed twelve stone six pounds;
and TOM JONES but ten stone five pounds weight.
It should not escape the memory, that JONES stood
up to *Belcher* (before that distinguished pugilist lost
his eye) *a considerably* LONGER TIME *than any other
man ever did!*

Bitton, the Jew, a pugilist of considerable celebrity, entered the lists with TOM JONES, upon Wimbledon Common, for twenty guineas a-side, on July 31, 1801. *Jem Belcher* seconded TOM. It proved a well-contested fight—and some very excellent displays of the *science* were exhibited—but JONES not being able to come to time (half a minute) the battle was decided against him.

Notwithstanding the numerous lists of battles which have been mentioned, it does not appear that *Paddington* JONES ever made pugilism his *peculiar* profession; but has always industriously followed through life his occupation, and much respected by his friends for his civility and good nature. In point of appearance, JONES is a very good-looking man, and of prepossessing nature; and at the present period, (1821,) although in his 50th year, he is in full vigour, and seems little, if any, the worse for the various contests in which he has been engaged. In height about five feet seven inches, and in weight ten stone five pounds.

As a pugilist, JONES is entitled to the most honourable mention, in being perfectly master of the *science*, and with *bottom* of the first quality. He has turned out several good pupils. His guard is formidable and commanding, with his left arm firm and extended to protect his body from assault, while his right is on the alert to give the return instantaneously. TOM is a very hard hitter, can use his hands with equal facility, stands well upon his legs, and meets his man with fortitude; his positions are not only elegant, but calculated to do much execution in putting in his blows.

It was the opinion of most of the scientific amateurs, who knew the circumstances under which JONES entered the lists with *Jem Belcher*, that TOM was ill-advised. It was completely premature upon his part to have engaged in such a contest—as he was by no means in sound health, or in possession of that strength and firmness which so characteristically had hitherto marked his combats. From labouring under a long confinement, the system of JONES had lost its tone, and sufficient time had not been allowed to recruit its power, much more restore it to that pristine excellence which he formerly had enjoyed. Three weeks only had elapsed since his recovery, when he had to contend with a HERO, (who afterwards was truly distinguished among all the heroes of the pugilistic schools,) and who was then in the full vigour of youth, health, strength, and every requisite to stamp his character as the first of pugilists. Notwithstanding the evident disadvantages that JONES had to contend against—the disparagement of having been severely beat in numerous battles, and the hurts from street skirmishes, contrasted with *Belcher*, who had scarcely been *pinked*, and blooming from the country, TOM's conduct was far above *mediocrity*, and ought not to be forgotten.

JONES has proved the conqueror in all his numerous battles, excepting only *two* instances : and no man has appeared oftener in the character of a *second* than TOM JONES; and few, it is said, understand that duty better than he does. In most of *Randall's* battles TOM performed the above office.

Numerous indeed have been the *skirmishes* in which TOM has been engaged : and the *long tails* that he has borne off as trophies of victory from the *guardsmen* who have, in the neighbourhood of Paddington, at various times endeavoured to *serve him out*, because he was considered as a scientific pugilist, would not prove far short in furnishing half a company. It is impossible that we can take our leave of PADDINGTON JONES without characterising him as a BRAVE and *distinguished* PUGILIST, and who is well deserving to occupy a *niche* in the temple of fame.

ANDREW GAMBLE

Was a celebrated hero of the fist, who had not only distinguished himself with considerable success in Ireland, but had derived great reputation from his successful encounters in England as a first-rate boxer, and who was viewed rather in the light of a Champion. ANDREW was a native of the *sod*, and apprenticed to a stone-mason in Dublin, where his pretensions were first discovered as a pugilist; and his frequent skirmishes in the *Liberty*, and his exhibitions in the Phœnix Park, rendered him a bruiser of notoriety in Ireland. GAMBLE was about six feet in height, a very powerful man, but not well made, being much *knock-kneed;* yet, notwithstanding this peculiarity for an Irishman, he stood remarkably firm, and faced his man with the most determined boldness. *Victory,* for a number of years, crowned all his endeavours; and, it is affirmed, that he proved the conqueror in eighteen battles, and that over men distinguished in both countries. He had a most tremendous fist, and dealt out *punishment* with uncommon severity. GAMBLE's knowledge of the *science* was considerable, and in *sparring* he was excellent;—his guard was correct and formidable, and his body so well protected from assault, that it required considerable talent to put in a *hit* with any degree of success. In all his battles, excepting with *Jem Belcher*, he displayed some heroism ; but, in the fight with that celebrated pugilist, his friends could scarcely refrain from believing that he had played a *cross*, such a strange alteration appeared in his character; but it is well known since, that he was conquered against his inclination. GAMBLE was a hard but slow hitter, and lost his consequence, as a pugilist, soon after the above defeat.

GAMBLE fought with *Stanyard*, a Birmingham pugilist of considerable celebrity, on September 5, 1792, on a stage twenty-one feet square, at Bentley Green, a few miles from Colchester. GAMBLE had for his second and bottle-holder *Williams* and *Ryan ;* and *Stanyard* had for his attendants *Joe Ward* and *Hooper.*

Upon their *setting-to*, GAMBLE was the favourite, and the odds were sported high that he proved the conqueror : but *Stanyard*, from his great strength and *bottom*, in the course of a few rounds, brought the betting level. The *science* of ANDREW began now to appear conspicuous, and the advantages were once more on his side, and the bets were five to four in his favour. *Stanyard* showed off his *game* in good style ; and several rounds were manfully contested, and some desperate blows were exchanged ; when the odds turned again upon the latter. In the eighteenth round, *Stanyard* struck a foul blow; but it did not terminate the battle; and GAMBLE continued the fight for one more round, when *Stanyard* fell, and ANDREW, considering himself the conqueror, left the ring. Considerable dispute took place, concerning the propriety of the circumstance, when at length it was determined a *drawn battle!* It was a good contest, and lasted for twenty-five minutes.

GAMBLE was matched to fight *Noah James*, (who had

been one of the Horse-Guards) for one hundred guineas, and which battle was decided upon Wimbledon
Common, July 1, 1800. Several thousands were betted
upon the event. From the celebrity of the combatants,
a great trial of skill was anticipated. *James* was a pugilist well known. He had fought no less than seventeen pitched battles, and had shown himself not only a
scientific boxer, but supported by a thorough *bottom*,
rarely equalled, and never excelled. GAMBLE was
seconded by *Stanyard*, and *Jack Bartholomew* performed the office of bottle-holder; *James* had for his attendants, *Joe Ward* and *Hall*

On entering the ring, *James* was the favourite, six to
four. Neither *science* nor *bottom* were wanting on either
side, and they *set-to* in the most determined manner.
For several rounds the success was alternate; and severer *punishment* had never been exhibited in any contest
whatever. In the twelfth round, GAMBLE put in a tremendous *facer*, that split his opponent's nose, and the
claret flew in all directions. The fight now raged truly
desperate, and every round was contested with the most
determined resolution and heroic firmness. In the twentieth, GAMBLE gave *James* a desperate blow, the
effects of which broke his collar-bone; and, in the next
round, ANDREW, with a *hit* equally terrible, shattered
his jaw-bone. The *bottom* of *James* had already been
considered of the primest quality; but his extraordinary
fortitude astonished all the beholders, by his continuing
the contest for four rounds after, undismayed by the circumstances, till he fell nearly without any signs of life.
The above battle was, in point of desperation, somewhat
similar to the one between the *Ruffian* and *Maddox*.

James had suffered so severely in the conflict, that the
surgeon who attended him gave no hopes of his recovery: upon which information, he sent for his opponent, and every thing passed between them that reflected honour on brave men. GAMBLE, it is said, touched
with the pitiable situation of his brave but unfortunate adversary, generously made his wife a handsome
present towards the support of her husband.

GAMBLE's next *set-to* was with *Jem Belcher;* in which
contest he was so soon deprived of his laurels, as to create the most dreadful murmurings among his countrymen, many of whom were nearly ruined from GAMBLE
being defeated.   *St. Giles's* was in a complete uproar
upon this occasion, and the *Paddies* had not been so
neatly *cleaned out* since the days of the renowned hero,
Peter Corcoran! It proved a most woful day for the
Irish indeed; the dealers in *wild ducks* had not a *feather
left* to *fly with;* the rabbit merchants were so reduced as
to be even without *poles,* and not a *copper* to go the next
morning to market; never were men so completely
dished and *done up!* ANDREW's name had hitherto
been a tower of strength; he was the *tight Irish boy,*
and the *darling* of his country—but, alas! the scene
was changed; he was now called *a cur,* an overgrown
thing, a mere *apology;* and was in danger of being
tossed in a *blanket,* by his enraged and disappointed
backers. GAMBLE from this defeat lost the *warm hearts*
of the *Paddies* ever afterwards.   GAMBLE appeared
truly contemptible in this fight, in comparison with
even the worst of his former displays—and it was the
opinion of the amateurs, that the evident superiority
of *Belcher* completely frightened all GAMBLE's courage
and *science* out of him.

ELISHA CRABBE, *the Jew,*

Was a professor of some notoriety in the gymnastic art, and, if not an immediate pupil of *Mendoza*, it is certain that he derived a number of embellishments from that celebrated boxer. In those days when *pugilism* was a distinguished feature of attraction, and when most of its professors were men of eminence—when *Humphries* claimed attention from his gentleman-like conduct, courage, and elegance as a pugilist—and *Mendoza*, for his superior knowledge of the *science*, by his communicative display in teaching the art of self-defence—when *Johnson* became conspicuous from his fine stamina, and intuitive excellence as a boxer —and *Ryan*, in uniting theoretic information with the best practical display of intrepidity and art, gained considerable notoriety—when *Jackson*, whose fine symmetry, manly fortitude, scientific attainments, and attractive heroism, made a lasting impression upon the spectators—and *Big Ben*, for his valour and tremendous qualifications, was looked upon as a phenomenon—yet, notwithstanding the well-merited reputation of the above pugilists, and however admired by their numerous adherents, CRABBE raised himself, even at this period, far above mediocrity, and proved worthy of honourable mention in the annals of pugilism.

ELISHA was possessed of so much *pluck*, that he had the fortitude to enter the lists with *Death*, (*Stephen Oliver*,) upon Blackheath, on April 17, 1788. *Death* was a powerful competitor, and it required no small de-

gree of courage and *science* to overcome so formidable a
rival, who had often knocked down many a brave
fellow, and had contended in the field of glory with
most of the distinguished pugilists, for a series of years,
with unexampled resolution and various success. As a
boxer, the experience of *Oliver* gave him the preference, and for the first part of the fight he appeared to
have had the advantage; but, in closing, the superior
strength of CRABBE was manifest, and the latter threw
his antagonist with considerable ingenuity, generally
falling upon *Death*, to the discomfiture of his wind.
Oliver endeavoured to *punish* CRABBE severely; but the
science of the *Jew* adroitly warded off his attacks, and
returned some truly desperate *facers*, that changed *Oliver's death-like* appearance to a more *crimson* hue. After a contest of upwards of half an hour, when one of
DEATH'S *peepers* was nearly closed-up, and upon receiving a tremendous *hit* that *levelled* him with his mother
earth, he declared the *Crabbe* was too *sour* for him,
when the *Jew* was proclaimed the conqueror. Royalty
witnessed the above trial of skill, surrounded by distinguished amateurs and first-rate boxers; and an innumerable concourse of spectators attended to do honour
to the combatants. CRABBE, in beating *Death*, obtained considerable fame as a pugilist; and was, soon
afterwards, matched against *Watson;* but with whom he
was not so successful, and, though he contested the
ground manfully, CRABBE was compelled to *give-in.*

CRABBE was also conquered by *Tom Tyne.*

ELISHA had been successful in several battles, and
had paid great attention in acquiring the *science.* He
was in height about five feet eight inches. For some

years before his death (which took place suddenly, June 18, 1809, on his return to London from Gravesend, on board the packet) he resigned all pretensions to pugilism, to perform the duties of a city officer, which situation he filled with considerable credit; and, in his character as a publican, in Duke's Place, he was civil and obliging to all his customers; and had been an object of considerable attraction, as a pugilist, among the members of his own persuasion.

ISAAC PERRINS

Of Manchester)

Was one, if not the most formidable pugilist of his time, and the distinguished opponent of the late *Tom Jóhnson*. In appearance, PERRINS was a perfect Hercules, well formed, and of an imposing and pleasing nature. The superior strength which he possessed over other men, resembled, by comparison, that of a giant to the usual portion allotted to mankind in general; but PERRINS was blessed with a mind which corrected this advantage, by evincing in his temper and manners the placid-like behaviour of a lamb. In Birmingham, where he long followed his occupation, in superintending a large manufactory, he was respected by his employers, and beloved by those men whom his situation gave him the power to command; and at Manchester, where he resided some years, he was an object of considerable regard and attention.

The most triumphant heroes of the adjoining counties, who had acquired considerable fame as first-rate pugilists, were rendered perfectly *insignificant* in his

presence; and his prowess was so uncommonly great,
that few, indeed, could be found possessing fortitude
enough to meet him. PERRINS was above the ordinary
size of pugilists, he was upwards of six feet two inches
in height, and was the unusual weight of seventeen
stone; but, notwithstanding his bulk, he was by no
means inactive, neither did he entirely depend upon
his *strength* for victory, having made himself tolerably
well acquainted with the *science.* The superior conduct
of PERRINS in his memorable contest with *Johnson,*
gave rise to considerable animadversions at that time,
respecting the merits of the two combatants—to *Tom
Johnson,* as he richly deserved, every praise was granted,
in his being able to accomplish so complete a victory
over such a hero as ISAAC PERRINS; and the prodigies
of valour which *Johnson* performed can never be forgotten, while life remains, in the minds of those amateurs
who witnessed that most tremendous battle. In speaking of PERRINS it was observed, that throughout the
fight his manner was above all praise—such an heroic
intrepidity, admirable fortitude, and contempt of danger had never been portrayed by any man, rivetting
the spectators with astonishment and approbation;
and it was asserted, that had *Johnson* fought like himself, as he had hitherto done, in boldly facing his man,
instead of resorting to those manœuvres that pugilists
are compelled to do who feel themselves *over-matched,*
impressed with a kind of fear of their antagonist's
superiority in any particular respect, PERRINS must
have beaten him off-hand.

PERRINS was far from an illiterate character, and in
his general conversation was intelligent, cheerful, and

communicative, and possessed a considerable share of discernment, which proved of great service to him in his character as a publican. His house at Manchester was well attended, and his customers were rather of a superior class. ISAAC had some pretensions to music, and, at one period of his life, was leader of a country choir. In company, PERRINS was facetious, full of anecdote, and never tardy in giving his song; and was a strong instance in his own person, among many others which might be cited, if necessary, that it does not follow as a matter of course (as is the too general opinion of the uninformed) that all PUGILISTS are *blackguards!*

In selecting the following anecdote from a very popular and amusing work, entitled " *The Itinerant*," which not only places the good temper and amazing strength of PERRINS in a conspicuous point of view, but, in its connexion with the above pugilist, exhibits one of the peculiar traits of character of the most natural actor that has adorned the English stage for some years past, (when all restraint of behaviour is forgotten in the gay and thoughtless moment of dissipation,) and, independent of the above circumstance, from the excellent specimen of spontaneous wit it contains, is truly worthy of promulgation :—" It happened that PERRINS, the noted pugilist, made one of the company this evening; he was a remarkably strong man, and possessed of great modesty and good nature ; the last scene took such an effect on his imagination, that he laughed immoderately.— *Cooke's* attention was attracted, and turning towards him with *his* most bitter look, 'What do you laugh at, Mr. Swabson, hey? Why, you great lubber-headed

thief, *Johnson* would have beat two of you! laugh at
me! at *George Cooke!* come out, you scoundrel!'

"The coat was again pulled off, and, putting himself
in an attitude, exclaimed, 'This is the arm that shall
sacrifice you!' PERRINS was of a mild disposition, and
knowing *Cooke's* character, made every allowance, and
answered him only by a smile, till aggravated by language and action the most gross, he very calmly took
him in his arms, as though he had been a child, set him
down in the street, and bolted the door. The evening
was wet, and our hero without coat or hat, unprepared
to cope with it; but entreaty for admission was vain,
and his application at the window unattended to. At
length, grown desperate, he broke several panes, and,
inserting his head through the fracture, bore down all
opposition by the following witticism:—'Gentlemen,
I have taken some *panes* to gain admission, pray let me
in, for *I see through my error.*' The door was opened,
dry clothes procured, and about one o'clock in the
morning we sent him home in a coach."

PERRINS died at Manchester, in the fiftieth year of
his age, in December, 1800, sincerely regretted by all
who knew him. His death was unfortunately occasioned
by his laudable exertions in endeavouring to save the
lives and secure the property of persons who were in
danger of destruction from the ravages of fire at that
place. The character of PERRINS was never sullied
from acts of intemperance, and though fond of the
gymnastic art as a *science*, it is but justice to observe
that he was too well acquainted with men and manners
either to offend the one or disgrace the other

JACK DOYLE

Was a bruiser of some celebrity, and had distinguished himself in several desperate conflicts, and obtained the appellation of a good fighter. Doyle was determined in his manner, and *set-to* with a resolution perfectly undaunted; and although not one of Fortune's favourites in receiving the smiles of victory often, yet Doyle is most honourably entitled to respectful mention in the annals of pugilism. In height about five feet eight inches, and well versed in the *science.* His name is rendered conspicuous from his memorable contest with *Jack Drake,* upon Blackheath. According to the amateurs, a better battle was never witnessed; and, for *thirty minutes,* the time it lasted, it was impossible to declare which was the greatest hero. Every exertion was made by *Doyle* to hear his opponent cry out, *Enough!* and Drake, with equal intrepidity, endeavoured to improve every chance, till he had perfectly satisfied *Doyle* there was no alternative left but that of *giving in!* It is supposed, for the time the above battle was contested, it was equal, if not more furious and determined than the one between the *Ruffian* and *Maddox.*

Doyle entered the lists upon Blackheath, with a man of the name of *Chitty,* a coal-heaver, for twenty guineas, on December 19, 1786. It was a terrible conflict, and contested with the most determined resolution, for a considerable time, on both sides;

but, in the event, DOYLE was proclaimed the conqueror.

DOYLE entered the lists with *Savage*, in Stepney Fields, on November 22, 1787. It was a most desperate conflict, and continued for near fifty minutes, with great impetuosity, and victory for a long time appeared doubtful; and not till DOYLE was terribly *milled*, did he observe that he had got *enough*. *Ryan* seconded DOYLE; and *Tom Johnson* performed the same office for *Savage*.

Bill Dean fought with DOYLE, in Harley Fields; and a most admirable specimen of valour was experienced in both the combatants, during a long and arduous contest. DOYLE strove hard to obtain the pleasing sound of victory; but *Dean* put in a superior claim, and had the satisfaction of hearing DOYLE observe—ENOUGH!

DOYLE was engaged in several other contests, and conducted himself with great spirit, and in no instance have we learned that he ever disgraced his character—of *a good pugilist*.

JACK BARTHOLOMEW

Was a pugilist of considerable pretensions, and had contended in the field of glory with several first-rate boxers. BARTHOLOMEW was a native of Brentford, and he had convinced many persons in and contiguous to that neighbourhood of the potent qualities of his arm. In height about five feet nine inches and a half, weighing about thirteen stone and a half, well versed in the *science*, and possessing most excellent *game*. BARTHOLOMEW was considered a very hard hitter; extremely active and formidable in all his battles; and perfectly entitled to the appellation of a sound and complete boxer.

Fearby (denominated the *Young Ruffian*) entered the lists with JACK BARTHOLOMEW, on Hounslow Heath, on Monday, June 8, 1795, for a trifling sum of money; but, nevertheless, it proved a most severe and determined contest, and FAME seemed considerably more the object in view than the deposit. The *junior Ruffian* displayed all those qualities, on which he valued his reputation, and endeavoured to persuade JACK that he must surrender his laurels to *his* superior acquirements; but BARTHOLOMEW was not to be *ruffianised* out of his skill easily, and met his opponent's impetuosity with firm and manly intrepidity. After a severe *mill* of fifty minutes, the *Ruffian* acknowledged his *gluttony* was perfectly *satisfied!*

BARTHOLOMEW had a *set-to* with *Bill Wood;* but, in consequence of some foul blows upon the part of JACK, *which* was the best man was not decided; though *Wood* was declared the conqueror.

Tom Owen, the conqueror of *Hooper*, the tinman, challenged BARTHOLOMEW for twenty-five guineas, This battle was decided on Sunbury Common, on August 22, 1797. Previous to the *set-to*, the odds were considerably in favour of *Owen;* who, upon the commencement of the fight, endeavoured to show that his vast *strength* would soon render unavailing the *scientific* efforts of BARTHOLOMEW. *Owen* was a troublesome customer, and required such a prodigious deal of *serving out*, that JACK had not a minute to lose with him. It was a truly manly fight, and *Owen*, full of vigour and resolution, met his opponent like a hero. BARTHOLOMEW, with all the experience of a veteran, received *Owen's* attacks with fortitude, and returned them with a noble and daring spirit; *strength* at last gave way, and *science* proved the master. BARTHOLOMEW, after a most desperate fight of thirty minutes, was declared the victor. The above battle was highly spoken of by the amateurs.

In tracing his two contests with *Jem Belcher*, BARTHOLOMEW is entitled to the most honourable mention; and, although defeated, his character as a pugilist was not in the slightest degree tarnished, by the manliness of his behaviour throughout the above battles.

It was no great length of time after his contests with *Belcher*, that JACK began to decline considerably in health. He had fought several severe battles, and his constitution had suffered materially from their violent effects. He received his final *knock-down* blow in July, 1803, in the Almonry, at Westminster. On opening his body, after his demise, at his own particular request, JACK's liver was found to be scirrhous. In briefly taking our leave of this hero—JACK BARTHOLOMEW ranked as a first-rate pugilist.

DAN MENDOZA.

" ————I have heard it said,
There is an Art, which in its piedness shares
With great creating Nature :
Yet Nature is made better by no mean,
But Nature makes that mean ; so, over that Art,
Which, you say, adds to Nature, is an Art
That Nature makes. This is an Art
Which does mend Nature, change it rather ; but
The Art itself is—NATURE !"

BOXING, the first principles of which are, most
unquestionably, derived from NATURE; and its effects
are so *early* and strongly implanted in the human frame,
as to portray its original and impressive qualities in the
most conspicuous point of view. It may be witnessed
in the INFANT, who can scarcely walk, and who is
seen to lift up its little arm indignantly against the
object that attempts to deprive it of its playthings ;
the BOY of riper years, in order to protect his top or
marbles from some lad of superior size, evinces his
native courage, by putting himself in a posture of defence, and daring his oppressor to the hostile combat ;
and the more matured MAN, who, acting from the impulse of his feelings, anxiously endeavouring to avoid
the imputation of *a coward*, disincumbers himself without hesitation of his apparel, and soon promulgates his
manhood, by an appeal to blows. So far the *natural*
appearances of PUGILISM ; in which original state,
strength and *activity* have generally prevailed, to the

manifest injury of the innocent and unoffending ; and
who, from not being able to contend against men of
athletic powers, (and perhaps, added to furious and
illiterate dispositions,) have also taken advantage of the
above requisites, which the *weak* have not been able
to resist, and have, as a matter of prudence, been compelled to put up with gross indignities, by not being
in the possession of the resources to resent it with any
degree of chance ; this it was which gave rise to ART,
and, ultimately, produced the *Science* of SELF-DE-
FENCE ; and thus it is, whereby NATURE is improved
from an union with ART.

It might be asked, what is an Admiral without tactics?
or a General without scientific precision ?   Where it
has appeared that downright *force* has succeeded once
—*skill*, it will be found, has produced victory a hundred
times.   Courage would degenerate into mere ferocity,
if not tempered with judgment, and brutality be the
most prominent feature in all contests.   The General
who leads on his men to the attack with an intrepidity
almost bordering upon enthusiasm, has never failed in
obtaining praise for his gallantry of spirit; but *that*
Commander, who has gained the victory from his consummate skill, in not losing the life of a man unavoidably, will not only insure the admiration of the dis-
cerning, but stamp his pretensions to the advantages
of *science* over impetuosity, in producing those brilliant
results which are never forgotten.   LEARNING has
its incalculable importance—and GENIUS its powerful
claims—but when united, they become truly irresistible.

MENDOZA was considered one of the most elegant
and scientific Pugilists in the whole race of Boxers,

and might be termed a complete artist. His theoretic acquirements were great, and his practice truly extensive. He rose up like a phenomenon in the pugilistic hemisphere, and was a star of the first brilliancy for a considerable period; but subject, like other mortals, to the influence of time, *another*, and ANOTHER, have appeared, whose feats of glory have rendered the heroic deeds of DAN rather dim, and almost to produce a total eclipse. Yet BOXIANA will endeavour to be grateful, and not hurried away by the almost irresistible charms of novelty; but hails the pleasing task of rescuing the deeds of the valiant from silent and unmerited oblivion.

The name of MENDOZA has been resounded from one part of the kingdom to the other; and the fame of this once-celebrated pugilist was the theme of universal panegyric—and, though not

> "The Jew
> That Shakspeare drew—"

yet he was that *Jew*, the acknowledged pride of his own particular persuasion, and who, so far interested the *Christian*, that, in spite of his prejudices, he was compelled to exclaim—" MENDOZA *was a pugilist of no ordinary merit!*"

DAN was, most undoubtedly, a new and prominent feature in pugilism, and his style of fighting has given rise to considerable animadversions among the amateurs, as to the utility and excellence of its practicability. As far as it could be ascertained in his own person, it was substantial and complete; and, perhaps, it may be but candid to allow, that whenever MEN-

DOZA failed in the promulgation of its effects, it proceeded more from a physical cause than from the insufficiency of his attainments—(not unlike a frigate,
well manned, a good commander, and a fast-sailing
vessel, that could perform her manœuvres with more
adroitness than a ship of superior metal, and which,
ultimately, has been obliged to knock under from the
overwhelming strength of a first-rate, affords no proof
whatever of its not possessing a superiority of talent
or courage—so with DAN, as far as *art* was necessary
to insure victory, he possessed it; and even *bottom* was
by no means wanting to second his efforts upon most
of his trying occasions; yet still *Fortune* was not
always propitious.) In those conflicts where art could
so far deprive his opponents of the advantage of their
strength—MENDOZA was eminently conspicuous, in
not only portraying the advantages of his peculiar
skill, but in almost rendering victory certain. In tiring
out a man's strength, who depended upon that particular circumstance to stamp him a formidable boxer,
by acting on the defensive till the assault in turn could
be practised with success, was one of MENDOZA's prominent traits; and then, from his own superior *science*,
united with his physical powers, gave him the pre-
eminence, in every way, over his adversary, which soon
made the object in view safe and practicable. Where
science and strength were opposed to his dexterous
efforts, he availed himself of his genius and *bottom*,
and was not wanting either in intrepidity or bravery,
and lost no time in combating the mighty prowess,
with which he has so often been assailed.

MENDOZA has contended with heroes of the first

class, and success has crowned most of his daring attempts; and in all of them he proved himself not *wanting*, although at times in defeat. His battles with *Humphries* were of the first order, and much as his skill was entitled to praise, his humanity had a brighter and more lasting claim to remembrance. In his contests with *Bill Warr*, his excellence was so superior, that it was like a *diamond* in contact with paste, contending for brilliancy or value; the scientific *Bill*, who knew *how* to WIN better than any other man in the kingdom, from his perfect acquaintance with the manœuvres of shifting and dropping from the prowess of his antagonist, when necessary—with MENDOZA was put to a stand-still—the perfections of the master stared him so strongly in the face, that the impression proved too weighty upon his mind, particularly in the second contest, that he stood no *chance*, and his inferiority was glaring.   DAN, in his trial of skill with *Jackson*, had to encounter serious difficulties—and it is but justice to state, that the attempt was a bold one; if MENDOZA valued himself upon his superior knowledge of the art, *Jackson's* pretensions to the *science* were impressive and commanding—but DAN's *game*, though good, was not capable of resisting the strength and activity of his opponent; and MENDOZA, in surrendering to such a distinguished hero as *Jackson*, was by no means disgraced; in fact, it was great temerity in entering the lists with so formidable a character.

In viewing MENDOZA as a teacher of the gymnastic art, it might almost be said, that he was without a competitor, and turned out some excellent pupils.   It has been contended, there was more elegance about his positions than an indication of strength; and more show

than utility.   No pugilist ever stopped with greater
neatness, hit oftener, or put in his blows quicker, than
MENDOZA; but they often failed in doing that execution which might have been expected, from their
want of force.   In height about five feet seven inches,
with a well-formed manly chest, and arms of a strong
athletic nature; a *bottom* never impeached; and possessing wind that was seldom disordered.   His battles
have been very numerous, and well contested; and we
have selected the following as the most prominent, and
entitled to notice :—

Martin, the Bath butcher, a pugilist of considerable
fame, entered the lists with MENDOZA, on Barnet Race-
ground, on April 17, 1787—it was well contested, and
MENDOZA exhibited those early specimens of excellence, which soon afterwards ripened into perfection.
In the event, the *butcher* acknowledged that he was
satisfied.

MENDOZA, in fighting *Humphries* at Odiham, was
defeated; but felt confident of success in the event of
another attempt, which took place at Stilton, on May 6,
1789, in Mr. Thornton's Park.   In order to accommo-
date the spectators, a building was erected, enclosing
a space of forty-eight feet in circumference, with seats
like a gallery, raised one above another, capable of containing nearly three thousand spectators, where every
person could see without the least interruption.

Humphries, attended by *Tom Johnson*, as his second,
entered between one and two o'clock, followed by *Butcher*, as his bottle-holder, and *Harvey Christian Coombe*,
Esq. as his umpire. MENDOZA immediately afterwards
made his appearance, attended by Captain *Brown* and
Michael Ryan, as his second and bottle-holder, having

for his umpire, *Sir Thomas Apreece.* The seconds,
according to an agreement, retired to separate corners
on the *setting-to* of the combatants.—The moment became interesting, and anxiety was upon the utmost
stretch—the opinions of the amateurs had undergone
various changes since the last combat; and the issue of
the contest was extremely doubtful—MENDOZA was
considered a formidable rival, he had rather risen into
estimation than otherwise since the first battle, and the
betting had no stability about it. *Humphries* appeared
strong and elegant in his position, and endeavoured to
put in a *facer;* but DAN, on the alert, stopped it with
great neatness, and returned a sharp blow, that *levelled*
his opponent. MENDOZA, elated with the attempt,
concluded the second and third rounds in the same
style. It soon began to appear that the *Jew* possessed
considerable confidence in his own powers; and, although the success was alternate in the various rounds,
for upwards of half an hour, the advantages were upon
the side of MENDOZA; the science of the latter made a
strong impression upon the spectators, by the neat manner of stopping the blows on his arm, and giving the return so instantaneously, as to bring his adversary down;
and even in point of throwing, DAN possessed the superiority. In the twenty-second round it appeared that
the articles were violated (which specified particularly,
that if either of the combatants fell without a blow, he
should lose the battle) by *Humphries* falling without a
blow; upon which circumstance a complete uproar ensued, and nothing was to be heard but the cries of *"foul!
foul!"* and MENDOZA's friends insisted that he had won
the battle. Upon the other side, it was as obstinately

contended, that the blow was "*fair*," inasmuch as that *Humphries* had stopped it before he fell. *Tom Johnson* was particularly positive as to the fact; but MENDOZA's umpire declared it to be foul: an appeal was then made to Mr. *Coombe*, who would not decide upon the case. The *row* was now beyond all description, *blows* had subsided, and *tongues* were in full and violent motion, and respect to person seemed out of the question. A warm altercation took place between the seconds, each supporting their *interested* side, when Captain *Brown*, full of *pluck*, called the veteran *Tom Johnson* a blackguard, and that he would kick a certain place, if he gave him any more of his impertinence—these were words *Tom* was not in the habit of swallowing, (the seat of honour to be disgraced,) and intimated to the *Captain*, that they would try as to the capability of his assertion, and put himself in a posture of defence. The quarrel had now grown important, and a battle was expected; but Captain *Brown talked* of fighting him at some more *convenient* period, for 1000 guineas, which operated only as the *flourish of the moment*, in never being mentioned afterwards! *Humphries* insisted on the fight being renewed, and taunted MENDOZA to *set-to* again; but the friends of the latter would not suffer him, being satisfied, in their own opinion, that he had won the battle. The spectators growing impatient for the decision, *Humphries* threw up his hat in defiance, and endeavoured to provoke the *Jew* to renew the combat. MENDOZA, considering that an unfavourable impression might go abroad against him, in refusing, or in its being decided as a drawn battle, consented to finish the contest. Silence was once more restored, and the combatants again *set-to*. DA *showed off* in good style, and went in with the most determined spirit, and finished the round by knocking down his opponent. In the next, he repeated the dose, and continued, during the remainder of the fight, to have the advantage. After thirty minutes had elapsed, *Humphries,* either from accident or design, committed the same error in falling without a blow—MENDOZA had put in some tremendous *hits,* and, in following them up, *Humphries* retreated and fell; when DAN, without the slightest murmur, was deemed the conqueror.

It was the opinion of the amateurs, that MENDOZA displayed the greatest *science* in the above battle; and he was considerably improved since his last fight at Odiham; that hitherto determined spirit seemed now moderated by steady and decisive judgment, and the skill and fortitude he displayed were truly entitled to respect and attention. *Humphries* had lost that commanding style which was so prominent in his last attack; and he seemed to labour under an impression he had a *superior* to encounter with; he did not maintain his ground with his usual confidence, but suffered his opponent to drive him, and even, upon some occasions, there was a sort of shrinking from the blows of his adversary MENDOZA looked upon victory as certain, and, in many instances, treated the guard of his opponent with much *sang-froid;* yet, notwithstanding, whether from prejudice, or *Humphries* being such a distinguished favourite, cannot be ascertained; but it is certain, the betting continued in his favour.

MENDOZA, from his superior style of *stopping,* received scarcely any blows of consequence, excepting a severe one on his cheek; and had not DAN displayed so much adroitness in the above respect, in all probability, he might have lost his life, as *Humphries* endeavoured to put in some tremendous blows at the pit of the stomach.

The head of *Humphries* exhibited severe symptoms of punishment, his face was much disfigured, one of his eyes completely closed up, and his forehead and lip very much lacerated. Upon the whole, there was a great falling off in his manner of fighting.

The *pugilistic world* were not quite satisfied with the decision of the above contest; and it was deemed expedient to set the matter to rights by a *third battle*, which would finally declare the merits of the respective combatants as to the appellation of conqueror. *Humphries* felt eager for the fray, and MENDOZA instantly acquiesced in the challenge, confident of success. September 29, 1790, was the day fixed for the decision of this grand combat, at Doncaster. To prevent interruption from the populace, and to render the accommodation more secure and complete for the subscribers, who had purchased their admission at half-a-guinea each, a large yard, belonging to an inn, at the above place, was selected for the scene of action, which was enclosed on one side by numerous houses, and upon the other by the river Don, secured by a strong paling. But perseverance and curiosity frequently overcome all impediments; and so it was in this instance :—water proved no hindrance, nor thick boards any obstacle to the anxiety of JOHN BULL to witness this heroic contest. Hundreds were rowed over from the other side to the paling, who lost no time in removing the obstruction to their wishes. Independent of those intruders, upwards of five hundred tickets were sold and admitted; and no confusion took place. Between the hours of ten and eleven the combatants mounted the stage, amid thunders of applause : *Humphries* displayed considerable agility in springing up; and MENDOZA was equally anxious to display his good spirits. The stage was twenty-four feet square, and raised four feet from the ground. *Tom Johnson,* who had in the last contest been so anxious in the cause of *Humphries,* now appeared as second to MENDOZA, accompanied by *Butcher* as his bottle-holder; *Sir Thomas Apreece* in his former capacity of umpire; *Humphries* was attended by *Ward* and *Jackson;* and Colonel Hamilton took upon himself the office of umpire; but, in case of any dispute arising between the chosen umpires, Mr. *Harvey Aston* was appointed as the third, whose decision, if appealed to, must be final.

The odds were five to four upon MENDOZA ; and *Humphries's* friends, still sanguine of his success, took them with avidity. MENDOZA, respecting his superior pretensions to the *science* was readily admitted; but the fortitude and *bottom* of *Humphries,* and other excellent qualities as a pugilist, that he was known to possess, had made an impression upon his admirers not easily effaced, and who entertained a strong opinion that he would ultimately gain the day.

The awful *set-to* at length commenced, and every eye beamed with anxiety ; the moment was interesting and attractive, and each party was lost in suspense. The combatants were heroes of no common stamp, and every feint was regarded with respect and attention; money was a secondary consideration in this case ; towering *fame* was attached to the issue of the contest ; and the

proud title of conqueror rested upon its termination —
they both felt its consequences, and were determined to
gain or *lose* it, honourably. *Humphries,* full of confidence
in his powers, went boldly in, and attacked his opponent
with great impetuosity; but Mendoza, prepared, met
him with equal temerity, when they closed and fell.
The second round was equally bold and determined upon
both sides; and though *Humphries* appeared to put in
the most blows, yet they did not seem of much effect.
The combatants, aware of each other's excellence, began to think a little of what they were about, and called judgment to their aid, it was *stop* for *stop*, and *blow*
for *hit*, for some time, when, an opportunity offering,
Mendoza concluded the third round by *knocking down*
Humphries. The fourth was of no import; but in the
fifth round, *Humphries* endeavoured to put in a tremendous *stomacher*—the *Jew* knowing this favourite attempt
of his opponent, stopped it with uncommon neatness,
and returned the compliment for his attention with a
facer—*Humphries* full of *game* in answering it, fell. It
now began to appear that *Humphries* was on the decline—he had not lost his gaiety, but still there was a
certain something that told the amateur he was *going!*
The odds rapidly rose upon Mendoza, till they arrived
at ten to one; and *Humphries's* inferiority soon became
manifest. Mendoza scarcely ever failed in bringing him
down whenever he hit him; and who frequently fell
from even a feeble touch, and sometimes without any
whatever; but the conquest appeared so secure and
safe to Mendoza that it was never noticed. If *Humphries* was compelled to acknowledge the superiority
of his opponents abilitie's respecting his improve-

HUMPHRIES & MENDOZA.

In their third public contest for superiority, on Sept. 29, 1790.

Publish'd Jan.1.1812, by G. Smeeton, 139, St Martins Lane.

ment in the *science*, it must not be forgotten that *Dick* never lost his greatness as a man : his fortitude was still the same, and the reluctance he manifested in giving up the contest, even when pressed so to do by his friends, who saw that no chance was left, yet he wished to fight longer, although he had scarcely any vision left, was an unequivocal proof of his excellent *game*.

MENDOZA, in conquering so noble and distinguished a competitor, added considerable fame to his pugilistic achievements; but the greatest merit attached to the conquest was the *manner* in which it was obtained. Prejudice so frequently distorts the mind, that, unfortunately, good actions are passed over without even common respect; more especially when they appear in any person who may chance to be of a *different* COUNTRY, *persuasion*, or *colour*. MENDOZA, in being a Jew, did not stand in so favourable a point of view, respecting the wishes of the multitude towards his success, as his brave opponent—the feelings are somewhat raised when we read :—

> You may as well go stand upon the beach,
> And bid the main flood bate his usual height;
> You may as well use questions with the wolf,
> Why he hath made the ewe bleat for the lamb;
> You may as well forbid the mountain pines
> To wag their high tops, and to make no noise,
> When they are fretted with the gusts of heaven
> You may as well do any thing most hard,
> As seek to soften (than which what's harder)
> His Jewish heart!

But truth riseth superior to all things, and the humanity of MENDOZA was conspicuous throughout the above fight—often was it witnessed that he threw up his arm

when he might have put in a most tremendous blow upon
his exhausted adversary, who perceiving that the victory was certain, nobly disdained to hear it observed,

————————'Tis a cruelty
To load a falling man.

Both the combatants displayed severe marks of punishment:—*Humphries's* nose was much disfigured, and appeared as if cut with a sharp instrument: his right eye
was completely closed, and his forehead was dreadfully
lacerated over the left; he had also received some heavy
body blows; a few ugly touches were observed under his
left arm, and his upper lip was split; in fact, he was so
exhausted as to be carried by his friends to a carriage,
the more speedily to obtain medical assistance.   MEN-
DOZA, who gained strength by the exhilarating sounds
of victory, sported his figure upon the race ground for
a short time after the combat, but not without symptoms of uneasiness—his head was much bruised, and
his left eye and ear portrayed the vigour of his opponent's fist.   His ribs were also in a tender state.

Bill Warr was matched against MENDOZA, to fight at
Stoken Church, Oxfordshire, June 22, 1791, but notice
being given of an intended visit from the magistrates,
it was agreed by the friends of both parties that the contest should stand over till the ensuing September, and
be decided at Doncaster, when it was again put off till
May 14, 1792, for Smitham-bottom, near Croydon. The
road from London to the above place beggared all
description.   Pedestrians out of number, and vehicles
of every quality were seen in rapid motion, eager to
arrive at the destined spot.   Between one and two the
combatants appeared upon the stage, and were greeted

with shouts of applause: MENDOZA had for his second and bottle-holder, *Tom Johnson* and *Butcher*, and *Harvey Aston, Esq.* as his umpire: *Warr* was attended by *Joe Ward* and *Jackson*, and *Mr. Watson* as umpire.

At the commencement of the fight, the odds were considerably upon *Warr;* and much was expected from his well-known acquirements; and it is but fair to state that he endeavoured to prove the conqueror, and used every exertion he was master of to obtain so desirable an end. For the first eight rounds of the battle he was an object of attraction, and dealt out some tremendous blows; particularly in the fourteenth he gave MENDOZA a dreadful *hit* upon the jaw, that knocked him off his legs like a shuttlecock, and DAN came down with uncommon violence. *Warr's* friends were now in high spirits, and the betting went forwards, as it was thought that DAN had received rather a *sickener*, but his *game* soon brought him about, and he went in with the most determined resolution, and gave *Warr* a *knock-down* blow. The superiority of MENDOZA now became manifest; *Warr* perceived he was in the hands of his master, and the spectators began to change their opinions. MENDOZA *levelled* his antagonist every round, though, notwithstanding, *Warr* put in some good *hits.* In the twenty-third round the combatants closed— *Warr* was completely exhausted, and, upon MENDOZA falling on him, he reluctantly GAVE IN. The above contest established DAN'S fame, and his scientific excellence was generally acknowledged.

Bill Warr thought that in another trial he might regain his laurels, and accordingly a match was made, to take place in January, 1794, contiguous to Hounslow, but the magistrates interfering, it was postponed till the 12th of November following, when it was decided upon Bexley Common.   The *set-to* was good, and *Warr* seemed to feel that he should be able to accomplish his wish; and, as before, in the first rounds he was successful, and his opponent fell before him; whether MENDOZA permitted him to show himself off in the above manner, that he might be enabled to exhibit his great superiority afterwards, or that DAN could not resist the efforts of his antagonist, has not been ascertained; but it was evident that he treated all the attempts of *Warr* with the most perfect *sang-froid;* stopped the *hits* of his opponent with great neatness and ease, and returned such tremendous blows so instantaneously, that he was disposed of in the short space of *fifteen minutes!*   In the above contest, *Warr*, who had hitherto been looked upon as a hero, was rendered so insignificant by comparison, as to appear little better than a mere *tyro!*   MENDOZA's confidence completely overawed him; and it was visible that he laboured under its depressing effects throughout the fight.

   But MENDOZA, amid all his glory, was doomed to experience the vicissitudes of fortune by a mortifying defeat in his contest with *Jackson*, at Hornchurch, on April 15, 1795.   It preyed so much upon his feelings that seven years had nearly elapsed since the above battle, when they burst forth with considerable fury, occasioned by the following circumstance: *Jem Belcher* after beating *Burke*, at Hurley Bottom, challenged DAN to fight, who immediately replied, that he had given up pugilism, and supported, by his industry, as a publican, at the Lord Nelson, in Whitechapel, a wife and six children, and only wished to fight *Jackson,* who had dealt unhandsomely by him as a pugilist ; and he now publicly declared himself ready **to enter the** lists with him for one hundred guineas, provided that he would not take the unmanly and cowardly advantage of holding his hair. This oration of MENDOZA's was soon trumpeted abroad, and some busy persons inserted a sort of challenge to *Mr. Jackson* in the *Oracle, or, Daily Advertiser*, which was immediately answered by the latter, (supposing it appeared in the Newspaper under the direction of MENDOZA,) and which occasioned in return the following letter :—

MR. EDITOR,

It was with inexpressible concern that, in your paper of Wednesday last, I observed a letter, signed "John Jackson," purporting to be an answer to a supposed challenge from me, inserted in your detailed account of the recent pugilistic contest at Maidenhead. Mistake me not, Sir, I was not concerned at the contents of Mr. Jackson's elegant effusion, nor in the least affected or surprised at the opprobrious falsity, brazen impudence, or malignant calumny of his assertions, which I deny IN TOTO ; but felt particularly hurt at the idea that I was compelled either to sit down tamely under injury, or incur the risk of offending my best friends, and particularly the respectable magistrates of this division, by resuming a profession which, both from principle and conviction, I had wholly relinquished.

In order satisfactorily to refute Mr. Jackson's allegations, it is only necessary to observe, that a month after our battle at Hornchurch I waited on him, upbraided him with his unmanly conduct, by laying hold of my hair, and offered to fight him for two hundred guineas—Jackson proposed to fight for one hundred guineas ; and upon that sum being produced, declined fighting under five hundred guineas!! Here was courage! Here was consistency! Here was bottom! and yet Mr. Jackson is a man of honour, AND OF HIS WORD !!!

MR. EDITOR, after this I left London for five years, which may easily account to Mr. Jackson for the interval of silence. I have fought thirty-two pitched battles—four with *Humphries* (three of which I won) and two with *Will Warr*, in both of which I was victorious : these two men were both game, and good fighters, and, of course, having received so many blows, my only motive for wishing again to fight *Mr. Jackson* must be that spirit of honour and retaliation ever inherent in the breast of man.

MR. EDITOR, I again repeat, that I am delicately situated; that I wish to fight *Mr. Jackson*, and intend it ; but that, from a dread of injuring my family, by offending the magistrates as a challenger in a newspaper (which would be indecorous in a publican), I can only observe, that I should be very happy to see, as soon as possible, either *Mr. Jackson* or his friends, at my house, where they shall receive every attention from me, as I wish most earnestly to convince the world what a deep and just sense I entertain of all *Mr. Jackson's* favours conferred upon

DANIEL MENDOZA.

Admiral Nelson, Whitechapel.

P. S. Allow me to thank you for your liberal impartiality ; and, through the medium of your valuable paper, to return my acknowledgements to the public for the many flattering marks I have experienced of their partiality.

MENDOZA, in the year 1806, again introduced himself to the notice of the public, by the following

APOLOGY, in stating his reasons for appearing once more in the character of a pugilist:—

MR. EDITOR,

After my frequent resolution never again to appear before the public in the character of a fighter on the stage, and which resolution I have for years carefully and rigidly persevered in, it may perhaps be incumbent upon me to state to that public, whose partiality I have so often experienced, the cause of my acceptance of a challenge from a person by no means entitled to the smallest lenity.

Some weeks ago, I unfortunately visited *Harry Lee*, then in temporary lodgings under the roof of a Sheriff's Officer; he was then in DURANCE VILE on two actions; he told me a long and piteous tale about his hardships, and the injustice and cruelty of his creditors; he assured me, that if I would become one of his bail, he would then be enabled to obtain his liberty, and that he would take special care that I should not suffer, as he would settle, or discharge, both actions as soon as he got out of his present confinement.

Notwithstanding I am not now very apt to act the part of a fool on such an occasion, having already sustained at various times considerable losses by former acts of credulity, and consequently become wiser by dear-bought experience, I listened to his statements, and gave an implicit belief to all his declarations. It being found that my bail alone would not give legal satisfaction, I persuaded my brother, and another friend, to join the bail-bond, giving them, like gentlemen in a certain great house, a bill of indemnity. I was induced to go this length to serve him, because *Harry Lee* assured me that he had no persons to befriend him; that the officers would not take his word for a single copper; and that unless I stood up to *John Doe* and *Richard Roe*, through the medium of my two friends, he would be immediately committed to prison, whence, with detainers, &c. &c. it would be impossible for years, perhaps, for him to obtain a release. All the ceremonies which the law requires being gone through, *Harry Lee* marched out with all the honours usually attending such a war.

But mark, gentle readers! as soon as the said *Harry Lee* obtained his liberty, he refused to comply with his solemn engagements; he, indeed, settled one of the actions; but would neither surrender himself nor settle the other. The consequence was obvious; having indemnified my brother and friend, we were obliged to pay, and, with the exception of fourteen pounds, the whole sum as smart money, for having been duped by *Harry Lee*.

Now, *Mr. Editor*, I am of opinion that if a man cannot satisfy his creditors, he ought, in honour, to release his bail by the surrender of his person, which *Harry Lee* positively refused. He was, however, not contented with this abominable usage of me, but went up and down the town circulating calumnies and lies against me, and threatened to beat me as soon as he found an opportunity; in short, he gave me such a challenge that I could not, consistent with honour or propriety, refuse.

The black ingratitude of *Harry Lee* is now very conspicuous; after cheating, deceiving, and I may say robbing his friend in need, he now wants to give him a kicking into the bargain; but I have no doubt but that I shall stop his career, and put in a blow of just indignation and honourable resentment, against a man whose conduct is a disgrace to any rank of life. I am, much against my inclination, forced to the fight, not from any fear of *Harry Lee*, but from a sense of violating those rules and peaceable conduct in which I had resolved to pass the remainder of my life. He who has been successful in upwards of 30 pitched battles; he who has disputed the palm of victory with the first and ablest men of his time, cannot surely be apprehensive of danger, either to his person or reputation, from *Harry Lee!!* I know that " The race is not to the swift, nor the battle to the strong; but that time and chance happeneth

to all men;" barring however all unforeseen accidents, I am
fully persuaded that I shall make *Harry* sorely repent his
unprovoked insolence; but I shall not gain by the contest the
smallest sprig of laurel, because *Harry Lee* has none to lose.
I am sorry thus to occupy the time of the public; and am,

Mr. Editor,

DANIEL MENDOZA.

No. 5, *Webber-row, Blackfriars'-road.*

[We feel induced to insert the epistolary effusions
which transpired between these modern heroes of the
fist, in order not only to form a contrast to those
laconic specimens of more ancient days, but also to
show the great deference, manifested at all times, to
preserve a good character, and stand well in the
opinion of the public—*even* by Pugilists!]

MR. EDITOR,

I have to thank you for your candid and manly manner
in which you announced your intention to afford me an opportunity of confuting the charges brought against me by *Daniel
Mendoza.*

Among the extraordinary events that fate or folly produce,
I believe insanity itself never dreamt of an epistolary correspondence between *Daniel Mendoza* and *Harry Lee.* What
Devil could have provoked him to exhibit his wonderful stock
of honour, virtue, and benevolence in so public a manner, I
am at a loss to divine; but clear and certain I am, that all
the advantage he promised himself he has already enjoyed;
it is the curse of fools to be the heralds of their own disgrace;
for mark, Mr. Editor, how a plain undisguised story, delivered by a plain unlettered matter-of-fact man, shall set him
down.

Mr. *Mendoza* has thought proper to pester the public with a
long narrative of his extravagant acts of kindness towards me;
that he rescued me from the hands of a bailiff, the confines of
a prison, and other disastrous perils. However, not to retail all
the haberdashery of complaints he has thought proper to extend to an unreasonable length, I shall content myself with
briefly answering the essence of his charge against me, and, I
trust, I shall have credit for doing it with truth and candour,
without the aid of Mr. *Mendoza's* ingenuity.

It is true, I was arrested on two writs of ten pounds each;
a circumstance that has frequently happened to honester men
than either *Mendoza* or *Harry Lee*. It is also true, that I
called upon him to assist in procuring me my enlargement,
which, by the bye, was but a slender tribute to the gratitude
he owed me; he certainly procured me bail, upon my promise
of settling both actions. As Mr. *Mendoza* admits, I did pay
one; but I am very sorry, for his own sake, he did not keep a
little nearer truth, with respect to the state of the other, as that
might have relieved him from the reprobation that injustice,
fallacy, and ingratitude merits.

The second action, upon which I am accused of having
run from my bail, and left Mr. *Mendoza*, under all the piteous,
lamentable, and ruinous circumstances, to pay, stood exactly
thus, at the time of his letter:—the debt and costs came to sixteen pounds, the alternative was paying it or going to prison;
fourteen pounds I raised and paid, so that all *Mendoza* could
possibly be liable to, was the vast sum of two pounds, which I
have also paid. And here, Mr. Editor, you must give me leave
to declare, that I think no man living abhors the idea of de-
serting his bail, or deceiving his friend, more than I do. How
far I have done either, in the present case, I leave to the determination of any man, *Dan Mendoza* excepted. Admit it,
for a moment, Mr. Editor, that I had left Mr. *Mendoza* to pay
a few pounds for me, for what he terms fixing my security,

the offence, surely, could not be held in any very heinous light
by him, if he will have the goodness to call to his recollection
the situation in which he left all his friends who were security
for his integrity when he commenced Sheriff's Officer. And
now, Mr. Editor, I crave your attention to a few words more,
which, I trust, will quench the thirst of Mr. *Mendoza* for literary
fame, and exhibit him as a paragon of ingratitude. I make
great allowances for the passions of a man labouring to prove
himself more conscientiously honest than myself; but I cannot
help lamenting that he chose the subject of ingratitude for his
purpose; and the dæmon who whispered it in his ear was certainly unacquainted with the account current between him and
myself upon the article of gratitude, which, in fairness, ought
to have been stated. In fine, Sir, Mr. *Mendoza* has, upon
some very urgent occasions, been driven to the solitary friendship of *Harry Lee*, who afforded it him in the most ample
manner his capacity would permit. However, fortunately for
Mendoza, it was sufficient for all his purposes. Upon two several occasions have I solicited the pecuniary assistance of my
friends, in aid of what my own abilities could afford; and this,
too, for the purpose of extricating him from the most irksome
of all personal inconvenience, as well as to succour his almost
famished family. Believe me, Mr. Editor, it is painful to me
to upbraid a man with the services I have done him: nor
should any consideration whatever have induced me to reveal
them, had he not goaded and scourged me into the measure.
Perhaps *Mendoza* has forgot the letters in my possession, ex-
pressive of the great obligation I had conferred on him, and
which, I trust, will put both him and the Devil who instructed
him to turn author, to the blush, upon a perusal, whenever he
finds it convenient to give me an opportunity to publish them.

With respect to the language that may have passed between
us, I admit it may not have been the most chaste; but, considering all things, not very illy adapted to our professions and

habits of life. It is sufficient to say, that the public have learnt from *Mendoza's* statement, that it has brought about a challenge, which has been accepted, to determine the dispute by manual argument, and I will not envy the laurels he may gather on the occasion. I can only promise that I will do my utmost to prevent his tearing a single sprig from the brows of

Your most obedient humble Servant,

H. LEE.

Antigallican, Temple Bar.

As might be expected, a challenge was the result of the above correspondence; and the KNOWING ONES entertained an opinion, from a comparison between the combatants, that MENDOZA would win it all to nothing. *Harry Lee* was well known as an excellent sparrer, but had never publicly entered the lists as a boxer; and although extremely well-made, and having the advantage of height and length of arm over his antagonist, yet his not having the experience of MENDOZA, or his *game* put to the test, he was considered, in every point of view, inferior. On March 21, 1806, at Grimstead Green, a short distance beyond Bromley, in Kent, the combatants met, and fifty guineas were the stakes deposited. It was a roped ring of twenty-five feet—MENDOZA had for his second, *Bill Warr*, and his bottle-holder, *Bill Gibbons; Harry Lee* was attended by the *Game Chicken* and *Gulley*. The odds were three to one that DAN proved the conqueror:—

First round.—Mendoza looked at his opponent with great insignificance, and seemed to feel a more than usual degree of confidence upon this occasion. Lee, however, soon made it appear that he was no novice in the art, and protected himself with his left-arm extended, and endeavoured to put in some prod *hits;* but Mendoza stopped them, and brought Harry a wil. The odds rose ten to one on Dan, and the bets were decided respecting the first *knock-down* blow and drawing of blood.

Second.—Lee rose in a furious state, and the blood pouring down copiously—Mendoza made a *hit,* which was neatly returned by Lee upon Dan's nose; when they closed and fell.

Third.—Lee, out of temper, went in to *mill* away; but Mendoza *punished* him right and left for his temerity, when he fell.

Fourth.—Lee now convinced the spectators that he was something more than a *sparrer,* by showing *game,* and put in a good *hit* over the left eye of Mendoza; but, in closing, Dan threw him. The opinions of the amateurs began rather to change, as it appeared not quite so easy a thing as they hitherto imagined; and two to one was sported that Mendoza did not conquer Lee in half an hour.

Fifth.—Lee, not destitute of *pluck,* attempted to rally; but Mendoza, aware of his intentions, put in so severe a blow, that sent Harry under the ropes. Three to one against Lee.

Sixth.—Mendoza, experienced in all the manœuvres of the art, from the many heroes he had contended with for glory, and with all the coolness of the veteran, judging that his opponent would attempt another rally, waited for him with the greatest composure, and put in a tremendous *hit* over Harry's nose, and threw him.

Seventh.—Of no account whatever.

Eighth.—Lee, trusting to impetuosity more than judgment, went in rapidly to his opponent; but the folly of such conduct was self-evident—Mendoza *hit* him away with the greatest ease, following him, and, in the event, gave him a cross-buttock. Lee's *frontispiece* had now a variegated appearance, from the celerity of Dan's fist.

Ninth.—Lee, full of gaiety, rallied—but Mendoza hit him sharply over the left eye, which was already swelled terribly. Five to one on Mendoza.

Tenth.—Dan laughed at his opponent; who made a feeble hit, and fell upon his knees.

Eleventh.—It appeared from Lee's conduct, that he entertained an idea that his opponent was to be conquered by impetuosity, and rushed in most furiously upon Mendoza, when the latter *hit* him, and Harry retreated, and took return upon the ground.

Twelfth.—Mendoza thought it was necessary to show a little fight, and, in a sharp rally, soon *punished* his opponent out of the ring.

Thirteenth.—Rallying was the order of the day with Lee, when Dan put in a severe *hit*, and, to avoid going down, Harry caught hold of his opponent.

Fourteenth.—Mendoza struck his adversary, who, to the astonishment of the spectators, went and laid himself down, as before. Some hisses and disapprobation occurred—and cries of " foul—take him away !"

Fifteenth.—Trifling away time ; Lee went down without a *hit*, and Dan laughed at his pretensions. Six to one against Lee.

Sixteenth.—Mendoza, waiting for his opponent, *hit* him in the throat, which more than *tickled* him, and he fell from its effects, to all appearance extremely weak. The odds now were out of comparison—and a guinea to half a crown was offered.

Seventeenth.—Lee went to the ground upon the first blow.

Eighteenth.—Mere flourishing—they closed and fell.

Nineteenth.—Harry, quite gay, tried what effect another rally might produce : but Mendoza's sagacity rendered the attempt futile, and gave Lee a desperate blow upon the chin, which not only cut it severely, but sent him under the ropes.

Twentieth.—Mendoza laughing at the insufficiency of his opponent's attempts—who now appeared quite passionate—stopped Harry's blows with the greatest *sang froid;* when, in closing, they both went to the ground.

Twenty-first.—Dan gave Lee so severe a *hit* upon the body, that it instantly *levelled* his opponent. All betters, but no takers.

Twenty-second.—Mendoza, in offering to strike his opponent, Lee fell down—cries of " foul !"

Twenty-third.—Of no consequence--both closed and fell.

Twenty-fourth.—Lee, still fond of rallying, tried it on—but Mendoza *hit* him away easily, when Lee slipped down.

Twenty-fifth.—Mendoza, as if expecting Lee would rally again, was perfectly prepared for the attempt, and *punished* him right and left, when Harry went to the ground, and appeared much exhausted.

Twenty-sixth.—Dan, full of spirits and vigour, as soon as Lee stood up, gave him a *leveller.*

Twenty-seventh.—Lee, in making a *hit*, lost his distance, and fell.

Twenty-eighth.—This was a most singular round. Harry went in to his opponent, and by main force pulled him down by the arm.

Twenty-ninth.—A rally on both sides—Lee, not dismayed, put in several *hits*, when, in closing, Mendoza fell uppermost.

Thirtieth.—The *science* of Dan was truly conspicuous, he stopped every blow; but happened to slip, when Lee put in some *facers* as Mendoza was going down.

Thirty-first.—Of no note whatever.

Thirty-second.—Dan rather appeared fatigued, and, in making a blow, went down upon his knees.

Thirty-third.—Lee now endeavoured to show that his spirits were in good trim, and made the best use of his knowledge, which was by no means beneath mediocrity; but it was mere pretence to strength, his weakness was palpably visible. His face was much altered.

Thirty-fourth.—Both the combatants fought well; but the event was in Dan's favour.

Thirty-fifth.—Mendoza sent Lee under the ropes, from a well-directed blow.

Thirty-sixth.—Dan repeated the dose.

Thirty-seventh, thirty-eighth, and thirty-ninth.—In all these rounds the superiority of Mendoza was manifest:—Dan stopped and *hit* as he pleased.

Fortieth.—Mendoza *punished* Lee's ribs severely, and from the effects of the blows he fell.

Forty-first.—Lee was now getting in a very exhausted state, and fell from a mere touch that Dan gave him.

Forty-second.—Lee began to perceive that the chance was against him, and his exertions were on the decline—Mendoza did as he pleased, and closed the round by throwing him.

Fifty-third.—For the last ten rounds, Lee had not the smallest prospect of success; but still his *game* prompted him to continue the fight, in hopes that some lucky chance might offer; but having fell a second time without receiving a hit, Mendoza was declared the conqueror.

The amateurs were completely surprised at the protraction of the above fight, for one hour and ten minutes. It is certain that *Lee* was not equal to the task of encountering so experienced and finished a pugilist as MENDOZA; but it is equally true, that his conduct was entitled to honourable mention, and, considering it his *first appearance* in the ring, *Lee* acquitted himself rather in a superior manner. That he was not wanting either in courage or resolution, was evident; and his scientific efforts, in several instances, were entitled to much praise; and he completely eradicated the idea (which had gained so much ground) that he was nothing more than—*a sparrer!*

It has been a tolerably general expressed opinion that no pugilist whatever, since the days of *Broughton*, (or *even Broughton* himself,) has ever so completely elucidated or promulgated the principles of boxing as DANIEL MENDOZA; and, if his own public assertion proves the fact, which, we believe, has never been contradicted, we never heard of any boxer who could make use of any thing like the following declaration, wherein he says, " *he who has been* successful *in* upwards *of* THIRTY PITCHED BATTLES; he who has disputed with the first and ablest men of his time!" It may be equally admitted, that he has also given more lessons upon the art than any other professor in the kingdom. MENDOZA for several years relinquished the profession of pugilism for the occupation of a publican, to support a wife and eleven children. He is an intelligent and communicative man.

Engraved from the Original in the Possession of

SIR HENRY SMYTH, BART.

Published April 5, 1813, by George Smeeton 139, St Martins Lane.

T.L.Busby. Sculp.

JOHN JACKSON.

All fame is foreign, but of true desert,
Plays round the head, but comes not to the heart:
One *self-approving* HOUR whole years outweighs
Of stupid starers and of loud huzzas!

IT has been observed, by the inimitable STERNE, that "you may travel from Dan to Beersheba, and cry all is barren—and so it is!" and the *Critic* may, in his closet, with equal facility assert, there is not one *single feature* in the whole race of Pugilists attractive enough to save the practice of boxing from condemnation; which declaration, however fallacious, may be received as truth, if the MIND of the traveller, unfortunately, prove *barren*. and throughout a long journey he is only aroused from his apathy upon the appearance of a *finger post*, or in enumerating the *mile-stones* which he has passed.

ZIMMERMAN boasted the advantages that *solitude* afforded to become virtuous and improve the understanding over an intercourse with society; and of the absolute necessity of contemplating in silence (when abstracted from the circles of gaiety and dissipation) the *materials* which are so essential to form a good character: but that great Master of the Passions, soaring above those precise modes and symptoms which tend to infer that mankind can only be correct in *private*, has evinced, by his grand and instructive displays of human nature (which have so often elicited the tear from the most obdurate) in delineating the heart of man in all its extensive variety of feelings, could never have been obtained nor promulgated in solitude, nor that fine stamina acquired which pervades the works of the immortal SHAKSPEARE—(who, we are told, in the early part of his life was a deer-stealer, and even the gayest of the thoughtless). It was our immortal Bard's intercourse with men and manners, that enabled him to treasure up those powerful observations which have so eminently marked his irresistible portraits, containing the very essence of all that is beautiful and impressive, enriched with those exquisite touches of colouring that never fade, having for their basis — NATURE!

It has been the leading feature of BOXIANA to expose the sophisticated attempts of those writers who have endeavoured not only to traduce the Patrons of Pugilism, but to annihilate, if possible, the practice of the manly Art of Self-defence—one of the most noble, invigorating, and national traits in the English character. If it should appear that the *mind* is debased from witnessing such public displays ; if the *customs* and *manners* of society were infringed upon by such exhibitions; and if the feelings of men were so blunted from these specimens of hardihood and valour, as to prevent them from fulfilling those public situations in life, which many are called upon to perform, with fidelity, justice, and reputation—then would Pugilism be a disgrace to that country where it is permitted, and boxers rendered obnoxious to society !

However, in point of argument and fact, it has perhaps become necessary to inquire, how far, in patronising Pugilism, the effects of which manly art have operated upon those minds, so as to reduce their consequence in the estimation of their friends, or injure their public character with society in general, have taken place?

It is an incontrovertible fact, that one of the most celebrated and exalted civil characters in the nation, whose patriotic attention toward the preservation and due administration of the laws ; whose firmness in supporting, upon all occasions, the liberty of the subject ; whose dignity and consistency of conduct in representing the first city in the world in Parliament; also in fulfilling one of the most important official situations, the Lord Mayor of London; that, upon his retiring from that most arduous and honourable situation—(a situation rendered difficult and of imminent peril, from the badness of the times and scarcity of provisions,) which he filled with so much humanity toward the consideration of the people, and so perfectly constitutional in its practice, adding stability to the civil power, and reflecting lustre upon the protection of the laws—it is upon record, no individual ever received more public thanks.   His patriotic conduct was not only admired throughout England, but, on being presented to the First Consul, Buonaparte, at Paris, his fame had so far ran before him, that he was complimented by that celebrated character in the following words, " that while the *civil power* was strong enough, never to call in the aid of the military!"   It appears, then, that the name of HARVEY CHRISTIAN COOMBE never suffered the slightest tarnish from his patronage of the OLD EN-

GLISH *custom of* BOXING in the early part of his life,
but through a long and distinguished career portrayed
such fortitude of disposition, and proved his pretensions
so clear to the character of a real Englishman, an honest
citizen, and an independent senator, that, on October
12, 1812, Alderman COOMBE was placed at the head
of the poll, by the voices of 5125 independent livery-
men, creating a majority of 548 votes over the highest
ministerial candidate.   He was also returned a fourth
time as member for the City of London, for his past
services, and as a conspicuous and interesting ornament
to the nation.

If the opinion of that senator be of any weight,
whose speeches have been so often loudly cheered in the
House of Commons, whose enlightened mind, classical
acquirements, and transcendant talents have so delighted and refined the senses of his auditors by his
brilliant wit—his figurative imagination, and irresistible eloquence—a mind stored with researches from
ancient and modern literature, united with a conversant
practice of the character and knowledge of mankind,
in all its various gradations, from the *rusticity* of a
cudgelling bout at a country fair—the humours of a
bull bait—the *minutiæ* of a boxing match, down to the
finished elegance of ROYALTY—he has thus publicly
declared his sentiments :—

" A smart contest, this, between Maddox and Richmond !
Why are we to boast so much of the *native* valour of our
troops, as shewn at TALAVERA, at VIMEIRA, and at MAIDA,
yet to discourage all the practices and habits which tend to
keep alive the same sentiments and feelings ? The sentiments
that filled the minds of the three thousand spectators who
attended the two Pugilists, were just the same in kind as

those which inspired the higher combatants on the occasion before enumerated.—It is the circumstances only in which they are displayed that make the difference.

> " He that the world subdued, had been
> But the best wrestler on the green."

There is no sense in the answer always made to this, ' *Are no men brave but boxers ?*' Bravery is found in all habits, classes, circumstances, and conditions. But have habits and institutions of one sort no tendency to form it more than of another?—Longevity is found in persons of habits the most opposite; but are not certain habits more favourable to it than others? The courage does not arise from mere boxing, from the mere beating, or being beat : but from the sentiments excited by the contemplation and cultivation of such practices. Will it make no difference in the mass of people, whether their amusements are all of a pacific, pleasurable, and effeminate nature ; or whether they are of a sort that calls forth a continued admiration of prowess and hardihood ?"

Then, if such an enlightened senator as the late Right Hon. W. Windham felt no hesitation in promulgating the above sentiments respecting the utility of Pugilism as a *national trait*, there appears no necessity whatever, that any of its *professors* stand in need of an Apology !

> Strange is it, that our bloods,
> Whose colour, weight, and heat pour'd out together,
> Would quite confound distinction, yet stand off
> In difference mighty. But do not so—
> From lowest place, when virtuous things proceed,
> The place is dignified by the doer's deed.
> Where great addition swells, and virtue none,
> It is a dropsied honour ; good alone
> Is good, without a name; vileness is so :
> The property, by what it is, should go,

Not by the title.   Honours best thrive,
When rather from our acts we them derive
Than our foregoers : the *mere* word's a slave
Debauch'd on every tomb, on every grave;
A lying trophy, and as oft is dumb,
Where dust and damn'd oblivion is the tomb
Of honour'd bones indeed!

No task can prove more pleasing to the dictates of
the biographer, in his developement of characters, than
when the circumstances of the case perfectly permit
him, in unison with truth, "nothing to extenuate, or
set down aught in malice!" and whether called upon
to portray the splendid achievements of the hero, or
exhibit the unsophisticated traits of the pugilist, provided that society are gainers by the publicity of their
efforts, the end in view is obtained. *Sophistry* has done
so much to obscure and place in the back-ground a certain class of mankind; and *Calumny* assisting with all
her venom, to produce, if possible, complete oblivion;
that CANDOUR scarcely possesses fortitude enough to
resist the torrent, but is carried placidly along with the
stream. Yet, notwithstanding, *prejudice* too often may
deform, as well as panegyric too highly adorn the picture; but while the original daily appears before the
public eye, nothing can prove easier in ascertaining
the fidelity, or of impeaching the integrity of the artist.

Marrying a woman for her beauty, it has been said,
is like eating a bird for its singing; and complimenting
a man, *merely*, upon the symmetry of his form, would
prove equally as absurd and ridiculous. It is most
undoubtedly true, that JOHN JACKSON, in the early
part of his life, was fond of the gymnastic science, and,

in the hey-day of youth, made three public displays of the art, much to the satisfaction of the spectators, and acquired the reputation of a scientific pugilist.

In the pugilistic hemisphere, JACKSON has long been viewed as a fixed *star*, and the other bodies may be compared to so many satellites revolving round the greater orb, deriving their principal vigour and influence from his dominion. To Nature he is indebted for an uncommonly fine person; his symmetry of form is attractive in the extreme, and he is considered one of the best-made men in the kingdom, standing five feet eleven inches and a half in height, and weighing about fourteen stone; with limbs elegantly proportioned, and an arm for athletic beauty that defies competition: such an exterior cannot but prove prepossessing, and such an exterior has had its weight in that peculiar respect.

It appears that JACKSON has *lived* all his life; and, to use the expression of the poet, he has " *caught the manners living as they rise,*" and not content with having it observed alone, that he is one of the best-made men in the kingdom, but wisely endeavoured to unite with the above expression, that of being one of the best-behaved men also. In fact, JACKSON possesses a *mind* that penetrates farther than the surface, and being well assured, from his intercourse with polished society, that gentlemen, however fond of PUGILISM they may be, cannot discourse upon *fighting* every minute in the day, begin again the next, and so go on to the end of the chapter, has prevented any such chasm from appearing in his composition. The advantages of good company have therefore proved obvious to him, and by appreciating its consequences he has turned it to a proper account, in foreseeing that the recommendations of being a first-rate Pugilist were of too transitory a nature to rely upon those qualifications *alone;* and although the term *thorough-bred* may have its importance in the *ring,* (and so essentially necessary in matters of a sporting description,) yet there are two more little words requisite to render the man complete, and pass him current through the world, denominated— GOOD BREEDING. If his pedigree cannot be traced with all that accuracy which herald-painters require in delineating ancestry, few men, who are aware of the necessity of so important a feature in exalting their character, have exerted themselves more to obtain the possession of such an invaluable and pleasing trait, and in adopting those celebrated maxims, than Mr. JACKSON has done :—

> Give thy thoughts no tongue,
> Nor any unproportion'd thought his act;
> Be thou familiar, but by no means vulgar.
> The friends thou hast, and their adoption tried,
> Grapple them to thy soul with locks of steel;
> But do not dull thy palm with entertainment
> Of each new-hatch'd, unfledged comrade.   Beware
> Of entrance to a quarrel; but, being in,
> Bear't, that th' opposed may beware of thee.
> Give every man thine ear, but few thy voice;
> Take each man's censure, but reserve thy judgment.

JACKSON has been far from an inattentive observer of the above requisites, and acquired considerable proficiency in his manners and address. He has let no opportunity slip whereby he might obtain knowledge and improvement : and who, we are informed, was born in the Metropolis, (but whose progenitors were natives of

Worcestershire,) was reared to the occupation of a builder. JACKSON had only attained his *nineteenth* year, when he entered the lists with that formidable boxer *Fewterel.* At that period he was an entire stranger to the sporting world; and, if we are not misinformed, it was owing to the late unfortunate Colonel HARVEY ASTON (one of the most steady and firm patrons of pugilism) that he was induced to try his skill in a public pugilistic encounter; and from this introduction he was accordingly matched to fight *Fewterel.* The style and fortitude displayed by JACKSON in the above contest, proved of so attractive a nature, as to be a recommendation to the *Fancy* in general, and which has proved a lasting acquaintance with the higher patrons of the pugilistic art. However, in his *set-to* with *Fewterel,* his most sanguine friends entertained doubts of his success, owing to the disadvantages he had to contend against; but his *science* and intrepidity throughout the fight entitled him to general approbation and conquest.

JACKSON, from his care and attention, soon became the proprietor of a most respectable inn in Surrey; and in that situation he is remembered with respect, from a general line of conduct which always manifested itself, in a desire to serve and please those persons whom curiosity or business led to visit his house. Fortune has been propitious to his views, and he has not been unmindful of her favours. In himself, JACKSON has proved " ALL *is not barren!*" and that, however terrific and formidable the *pugilist* may appear in combat, yet the same individual may be tempered with those sensibilities which make man-

kind valuable and interesting.   The hitherto rude and
massy piece of stone, obscured by the dirt, when removed and polished by the hands of the sculptor,
ultimately becomes the finished and beautiful statue,
attracting the gaze and admiration of all who witness
so exquisite a production; and which, but for the
mind of the artist, who saw the figure in the stone, it
must have remained unmeaning and unnoticed.   Human nature, however harsh the term may appear,
without some degree of intellect, can only be viewed
as little better than a mere piece of clay—the *General*
would never acquire greatness—the *Poet*, sublimity—
the *Senator*, independence—the *Painter*, excellence—
the *Architect*, grandeur—the *Warrior*, bravery—or
the *Historian*, impartiality—if they merely passed
over objects as they first presented themselves, (either
fascinatingly elegant, or most horridly deformed,)
without the application of a lively and *appropriating*
MIND.

In relinquishing his pretensions to PUGILISM, and
giving up all the honours attending on conquest, it
is but common justice to observe, that JACKSON has
practically realised the character of a gentleman;
equally respected by the rich and poor; and ever
ready to perform a good action.   Were it necessary,
numerous instances might be quoted, in verifying the
excellence of his heart, and the sensibility of his disposition: and in him also the Pugilists experience a
steady and warm friend.

JACKSON is personally known to most of the first
characters in the kingdom; and the circles he now
moves in are of the greatest respectability, and whose

recommendations to whom have not occurred *merely* from the scientific acquirements of Pugilism, but upon pretensions which are of the most firm and durable nature: a pleasing address; an intelligent and communicative disposition; and which have rendered him in society a cheerful and agreeable companion. Mr. JACKSON possesses sufficient property to render him an independent character, and to support that station with stability. In offering advice to the Pugilists of the present day, it cannot be expressed in more concise or appropriate terms than " *Go thou and do likewise.*"

JACKSON fought with *Fewterel,* a Birmingham hero, whose fame ran before him, having proved victorious in near twenty battles. Great expectations were formed upon the contest, and numerous bets were depending upon its issue. The battle took place on June 9, 1788, at Smitham Bottom, near Croydon, in Surrey; *Fewterel* was attended by *Warr* and *Dunn;* and JACKSON had for his second *Tom Johnson,* and *Humphries* officiated as his bottle-holder. It was apprehended that JACKSON would never be able to knock *Fewterel* down, as the latter was a man of great bulk and uncommon strength; but this opinion was soon rendered fallacious, by JACKSON levelling him frequently, in the course of the fight. *Fewterel,* with all his powers, was perfectly incompetent to enter the lists with JACKSON, either in point of *science* or *bottom,* and had recourse to shifting, and falling down often without a blow; trying every manœuvre to win; and even infringing on the time allowed between each round. The contest lasted a few minutes above an hour; but *Fewterel* was considerably *punished* before he *gave in.* His Royal Highness the Prince of Wales was much pleased with the intrepidity displayed by JACKSON, and acknowledged it to the latter by a small present.

JACKSON next fought *George Ingleston* the Brewer, at Ingatestone, in Essex, on March 12, 1798—where he met with the unfortunate accident of dislocating his ankle, and breaking the small bone of his leg: but notwithstanding which circumstance his fortitude was truly conspicuous. See page 223.

The amateurs were much interested in the contest between JACKSON and *Mendoza*, for 200 guineas a-side, upon a twenty-four feet stage erected at Horn-church, in Essex, on April 15, 1795. *Mendoza* was seconded by *Harry Lee*, and *Symonds* officiated as bottle-holder; and JACKSON was attended by *Tom Johnson* and *Bill Wood*. Mr. Smith and Mr. James Nayler acted as umpires upon this occasion; and both the combatants were loudly cheered upon their appearance. The bets were in favour of *Mendoza*.

First round.—The spectators were more than commonly interested, from the celebrity of the combatants.—Judgment was not wanting on either side, and a fine display of the art was witnessed—the amateur experienced a rich treat in the development of the science in all its characteristic minutiæ —a minute had expired, and both waiting for the advantage, when *Jackson* put in a tremendous hit, that laid *Dan* prostrate on the stage.

Second.—In this round Mendoza showed the advantage of the *science* to perfection, by stopping the blows of his antagonist with great neatness, and in returning several good hits.

Third.—Both on the alert, and *pelting* away without ceremony—Jackson put in several severe *hits*, and Mendoza was not behind in returning the compliment; but in the termination of the round Dan went down. Notwithstanding, the odds rose two to one on Mendoza.

Fourth.—This was the heat of the battle—fear was out of the question, and the combatants lost to every thing but victory. Jackson, confident of his powers and knowledge, went in with great courage, treating the *science* of Mendoza with indifference, and *punishing* him most terribly, when Dan fell from a severe blow on the right eye, which bled profusely. The odds rose upon Jackson.

Fifth.—The scene was now considerably changed, and some murmurings were expressed by the friends of Mendoza, on witnessing Jackson take hold of his opponent by the hair, and *serving him out* in that defenceless state till he fell to the ground. An appeal was made to the umpires upon the propriety of the action, when it was deemed perfectly consistent with the rules of fighting, and the battle proceeded. The odds were now changed two to one on Jackson.

Sixth to Eighth.—Mendoza was getting rather exhausted, and endeavoured to recover his strength by acting on the defensive ; but he could make no way against the superiority of Jackson.

Ninth and last.—Mendoza stood no chance—Jackson appeared in full vigour, and *hit* away his man with great ease. Dan suffered considerably. and after falling completely exhausted, acknowledged he had done.

The above contest, for the time it continued, *(ten minutes and a half,)* was never exceeded in point of severity; but JACKSON was little the worse for it, and jumped from the stage with great activity. It *was* quite otherwise with *Mendoza,* who was very much beaten. Numerous indeed were the patrons of pugilism present upon this occasion, among whom were the Duke of Hamilton, and several other noblemen and gentlem n amateurs.

A paragraph, near seven years after the above combat, appearing in some of the newspapers, purporting that a fight would take place between *Mendoza* and JACKSON; the latter, by way of a FAREWELL EPILOGUE to the public, informing them of his determination, inserted the following letter in the *Oracle*, or *Daily Advertiser*, on Wednesday, Dec. 1, 1801.

TO THE EDITOR.

Sir,

I was somewhat astonished, on my return to town on Saturday, to learn that a challenge was inserted in your paper on Thursday last, as if from Mr. Mendoza. Should I be right in my conclusion, by believing that it comes from that celebrated pugilist, I beg you will inform the public, through the medium of your paper, that for some years I have entirely withdrawn from a public life, and am more and more convinced of the propriety of my conduct, by the happiness which I enjoy in private, among many friends of great respectability, with whom it is my pride to be received on terms of familiarity and friendship : goaded, however, as I am to a petty conflict, I hope that it will not be considered as too much arrogance on my part, simply to observe, that, after waiting for more than three years to accept the challenge of any pugilist, however dexterous in the science, and however highly flattered by his friends, I think it rather extraordinary that Mr. Mendoza should add a silence of four years to those three, it being nearly seven years since I had the satisfaction of chastising him for his insolence ; but Mr. Mendoza derived one great good from the issue of that contest —he was taught to be less hasty in forming his resolutions, more slow in carrying them into effect.

This cautious and wise principle of action deserves much commendation ; and having served an apprenticeship of seven years to learn a certain portion of artificial courage, he now comes forward with a stock of impudence (the only capital which during that time he seems to have acquired) to force me to appear once more in that situation which I have for years cheerfully avoided.

Reluctant, however, as I am, to attract again, even for a moment, the public attention, I shall have no objection to vindicate my character, by a meeting with Mr. Mendoza, when and where he pleases, PROVIDED he'll promise to fight, and provided he'll also promise not to give previous information to the magistrates of Bow-street, or elsewhere.

Flattering myself that your readers and the public will pardon this intrusion on their more precious time,

I am, Sir,

Yours and theirs, most respectfully,

Nov. 20, 1801.   JOHN JACKSON.

Notwithstanding the appearance of the above letter, it produced no battle, neither has JACKSON been engaged in any contest whatever for upwards of twenty-six years. It has been observed of him, in reference to other men, that few pugilists have appeared but what have been distinguished for some peculiar trait of excellence appertaining to the art of self-defence; some for superior *strength;* others for intuitive *science;* and many for extraordinary *bottom;* but JACKSON has the whole of them united in one person. His agility is truly astonishing, and there are few men, if any, that can jump farther than he can; in point of strength, he is equally gifted. A cast has been taken from the arm of JACKSON, on account of its fine proportion and anatomical beauty, and of its athletic and muscular appearance, only twenty copies of which have been distributed among his most particular friends.

We cannot pass over the following patriotic trait displayed by JACKSON in the year 1811, in procuring a benefit at the Fives' Court, in St. Martin's Street, towards aiding the public subscription tending to alleviate the sufferings of the Portuguese, whose towns had been destroyed by the French. This benefit produced the sum of *one hundred and fourteen pounds*, and was paid to the committee for conducting the same.

In thus paying attention to the wants of our suffering allies, JACKSON's humanity would not let him prove unmindful towards his unfortunate countrymen, the *British Prisoners in France.* In consequence of which, another benefit was produced in the beginning of the year 1812, when the respectable sum of *one hundred and thirty-two pounds, six shillings*, was the receipt thereof, which was immediately applied in aid of that laudable purpose. To the credit of all the pugilists be it remembered, that, on the first intimation of such a plan, they all cheerfully volunteered their services by seconding the efforts of so disinterested a proposition.

In taking our leave of the above person, we have only to observe, that BOXIANA would not have done his duty to the public in omitting the pretensions of JACKSON to pugilism, notwithstanding his long retirement from the scene of action; and, whether as a pugilist, or in any of the capacities he has filled, we feel no impropriety in concluding, that,

> Take him for all in all,
> We shall not look upon his like again.

TOM TRING.

Out, out, brief candle!
Life's but a walking shadow—a poor player,
That struts and frets his hour upon the stage,
And then is heard no more!

SUCH is the influence of Time! Notwithstanding the above pugilistic hero has occupied the pencils of some of our first-rate English artists; and also, at one time, challenged all England, (excepting his most intimate friend, the late *Tom Johnson,*) for *one thousand guineas,* he is, at the present period, almost totally forgotten!

No boxer, it appears, possessed such attractions to publicity as TOM TRING. As a pugilist, his qualities were of a most tremendous nature, and few men appeared who were capable of resisting his mighty prowess. His figure was of an Herculean stamp, which rendered him conspicuous; and, in being clad with the rich paraphernalia of ROYALTY, (of which he was one of its *striking* appendages,) TOM obtained considerable notoriety.

TRING is a native of Leighton-Buzzard, Bedfordshire; his prize-fights were but few, but his *skirmishes* numerous indeed. His first *set-to* in London was with one *Tom Pratt,* in Baker's Fields, Bayswater, in 1787. *Pratt* was a very formidable man, being upwards of six feet in height, and stout in proportion; but TRING felt so confident in his own powers, that he fought him a guinea against five shillings. TRING proved perfectly correct in his idea, and dealt out such tremendous

VOL. I.   2 T *punishment* in the course of five minutes, that *Pratt* made the best use of his heels, and left TOM in possession of the ring!

Some difference of opinion having taken place between TRING and one *Harry Norfolk*, a bricklayer, a regular *set-to* immediately commenced in the streets. *Norfolk* was a thorough *game* man, full of activity, and not destitute of *science;* and, in an accidental *turn-up*, was an *ugly customer.* Such a *street*-fight had not been witnessed for many years. Notwithstanding the ponderous blows of TRING, *Norfolk* never flinched from his adversary, but returned *hit* for *hit* with uncommon severity; and possessed such an *appetite*, that it was nearly an hour before he was *satisfied!* TRING felt the effects so severely of his opponent's fist, that he wore one of his arms in a sling for a considerable time afterwards.

But the most desperate conflict in which TRING was engaged, was with *Big Ben*, at Dartford, for ten guineas a-side. TRING had for his second *Joe Ward*, and *Sibley* for his bottle-holder; and *Ben* was attended by *Martin*, the Bath Butcher, and *Fry*. No *flinching* was observed in this contest, and a more determined battle was never witnessed. *Ben*, always a hero, displayed courage of the finest quality; and the fortitude of TRING was equally attractive. The blows that passed between them were tremendous in the extreme; and they alternately *hit* each other away with the most remarkable facility. Both the combatants exhibited dreadful marks of *punishment;* and the contest was for a considerable time doubtful—*Ben* was nearly blind; and it was not till TRING had completely lost all vision that he *gave it in.* Two such hard *hitters* were scarcely ever matched, and, during the nineteen minutes which the battle continued, the *punishment* might be said to be reciprocal.

As a pugilist, if TRING did not possess the scientific minutiæ of a *Mendoza*, his *game* was of the richest quality, and he was not without some pretensions to a knowledge of the art. TOM was one of the hardest *hitters* of his time; and *Big Ben*, whose judgment in those matters could not be impeached, not only refused to enter the lists a second time with TRING, when he was challenged, but declared, before his death, that his constitution had suffered most materially from the severe blows which he had encountered at Dartford.

In the early part of his life, TRING was, in the opinion of some of the most distinguished artists, the finest made man in the kingdom. In height, six feet one inch, and weighing fifteen stone; his symmetry of form was considered so completely athletic, and so much admired, that he was selected as a peculiarly fine subject to stand for a painting of HERCULES, which was afterwards publicly exhibited at the ROYAL ACADEMY:

> Dignity and grace
> Adorn his frame, and manly beauty join'd
> With strength Herculean.

Nor was the figure of TRING confined to the picture of *Hercules*, as he stood several times, in various attitudes, at the above Academy, to exhibit the beauties of the human frame, for the instruction of the numerous students, and improvement of the professors. Among the works of the late President, Sir *Joshua Reynolds*, *Hopner*, *Beechey*, &c. the athletic form of TRING may be traced. A fine bust was also taken of him, by a celebrated artist.

TRING lived in the capacity of Chairman to his

Royal Highness the Prince of Wales, for fifteen years; and we understand, that had he not been expressly prohibited, his pugilistic encounters, in all probability, would have been more numerous.

He was a civil, well-behaved man, but unfortunately reduced, in the decline of life, to procure a livelihood from the casual employment of carrying heavy loads, in the capacity of a street-porter:

> When men once reach their Autumn, sickly joys
> Fall off apace, as yellow leaves from trees,
> At ev'ry little breath misfortune blows;
> Till, left quite naked of their happiness,
> In the chill blasts of winter they expire.
> This is the common lot.

Tring died in 1815.

FEMALE PUGILISM.

To show the *nationality* of boxing, and that it is not merely confined to *heroes*, we have extracted the following copy of an advertisement, which appeared in a diurnal print, in June, 1722, upwards of *ninety-nine years* since, when even heroines panted for the honours of pugilistic glory!

CHALLENGE.

I, Elizabeth Wilkinson, of Clerkenwell, having had some words with Hannah Hyfield, and requiring satisfaction, do invite her to meet me upon the stage, and box me for three guineas; each woman holding half-a-crown in each hand, and the first woman that drops the money to lose the battle.

ANSWER.

I, Hannah Hyfield, of Newgate Market, hearing of the resoluteness of Elizabeth Wilkinson, will not fail, *God willing*, to give her more blows than words—desiring home blows, and from her, no favour: she may expect a good thumping!

CALEB BALDWIN.

WILLIAM WOOD.

Publish'd Oct.21.1812. by G.Smeeton. 139.St.Martin's L.x

CALEB BALDWIN

(The Veteran CHAMPION of WESTMINSTER.)

Of Caleb's deeds I'll now relate,
A fighting hero of the state—
Whose pugilistic feats I sing,
And great achievements in the *ring :*
Of FORTITUDE that never shrink'd,
Of many *mill'd*, and numbers *pink'd ;*
CUSTOMERS *served*, both right and left:
And GLUTTONS *fed*, till they have *wept !*
A child of Nature—full of *game*—
Entitled to the smiles of Fame ;
Of BALDWIN's prowess then be brief—
And chaunt the battles of this CHIEF !

IT has been remarked by the incomparable Goldsmith, *that* ONE HALF *of the world are ignorant how the other* HALF *live !* and, perhaps, the observation may not be a great way off the truth in stating that the *unacquainted* HALF never think it worth their while *to inquire.* In fact, the times are so accommodating in which we live, and so many opinions are offered to us, ready *cut* and *dried* for our acceptance, that we have scarcely time to peruse one-third of those crudities, much more to *think* upon, or digest, any of them !

It has been emphatically asserted by a great political writer, Mr. Cobbett, that the study of the learned or dead languages is unnecessary; and although that classic *sprig* of literature, Leigh Hunt, has, with the *flourish* of his pen, completely condemned the manly and national practice of Boxing, as debasing the finer feelings of our composition, and tending to degrade

the character of Englishmen to that of mere brutes;
yet, they are not decidedly facts, because thus boldly asserted by those public caterers. Admitting that the
strong *genius* and *industry* of the one have so far carried
him through all his difficulties, and placed him upon a
towering eminence, without the *finish* of a University,
his argument gains no strength whatever by the solitary
instance of *his* extraordinary success : and, granting
that the *classical acquirements* of the other have raised
him to an unexpected importance in promulgating sentiments tolerably approved of, it by no means decides
that Pugilism is a barbarous trait, because it does not
accord with his *imperative* notions ! Nor is the old intuitive English spirit of Boxing to be suppressed, or the nation suffered to become effeminate, because the *refined*
pages of a newspaper (the *Examiner*) are not to be sullied
with the details of a pugilistic contest—public opinion
is not yet so completely shackled as to take for *data* all
their productions; but, although we differ in opinion
from those champions of the press, we do not detract
from their merits, and feel strongly impressed that the
world is much indebted to their united exertions.

LEARNING will always ensure respect, and GENIUS
claim admiration; but we are well convinced, agreeing
with the doctrine of the great Bacon, that books *alone*
will not inform us of the true state of things, without an
intercourse with that book of books, REAL LIFE; from
which we are taught to appreciate and become acquainted with ourselves.   It becomes, then, our duty to observe well the passing scene, and not let it slip away
without some remembrance of its importance; and it is
not because we may have had the good fortune to acquire

a slight acquaintance with Greek, a smattering of Latin, or picked up a few phrases of French, that we are to look down upon the rest of mankind with contempt who have not had the same opportunities of *exercising* their MINDS. Whether in our mixture with society we come in contact with the *erudite* index of a Horne Tooke, or the rough *nob* of CALEB BALDWIN, the observer will not lose any thing, if it should not prove too much trouble to make a comparison; he will find, in the course of his investigation, that, in the one, to what a pitch of excellence human nature can arrive at by study; and he will also experience in the other that even the wild flowers of Nature possess a certain indescribable something, which will arrest the traveller's attention so as not to pass them by with indifference :—

> Know NATURE's children shall divide her care,
> The fur that warms a Monarch warm'd a Bear.

Paddington boasts its HERO, and *Westminster* her CHAMPION ; and it is rather a *knotty* point to decide which of those brave pugilists has fought the most battles.

CALEB STEPHEN RAMSBOTTOM (otherwise BALDWIN) was born in Westminster, on the 22d of April, 1769, and is in height five feet six inches and a half, weighing nine stone eleven pounds; though in his regular battles he never weighed so much by four pounds.

The renowned CALEB has been considered one of the best *bits of stuff* in the kingdom ; and, we believe, we are tolerably correct in asserting, that, notwithstanding his numerous contests, he has proved the conqueror in all of them, excepting one *solitary* instance; and even in *that* we shall endeavour to prove, in its proper place, he was entitled to victory.

Whether George Colman, the Dramatist, had CA-LEB in his eye when he penned the following lines, we cannot ascertain :—

> Yet some affirm no enemies they are,
> But meet just like prize-fighters in a fair ;
> Who first shake hands before they box,
> Then give each other mighty knocks,
> With all the loving kindness of a brother !

We are well assured, that he has *peeled* oftener than any other pugilist whatever, although possessing a disposition far from irritable, and not following pugilism as a profession. It would require a small volume to detail his heroic achievements, and the various CUSTOMERS he has *disposed of*—the numerous GILLS he has *punished*—the LUSTY COVES he has *milled*—the RUFFIANS he has *doubled up*—the SAUCY SWELLS he has *pinked*—the BOUNCES that he has *hit-away*—and the FIGHTING MEN whom he has *conquered!* We shall endeavour to give the most prominent of his encounters.

CALEB's first *set-to* was about the year 1786, when a mere stripling, with one *Gregory*, on his native soil, Tothill Fields, for half-a-guinea; and, from the early specimens of the *science* exhibited by CALEB in *punishing* and conquering *Gregory*, who was every way his superior in point of manly proportion, CALEB was considered as a promising pugilist.

CALEB had a sharp battle with *Jem Jones*, a sweep, upon Wimbledon Common, for a guinea a-side; but it appeared that the *Sweep* would have been more profitably employed, had he have continued follow

ing his occupation in crying, " SWEEP, SOOT, HO !''
than in encountering the potent fists of CALEB, to
whom he *surrendered*

The veteran *Tom Johnson*, valuing the qualities of
CALEB, backed him for ten guineas against *Arthur
Smith*, a gipsey. This contest was decided near the
Plough, Kelsey Green. It was a good battle; but the
Gipsey had not only to return to his tribe with severe
marks of *punishment*, but was also defeated.

Jerry Matthews, a pugilist of some note, and who
had acquired considerable fame in contending against
Mendoza for two hours, challenged CALEB for ten
guineas. This contest was decided in Hyde Park.
Poor *Jerry* was completely distanced and confounded;
CALEB *punished* him so severely in the course of fifteen
minutes, that *Jerry*, quite *panic-struck, bolted* out of
the ring with all convenient speed, to the no small
astonishment of the spectators, who expected quite a
different termination.

CALEB fought a glass-blower, of the name of *Bill
Burke*, on Beekley Heath, for ten guineas. It was a
well-contested battle; but, in the event, the *Glass-
blower* lost his wind, and acknowledged the superiority
of CALEB's *bellows*.

A most desperate *turn-up* took place in Peter-street,
Westminster, between one *Wadhams*, a grenadier, (six
feet high, well proportioned, plenty of *pluck*, and
gifted with prodigious strength,) and CALEB BALD-
WIN. The *Grenadier* charged upon his enemy with
uncommon fury, and it required no small fortitude to
withstand the impetuosity of the shock; but CALEB,
never afraid, notwithstanding the great difference of

size and weight between him and his opponent, relied upon his judgment to get rid of this *glutton*. The *science* of CALEB at length prevailed, and he so *punished* the *nob* of the *Grenadier*, that he could not put on his cap; but the soldier was so determined upon beating his opponent, that he did not cry out ENOUGH, till he was totally blind.

CALEB entered the lists with *Bob Packer*, on Hounslow Heath, for twenty guineas. This was a well-contested battle throughout; and it was not till after forty-five minutes had elapsed of most severe fighting that *Packer* gave in.

A *Coal-whipper*, weighing fourteen stone, in Pyestreet, Westminster, threatened, upon a trifling difference of opinion, to give CALEB a *hiding;* but the CHAMPION of that quarter was not thus to be frightened out of his title. CALEB's *bottom* was of too staunch a quality to put up with an affront pusillanimously, and he, without further hesitation, *peeled*, when a regular *set-to* commenced. It required all the *game* CALEB was master of, as well as *science*, to contend against the *Coal-whipper*, who displayed great courage and *gluttony*. The latter endeavoured to dispose of BALDWIN by sheer strength, and contended for *an hour*, although *punished* dreadfully, and hurt from severe falls. It was one of the most desperate street-fights ever witnessed: and had it not have been for the superior *science* manifested by CALEB, he must ave been crushed, from the ponderous efforts of his opponent.

One *Jones* and BALDWIN had a *turn-up* also in Pyestreet, which continued for three quarters of an hour.

The combatants were nearly upon an equality, *Jones* being five feet eight inches, not destitute of *bottom*, and with pretensions to the pugilistic art. It was a good fight, and some alternate turns of success were experienced; but the superiority of CALEB, for the last ten minutes, was evident, and *Jones* was *satisfied* that he was conquered.

On December 22, 1800, one *Keiiy*, an Irishman, fought CALEB, at Wimbledon, for twenty guineas a-side. The battle was decided in a quarter of an hour; during which short time, twelve rounds were most sharply contested, and CALEB showed himself off in a superior style, by *punishing* his opponent severely.

Upon the same stage on which *Belcher* and *Berks* fought, at Hurley-bottom, on November 25, 1801, CALEB fought *Lee,* a butcher. The battle lasted for nearly half an hour, and was well contested by both the combatants—*skill* nor *bottom* was not wanting on either side; and it was not till about the seventeenth round that it was decidedly in favour of BALDWIN, who proved the conqueror.

O'Donnel, a pugilist of considerable repute, was matched against CALEB, for a purse of fifty pounds, and which was decided upon Wimbledon Common, October 21, 1803. The odds were considerably in favour of BALDWIN.

First round.—Upon stripping, it was thought by some of the best informed of the *Fancy,* that, notwithstanding O'Donnel had proved successful in severe battles, yet he appeared somewhat impressed with the superiority of his opponent's acquirements; however, after some little sparring, he put in the first *hit;* which was sharply returned by Caleb, and who, in closing shortly afterwards, threw O'Donnel.

Second.—The shyness of O'Donnel was immediately visible,

and Caleb, who is always *awake* to what is going on in these matters, endeavoured to convince O'Donnel that his fears were too well grounded, by sticking to him very close, and putting in some severe blows; but O'Donnel, from his knowledge of the *science*, warded off most of their serious effects: excepting a severe body-blow, which *levelled* him.

Third.—O'Donnel was up to his time; but he was in no condition to face his opponent; and Caleb, like a skilful general, endeavoured to improve upon so favourable an opportunity of making his conquest sure, and *punished* O'Donnel most severely, who could not get away from Caleb. In closing, O'Donnel went down. Four to one on Baldwin.

Fourth.—O'Donnel, rather recovered, began to exhibit a little gaiety, and his friends entertained hopes of a successful change, by the manly manner in which he contested this round. Caleb received several severe blows from him, one of which cut his right-eye, and, at the termination of the round, was thrown for the first time.

Fifth.—O'Donnel had the worst side, from the strong effects of the sun upon his face, and, with a deal of ingenuity, tried to manœuvre the Veteran out of his position; but Caleb was too good a judge. Several hard blows were exchanged, and one of them *levelled* Baldwin. The *Paddies* were now all in high spirits, and they flattered themselves their Champion would once more come through the piece, and began to bet a little.

Sixth.—O'Donnel now felt somewhat more confident, and went in to his man full of gaiety; but Caleb welcomed him with some prime salutes—O'Donnel, notwithstanding, put in such a tremendous *hit*, that made Caleb reel again; but who, on recovering the shock, with more temerity than judgment, dashed in, and knocked down O'Donnel.

Seventh.—O'Donnel, full of *pluck*, displayed some excellent *science;* and Caleb was not behindhand in showing his experience and abilities; and O'Donnel had so far gained upon his friends, that the betting was nearly even. Caleb, on the lookout, perceived an opening, and put in a tremendous *hit* upon the kidneys of his opponent, that made him grin " a horrid ghastly smile!" and seemed nearly to deprive him of his faculties, and, in closing, Caleb threw O'Donnel with great ease.

Eighth and last.—O'Donnel came to his time; but evidently under symptoms of great pain, and could scarcely stand upright; while, on the contrary, Caleb, full of gaiety, showed off his powers in good style, and *punished* his opponent almost as he pleased; and, by way of a *finisher* to the contest, gave O'Donnel a severe cross-buttock; who immediately *gave in!*

In the above contest, CALEB distinguished himself considerably; and in conquering O'Donnel raised his character as a pugilist.

CALEB now entered the lists with *Dutch Sam*, at Woodford Green, near Hornsey, on August 7, 1804. It was a battle that had long excited considerable attention in the sporting world, from the great celebrity of the combatants. CALEB had for his second the veteran *George Maddox*, and *Paddington Jones* for his bottle-holder; and *Dutch Sam* was attended by *Bill Wood* and *Puss*. Upon stripping, the odds were in favour of CALEB BALDWIN.

First round.—The spectators were extremely anxious to witness on which side the first advantage appeared—great expectations were placed upon Caleb, whose experience, well-known *bottom*, and scientific accomplishments rendered him a finished pugilist; and Dutch Sam was an object of considerable attraction among the *Fancy* in general; after some displays of the art, Sam made a *hit*, which did not tell; but Caleb, eager for the fray, returned the compliment extremely sharp, and put in a desperate facer, that *levelled* his opponent. Three to one in favour of Caleb.

Second.—Sam felt impressed that he had a *trump* to deal against, and appeared rather shy of Caleb: when the latter, full of spunk, and knowing there was no time to lose, when a favourable opportunity offered, *punished* away both right and left, treating Sam with a *prime taste* of his *milling* qualities, that *levelled* him once more with his mother earth.

Third.—Sam displayed a little more confidence, and put in some *hits;* but the superiority of CALEB was now manifest, who dealt out *punishment* so severely upon his opponent's frame, that, upon the termination of this round, Sam positively declared to his second, he was beaten, and must GIVE IN: *but* Bill Wood *smothered the sound, and brought him forward again to face his man!*

The fourth, fifth, and sixth rounds were all in favour of

Caleb, and Sam was so perfectly convinced in his own mind it was against him, that he declared once more to his second he could fight no longer; when Bill Wood *clapped a hand-kerchief upon his mouth, and would not let him speak, and assisted by* Puss, *they again brought him up to renew the contest!* which was continued with uncommon severity and both bleeding profusely, till the

Ninth.—When, after the exchange of some good blows, Caleb put in a tremendous *hit* on Sam's temple, that brought him down instantly: and Sam appeared considerably depressed from its effects, and till the

Thirteenth.—The superiority of Caleb was manifest to all the spectators; and with the experience of a veteran pugilist, endeavoured to improve every favourable turn that presented itself. Caleb displayed good science, and Sam considerable talent; and the judgment and bottom exhibited on both sides were of the first quality—stopping dexterously, and returning sharply were often discernible in both the combatants, till the

Twentieth.—When Caleb for the first time began to show some slight symptoms of fatigue; and Sam seemed rather to be gaining ground, till the

Twenty-third.—When the Champion of Westminster was considered something on the decline, and although he put in several blows, they were not of any serious effect; while, on the contrary, Sam appeared to increase in gaiety, and dealt out his hard blows with considerable success, till the

Twenty-sixth.—When the decision of the battle was nearly left to the effect of chance, as both the combatants were so completely exhausted *as not to be able to stand up at the appointed time*—and in this precarious state of things, if any proper criterion could have been established to form a judgment, which was the most likely of the two to prove the conqueror, it was Sam, whose exterior did not appear quite so much disfigured as his opponent; and it ought not to be passed over here without honourable mention, that Sam's conduct was highly praiseworthy, and his humanity conspicuous, in nobly disdaining to *hit* his brave adversary, who was already stunned from a severe blow of his left hand, and nearly in the act of falling, when Sam, instead of following up the advantage with his right, with a manly feeling made no use of it.

Thirty-seventh.—For the last ten rounds, Caleb was much distressed, and that true *game* which had been so much distinguished in all his other battles, here, if possible, showed itself greater than ever. From his exhausted state, the blows of Caleb, although well meant, lost their effect. And it was with the greatest reluctance that his brave heart acknowledged that he was conquered, who had so long, and so often been *accustomed to the shouts of victory.*

Sam, in proving the victor, had not much to boast of; and who was so severely *punished,* that he could not have lasted much longer : and so strongly was he impressed with the valour and hardihood of CALEB, (who was by no means in good condition, from bad health, at the time he fought,) that, upon being matched to fight in the ensuing September, at the particular challenge of BALDWIN, for twenty guineas, *Sam* forfeited his deposit and declined.

CALEB entered the lists with BILL RYAN, on Blackheath, August 6, 1805. This contest had been a long time in agitation, and a good fight expected. *Ryan* was the son of the celebrated pugilist of that name, and who had acquired considerable reputation as a good boxer, and the amateurs in general flattered themselves with a grand display of the *science.* CALEB had for his second the *Game Chicken;* and *Paddington Jones* performed that office for *Ryan.* The odds were rather in favour of CALEB.

First round.—Considerable *science* was displayed between the combatants, and every manœuvre was tried for the first advantage, when Caleb put in right and left, and closing, they both fell.

Second.—Caleb, full of spirit, put in a good blow, and during the act of closing, Ryan gave his opponent a severe facer, when they both went down.

Third.—Caleb showed himself well versed in the art, and put in some severe body blows with considerable neatness ; when Ryan, quite impetuous, rushed in and threw his opponent.

Fourth.—Caleb, full of gaiety, and taking the advantage of an opening. gave his adversary a severe blow over the eye, which soon puffed it up, and put it into *mourning*—some good blows were exchanged between the combatants, but Caleb took the lead, and finished the round in style, by making Ryan perform a somerset against his will.

Fifth.—Pelting away on both sides, and firmness was the order of the day; but Caleb was the most prominent in the scene; and in closing, fell uppermost.

Tenth.—During the last four rounds, Caleb was the hero of the tale, and it was difficult which to admire the most, the *science* he displayed, or the courage he exhibited; and proved himself perfectly entitled to the term of a thorough-bred boxer.

Eleventh.—Caleb went in with great celerity, and treated the spectators with another pantomimical touch, by making his opponent display another somerset.

Twelfth.—Reflection manifested on both sides, and some good sparring witnessed: Ryan having felt the severe effects of Caleb's powers, appeared rather shy, which Caleb observing, as if to increase his terrors, put in a dreadful *hit* upon his *nob* that *levelled* him in a twinkling.

Thirteenth.—Caleb, elated with his success, repeated the blow with increased advantage, and Ryan fell from its great severity.   Five to one on Caleb.

Fourteenth.—Caleb still keeping the superiority.

Fifteenth.—Ryan did not much like his opponent, and was rather shy upon *setting-to;* but, rising superior to any thing like despondency, he made a good rally, and brought the old adage to the mind of the spectator, that *a battle is never won, till it is lost!* and put in some good *hits*. It was thought that a little falling off appeared about Caleb: he had been uncommonly active, and seemed to feel the effects of his efforts.

Sixteenth.—Ryan, a little renovated, became an object of attraction in turn, and endeavoured to show that he was *now* the strongest man: and gave convincing proofs of it, till the

Twenty-first.—When Ryan, although much exhausted, portrayed the most gaiety, and showed that he still possessed strength enough to throw his opponent.

Twenty-second.—Caleb, like a hero of the first stamp, who, upon finding the citadel in danger, summoned all his courage to prevent demolition; but he had to contend against a more powerful opponent than his daring adversary. Nature was on the decline, and he was compelled to substitute *spirit* for STAMINA—the *science* of CALEB was still the same, but the *strength* of BALDWIN was going, if not almost extinct; yet he, nevertheless, put in some well-meant blows, but they were of no effect; and *Ryan* not only *punished* but *levelled* the brave veteran.

Twenty-sixth.—Caleb, still *game*, came again to the scratch, but while falling, from exhaustion, his opponent struck him. "Foul, foul," was vociferated, and, *sans cérémonie*, the ring was instantly broken. It is utterly impossible to detail any thing like the *arguments* that were made use of to convince each other of their opinions being grounded in error—*Babel* could not have been worse; and how it would have terminated, it is difficult to conjecture, had not the dragoons, at this precise juncture, interfered and closed the debates.

The battle was decided as *drawn*—and both the combatants, if they gained nothing else, retired with the receipt of plenty of hard blows, after half an hour's complete *milling*.

CALEB has long been an interesting and attractive object in the *Fancy*, and a public character in the Metropolis, as one of the most lively of the race of *costard-mongers*. As a pugilist, CALEB stands high upon the roll of fame: and

His *pugilistic* deeds have rank'd him with the great!

Though not the proud and elevated Champion of England, yet let it be remembered that he retained for many many years the title of *unconquered champion* of his native soil, WESTMINSTER. His courage has never been doubted; his pretensions to the *science* never questioned; and throughout the whole of his very extensive practice universally admitted a sound pugilist, possessing an integrity unimpeachable.

Either for a *turn-up*, a fight in the ring, or *set-to* upon the *stage*, CALEB is perfectly *at home!* and never shy in sporting his *canvass*, when the necessity of the case demands an *appeal* for decision. For his weight, few *harder hitters* are to be found; and some of his pupils

have turned out to be *milling coves* of first-rate pretensions. Also in his dominions considerable allegiance
is paid by the *natives* to their avowed and admired
CHAMPION; and whose *opinion* in matters of *sport*
commands great attention and deference: to which
place all sorts of the *Fanciers* resort to witness the
exhibition of some of the *primest* of the OLD ENGLISH
SPORTS, and to partake of a *bit of life!*

Tothill Downs has long been a favourite spot for rich
scenes, and where the game *donnok* is frequently baited
with all its *rich* accompaniments; the badger *drawed*
in prime style—and where *neddies, after* the manner
of *Chilibi*, leave their unsophisticated riders behind
them. *Tykes,* sported by their *elegant* proprietors,
boasting of their pedigree, equal to a race-horse. On
these Downs many a *novice* has stripped to show fight,
who has soon been matured into a good boxer. The
groups of characters, assembled here at times, are some
of Nature's rarest moulds—from the *bit* of blood, down
to the flash kid: and, in short, it only requires a *peep*
into those dominions, to prove that *one half of the
world is ignorant how the other half lives!*

CALEB, although perhaps not so conversant in *high
Kent* as the late celebrated Bamfylde Moore Carew, or
flash Parker, yet he is *down as a hammer* to the *slum* of
the modern Greeks —and who has an undisputed claim
to the title of an—ORIGINAL. In private life he is a
civil well-behaved man; remarkably inoffensive; and
notwithstanding he possesses all the qualities of a distinguished pugilist, no man is more attentive or industrious to obtain a livelihood by his calling, than the
veteran Champion of Westminster, CALEB BALDWIN.

CELEBRATED PUGILISTS

SINCE THE DAYS OF THE RENOWNED

CHAMPION, JAMES BELCHER.

I'll read you matter, deep and dangerous,
As full of peril and advent'rous spirit,
As to o'erwalk a current, roaring loud,
On the unsteadfast footing of a spear.

JACK O'DONNEL.

Thumps follow thumps, and blows succeeding blows,
Swell the black eye, and crush the bleeding nose;
Beneath the pond'rous fist the jaw-bone cracks,
And the cheeks ring with their redoubled thwacks!

O'DONNEL was a native of Ireland, but, it seems, he left the *sod* at a very early period of his life, in quest of fame, and was not long in finding his way to the *long town*, (London,) entertaining a tolerably sound opinion, that if an individual is to obtain notoriety in any science whatever, it is in the Metropolis, where it will be quickly discerned, and his friends augment in proportion as he advances towards perfection. O'DONNEL was not deceived in this respect, and upon portraying some pretensions to the gymnastic art, several patrons stepped forward, and placed him under the tuition of an eminent boxer. He improved so fast in the *science* as to stamp him a pugilist of considerable rank, and also to raise him in the eyes of his countrymen as their future Champion, reminding them of their proud days, when Peter Corcoran flourished in all his greatness. At the age of eighteen, O'Donnel was matched against *Pardo Wilson*, (related to the family of the Belchers,) for twenty guineas a-side, to fight at Wormwood Scrubs, on October 26, 1802. *Pardo Wilson* was a pugilist of some experience, and displayed considerable *science* throughout the fight; but, after ten rounds of hard fighting, during which O'Donnel evinced great superiority of skill and strength, *Wilson* surrendered, completely exhausted. The *Paddies* were so elated that they carried their hero off in triumph.

In about three weeks after the above contest, O'Donnel entered the lists with one *Smith*, a boot-closer, at Wormwood Scrubs, on November 15, 1802, for twenty guineas. This was not only a sharp but scientific conflict, and O'Donnel raised himself considerably in the estimation of the *sporting world*, by the talents and *bottom* he displayed throughout *forty-eight* rounds, occupying one hour and twenty minutes. O'Donnel was borne off amidst the smiles of victory, and the praises of his countrymen.

O'Donnel was to have fought one *Henigan*, on January 18, 1803; but, upon the night previous, they were both bound over to keep the peace.

O'Donnel was matched against *Caleb Baldwin*, (see p. 307,) but being defeated—mark the difference!!!—*No smiles! no shouts! no shoulders offered to support the drooping hero!* but he was placed in a nackney coach, to groan and reflect upon the reverse of fortune! Any further comment is unnecessary!!!

O'DONNEL contended with *Tom Belcher* for a subscription-purse of twenty guineas, at Shepperton Common, Surrey, on April 27, 1805, but was compelled to surrender to the superiority of that distinguished hero.

O'DONNEL (who had been defeated by one *Emery*, a man much stronger, taller, and heavier by one stone, than himself, when in a bad state of health) now entered the lists with *Emery*, at Hodgsdon Green, near the Six Bridges of the Paddington Canal. O'DONNEL had for his second, *Tom Blake*, and his bottle-holder, *Bill Ryan;* and *Emery* was attended by *Tom Jones* and *White*. It was for fifty guineas, and took place on December 5, 1805. This was a contest of *strength* against *skill*, and, for the first part of the battle, *strength* prevailed ; but when that quality lost its force, *science* appeared with double advantage in acting on the defensive, and, at the same time, putting in the most tremendous *punishment*. At the expiration of forty-nine minutes, *Emery* was so completely *served-out* that he could scarcely stand, acknowledging he was beaten.

O'DONNEL fought a novice, at Wilsdon Green, on June 3, 1806, of the name of *Wasdale*, a Spitalfields Weaver, for twenty guineas. *Wasdale* had *milled* several of his neighbours, and, from his size and weight, having created considerable terrors, he flattered himself he had some pretensions to pugilism, and was weak enough to risk twenty guineas against so accomplished a pugilist as O'DONNEL. The *Weaver* was completely in the *basket*, and never was any attempt so wretched ; O'DONNEL *milled* him in all directions, and perfectly

convinced *Wasdale* how much he had deceived himself
when he imagined he could fight. The odds were
twenty to one on O'DONNEL, after three rounds.

O'DONNEL had been engaged in several other contests, and was looked upon as an elegant fighter.   He
ranked as a pugilist of considerable pretensions, received great encouragement, and might have insured many
friends, had not his laurels been blighted, by the des-
picableness of his conduct, in taking possession *of what
was not his own!* However painful it is to state, it becomes our duty not to withhold the truth, when it may
operate as an example, tending to benefit and deter
others from falling into the same error :—

> The purest treasure mortal times afford
> Is spotless reputation : that away,
> Men are but gilded loam or painted clay.

JOE BERKS, otherwise BURKE,

WAS rendered an object of considerable notoriety in the
sporting world, from his daring conflicts with *Jem Belcher*, and his tremendous battles with the *Game Chicken*.
Although victory stood aloof from his brave endeavours,
yet it must be allowed that BERKS was a boxer of extraordinary fortitude, and displayed *game* upon the
above trying occasions almost unequalled.   It is difficult to ascertain (in the pugilistic phrase) whether he
was the greatest *ruffian* or *glutton ;* but such an union
of those powerful qualities were scarcely ever observed
in one man :—IMPETUOSITY was his forte ; *science* he
smiled at, although he fell so often from its decisive effects ; and, throughout all his battles, he was DESPERA-

TION *itself!* BERKS undoubtedly was one of the most tremendous boxers in the whole race of modern pugilists, and who required no trifling *punisher* to make him cry out—*enough!* Notwithstanding the dreadful *millings* he received from *Belcher*, the *Chicken*, and *Gregson*, the quickness of his recovery was astonishing, portraying the hardihood of his nature, and the excellence of his constitution; in short, to sum up his pretensions to pugilism, it is but common justice to state, that BERKS, though he could not claim eminence as a *scientific* boxer, yet he stood as high as any of them upon the list, in point of bravery.

BERKS was a native of Shropshire, born at a place called Wem, of Irish descent, extremely well made, and of muscular appearance, not far off of six feet in height, and in weight about thirteen stone. The severe cut across his nose (which is observed in the likeness we have given of him, and the only one that was ever taken) he received in one of his battles with *Belcher.* BERKS, whether from his numerous *defeats*, or conceiving himself *neglected*, we cannot ascertain: however, unfortunately for himself and character, he deviated from that path of rectitude which no man ought to lose sight of in every station of life, or even labouring under the greatest extremity, but should endeavour to make INTEGRITY conquer *difficulties!*

'Tis GOLD
Which buys admittance, oft it doth, yea makes
Diana's rangers false themselves, and yield up
Their deer to th' stand o' th' stealer: and tis gold
Which makes the true man kill'd, and saves the thief;
Nay, sometimes hangs both thief and true man; what
Can it not DO, *and* UNDO?

Through the great exertions and humanity of Mr.
Jackson to alleviate the sufferings of a fellow-creature
in distress, we understand, BERKS was liberated from
his unhappy state, and obtained the situation of a non-
commissioned officer in one of his Majesty's regiments
on foreign service.

DUTCH SAM.

The *primest* BOXER on the list—
And *hardest hitter* with the fist;
The knowingest COVE for a *mill!*
Stored with *flash*, and stock'd with *skill*,
For *stopping*, *hitting*, down to *fib*—
Not inferior to mighty CRIBB
Bold and humane throughout the fight,
Judging his *distances* ever right;
A pugilist that's firm and tough,
Who ne'er cried out, *Hold!*—ENOUGH

His want of height and weight preclude him from obtaining the elevated title of CHAMPION—but his pretensions to pugilism, in every other point of view, render
him, by comparison, one of the best fighting men in
the kingdom. In the pugilistic world he is viewed as a
phenomenon, and it is the opinion of the *Fancy*, that,
since the days of *Jem Belcher*, few men have put in
such strong claims to excellence in boxing as DUTCH
SAM, whose knowledge of the *science* is generally admitted complete, and his style of fighting, in many instances, perfectly original.

It appears that SAM was first noticed by *Harry Lee*,

DUTCH SAM.

JOHN SMITH, Generally called BUCKHORSE.

Published Oct 7, 1812, by G. Smeeton, 139, St Martins Lane.

and, under his auspices, from the following circumstance, he was introduced into the circle of Boxers:— *Lee,* on his return home from Enfield, on the day that *Belcher* and *Burke* were to have fought, (October 12, 1801,) witnessed SAM fighting with a man by the roadside, very much his superior as to size and weight, and, from the excellence which he displayed in that contest, *Lee* distinguished those peculiar traits in the youthful *tyro* which have since proved his judgment correct, and, matured by time and practice, placed SAM as a first-rate boxer, and stamped him a complete pugilistic HERO.

SAM is in height about five feet six inches and a half, weighing only nine stone four pounds, (never exceeding eight,) and rather of a robust make; and who has, notwithstanding, vanquished some of the best *ten* and *twelve* stone bruisers in the country.

Possessing a sharp and penetrating eye, he watches the movements of his opponents with considerable accuracy, and his potent arm is ever ready to second so invaluable a director. In general, his *distances* are excellently well judged, rendering his blows powerful and effective; and it is thought that few boxers throw less *hits* away than DUTCH SAM; and though manifesting great ingenuity in avoiding the blows of his adversary, his facility in giving most severe *punishment,* in the return, is truly prominent. Ever on the wing, he assumes, as the necessity of the moment requires, either an offensive or defensive position with much adroitness.

As a *hard hitter,* we except no pugilist whatever— *Gulley* never struck with more force, or *Cribb* with greater ponderosity than SAM, whose blows are truly dreadful to encounter; and it has been the public-ex-

pressed opinion of one of the most experienced and
scientific pugilists in England, that he would be a complete match for the mighty *Cribb*, provided they were
only to strike blow for blow. *Cropley*, who has entered
the lists with *Tom Belcher* and DUTCH SAM, has since
declared, that he would sooner receive HALF AN HOUR'S
milling from the former, than FIVE MINUTES' *punishment* from the latter boxer.

Among his own persuasion (the Jews) he is an object
of great notoriety, and no money is ever wanting to
back him upon any pugilistic occasion, his INTEGRITY
having been proved of the first quality :—

> Good name in man or woman
> Is the immediate jewel of their souls:
> Who steals my purse steals trash, 'tis something, nothing;
> 'Twas mine, 'tis his, and has been slave to thousands;
> But he that filches from me my good name,
> Robs me of that which not enriches him,
> And makes me poor indeed!

We have been credibly informed that SAM was once
tampered with by the offer of A THOUSAND POUNDS to
lose a battle, on which great sums had been betted;
but he spurned such a base attempt to degrade his
character with becoming spirit and indignation; and
thereby preserved an unsullied reputation.

No pugilist appears to *time* his fights with so much
solid judgment as SAM; in fact, he almost reduces his
conquests to a certainty, by weighing them well in his
mind, that if the pending battle in which he may be
engaged does not appear quite clear to him, he is off,
and forfeits his deposit.

NATURE has done wonders for him respecting a most

excellent constitution; but to such a fine requisite he pays no attention whatever towards its preservation—*training* to SAM is but of little use, as his existence might be endangered from indigestion, if the coats of his stomach were not well diluted with *copious libations of Deady's brilliant fluid;* and which must be procured for him at all events, either directly, or under the *rose!* Those who know him best, would feel no hesitation whatever in (if not give a preference to) matching him at a day's notice, instead of a month's *training!*

Regarding his mental acquirements, SAM is *flash* to the very ECHO; and, it is thought, that no individual could portray in richer colours the *adventures* of a CABBEROOSE than the character in question, and who, in the *slang chronicles,* would be denominated a GAMMONER of the first brilliancy; *down* to all the tricks of life, and not to be *had* upon any *suit* whatever!

SAM's first regular *set-to* was with the veteran *Caleb Baldwin,* see page 309.

SAM entered the lists with *Britton,* a Bristol hero, (a pugilist of no mean pretensions, and who had fought *Jem Belcher* for half an hour when *Jem* was in his prime,) on April 27, 1805, at Shepperton Common, Surrey. It was a well-contested battle—and, after considerable *game* and *science* being displayed on both sides, during thirty rounds, SAM was declared the conqueror.

SAM was, at length, matched to fight with *Tom Belcher,* for one hundred guineas, on February 8, 1806, at Moulsey Hurst, in a roped ring. *Gulley* seconded *Tom Belcher,* and *Dick Whale* was his bottle-holder; and the attendants upon DUTCH SAM were *Mendoza* and *Tom Blake.*   Bets were extremely *flush*, but no odds offered.

First round.—Great expectations were formed of a complete display of the *science*, and the eyes of every spectator were on the alert, in viewing the attempts of his favourite hero—Sam threw out a lure; but Tom was not to be *had*, and made a good *hit*, which was quickly returned by the Jew; and Belcher, in endeavouring not to be behind hand, lost his equilibrium in putting in a blow, and fell.

Second.—Belcher, extremely active, and with good effect, hit his opponent right and left—Sam slightly returned, when they closed and fell.

Third.—Sam tried to *punish* Tom's ribs; but Belcher's guard was too secure, and gave him a good *hit* for his intention; they closed and fell.   Five to four on Belcher.

Fourth.—In this round Tom proved himself to be a first-rate pugilist, his *science* was truly eminent, and he appeared the most prominent hero of the two; notwithstanding Sam's rallying, he warded off his strength with great dexterity, and *punished* away with his right hand; but Sam, by dint of stamina, threw his opponent.

Fifth.—Of no importance.

Sixth.—Both the combatants intent upon losing no time, and several severe blows were exchanged, but in favour of Tom, who stopped the desperate *hits* of his antagonist with singular adroitness.

Seventh.—Tom, in a rally, made his opponent's head rattle again; but Sam received the shock undaunted, and hit Belcher on the eye; in closing they both went down.

Eighth.—Both pelting away, when Belcher threw Sam. Two to one on Tom.

Ninth.—Belcher some little the worse for his exertions, which Sam perceiving, ran in, and knocked him down.

Tenth.—Belcher tried to *punish* his opponent's *nob*; but without effect, and fell through exhaustion, after Sam had rallied.   The odds now shifted, and seven to four were offered upon Sam.

Eleventh.—Hitting and stopping on both sides dexterously managed ; and in closing, Sam fell uppermost.

Twelfth.—Belcher made the best of himself, and showed off

rather gay ; but his blows were without effect, and he fell, to all appearance, much enfeebled. Two to one on Sam.

Thirteenth.—Tom, somewhat recovered, made his opponent's head feel the effects of it, which rendered him so shy, that Belcher went in, and without difficulty threw him.

Fourteenth and fifteenth.—Belcher was again looked up to, and Sam still shy. Even betting.

Sixteenth.—Sam, impetuous, endeavoured to *serve* Tom out, and followed him round the ring ; but Belcher paid him for his temerity.

Seventeenth.—The *science* displayed by Tom in this round was truly excellent—his *distances* well judged, and his blows told. Odds six to five on Belcher.

Twenty-fourth.—In the last six rounds, Belcher took the lead—but both the combatants were on the decline, and though several *hits* were exchanged, they were not effective.

Twenty-fifth.—Belcher, although weak, appeared so formidable in the eyes of his opponent, that Sam did not like to meet him.

Twenty-sixth.—Belcher, without hesitation, put in a good *facer*, and concluded the round by throwing Sam. Tom the favourite, and the odds laid upon him.

Twenty-ninth.—In the last two rounds, Belcher continued to exert himself in the best manner; but still he betrayed great weakness.

As far as *science* could protract, and *bottom* render it assistance, they were manifested by *Tom Belcher* in the above contest, who continued fighting till the FIFTY-SEVENTH round, when Nature so completely forsook him that he was compelled, though reluctantly, to *give in*.

The friends of *Belcher* were not satisfied as to the result of the above battle, and *Tom* was backed for two hundred guineas to fight DUTCH SAM, on July 28, 1807, at Moulsey Hurst, in a twenty-eight feet roped ring. SAM had for his second, *Mendoza*, and *Bitton* for his bottle-holder; and *Belcher* was attended by *Bill Warr* and *Watson*.

First round.—Eager to commence offensive operations, Sam attempted to plant a severe blow on his opponent's ribs; but failed, when Tom *nobbed* him with two terrible *hits*, and got away:—*science* now made its appearance for a short period, when Sam rallied, and, in closing, he fell uppermost.

Second.—Sam incorrect in his *distance*, but, notwithstanding, put in a severe right-handed blow on Tom's loins, which Belcher returned by a tremendous *facer*—some sparring now took place, when Sam put in so severe a blow upon his adversary's neck, that brought him down.

Third.—Sam firm and confident, and Belcher equally *game*, both pelting away, and good judgment displayed on both sides; in closing, Belcher was thrown.

Fourth.—Both the faces of the combatants betrayed visible alteration—Belcher's nose bled copiously; and Sam's eye was much swelled. Belcher put in a hard *facer*, and Sam, in closing, threw his adversary with great violence.

Fifth.—A better round was never witnessed in any fight whatever—*science*, activity, and *bottom*, were all upon the alert —Sam made a rally, and many good *hits* were exchanged, when they closed; but, on disengaging themselves, Tom rallied, who, nevertheless, had the worst of it, and went down from a slight blow from his opponent. Five to four on Sam.

Sixth.—Both on their mettle, and good *hits* exchanged.— Belcher stopped some severe blows; but fell rather weak. Six to four on Sam.

Seventh.—Rather an irregular round; but, in closing, Sam threw Belcher on his head.

Eighth.—Of no note.

Ninth.—Belcher planted two severe *hits*, right and left, in his antagonist's face, and threw Sam most desperately.

Tenth.—Sam, in return, after putting a heavy blow in the body, threw Tom.

Eleventh.—Belcher stopped his antagonist's *hits* with great *science;* and, in closing, Sam went down.

Twelfth.—Belcher on the look-out, anxiously endeavouring to save himself; but Sam followed him, and brought him down.

Thirteenth.—Tom stopped two blows with great neatness, and returned a most desperate *hit;* the effects of which Sam felt severely, and soon after fell, much exhausted.

Fourteenth.—Sam's eyes were now in *mourning*, and Tom's left side showed the marks of his antagonist's fist, upon which place Sam put in a severe blow, when they closed, and Sam went to the ground.

Fifteenth.—Extremely irregular—retreating, hugging, &c. Tom fell, from weakness. Seven to four on Sam.

Sixteenth.—Rallying on both sides, and several severe *hits* were exchanged; in closing, Belcher threw his opponent.

Nineteenth.—Hard fighting, and both of the combatants, trying for superiority at arm's length, fell from each other's blows.

Twentieth.—Sam put in a blow on his opponent's nose; but, in closing, Sam went down.

Twenty-first.—The conflict was now desperate; hitting and stopping without delay; but rather in favour of Sam.

Twenty-sixth.—Belcher, full of courage, showed himself master of the *science*, by his dexterity in stopping, and returning with severity.

Twenty-seventh.—Belcher on the decline; and his friends not sanguine; Sam hit him three desperate blows on his already *punished* side; but Tom, notwithstanding, threw his opponent.

Twenty-eighth.—Belcher fell from the severe *hits* he received upon his head. Three to one upon Sam.

Twenty-ninth.—The *science* of Belcher was still prominent; but he wanted strength to render it effective, and was thrown.

Thirtieth.—Sam's eyes were nearly darkened; but he was still gay, and, in rallying, knocked Tom down. Four to one upon Sam.

Thirty-first.—Tom now convinced the spectators that he was not only entitled to the character of a scientific, but a *game* pugilist—his courage was truly admirable; but the chance was positively against him, and Sam was no stranger to the circumstance.

Thirty-second.—Belcher, in rallying, fell from weakness.

Thirty-third.—Tom's exhausted appearance was visible; but his brave heart, still anxious to contend, although Nature refused to second his efforts—his blows were of no effect, and he fell from complete inability to proceed.

Thirty-fourth, and last round—Which terminated in a manner quite unexpected—Tom, in making a *hit* at his opponent, fell upon his knees; and Sam in returning struck him—upon which the cries of " foul" were immediately heard.   It was a sort of straw to catch hold of, and advantage was taken of the circumstance.   The umpires, in giving their opinion, were in opposition to each other, and it was some difficulty to get that *point* settled to the satisfaction of all parties; it was then decided in favour of Sam, subject to future consideration.   After considerable arguments at various meetings, and PRECEDENTS resorted to, upon similar occasions, it was finally decided as a *drawn battle*, and that a THIRD appeal should be made, which took place

On Friday, August 21, 1807, on Lowfield Common, near Crawley, in Sussex, in a thirty-feet roped ring, and that the following article of *Broughton's* rules was to be decisive :—

7. That no person is to hit his adversary when down, or seize him by the ham, the breeches, or any part below the waist: a man on his knees to be reckoned down.

DUTCH SAM was seconded by *Mendoza,* and *Bitton* was his bottle-holder; and *Tom Belcher* was attended by *Gulley* and *Ward.*

First round—Considerable anxiety was manifested upon the combatants *setting-to*, and the *interested* spectators were much agitated with hopes and fears, upon the decision of this THIRD contest between two such distinguished pugilists:—Sam made a feint with his left hand, and endeavoured with his right to *hit* Tom's ribs; but they were stopped, and Belcher returned feebly with his left hand, and, in closing, Sam was underneath.

Second.—Sam going in to rally, Tom *hit* him right and left, and likewise stopped two blows.   In closing, Belcher was thrown.   Betting now commenced—Five to two on Sam.

Third.—Sam extremely cautious till he had got his proper *distance*, when, after making a left-handed feint, he put in a terrible blow under Belcher's left eye, that brought the *claret* out in abundance, and its effects were so severe, that Tom was confused, and who, upon exchanging a *hit*, was thrown. Three to one on Sam.

Fourth.—Both rallying, and exchanging *hits* at arm's length —no advantage on either side; but the strength of Sam was prominent in closing, who threw his opponent.

Fifth.—A most excellent round; but rather in favour of Belcher. Sam rallied, but without effect, as Belcher hit him off; notwithstanding, Sam closed, disengaged, and commenced another rally, when Tom put in a most tremendous blow upon the left eye of his opponent, and also threw him a heavy fall.

Sixth.—Desperate fighting—both exhausted, and fell together.

Seventh.—Belcher put in two slight *hits:* when they closed irregularly, and fell.

Eighth.—Rallying and good *science* prominent on both sides —hitting and stopping in good style, till they both fell. Belcher manifested first weakness.

Ninth.—Sam incorrect in his *distances,* his blows did not tell, and Belcher gave him a severe fall. Four to one on Sam.

Tenth.—Belcher *hit* his opponent slightly, when Sam threw him.

Eleventh.—Sam, full of strength, rallied desperately, which was followed up by Tom, but in favour of the Jew. Sam's blows were dreadful, and Belcher's face and body suffered materially, when he fell from weakness.

Twelfth.—No blows were given. Tom ran himself down. All betters, but no one sanguine enough to take them.

Thirteenth.—Sam followed the steps of his opponent, and ran himself down.

Fourteenth.—Belcher, somewhat shy from the severe beating which he had received, fell from two of Sam's right-handed body blows.

Fifteenth.—Belcher made every effort to put in some good *hits:* but they were too feeble to do any execution, and fell from weakness while rallying.

Sixteenth.—Of no importance, except both the combatants, after closing, appeared to fall from exhaustion.

Seventeenth.—Belcher, in attempting to *hit* his opponent, was stopped, and, in closing, Tom fell between his adversary's arms on his knees: but Sam, who was too strongly impressed with the articles, held up his hands, to show that no foul blows should put an end to this contest.

Eighteenth.—Sam, in closing, got his opponent's head under his arm, and *fibbed* Belcher so severely that he dropped.

Nineteenth.—Tom fell on his knees, but Sam was on his guard, and only smiled.

Twentieth.—Sam beat his opponent to the ropes with considerable ease.

Twenty-first.—Belcher still suffering under Sam's superior strength.

Twenty-second.—Belcher, rather recovered, obtained some little advantage.

Twenty-third.—Belcher, still livelier, contended spiritedly, till they both fell, and lay all along on the ground.

Twenty-fourth.—Belcher completely astonished his friends by his fine *game* and resolution, and obtained considerable advantage in a desperate rally, when they both fell quite exhausted.

Twenty-fifth.—Tom's superiority in the *science* of boxing was truly conspicuous in this round, his blows were well-directed, but not effective.

Twenty-sixth.—Belcher still the best, and Sam, to avoid Tom's favourite right-handed body blow, threw himself on his face.

Twenty-seventh.—Sam received a heavy fall after some irregular fighting.

Twenty-eighth.—Belcher claimed considerable respect and attention from the fine style in which he gained the superiority over his opponent, and also in giving Sam a very severe fall.

Twenty-ninth and thirtieth.—Good rallies took place in both these rounds, but rather in favour of Belcher.

Thirty-first to thirty-sixth.—It was evident to the spectators that Belcher could not win. The ferocity of Sam was tremendous in the extreme; he followed his opponent to all parts of the ring, putting in dreadful *facers* and body blows, dealing out death-like punishment, till his brave opponent fell quite exhausted, when his brother Jem took him out of the ring in the most feeble state, and placed him in a gentleman's chariot. It was on the left side, from the kidneys to the crown of the head, where Tom was so severely beaten. Sam's principal injury was a blow under the left eye, and some trifling marks, who dressed himself with perfect indifference before he left the ring.

Sam entered the lists with *Bill Cropley*, on May 10, 1808, in Sir *John Sebright's* Park, Hertfordshire. *Cropley* is a fine well-made young man, and possessing stamina of so fine a quality that an opinion was entertained by several of the amateurs that Sam would never be able to overcome such an invaluable requisite. It was a well-contested battle for twenty-five minutes; but Sam was the favourite after the first three rounds, and not declared the conqueror till *Cropley* was quite exhausted.

A match was made between SAM and a respectable tradesman, for two hundred guineas, of the name of *Medley*, which took place at Moulsey Hurst, on May 31, 1810. Whether it was owing to a quarrel between the parties, or merely respecting the honours of pugilism, we have not ascertained, but considerable interest was excited in the *sporting world* as to its issue, *Medley* being a heavier man than SAM, and felt so confident as to his powers that he put down his own stake: as a *sparrer* he had given convincing proofs of his knowledge of the *science*, but his manhood had never been practically put to the test; yet SAM did not view him with indifference —and in the first instance forfeited his deposit. SAM was seconded by *Harry Lee*, and *Puss* was his bottle-holder, and *Medley* was attended by his brother *Phips*, and *Cribb*. The odds were greatly in favour of SAM Throughout a long fight of *forty-nine* rounds, SAM maintained the superiority—his *punishment* was dreadful in the extreme, and it was owing to this gift that he obtained the victory. *Medley's science* was by no means superficial, and his *game* would have done honour to the first-rate boxer, but his blows, however well-directed, were not effective—they were showy instead of telling; his appearance was truly ghastly, and he bled in every direction. SAM's humanity was nobly exemplified in the above contest, and much as his abilities were to be admired, his feeling claimed greater attention.

That respect we owe to *impartiality* forbids us to pass over the following *turn-up* without some comment, in which the laurels of DUTCH SAM were in danger of being wrested from his brow. In passing over Wimbledon Common, in 1805, near to which he was in *training*, he met with a butcher, of the name of *Jem Brown*, of Wandsworth, and, after a few words having passed between them, an immediate appeal was made to the *fist*.

The *Butcher*, most certainly, had the best of it, and *levelled* his opponent two or three times—when SAM *declined proceeding any further at* THAT *time*. Whether from INABILITY, or from feeling the impropriety of risking the issue of a private *row*, which might have prevented him from fulfilling his public engagement, and in the event of it, perhaps, made him lose *that* battle, can only be decided by himself—but a tolerably general opinion has been entertained that *Brown*, in a regular contest with SAM, would soon be disposed of.

In the vicinity of St. George's Fields, a man of the name of *Jones*, a Limner, and a neighbour of DUTCH SAM's, who valued himself upon his *milling* qualities, publicly declared that he was the Champion of that quarter, and had frequently importuned SAM to have a *set-to*, but who always declined. It happened that one evening, shortly after the above declaration, SAM was regaling himself at a public-house near the *Limner's* dwelling, till glass succeeding glass of *Deady's brilliant fluid*, had nearly obliterated all the things of this world from SAM's pericranium, when *Jones*, learning the circumstance, soon entered the premises, and endeavoured to provoke him, in this debilitated state, to a combat, but in vain, upon which *Jones* immediately struck him. This was too much, and SAM, reeling to and fro, returned it, and, scarcely intelligible, inquired " whether he was doing right or wrong to defend himself," and who immediately went into the street to decide it. SAM, notwithstanding his intoxicated state, appeared to have the advantage, when *Jones* seized him by the hair of his head, threw him down, and beat him violently upon the stones. This act of cruelty operated contrary in its effects to what was expected by its perpetrator, by awakening SAM to a better recollection of what he was about, who started up, exclaiming—"Take care, take care, for now I'm coming!" and put in such a *stomacher* as nearly deprived *Jones* of his breath, and following it up by a tremendous *hit* over his eye, *levelled* this brute with the mud. The painter was so completely *satisfied*, that he would not encounter SAM's fist any more. *Jones* weighed thirteen stone six pounds; and, though destitute of propriety, was not without considerable pretensions to the *science;* but who was severely taught the folly of vain boasting!

BOXING is not only a *national,* but a noble propensity; and, in its proper application, has raised the valour and manly intrepidity of the English nation, eminently conspicuous over all others, from its practice; but when unfortunately perverted by any of its professors, who turn it into an engine against that public by whom they have been supported and cherished, it degenerates into brutality, and renders its name despicable. PUGILISM, we are sorry to observe, never lost its importance so much in the esteem of the nation, as in the O. P. disturbance of Covent-Garden Theatre, when some of its first-rate professors *suffered themselves to be* HIRED *to* intimidate *and* impede *the people from obtaining their rights and liberties!* Names might be mentioned, as we are in possession of them; but we trust that a friendly hint will prove more than sufficient to point out the impropriety of such pro-

ceedings, and that, in future, good sense will reign
predominant, by preventing the repetition of such
disgraceful conduct.

> 'Tis a knavish piece of work : But what of that ?
> *Those* (PUGILISTS) that have free souls, it touches not,
> Let the gall'd wince, our withers are unwrung !

TOM BELCHER.

> From SLACK descended—mighty name !
>   Great Hero of the Fist—
> Conquering BROUGHTON, raised *his* fame
>   *Then* first upon the list.
>
> His grandson, JEM—a Champion rare !
>   Did honour to the cause—
> And TOM and NED, with anxious care,
>   Increasing the applause.
>
> Their deeds of valour long will grace
>   The pugilistic page,
> These heroes of the *milling* race—
>   In a succeeding age.

HOWEVER celebrated the heroic achievements of his
great pugilistic ancestors have been, and however the
distinguished conquests of his brother JEM may have
been extolled—it is but fair to state, that TOM BEL-
CHER does not derive his present celebrity from their
actions ; on the contrary, TOM has been the architect
of his own fame, and, in emulating the noble deeds of
his brave grandsire and brother, he has not only showed
his own passport to excellence as a pugilist, but added
fresh laurels to the already proud name of BELCHER.

T. BELCHER.

R. GREGSON.

Published Feby 1 1815 by G. Smeeton, 139 St Martins Lane.

TOM has been engaged in TWELVE prize combats, out of which number he has proved the conqueror EIGHT TIMES; and out of the other four, *one* has been decided as a drawn battle.

His first *set-to* was with *Jack Warr*, (son of the noted pugilist of that name,) for a subscription purse of fifty guineas, in Tothill Fields, in a roped forty-feet ring, on June 26, 1804. *Warr* was the stoutest, but BELCHER the tallest man; and upon whom the odds seemed rather to incline. From the sound pedigree of both of the combatants, great expectations were formed in the *sporting world* as to their abilities; and in the battle they gave ample proofs of their acquirements as to future excellence. It was a good fight throughout, and every round was not only manfully, but scientifically, contested; the blows of *Warr* were truly desperate, and in general directed at the body of his opponent; while BELCHER, on the contrary, fought at the head. The successes were alternate, and the betting varied accordingly; and it was not till after thirty-three minutes had elapsed, and nineteen rounds had taken place, that *Warr* gave in. He was carried off the ground almost lifeless. BELCHER obtained considerable fame by this contest.

TOM was now matched with *Bill Ryan*, (son of the celebrated *Michael Ryan*,) on November 31, 1804, for a subscription purse, on Wilsdon Green. BELCHER had for his second, *George Maddox*, and his bottle-holder, *Joe Norton;* and *Ryan* was attended by *Paddington Jones* and *Dick Whale*. The odds were six to four upon BELCHER, who felt confident of success.

First round.—Anxious to commence offensive operations, sparring was out of the question, hitting and stopping prominent upon both sides, when they closed and fell.

Third and fourth.—Several good blows were exchanged during these rounds, but terminated in favour of Ryan.

Sixth.—A better round was never witnessed, nor finer courage ever displayed; when, at length, Belcher hit his opponent so severely on the temple, as to knock him down: who appeared a little exhausted. Seven to four on Belcher.

Eighteenth.—For the last eleven rounds no visible difference was experienced—both of the combatants displaying those traits of courage and science which entitled them to the characters of *first-rate boxers*. Tom put in a desperate blow over the mouth of his opponent, when Ryan, in return, knocked him down; and took the lead, in point of superiority of strength, till the

Thirtieth.—Belcher was now much exhausted, and he appeared to be contending against nature, but his display of the science was elegant and attractive.

Thirty-first.—A few hits were exchanged, when Ryan put in a knock-down blow.

Thirty-second.—Ryan repeated his hit.

Thirty-third and thirty-fourth.—Belcher felt the severe effects of his opponent's powers; and was *levelled* in both these rounds.

Thirty-seventh.—Tom, full of heroism, nobly contended for glory; but it was against him, and he fell from inability.

Thirty-eighth.—Belcher put in an appearance, but it was only to be knocked down; upon which some little commotion took place, by the ring being broken, and the friends of Belcher declaring the last blow to be foul. The Umpire, however, decided to the contrary, and RYAN was declared the victor.

O'Donnel, the celebrated Irish hero, fought TOM BELCHER for a purse of twenty guineas, on Saturday, April 27, 1805, at Shepperton, Surrey. Considerable *science* was displayed by BELCHER upon this occasion; and *O'Donnel* showed himself entitled to respectable attention; but who was completely *satisfied* in fifteen rounds, when BELCHER was proclaimed the conqueror.

TOM BELCHER, anxious to recover the lost laurel, entered the lists once more with his late opponent, *Bill Ryan*, on June 4, 1806, at Leleham Burway, Surrey, for twenty-five guineas a-side. BELCHER had for his second, *Tom Blake;* and *Ryan* was attended by *George Maddox.* The odds were considerably in favour of *Ryan.* The battle lasted fifty minutes, during which time twenty-nine rounds were well contested, when BELCHER was declared the conqueror.

On February 8, 1806, he fought *Dutch Sam;* see page 323.

TOM BELCHER fought with a man denominated *Jack of the Green,* a pugilist of no note, and who was soon disposed of in the hands of such an able professor for his daring temerity.

BELCHER's second contest with *Dutch Sam,* was on July 28, 1807, which was decided a *drawn battle;* see page 326.

TOM's third and last contest with his brave opponent, *Sam,* was on August 21, 1807; see page 328.

On April 14, 1808, BELCHER fought with *Dogherty,* in a twenty-one feet roped ring, upon EPSOM DOWNS, near the Rubbing House. *Dogherty* was seconded by *Cropley,* and had for his bottle-holder, *Dick Hall;* and BELCHER was attended by *Mendoza* and *Clarke.* Odds six to four on BELCHER.

First round.—Above a minute transpired before any blows were exchanged, both sparring to obtain the advantage. Belcher stopped his opponent's hits with considerable neatness— a rally took place, when they closed, and disengaged. Some trifling hits took place, when they again closed, and Dogherty threw Belcher.

Second.—Belcher stopped a terrible left-handed *hit* which Dogherty aimed at his head; when the latter rallied, but Belcher *hit* him off his legs.

Third.—Skill and courage were pre-eminent on both sides: Dogherty rallied, but Belcher rendered his hits unavailing, and put in some severe blows on Dogherty's face, who, in terminating the round, threw Tom.

Fourth.—The talents of both the combatants were extremely conspicuous in this round; but Belcher had the best of it. Dogherty received a tremendous *facer* in endeavouring to plant a hit, and *Belcher* rallied in fine style, when Dogherty convinced him that he was no novice, by his dexterity in stopping —yet Tom, in following his opponent round the ring, *punished* his head most terribly; and brought him down by a blow under the jaw.   Three to one upon Belcher.

Fifth.—Belcher, with uncommon dexterity, broke through Dogherty's guard, and with his left hand planted a most dreadful blow in his throat, which so completely confused him, that he repeated the hit three times before Dogherty could recover himself, when they closed and fell.

Sixth.—Belcher upon *setting-to* dropped his opponent from the first two blows.

Seventh.—Dogherty's efforts were completely scientific, and he stopped Belcher's blows with great neatness; but notwithstanding Belcher *levelled* him.

Eighth.—Belcher had enough to do in warding off the well-aimed hits of his adversary—who now went in full of impetuosity, yet not without science; in closing, Tom was thrown upon the ropes by Dogherty, and, to all appearance, without any difficulty.

Ninth.—Several good blows were exchanged—but Belcher was not seen to so much advantage in this round; and in closing, Belcher fell underneath.

Tenth.—Belcher, rather careful, retreated; when Dogherty, conceiving something might be gained by following him, put in two good hits; but, on closing the round, Dogherty was thrown.

Eleventh.—Belcher put in two *facers*, when both the combatants fell out of the ring.

Twelfth.—Dogherty was again thrown; previously to which Belcher planted two good hits.

Thirteenth.—Dogherty, full of pluck, rallied, but Tom threw him with considerable force.

Fourteenth.—Tom, evidently superior in this round, rendered the rallying of Dogherty unavailing, and threw him again violently.

Fifteenth.—The *game* of Dogherty claimed admiration, and his appearance commiseration—his head was terrific, and his strength was nearly exhausted, yet notwithstanding he rallied; but his blows were of no effect, and he fell beneath the superiority of his opponent.

Sixteenth and seventeenth.—In both these rounds the feebleness of Dogherty was visible to all the spectators; and, to the honour of Belcher be it recorded, he disdained taking any more advantage than was necessary to insure his contest. Such traits of humanity ought not to be forgotten.

Eighteenth and nineteenth.—Dogherty's spirits were good, but his stamina was departed—his blows did not tell, although he stopped with considerable science; yet Belcher kept the lead in fine style; in closing they both fell.

Twenty-fourth.—Up to this round it was evident that Tom must win; but his brave opponent was determined to try every effort while the least chance remained of success. Tom put in three desperate *facers*, and also hit him so severely in the throat and stomach, that he fell in a manner quite bent and exhausted.

Thirty-third.—Dogherty, still determined, contended for the last eight rounds, but was nothing more than a mere object of *punishment* to his opponent, who continually *levelled* him with the most apparent ease, till Dogherty could not come again. Belcher was declared the conqueror, who, upon hearing the welcome sound, threw a somerset.

Cropley now entered the lists with Tom Belcher, for a subscription purse of fifty guineas, on October 25, 1808, at Moulsey Hurst, in a thirty-feet roped ring. *Cropley* was seconded by *Tom Jones*, and *Dick Hall* acted as his *bottle-holder;* and Belcher was attended by *Mendoza* and *Dutch Sam*. The combatants were looked upon nearly in an equal point of view, and considerable expectations of a fine display of the art of pugilism were entertained by the amateurs. The odds upon *setting-to* were in favour of Belcher. During a contest of thirty-four rounds, which occupied fifty-six minutes—it is but justice to observe that a more real scientific fight was never seen; and *Cropley*, although defeated, proved himself an excellent boxer, and possessing *bottom* of the first quality. His defeat was principally in bringing his head too forward when putting in his blows; which Belcher taking the advantage of, *punished* his face so dreadfully that scarcely any traces of its former appearance were discernible. It was with the greatest reluctance that *Cropley* GAVE IN.

One *Farnborough,* who rested his pretensions upon his *game,* had the temerity to fight TOM BELCHER, on Epsom race-ground, in a thirty-feet ring, on February 1, 1809. Upon the part of *Farnborough,* it was *mere* pretensions; BELCHER treated him with the most perfect *sang froid,* and in the course of twenty minutes, he so completely *punished* and disfigured him, that *Farnborough* was glad to cry for quarter; while, on the contrary, BELCHER was scarcely touched.

SILVERTHORNE, a pugilist of some practice and success, was matched for one hundred guineas, and a subscription-purse of fifty pounds, against BELCHER, which was decided upon Crawley-heath, near Copthall, on June 6, 1811; *Silverthorne* was seconded by the veteran *Caleb Baldwin,* and his bottle-holder, *Bill Gibbons;* and BELCHER was attended by *Gulley* and *Tom Jones.* Four to one upon BELCHER.

First round.—Belcher, upon the alert, stopped a tremendous blow aimed at his stomach by Silverthorne, and returned two sharp hits right and left in Silverthorne's face, which immediately produced a great discharge of blood; after disengaging themselves, Belcher pelted away most dreadfully, and putting in hits almost as quick as lightning; and it is supposed that such a *first round* was never before witnessed, wherein so much *punishment* was dealt out to one combatant. Silverthorne fell from the severe effects of Belcher's blows.

Second.—Silverthorne rose under evident symptoms of fear, and retreated from his adversary, who now hit him right and left upon the head. Silverthorne, in planting a hit upon Belcher's throat, was stopped; but who nevertheless put in a severe body blow, which Belcher returned by a *leveller.*

Third.—Silverthorne was covered with blood, and who rallied, but without effect—Belcher put in several severe blows. Silverthorne showed that he was not without *science,* in warding many of them off from doing great injury; and

Belcher in losing his distance, closed, and was thrown by Silverthorne.

Fourth.—It was now evident to the spectators that Silverthorne was much inferior to his brave opponent, who frustrated all his attempts with ease and security. Silverthorne endeavoured to plant a severe body-blow, which Tom stopped, when a rally commenced, which turned out to Belcher's advantage, who put in a terrible blow, then closed, and threw his opponent a cross-buttock enough to knock all the breath out of his body.

Fifth.—Silverthorne bled profusely, who received two *facers* from Belcher, and, in a rally, Silverthorne fell. All betters but no takers.

Sixth.—Silverthorne, notwithstanding the chance was against him, showed some little play, and stopped very neatly a right-handed blow which was intended for his head, but Belcher nevertheless put in a severe body-blow, and Silverthorne fell in attempting to return it.

Seventh.—It was now all over with Silverthorne, who was completely exhausted, but still wished to try another chance—Belcher did as he liked with his opponent, and finished the contest by a desperate hit in the throat, which knocked him down, when Belcher was proclaimed the conqueror, who instantly, to show how little he was the worse for the contest, threw a somerset.

In point of elegance of attitude and scientific precision, it is considered at the present period that Tom Belcher, as a pugilist, stands unrivalled. Throughout the whole of his twelve battles, his superior knowledge and practical display of the art over that of his opponents have been conspicuously prominent. The blows of Belcher are given with the rapidity of lightning, putting them in with his left hand straight, though he can use both his hands with equal facility, and are more numerous than any other boxer; his excellence in stopping is so truly admirable that he seems perfectly aware of the intention of his adversary, and might be said to be armed nearly at all points. No pugilist gives the *return* with greater celerity; and his *one*, TWO, are in general so well applied as to do considerable execution. His *game* is of the finest quality: and his resolution to persevere while a single *chance* remains to obtain the victory, has claimed universal admiration, and must ever render him an object of great attraction in the boxing circles. He is also a pugilist on whom great dependence may be placed. In some instances, an opinion has been entertained that TOM paid too much attention to trivial sparring; and in some of his contests it has been thought that his blows were not *weighty* enough to second the intention with which they were directed, or to produce that desired effect so much wished; but were his *physical* powers equal to his judgment. few men, it is supposed, would be able to stand any length of time in contact with his efforts. These circumstances cannot be stronger verified than in his distinguished combats with *Dutch Sam*, who, by comparison, as a *scientific* pugilist, is certainly inferior to BELCHER, but when judged of as the most *effective* boxer, *Dutch Sam*, without any question, takes the lead. In the present era of pugilism, no contests have engaged the conversation of the *Fancy* in general more than the merits of the *three* public displays of the above heroes.

It is well known that BELCHER entered rather prematurely into the FIRST battle with *Sam;* he had been living too gay, and his *stamina* was enfeebled from its debilitating effects. The time allowed for training was also too short to recover its proper tone, and in consequence of which he became the victim of the bad advice of his backer.

In the SECOND contest which was adjudged a drawn

battle, it was visible, that, notwithstanding BELCHER put in nearly three blows to one more than his adversary, they were compared more to a sort of slight *taps* than forcible hits, and operated upon the spectators more from their showy appearance, than by possessing any decisive qualities to the disadvantage of his opponent; but nevertheless it was a matter of considerable astonishment to every one who witnessed the fight, the manly fortitude displayed by TOM in resisting the severe *punishment* of *Dutch Sam.*

In the THIRD and last battle, BELCHER was by no means recovered from the severe effects of the former contest. In stripping, his body exhibited the bruised marks of the late combat, and he evidently fought under great depression and disadvantage. It has been strongly urged by the friends of TOM, that he *was never in* PROPER CONDITION, and in which opinion BELCHER himself acquiesces, and asserts, that *Sam has always had the best of him* in point of *condition!* while the admirers of *Dutch Sam,* with equal confidence, aver that BELCHER had not strength enough to reduce the ferocity of the above pugilistic phenomenon. It is only justice to state that much difference of opinion always existed upon this subject.

BOXERS, if they feel any sort of ambition to attain eminence, should endeavour to comply with a regular mode of living, and to bear in remembrance that the *stamina* is easier reduced than the tone of the system recovered. The constitution once touched, the mind or resolution also becomes enfeebled; and the frame, in losing its natural vigour, begets depression and fear, thus occasioning, in a great degree, exhaustion and premature defeat!

As a sparrer TOM is truly distinguished, and exhibits all the various traits of the art with the utmost elegance and perfection, and who has turned out a number of very expert and scientific pupils. In several of the principal towns of the kingdom, TOM has portrayed the utility of the SCIENCE OF SELF-DEFENCE with considerable respect and attention. BELCHER is in height about five feet nine inches, weighing nearly eleven stone. His appearance much of the gentleman, and his manners and deportment are of the most mild and inoffensive nature, well calculated to prepossess the stranger much in his favour, by experiencing in his company the perfections of the pugilist, without any of that ferocity which the unacquainted are too apt to imagine characterises the brave boxer.

NED *(the eldest)* BELCHER.

THE brave family of the BELCHERS have put in such strong claims to pugilistic excellence, that we cannot pass over the efforts of any of its members (however trifling) without preserving a small niche to perpetuate their well-merited fame.

NED, in all probability, might have proved himself equally as distinguished a boxer as either of his renowned brothers, had he not, in his youth, received a material injury in his right hand, which ever afterwards prevented him from making much use of it, and in fighting he could only hit with his left—his *bottom* was excellent, and, in the contests in which he was engaged, NED showed himself off in the true BELCHER style.

The only pitched battle, we have learned, that NED fought, was with one *Jones*, a hackney-coachman, on Epping Forest, on June 5, 1806, and which has since been spoken of as a spirited and well-contested battle, and that NED's pretensions to pugilism were far above mediocrity. NED so completely *punished Coachee*, that, in the event, he was declared the victor.

Although labouring under the disadvantages of a lame hand, he was not easily intimidated, and upon some difference of opinion taking place between him and the Young Ruffian, *(Fearby)* in Wardour-street, Soho, an immediate appeal was made to the fist. NED (like his brother *Jem*) soon *served-out* the *Ruffian*, and once more convinced him that the name of BELCHER was a tower of strength.

That notorious *glutton, Joe Berks,* having insulted two gentlemen, in a public-house, in Oxendon-street, in the presence of NED BELCHER, he immediately ex-postulated with *Berks* upon the impropriety of his conduct; but instead of getting any reply, the latter, without hesitation, (being rather in an inebriated state,) struck NED for his interference. This assault was not to be put up with passively; the name of BELCHER must not be disgraced, and NED instantly returned the favour. A regular *set-to* was the result, and *Berks* was so severely *punished* in the course of a few rounds, that he was glad to cry for quarter; and also make some acknowledgement for the error which he had committed.

NED died of a consumption, a few years since.

BOB GREGSON, P. P.

One of the most distinguished Champions of Lancashire,

AND

POET LAUREATE

TO THE HEROIC RACE OF PUGILISTS.

I dare do all that may become a man;
Who dares do more, is none.

In recording the most prominent traits of the cele-brated Pugilists, from the earliest professors of the Gymnastic Art, down to the present *milling* era, when passing in review, Boxiana has found none more entitled to peculiar attention than the hero of the present sketch.

Fig, for his superior skill and union of talents, in fencing, dexterity in cudgelling, and manliness of boxing, stood without a rival competitor; but who was succeeded in the latter acquirement by *George Taylor,* a pugilist of considerable repute, till the veteran *Broughton* appeared, who rose up like a phenomenon in the pugilistic hemisphere, and gave elegance and perfection to boxing, till he was unexpectedly *vanquished,* and retired from all contests, to make room for the mighty and decisive *Slack! Corcoran* performed prodigies of valour as a bruiser; but it was *Tom Johnson* that portrayed the soundness of the art, throughout an extensive practice, particularly in opposition to the manly and judicious efforts of *Michael Ryan. Humphries* gave dignity and grace to *positions*; and *Mendoza* enriched pugilism with superlative *science,* and rendered the acquirement of *self-defence* easy and practicable : while *Big Ben*

became attractive for his tremendous powers. *Bill Warr*
evinced the advantages of activity; *Hooper* astonished
by his uncommon *pluck;* and the fine symmetry and
strength of the human figure, was an interesting topic,
exemplified in the person of *Jackson*. A new epoch
took place in fighting, when *Jem Belcher* made his
appearance, and his *nouvelle* rapid style of execution
baffled all his competitors. For manly fortitude and
humanity, the name of *Pearce,* as a pugilist, can never
be effaced; while the *gluttony* of *Berks* will ever form
a *striking* subject for the *caterers* of that sort of food;
and, as a hard hitter, *Gulley* will long claim remembrance. The singularity of *giving, Dutch Sam* stands
as a prodigy, operating as a contrast to the neatness,
promptitude, and precision of *Tom Belcher.* For
hitting and getting away, *Richmond* is distinguished,
and the brave *Molineaux* keeps a strong hold in the
circle of boxers, as a pugilist of the first class; while
the CHAMPION OF ENGLAND stands unrivalled for his
punishment, game, and *milling* on the *retreat!* Yet, notwithstanding the above variety of qualifications, it has
been reserved for BOB GREGSON *alone,* from his
union of *pugilism* and POETRY, (to recount the deeds
of his Brethren of the Fist in heroic verse, like the
bards of old, in sounding the praises of their warlike
Champions,) whose pretensions to the former are beyond all dispute, and respecting the latter, one of the
most distinguished works of *sporting celebrity* has given
place to the poetic effusions of his muse.

BOB was born on the 21st of July, 1778, at Heskin,
three miles from Chorley, and ten from Preston, in Lancashire, descended from very respectable parents, and

who possessed a farm of considerable extent at that place. Bob's education was by no means neglected : and he filled the situation of Captain of the Liverpool Wigan Packet for several years with credit and respect, and was allied by marriage to a family of some importance in the above great mercantile town.

For the period of seven years, all the pugilistic heroes of Lancashire, as well as those from other parts, who met him in combat, surrendered to his conquering arm; and the name of GREGSON was resounded from one end to the other, as the proud CHAMPION of that most populous county. His pitched battles are numerous; but the skirmishes of BOB were by far too frequent for us to treat upon, and we have, therefore, slightly touched on those achievements which claim a prominency of feature.

BOB's pugilistic talents, perhaps, might have been for ever obscured from the world, and himself content to drag on a life of rustic insipidity, had not the smiles of the *fair sex* awakened his brave heart, and brought them into action. At the age of eighteen, GREGSON commenced, with all the impassioned ardour of youth, a Champion in defence of that sex, of whom the Poet has so emphatically portrayed :—

> WOMAN, the fountain of all human frailty !
> What mighty ills have not been done by WOMAN?
> Who was't betray'd the Capitol ? A WOMAN.
> Who lost Mark Antony the world ? A WOMAN.
> Who was the cause of a long ten years' war,
> A ad laid at last Old Troy in ashes? WOMAN!

BOB being at Bispham Green, near Ormskirk, in Lancashire, to participate in the rustic sports of a country wake, when he was rudely assailed by one *Harry Maudersley*, who attempted to take away the idol of Bob's heart from him, but GREGSON resented the insult so strongly, that a regular *set-to* immediately commenced. After half an hour's decent *milling*, notwithstanding *Maudersley* was a tall man, and weighing thirteen stone, his *amorous* pretensions were so completely taken out of him by Bob's potent fist, that he surrendered all claims to the female in question once more to the entire protection of her admiring hero. Bob's situation became more perilous than ever, as one *Ned Waller*, a sort of second Champion to the county, and a friend of *Maudersley*, rather jealous of Bob's success, instantly kicked up a *row* with him, which continued an hour and a half, during which time Bob was without his clothes. At length he entered the ring with *Waller*, and likewise gave him a severe beating. GREGSON's fame now rose so rapidly into notice, not only from this *affair of gallantry*, but his pretensions to boxing were considered so sound, that *Jas. Ayschroft*, the *Champion of Lancashire*, a Collier, weighing sixteen stone, surrendered his claim to that elevated title to Bob, who became the first pugilist in the county.

GREGSON was now rendered a public mark to *hit* at, and challenges came in thick and threefold:—*Ned Prescot*, a man of considerable size, and weighing fifteen stone and a half, entered the lists with Bob at Wigan Fair, but, in the course of twenty minutes, *Ned* was so completely *punished*, that he was glad to cry out ENOUGH! yet, in a short time afterwards, *Prescot* demanded a second trial, when Bob again disposed of him in quick time.

James Benton, a Collier, well known in Lancashire

as a pugilist of no mean stamp, fought with GREGSON, at Standish; but who, after a hard contest, *gave in.*

BOB also contended with one *Tom Dawber*, a boxer who had *milled* a few customers in his time. The latter felt so jealous of GREGSON's growing fame, that he challenged him to a public combat; but, in the event of which, *Dawber* paid most dearly for his temerity. He not only received severe *punishment*, but acknowledged that he had obtained a cure for his *jealousy.*

Robert Fance, who had a thirst for pugilistic honours, and weighing thirteen stone, contended with BOB at Chorley, but who also fell beneath the conquering arm of the latter.

A man, of the name of *Tom Wright*, (a particular friend of BOB's,) and who, from his various exploits in pugilism, was considered the only equal match that could be found for him in Lancashire, entered the lists with GREGSON, at Eccleston, upon an agreement that *they should fight without seconds*, and not *to be separated.* A most desperate conflict ensued, which continued for an hour and a half, when *Wright*, not till he was almost *annihilated*, reluctantly acknowledged BOB's superiority. GREGSON was also a considerable time before he recovered from the severe effects of this battle.

BOB was now engaged in a truly *nouvelle* contest with a farmer's servant, of the name of *Bill Hallsol*, at Scarsbrick Bridge, near Ormskirk. *Hallsol*, who was not insensible to the *widowed charms* of his mistress, and who aspired to the management of a good farm, &c. plucked up courage to make her an offer of his hand, but the *fair widow*, who was descended from a race of pugilists, would not agree to the terms of capitulation only upon the following condition, that he must conquer the Champion GREGSON, before she surrendered in due form to the completion of his wishes. LOVE and GLORY were two noble subjects, and, to prove that the "*Age of Chivalry*" was not over, *Hallsol* immediately challenged BOB to the field. GREGSON, always ready to the calls of honour, accepted the invitation instantly. *Hall* entered the ring with the enthusiasm of a *knight errant*, and bravely fought to obtain this *double conquest;* but his ambition proved too daring, and he was so completely punished out of all recollection of the cause in which he had been engaged, that his fall was truly desperate, and he was carried away nearly in an inanimate state. However, upon *Hallsol's* recovering a little from the severe effects of this battle, the prize was still so dazzling to his eyes, and the *charms of the widow* had made such a strong impression upon his feelings, that, before the week had elapsed, he sent a second challenge to GREGSON, who, very *politely*, gave him another chance to obtain the *fair hand* of his mistress; but poor *Hallsol* was again so miserably beaten, and his flattering dreams of joy so completely vanished, that his bold heart was almost broken at the cruel inflexibility of the *fair one*, by imposing upon him such an ungracious task, to procure the possession of her smiles.

The tremendous *Joe Berks* now made his appearance at Manchester, threatening destruction to all the pugilists in the county who should have the temerity to enter the lists with him, when GREGSON was once more called upon to avenge the honour of his native soil, and to expel, if possible, this daring invader. It was a truly brave contest, and the *gluttony* of this pugilistic *cormo-*

rant was never more completely *satisfied;* and he publicly declared, a short time afterwards, that his *appetite*
had never been good since that period. The battle
took place at Higher Hardwick, when, after forty
minutes had elapsed, *Berks* acknowledged GREGSON
to be his master.

Soon after the above circumstance, BOB's prospects
in life experienced a material change, owing to a severe
domestic calamity, in the loss of an amiable and affec-
tionate partner; and he now not only bid adieu to Lancashire, but, in all probability, to pugilism in future.
BOB was presented with a commission in the army,
which regiment, named after the county, was quar-
tered at Plymouth, to which place GREGSON repaired
to join the standard; but finding his finances were not
able to support the character of an officer with that
respectability which such a situation required, he relinquished the project. BOB, without any pursuit
before him, arrived in the Metropolis, (to use a sporting phrase,) nearly *cleaned out.* BOB now experienced
some vicissitudes—facts are stubborn things—and
it was from the necessity of the moment only, that
GREGSON was induced to enter the ring again as a
pugilist.

Upon BOB's first meeting with *Gulley,* at a public-
house, some harsh epithets passed between them, when
GREGSON, to show his strength, took *Gulley* up under his
arm, and threw him down on the ground; upon which a
match was the consequence between those heroes. But
BOB was not the man he had been, and what is termed
the *fight* had, in a great measure, been taken out of
him, from the numerous battles in which he had been
engaged for several years past, with all the strongest

and best men of Lancashire; yet, nevertheless, his contest with *Gulley* (see page 176) exceeded every other battle in the annals of pugilism for determined resolution and *bottom;* and the betting, which had been *twenty* to one, was reduced, towards the close of the fight, to *even;* and so exhausted were the combatants, that BOTH were expected to pronounce at the same time—ENOUGH! But the *time* being expired, and GREGSON not appearing exactly ready, the fortunate moment for *Gulley* was immediately seized upon by his friends, who carried him off as the conqueror; but who was so dreadfully beaten, that he lay for *five hours* afterwards so perfectly insensible, that little hopes were entertained of his recovery! In fact, such serious consequences were apprehended, that the partisans of *Gulley* had him taken to GREGSON, who was in a coach, to shake hands with him before he left the ground. In the second engagement with his brave opponent, the fortitude of GREGSON was truly conspicuous. In his memorable fight with the present CHAMPION OF ENGLAND, *Tom Cribb,* it was singular in the extreme that BOB lost the battle. In the round previous to the last, it was betted TEN to *one* that *Cribb* did not come again; and it is asserted, it was owing to an *accidental throw,* proceeding from a sort of entangling with their legs, which occasioned, unexpectedly, GREGSON to go down. The shock of which operated so forcibly upon his exhausted frame, that "*time*" had expired before he was ready again to *set-to.* *Cribb* was equally in as bad a state, but who, upon hearing the welcome sound of victory, *fell down,* and did not recover for some few minutes!

THREE such succeeding battles as the above had scarcely, if ever, been witnessed; and GREGSON, although in *defeat*, rose proudly as a most distinguished pugilistic hero. Two *out of the* THREE were truly the effect of *mere* CHANCE; and when the above contests are fairly analysed, when *impartiality* shall pronounce her unerring verdict, it will be seen that pugilism never had a braver supporter than BOB GREGSON. If BOB did not possess that accuracy of *science,* so very prominent as some of the first professors of the gymnastic art, yet his display of *bottom* and intrepidity, with those heroes of the fist, *Gulley* and *Cribb,* who experienced such difficulty in reducing his efforts—have completely stamped him a pugilist of no ordinary pretensions— and a boxer that is not often to be found.

Soon after the above period, BOB took a benefit at the Fives' Court, when he took his final leave of pugilism, as a public professor, to commence landlord of the *Castle,* in Holborn, since denominated, and better known by the appellation of

BOB's CHOP-HOUSE:

His house is known to all the *milling* train,
He gives them liquor, and relieves their pain.

And, although it must be admitted that it is not of equal notoriety with Lloyd's Coffee-house, yet it is of great *celebrity* in the SPORTING WORLD, and is viewed as a prominent feature in the Metropolis; and which has its subscription, commodious coffee-room, &c. attached to it. In the latter apartment are whole-length portraits of some of the celebrated pugilists, framed in the most superb style of elegance; and the landlord, as a convincing proof that he entertains no spleen or envy against his distinguished competitor, the CHAMPION OF ENGLAND, as well as showing great diffidence, has exhibited three portraits of CRIBB, to the *exclusion of his own likeness!* BOB's frequenters are of the most respectable description; and the various gradations of the *Fancy* hither resort, to discuss matters incidental to pugilism, and where every attention is paid to the casual visitor, that each department, it may be said, is conducted with cleanliness, propriety, and despatch.

GREGSON is in height six feet one inch and a half, and weighing about fifteen stone six pounds: to Nature he is indebted for a fine figure, and his appearance is manly and imposing. BOB has been considered so good an anatomical subject to descant upon, that Mr. CARLISLE, the celebrated Professor of Anatomy at the Royal Academy, has selected him to stand several times for that purpose; and who has likewise been the subject of the pencils of LAWRENCE, DAW, &c. &c. in their portraying the beauty of human proportion; with a constitution truly robust, a vivacious eye, calculated to dazzle every spectator with its importance, and an arm that is

"Active and strong, and vigorous to all its purposes."

Possessing good intellectual faculties, his general deportment is above all absurd affectation; nothing supercilious is to be found in his manner, and ambition, it appears, is totally exempt from his breast:— on the contrary,

Far other aims his heart has learned to prize—
More bent to raise *the* VALIANT *than to* RISE!

It seems that GREGSON was an independent pugilist—
he was not on the *flash* side, *i. e.* he was not *down* when
he entered the lists with the London Boxers; and it is
still said of him, that he remains as *perverse* as ever, in
obstinately judging for himself, in opposition to all
flash opinions, adhering to those old-fashioned notions
of *right* and *wrong!* but, notwithstanding these peculiarities of disposition, we are informed, he is humane,
friendly, and attentive to the professors of the fist,
but more especially at those periods when consolation
and comfort are necessary—the BRAVE in DEFEAT!

It has been urged that GREGSON must have won those
battles alluded to, had he have proved *scientific;* but
some allowance ought to be made, when it is considered
the difficulties he had to contend against, in divesting
himself of those *provincialities* in which he had been
reared, and all at once to commence the elegant, scientific, and finished metropolitan boxer. Every thing in
London must be excellent to gain eminence, and where
the exalted Champion of a County ranks *only* with
Champions of Counties, and is put upon a level with
other men, till he soars above those comparisons, and
some great event places him upon *that* elevated seat, the
most anxious desire of all pugilists to obtain. It is an
opinion strongly entertained in the Army, that it is much
easier to make a man a good dragoon who never mounted
a horse in his life, than a post-boy who has been riding
all his days; proving that instruction is acquired with
greater facility where there has been no particular bias,
than it is to dispense with accustomed peculiarities.

Respecting BOB's mental capacity, it will be found,
that he is an intelligent, well-informed person, and if he

cannot, by way of comparison, claim a superiority of *science* over his brethren of the fist, however, as a man of *nous*, he stands upon an elevated point. With a mind rather fond of inquiry, he has formed some acquaintance with that class of literature which tends to enlarge and dignify the human intellect ; and, although not possessing the terseness and originality of Dry-DEN, or the musical cadence and correctness of POPE, yet still he has entered into a peculiar subject with a characteristic energy and apposite spirit :

> The poet's eye, in a fine frenzy rolling,
> Doth glance from heaven to earth, from earth to heaven,
> And, as imagination bodies forth
> The form of things unknown, the poet's pen
> Turns them to shape, and gives to airy nothing
> A local habitation and a name.

Instead of that spirit of detraction which too often pervades the breast of a fallen competitor, GREGSON, it must be admitted, with a spirit of liberality, which few men possess, has not only endeavoured by his talents to increase and promulgate a *conquering* RIVAL's *fame*, but also to consolidate his great achievements. The *Herald's Office*, perhaps, might have been searched in vain to procure armorial bearings for the CHAM-PION's *coat of arms*, had not BOB's inventive genius rendered the application unnecessary, (assisted by the most natural comedian of the age, *John Emery*, to whose united efforts, the heraldry of *Tom Cribb* is indebted,) and which otherwise might have been for ever obscured from the world. The following poetic effusion was written by BOB GREGSON, in honour of the CHAMPION's victory over *Molineaux*.

VOL. I.   3 D

BRITISH LADS and BLACK MILLERS.

You gentlemen of fortune attend unto my ditty,
  A few lines I have penn'd upon this great fight,
In the centre of England the noble place is pitch'd on,
  For the VALOUR OF THIS COUNTRY, or *America's* delight;
    The sturdy Black doth swear,
    The moment he gets there,
The planks the stage is built on, he'll make them blaze and smoke,
    Then CRIBB, with smiling face,
    Says, these boards I'll ne'er disgrace,
They're *relations of mine,* they're OLD ENGLISH OAK.

Brave MOLINEAUX replied, I've never been denied,
  To fight the foes of Britons on such planks as those;
If relationship you claim, bye and bye, you'll know my name,
  I'm the Moorish milling blade that can drub my foes.
    Then CRIBB replied with haste,
    You slave, I will you baste,
As your master us'd to cane you, 'twill bring things to your mind:
    If from bondage you've got clear,
    To impose on Britons here,
You'd better stopp'd with Christophe, you'll quickly find.

The garden of freedom is the British land we live in,
  And welcomes every slave from his banish'd isle,
Allows them to impose on a nation good and generous,
  To incumber and pollute our native soil.
    But John Bull cries out aloud,
    We're neither poor nor proud,
But open to all nations, let them come from where they will:
    The British lads that's here,
    Quite strangers are to fear,
Here's TOM CRIBB, with bumpers round, for he can them *mill!*

Through the wide range of society the traveller may, at times, meet with something like the perfections of a GRANDISON; while, on the contrary, his journey will be repeatedly arrested by the frailties of a TOM JONES: human nature is so prone to error, and circumstance and situation operate so strongly upon the feelings, that we are too apt to "*put an enemy into our mouth to steal away our brains!"* and by so doing, commit those excesses, which, on mature reflection, our nature revolts at with disgust and unhappiness. *Alexander* killed *Clytus* when besotted with liquor, and his rational moments were ever afterwards embittered with sorrow and remorse, by the death of his best and most valued general—but, if every man was dealt with according to his deserts, "WHO *should 'scape whipping?"*

GREGSON, from his retentive memory, obtained considerable repute among that most honourable and ancient fraternity denominated Freemasons.

We cannot conclude without observing that no pugilist has had to contend against severer disappointments than GREGSON ; nor has any boxer, whatever, experienced more chilling and almost overwhelming defeats. But, in nobly buffeting the frowns of fortune, he displayed the struggles of a brave mind thirsting after victory, and evinced a *bottom* as sound as gold. In himself, BOB made a bold stand to obtain the honours of the Championship, and it was so *nice a point,* that it was the toss-up of a halfpenny whether it was decided for *Lancashire* or *Bristol;* and the specimens of fine resolution and *game* GREGSON has since introduced for pugilistic honours have by no means disgraced his patronage, or reflected any impropriety for portraying a partiality in favour of his native country. Since his residence in the Metropolis, BOB has been completely in the back ground respecting success in boxing affairs ; but who has amply succeeded in establishing a character for independence and honesty, that must ever render him one of the

soundest friends of pugilism, and whose name will
long live enrolled among the records of the brave.

> Hail, noble Albion! where no golden mines,
> No soft perfumes, nor oils, nor myrtle bow'rs,
> The vig'rous frame and lofty heart of man
> Enervate: round whose stern cerulean brows,
> White-wing'd snow, and cloud, and pearly rain,
> Frequent attend, with solemn majesty:
> Rich queen of mists and vapours! These, thy sons,
> With their cool arms compress; and twist their nerves
> For deeds of excellence and high renown.
> Thus form'd, our *Broughtons, Slacks, Johnsons,*
> Our *Belchers, Jacksons, Cribbs,* and our *Gregsons* rose.

TOM MOLINEAUX,

The Tremendous Man of Colour.

> The hero who, to live in story,
>   In search of honour dares to roam,
> And reaps a crop of fame and glory—
>   This is the warrior's harvest home.

UNKNOWN, unnoticed, unprotected, and uninformed,
the brave MOLINEAUX arrived in England: descended
from a warlike hero, who had been the conquering pugilist of *America*, he felt all the animating spirit of his
courageous sire, and left his native soil in quest of glory
and renown.   The British nation, famed for deeds in
arms, attracted his towering disposition; and his ambitious spirit prompted him with an ardent desire to
enter the lists with some of her most distinguished
Champions.   *Distance* created no obstacles, nor the
raging seas were no impediment to his heroic views,
and, like the daring adventurer who suffers nothing to

thwart his purposes, the object of his wishes were gained, and he, at length, found himself in the most enviable capital in the world—LONDON. MOLINEAUX was a perfect stranger, a rude, unsophisticated being; and, resting entirely upon his pugilistic pretensions to excellence, he offered himself to the notice of the public. He was soon noticed by the patrons of those gymnastic sports, which, from their practice and support, have instilled principles of valour into her hardy sons, that have not only added greatness, but given stability to the English character.

MOLINEAUX came as an open and bold competitor for boxing fame; and he challenged the proudest heroes to the hostile combat. Such declaration was manly, fair, and honourable, and entitled to every respect and attention among the pugilistic circles. It was, however, objected to MOLINEAUX, that he was too ambitious, by threatening to wrest the laurels from the English brow, and planting them upon the head of a foreigner—if so, dearly has he paid for his temerity; but if his claims to pugilism were of the first-rate quality which they have been represented, the greatest honour was attached to the conquest of such a formidable hero.

MOLINEAUX's first *set-to* in England was with a Bristol man, of robust make, and about six feet in height, in Tothill-fields, on July 24, 1810. *Richmond* seconded MOLINEAUX, and *Cribb* his countryman. It was a most *game* fight, and continued for an hour. MOLINEAUX *punished* his opponent so severely, that it was impossible to distinguish a single feature in his face. He also gave such specimens of dexterity and *science*, as to claim considerable attention from the

spectators, who viewed him as a pugilist of great
promise.   Upon MOLINEAUX being declared the conqueror, he was immediately matched to fight *Tom
Blake*, a man denominated, from his fine *bottom* and
resolution, *TomTough!* a boxer of great repute and
practice.

In less than a month from the above period, this
contest was decided upon the coast a few miles from
Margate, on August, 21, 1810, upon the same spot of
ground on which *Richmond* and *Maddox* had so bravely
contended.   MOLINEAUX was attended by his friend
Richmond; Blake had for his second *Tom Cribb*, and
his bottle-holder, *Bill Gibbons.*

First round.—The fame of Molineaux having got rather
spread abroad, considerable anxiety was manifest upon the
combatants *setting-to*—good sparring was exhibited for a short
period on both sides, when Blake showed himself completely
scientific in hitting right and left, and stopping the return of
Molineaux ; they closed, but Blake, in slipping from his antagonist, received a terrible *hit* upon the back part of his neck,
which was repeated by the Black so severely as to send Blake
down.   Even betting.

Second.—Blake soon discovered that his opponent was not
to be disposed of easily, and that his blows, however well directed, were not strong enough to knock his adversary down.—
Molineaux seemed to disregard the attempts of Blake, and
showed himself tolerably conversant in the science, by beating
down his adversary's guard with his left hand, and by a tremendous blow with his right *levelled* Blake.

Third.—Blake appeared rather exhausted, which Molineaux
perceiving, went in to improve upon the circumstance ; but
Blake *hit* him on the jaw ; when they rallied and fell, Blake
undermost.

Fourth.—A truly obstinate round ; but evidently in favour
of Molineaux, who broke down Blake's guard and *punished*
him severely in the face ; notwithstanding, Blake put in several body-blows, but they were not effective, and was ultimately
knocked down.   Five to two on Molineaux.

Fifth.—Blake covered with blood ; but with great resolution rallied, when Molineaux held him round the neck with his left arm, and *fibbed* him so tremendously, that Blake fell, completely exhausted.

Sixth.—Molineaux had it all his own way this round, and, without ceremony, went in and knocked down Blake's guard with his left hand, and with a terrible blow, put in with his right, *levelled* his adversary. All betters, but no takers, in favour of Molineaux.

Seventh.—Blake's *game* was not yet extinct, and he rallied with considerable spirit, and some good blows were exchanged; but who fell from weakness.

Eighth.—Molineaux, determined to finish the contest, went in with uncommon fury; Blake endeavoured to retreat from the violent efforts of his opponent; but was compelled to rally, and who put in a good blow upon the cheek of his opponent. Molineaux returned with a tremendous *hit* upon Blake's head, that completely took all recollection out of him; the effects of which he did not recover from so as to be ready to time, when Molineaux was proclaimed the conqueror.

In the above battle the amateurs were completely astonished at the improvement exhibited by Molineaux, and the *punishment* he dealt out was so truly tremendous, and his strength and *bottom* so superior, that he was deemed a proper match for the Champion, Tom Cribb; in consequence of which, a match was made for two hundred guineas a-side, and a subscription-purse of one hundred was to be given to the winner. It was now the jealousy commenced, and the aspiring ambition of Molineaux to obtain the Championship of England, excited considerable anxiety and interest in the *sporting world;* the honour of the country was at stake, and, it is supposed, that no boxer ever entered the ring with so many wishes for his success as *Tom Cribb.*

It was on December 18, 1810, at *Copthorn,* a few miles north-west of East Grinstead, Sussex, that TOM CRIBB, *in vanquishing* his brave opponent, Molineaux, *added fresh laurels to the* Championship, and honour to his country.

MOLINEAUX, notwithstanding his defeat, felt that he was entitled to another *chance,* and accordingly sent the following challenge in three days after the above battle :—

To Mr. THOMAS CRIBB.

St. Martin's Street, Leicester-square,
December 21, 1810.

SIR,

    My friends think that had the weather on last Tuesday, the day upon which I contended with you, not been so unfavourable, I should have won the battle ; I therefore challenge you to a second meeting, at any time within two months, for such a sum as those gentlemen who place confidence in me, may be pleased to arrange.

As it is possible that this letter may meet the public eye, I cannot omit the opportunity of expressing a confident hope that the circumstance of my being a different colour to that of the people amongst whom I have sought protection, will not in any way operate to my prejudice.

I am, SIR,
Your most obedient humble Servant,
T. MOLINEAUX.

Witness, J. SCHOLFIELD.

Since the defeat of MOLINEAUX, a young man of the name of *Rimmer,* a native of Lancashire, about twenty-two years of age, and who had distinguished himself in two or three battles in his own county, was matched against the competitor of the Champion, for one hundred guineas, under the auspices of *Gregson.* Moulsey-Hurst was the scene of action, in a twenty-five feet roped ring, on May 21, 1811. MOLINEAUX was seconded by his friend *Richmond,* and *Bill Gibbons* his bottle-holder; *Rimmer* was attended by *Powers* and *Jones.* Three to one in favour of MOLINEAUX.

First round.—Two minutes had elapsed in sparring, when Rimmer *hit* right and left ; but his *distances* were badly judged, and they proved of no effect, and got away—resuming a sparring attitude, when Molineaux put in a left-handed blow with great violence on his opponent's neck, which was returned very slightly by Rimmer, who fell upon receiving this blow. Molineaux the favourite, four to one, and Rimmer exhibited the first display of *claret*.

Second.—Rimmer hit right and left, made some play, and got away, but his distance was erroneous: Molineaux, on the look-out, made some excellent stops in a desperate rally which took place, but they both disengaged. Another rally immediately commenced, and here the *Black's* tremendous powers were witnessed, he *punished* Rimmer in all directions, and knocked him down finally by blows right and left, with uncommon celerity and science.

Third.—Molineaux now appeared confident that he was at home, from the success of the last round, and viewed his adversary with a supercilious grin, sparred low, as if treating Rimmer with contempt, and waited, as before, till his opponent made play, when the Black hit away, and followed them up so hard and fast that Rimmer, it appeared, went to the ground from a wish to avoid the *punishment* of his opponent.

Fourth.—The head of Rimmer was now completely *pinked*, and, from his manner, seemed at fault, from a severe blow he had received in the last round on the temple. Molineaux put in several severe hits, right and left, over his guard, when Rimmer instantly fell, as if shot. Molineaux was quite a hero, and punished his opponent with considerable ease and effect. Eight to one Molineaux was the conqueror.

Fifth.—Rimmer greatly distressed, and in making a hit fell.

Sixth.—Rimmer judged his distances very incorrectly, and fell from weakness.

Seventh.—Rimmer in this round appeared to the greatest advantage, and had the best of it,—he put in a good blow with his left hand, and rallied courageously—several good hits were exchanged, when Rimmer fell over his opponent's legs.

Ninth.—Rimmer strained every nerve to change the state of the battle, hit his adversary away in their rallying, and, in closing, threw Molineaux.

Tenth.—Rimmer's spirited conduct made Molineaux quite ferocious, who went in desperately, and was intemperate enough to make play, but pursuing Rimmer, and *punishing* him to all parts of the ring, at length *levelled* him.

Eleventh.—Rimmer showed himself entitled to the appellation of a *game* pugilist. Several good blows were exchanged; but Rimmer appeared to have a very incorrect idea of distance, and seemed impressed with the severity of his opponent's hits by holding his head down, which received several blows, when he fell,

Twelfth.—Rimmer was losing the battle fast, and hit his adversary's body without effect.—Passion now was uppermost with him, and he ran in after the *Lancashire* method, lifting Molineaux by the thighs of his legs, and throwing him down. Some murmurs broke forth of "Foul! Fair!" &c.

Thirteenth.—Rimmer hit his antagonist over the mouth, but was thrown by him.

Fourteenth.—Rimmer rallied and closed, when each tried to show his superior strength, but both fell in the attempt, owing to a Lancashire touch of Rimmer.

Fifteenth.—It was *all up* with Rimmer, who retreated to every part of the ring, followed closely by Molineaux, who put in a dreadful stomacher, which *floored* him. A scene now took place which beggared all description; during the time Rimmer lay prostrate on the ground, the ring was broken, owing, it is said, from the antipathy felt against a *man of colour* proving the conqueror :—if it were so, the illiberal were disappointed by this manœuvre, as those who had taken the odds gained nothing by the event. Rimmer was completely exhausted, almost in a state of insensibility. It would have been a fine subject for the pencil of Hogarth to have delineated. *Corinthians* and *Costermongers* in rude contact; *Johnny-Raws* and first-rate *Swells* jostling each other ; Pugilists and *Novices*, all jawing, and threatening, but no hearing. The confusion was beyond every thing ; sticks and whips at work in all directions, ten thousand people in one rude commotion, and those persons in the interior of this vast assemblage suffering from their attempts to extricate themselves from so perilous and unpleasant a situation. Twenty minutes elapsed in this *chaotic* manner, till the Champion of England, assisted by some brave followers, once more formed something like a ring. By the rules of fighting, if either of the combatants leave the ring, he is considered to have lost the battle. Molineaux and Rimmer again *set-to*, but it proved a short-lived advantage to the latter, notwithstanding extraordinary exertions were made to renovate Rimmer, and make him stand upon his legs, but it was all in vain. During six more rounds Rimmer was so severely *punished*, that he was unable to stand up, when he acknowledged that he had received *enough!*

From the above and other battles MOLINEAUX had given such tremendous specimens of *milling*, that since the defeat of *Rimmer* no other pugilist, it should seem, possessed temerity enough to call the *man of colour* to the field, till he once more entered the lists with the CHAMPION of England, at a place called Thistleton Gap, in the county of Leicester, on September 28, 1811, and was again vanquished; but in a much shorter space of time, the contest continuing only *nineteen minutes* and a *few seconds!*

The joy experienced upon the above occasion by the *flash* side cannot be described—and, considering all the disadvantages under which MOLINEAUX fought this battle, he performed wonders. It is not meant to be urged that MOLINEAUX had not fair play throughout the fight *in the ring*—it is well known that he had—but the *Black* had to contend against a prejudiced multitude; the pugilistic honour of the country was at stake, and the attempts of MOLINEAUX were viewed with jealousy, envy, and disgust: the national laurels to be borne away by a foreigner—the *mere* idea to an English breast was afflicting, and the *reality* could not be endured:—that it should seem, the spectators were ready to exclaim—

" Forbid it, heaven—forbid it, man!"

It was from this sort of impression, which operated upon the feelings of the auditors, that MOLINEAUX had more to fear than even the mighty prowess of his brave opponent—the applause and cheering were decidedly upon the part of the CHAMPION; in fact, the *man of colour* received, generally, a very different sort of reception, occasioned, we apprehend, from the extreme anxiety manifested by the friends of *Cribb* for the safety of his honour and renown; nor are these observations tended to detract one single jot from his well-merited laurels; but an impartial statement of a contest like the above, supersedes every other consideration. It would be absurd to remark, that MOLINEAUX underwent any thing like a regular *training ;* but, on the contrary, he indulged himself to excess—without a patron, he had to range from town to town, to support himself by exhibitions of sparring, and entering into all the glorious confusion of *larks* and *sprees* that might present themselves ; while, in opposition to such a line of conduct, how far different was it with the CHAMPION, placed under the immediate direction of Captain *Barclay,* and secluded from the world, at the estate of that Gentleman, his stamina became invigorated to the finest tone possible, his mind cheerful and independent, and feeling a confidence that every chance was in favour of his success. MOLINEAUX, in spite of his alleged ferocity, laboured under considerable depression; wherever he went, he was unpopular; which circumstance was considerably heightened upon his public appearance to face his antagonist. His constitution was by no means so good as in the former contest: but his efforts were tremendous and terrible, and for the first few rounds of the battle the *flash* side experienced great palpitation. Much more need not be observed than upwards of eighteen months elapsed (March 31, 1813) before MOLINEAUX met with a competitor, (in *Carter,*) though he had publicly challenged all England; but which contest did not take place, owing, it it said, from *Richmond's* arresting MOLINEAUX.

It appears that MOLINEAUX is never behind-hand
for a *brush*, and always ready to *set-to* whenever called
upon, which was witnessed in his *turn-up* with *Power ;*
the cause of which has been variously related.   The
latter, having been dealt with by *Richmond* not in a way
satisfactory to his feelings, had publicly declared
vengeance against the *man of colour;* and on meeting
with MOLINEAUX, at the house of *Richmond,* from
some reflections on complexion, which appeared too
pointed at the *Moor,* they immediately stripped, and
decided the affair of honour in the street.   It was a
most irregular contest, and impossible to be described
with any degree of accuracy ; but the *science* of *Power*
was visible, and he *milled* the *nob* of the *Black* in good
style, and got away; yet still MOLINEAUX was too
heavy for him, and upon closing in the crowd *science*
proved but of little advantage.   At times they both
fell; and after seventeen minutes of considerable confusion this *row* ended: the friends of *Power* interfered, deeming it advisable that he should no longer
contend with so powerful a man as MOLINEAUX.
Power's gallantry, notwithstanding an eye-lid rather *put
out of shape,* and a lip *damaged,* would not permit him
to break off an appointment that he had previously
made of accompanying four ladies to the theatre,
and whither this Hero of the Fist repaired, with the
most perfect *sang-froid,* to enjoy the company of the
fair sex, and the attractions of the stage.

MOLINEAUX, at all events, must rank high as a
scientific pugilist; and it is said, that if he could
receive punishment equal to the manner in which he
serves it out, it would be almost impossible for any

one to stand long against him.   In height, about five
feet nine inches; weighing between 13 and 14 stone;
twenty-eight years of age; inferior to none in point of
courage and *bottom;* and considered a most excellent
two-handed fighter.   Full of fight, he exchanges *hits*
with great alertness, and stops with considerable dexterity.   Remarkably civil and unassuming in his demeanour, considering his want of education, MOLI-
NEAUX has rendered himself to the *Fancy,* if not a
decided favourite, at least an object of considerable attraction.   To *Richmond* he is most undoubtedly
indebted for a considerable portion of that superior
pugilistic science which he possesses.

The following paragraph having appeared in the
Leicester paper of Feb. 3, 1813 :—"*Jay,* the pugilist,
has challenged MOLINEAUX to fight at any notice; but
Blackee remains both *deaf* and *dumb* to this challenge,
as he did to *Cribb's* immediate acceptance of a vaunting
challenge to him.   The Champion promises him a
love-dressing for his *bounces,* if he could be prevailed
on to come to London."

To which MOLINEAUX thus replied—" I, the said
MOLINEAUX, do declare, that I never received any
challenge but through the medium of your print, but
I am ready to fight him at any place, within the county
of Leicester, for a sum not exceeding £200, if accepted within one month of the above date. In opposition to that part of the paragraph which relates to
Cribb, I declare that I sent him a challenge within two
months, but I have received no answer; my friends
being mentioned in the challenge, who would back me

to any amount; and that I have never received any challenge from *Cribb* since I last fought him.

N.B. Letters left at the Post-Office, Leicester, will be duly attended.

The mark of

✗ THO. MOLINEAUX.

MOLINEAUX is also a good wrestler, and displayed great activity and powers, at the last Exeter meeting, July 27, 1812, where he entered himself for the public prize of Ten Guineas, but received a dreadful fall from *John Snow*, of Moreton.

CHARLES DIXON.

From recording the deeds of the athletic and powerful, whose strength and stamina have rendered them of such interesting notoriety, we are, for a short space, called upon to descant on pugilistic objects of less importance, though notwithstanding their efforts might be deemed Heroism in Miniature.

DIXON, whose weight was not above eight stone and a half, was as good a pugilist as ever exhibited in the lists of honour, his bottom was unquestionable, and his style of fighting not unlike that of *Tom Belcher*.

DIXON's first public *set-to* was on Feb. 8th, 1806, at Sendon Heath, near Virginia Water, with *Charles O'Shaugnessy*, a man considered so superior in every respect, that the bets were ten to one in his favour; but the skill and courage displayed by DIXON was of such peculiar excellence as to call forth the praises

of the most distinguished amateurs and experienced
pugilists. The *Game Chicken*, who was a spectator of
this combat, offered a great bet, that DIXON's body
was not so large as his thigh, as a proof of his diminutive stature. The fight was truly severe, and had
Charles not consented to have had his eyes lanced,
which were completely closed up, he must have lost
the battle; but on this experiment being performed,
he soon rendered the efforts of *O'Shaugnessy* unavailing, and was pronounced the conqueror.

In June, 1807, he entered the lists with *Lennox*, at
Moulsey Hurst, and after a sharp conflict, DIXON beat
his antagonist; in the July following, on the 28th,
at the same place, he also disposed of one *Groam*.

DIXON, on Feb. 9, 1808, at Highgate Common,
had the temerity to fight with a man of the name of
Smith, nearly two stone heavier than himself, and he
felt flattered that his knowledge of the *science* would
enable him to come through the *piece* with success;
but the superior strength of *Smith* gained him the
battle, by his throwing DIXON repeatedly, who could
not recover from the severe effects of such heavy
falls.

Soon afterwards, in 1808, at Wilsdon Green, he
again had the courage to meet a man, even heavier
than *Smith*, of the name of *Green*, and lost in a similar manner. DIXON fought both these battles against
the advice of his friends; and it is only fair to state,
that he contended for the honour of victory till
Nature was completely exhausted.

In the same year, in the month of November, DIXON
fought with one *Harris*, a soldier. The battle con-

tinued for two hours: and, in consequence of the behaviour of *George Rhodes*, who seconded *Harris*, and
finding that his man was dead beaten, endeavoured
to persuade the umpires that DIXON had given a foul
blow, who, however, declared otherwise. *Rhodes*, the
next day, arrested the stake-holder for the sum he
held on his account, and thus was DIXON deprived of
the fruits of his conquest.

At Wilsdon Green, April 12th, 1801, DIXON was
to have fought *Brannam*, for a subscription purse of
twenty guineas, and a great number of persons were
assembled to witness the conflict; but it having been
whispered that DIXON intended to play booty, and
that it was only to be a *sham* fight, which was perceived in the course of two rounds, as planting and
stopping were the order of the day; and after half an
hour's complete humbugging, *Brannam* retired from
the ring. The amateurs, conceiving themselves imposed upon, decided that neither of them should have
any of the money, as a lesson in future.

DIXON, to recover his reputation, entered the ring
on May 31st, 1801, at Moulsey Hurst, and, after a most
determined contest of nearly an hour, was compelled
to surrender to the superiority and *gameness* of *Ballard:*
but DIXON, not feeling satisfied, had another *set-to* in
the following November, at Old Oak Common, on
the 15th, when *Ballard* again proved the conqueror.

This was the last battle he fought: and it is painful to state, that, notwithstanding his *game*, he did
not possess *courage* enough to be correct in his deportment through life; and the Recorder of London was

compelled to send him to try the effects of another
climate.

CHARLES BRANNAM,

Commenced pugilist at an early period of life, when he
was only 14 years of age, and was the terror to most
of the growing young men in the parish of St. James,
Westminster: and at that age fought a man of the name
of *Davies*, for a guinea, in St George's Row, Paddington, which he won, after a well-contested battle of
thirty-five minutes. The advantage of strength was so
much against him, that, till within the last ten minutes
of the battle, he appeared to have no chance of success;
but having reduced his opponent's *strength* down to
his own level, BRANNAM's *science* caused him to prove
the victor.

In less than six months after CHARLES had been
placed out as an apprentice to a Carpenter, he entered
the lists with a man of the name of *John Redding*, better known by the appellation of *Jack in the Green*.
It was a truly severe contest, and BRANNAM was
knocked down nine times in succession, which had
nearly terminated the fight; and from the superior
strength of *Redding*, which was so convincing to every
one present, BRANNAM's friends insisted he should
no longer continue a battle, where there was no probability of success; but he was deaf to their remonstrances, and soon afterwards gave his opponent two
such tremendous *hits* on the nob, that nearly deprived
Jack in the Green of his senses: from this unexpected

circumstance BRANNAM now took the lead, and the bets immediately changed in his favour; when, after an hour and five minutes, BRANNAM was declared the conqueror: but so determined had been the heroes, that scarcely an original feature in either of them could be recognised. It was for two guineas, and considered the best battle that he ever fought. About eight months after this severe contest, BRANNAM, seconded by the elder Belcher, fought a tinman, of the name of *Thompson*, who was attended by *Tom Blake*, near the Queen's Head and Artichoke, for two guineas: in the course of twenty minutes the tinman was completely satisfied.

At this period, BRANNAM, according to his weight, was looked upon scarcely to have his superior, when *Jem Belcher* matched *George Humphries* against him for five guineas, but *Humphries* was the heaviest man by two stone, and the odds were two to one in his favour. The battle took place in Harper's Fields, near the New Cut, on Monday, January 8, 1807, in the presence of some thousands. After a severe conflict of fifteen minutes, BRANNAM was proclaimed conqueror, leaving *Humphries* on the ground almost lifeless. *Paddington Jones* seconded *Humphries*, and *Bill Ryan* attended BRANNAM.

It was not long after this battle, that BRANNAM, in returning from an ironmonger's shop, in Piccadilly, with several locks in his hand, accidentally touched against a *fille-de-joie*, who was escorted by a gallant *son of Mars:* it appears that BRANNAM begged pardon for the supposed offence, but this grenadier of the Guards, *sans cérémonie*, gave BRANNAM so severe a *facer*, that

made him instantly *bite the dust*, and the locks flew about
in all directions.   A gentleman, passing at the time,
observing the violent conduct of the grenadier, immediately insisted on his name, and what company he belonged to, that he might obtain redress from his officers;
but BRANNAM begged he would not interfere, declaring that he would soon *mill* the *swaddy* for his favour :
still the gentleman thought he had better complain to
his officers, than attempt to fight a man every way so
much his superior.   A small ring being formed, they
set-to, and in the course of the first round BRANNAM
so *nobbed* the soldier that his face was covered with
blood, and who felt so *satisfied*, that he declared he
would fight no more ; but some of his comrades passing, and feeling ashamed that a mere boy should beat
one of their regiment, made him continue the battle for
a quarter of an hour longer, when he was completely
blind.   BRANNAM received a guinea from the gentleman for his bravery, and who accompanied him
home to his master, to prevent his getting into
trouble.

On the 6th of September, 1808, BRANNAM entered
the lists with a *bottom* man of the name of *Renny*, for
ten guineas, at Wilsdon Green.   *Renny* had fought
numerous battles in his time, but never entered the ring
for a prize; yet still the odds were laid thick upon him.
In the first round BRANNAM showed himself off in
such good style, and his *science* appearing superior,
his friends backed him with spirit; *Renny* tried to
bore in upon his opponent, and dispose of him with
quickness and facility, but BRANNAM, being aware of
his intention, stopped *Renny's* hits with great adroit-

ness, and made some excellent returns, one of which he planted so severely on the head of his adversary, as to break a finger. This accident made a material alteration in the battle; the odds were now seven to four on *Renny,* who took the lead for the next quarter of an hour; but, notwithstanding BRANNAM's disaster, he maintained the contest with the greatest resolution for nearly two hours, when he was declared the victor, after having nearly killed his opponent, who was a truly *game* article. *Paddington Jones* and *Tom Blake* were seconds to BRANNAM, and *Jem Belcher* and *Dick Hall* supported *Renny.*

It appears that *Jem Belcher* was so disappointed in BRANNAM's beating *Humphries* and *Renny,* that he felt determined to try another subject for him, and accordingly selected one *Brook,* a brick-maker, and backed him for ten guineas, which battle was to have taken place on the 4th of October, 1808, on Finchley Common; but some peace-officers appeared, and showed their authority, to which they prudently bowed, and journeyed onwards to Barnet Common, where, a ring being formed, BRANNAM and *Brook* immediately set-to; but, after thirty-five minutes of good *milling,* the Mayor of Barnet and his officers compelled them to desist, which left this contest in doubt.

BRANNAM now entered the ring with a scientific boxer, *Jack Eldridge,* for ten guineas, at Wilsdon Green, on March 2, 1809. The true art of boxing was here displayed on both sides, and the amateurs and spectators were well satisfied with their efforts; but, after sixteen minutes had elapsed, BRANNAM gave his opponent so tremendous a cross-buttock, that his neck was nearly broken; and *Eldridge* reluctantly gave in!

BRANNAM, like other pugilists, whom Fortune had smiled on for a long time, was now doomed to meet a reverse of luck, by meeting with *Ballard*, a pupil of the veteran *Caleb Baldwin*, on Highgate Common, on January 1, 1810. The battle was fought with great spirit for forty-five minutes, when BRANNAM's hands refusing to do their office, he was necessitated to acknowledge that he was conquered.

JOHN FOSBROOK,

Although not publicly known in the Metropolis, is a boxer of considerable provincial reputation, and a native of Burton-upon-Trent, in Staffordshire, in height five feet eight inches, and weighing twelve stone; and considered equal to any pugilist of that weight in the kingdom. He occasionally visits the Metropolis, but has not been matched with any professed Metropolitan bruiser, although he has received considerable instruction from the Hero of Paddington, and in the prime of youth, being only twenty-three years of age.

At Burton-upon-Trent he has *milled* some of the primest fighters, and particularly one *Geery*, a navigator, with whom he maintained a most severe conflict for upwards of three quarters of an hour, when *Geery* was very glad to cry for quarter.

FOSBROOK also beat a man of the name of *Marriott* twice, who was considerably heavier and stronger than himself, in Cheshire, which added fresh laurels to his character in that part of the country.

JOHN FOSBROOK.

WILLIAM WARE.

Published Nov.ᵗ 13. 1812. by G. Smeeton, 139. St Martins Lane.

In Paddington Fields, one *Watts* challenged Fosbrook for ten guineas; but he was soon glad to give
it in. *Tom Jones* seconded his friend upon this occasion.

After a desperate conflict of fifty-eight minutes,
Fosbrook beat a hero of the name of *Gantliff*, in
Cheshire: and conquered one *Jack Heaps*, a boxer
of much celebrity, in Staffordshire, after an hour's
decent *milling*.

During the short time Fosbrook was engaged at
the Copper Mills, at Rickmansworth, he was violently
attacked by three navigators and a woman; but by
considerable judgment and courage he soon made the
navigators repent their conduct, and retreat from his
punishment, when he found no difficulty in *persuading*
the *lady* to follow their example!

At Shaffnel, in Staffordshire, he vanquished one
Tom Cock twice, who was thought to have considerable
pretensions to boxing.

TOM BLAKE:

(*Otherwise denominated* Tom Tough.)

Among the numerous pugilistic heroes, whose valorous deeds claim the recording pages of Boxiana, the
name of Blake deserves most honourable mention.
His combats have not only been numerous but uniformly
good; remarkably dexterous and scientific upon all
occasions; and possessing a *bottom* of the finest quality.
Tom Tough was a tremendous competitor to all those
who had the temerity to enter the lists with him:

and it must not be passed over, that the greatest
CHIEFS of the present period found it of the utmost
difficulty to make him pronounce the word ENOUGH!
In his contest with *Holmes*, BLAKE proved himself
Tough indeed—it was truly termed a slaughtering
conflict, which will be perceived in the recital:—in
his battle with *Tom Cribb*, his *science* and courage
were so truly excellent, that no odds were offered for
nearly twenty minutes, and an hour had elapsed before
BLAKE evinced distress. In the fight with *Molineaux*,
though upwards of forty years of age, it still appeared
that the *fight* was not taken out of him, and he proved
a considerable *teaser* to the *Black*, before he was disposed of.

At Wilsdon Green, on January 30, 1804, for a
subscription purse of twenty guineas, TOM BLAKE
entered the ring with a Coachman of the name of
Jack Holmes, known in the fighting world as a *bit of
stuff* that might be depended upon; but notwithstanding this high character, the odds were in favour of
BLAKE, six to four, on their stripping.

First round.—*Coachee* gave his opponent a severe hit upon
the *near* side, which shook his equilibrium, and pursuing this
advantage, planted a severe blow with his left hand, that
brought Blake down. The bets turned instantly, and *Holmes*
became the object of attraction, six to four.

From the second to the eleventh round,—Manliness and
heroism were the prominent features upon both sides; closing
was out of the question, and shifting seemed totally beneath
their courageous hearts; no pulling or hauling was resorted
to, but hitting and returning were followed up with great
spirit, and neither fell down without a knock-down blow.
Holmes being *levelled* successively the last three rounds, the
odds were now four to one against him.

Twelfth.—Blake, on setting-to, immediately knocked his
antagonist down.

Thirteenth.—Blake repeated this blow with the same success.

Fourteenth to the Seventeenth.—The combatants were completely upon equal terms during these rounds, which were most courageously contested.

Nineteenth.—Both on the alert, and for a short time it was impossible to distinguish which evinced the most bravery; at length the advantage appeared on the side of Blake. The spectators applauded loudly their manly efforts.

From the Twentieth to the Twenty-sixth—Was one continued scene of hardihood and valour, and the odds continued varying alternately. Never was applause more liberally and disinterestedly bestowed upon any pugilists, their exertions were far above the usual display of boxers. Blake's side was like a raw piece of beef, from the severe *punishment* he had received from *Holmes;* but yet the odds were considerably in Tom's favour.

Twenty-eighth.—Blake was nearly losing his nose this round, from a most tremendous blow which *Holmes* planted upon it, that fairly turned him round from its force; Tom instantly returned a severe hit upon the *Coachman's* side, but fell from his own blow. Three to one in favour of *Holmes.*

Twenty-ninth.—In the last fall, Blake had sprained his knee so severely that he was quite lame, and could scarcely move his foot from the earth without suffering considerable pain. His seconds wished him not to proceed, and his friends endeavoured to enforce it; but Tom insisted on continuing the battle, and patiently waited for his antagonist *setting-to,* when he threw out his left hand and *levelled* him. Still the odds were much against him.

From the Thirtieth to the Thirty-fourth—Blake's firmness was manifest, and he waited for the attack of his opponent.

Thirty-fifth.—Tom now appeared in better spirits, and somewhat recovered from his lameness, and praised, during this round, the courage of his adversary, but wished him to understand that he would be beaten. Odds in favour of Blake.

Forty-first.—Tom was knocked down in a rally, and *Holmes* had the best of this round. The battle was protracted till the

Forty-eighth.—When it would have appeared to a stranger like the first round, from the severity of the *punishment* which was dealt out upon both sides. Poor *Holmes's* face was now rendered perfectly unintelligible, not a single feature could be traced; and the side of Blake was terrifying to view. The odds were in favour of Tom.

Forty-ninth.—*Holmes levelled* his antagonist with considerable dexterity.

Fiftieth to the last.—Blake, being aware that *Holmes* was on the decline, showed great alertness, and planted a severe hit upon the *Coachman*, which the spectators thought must prove a *finisher*, but in this they were much disappointed, as *Holmes* rallied, and made a desperate attempt to gain the round, in which he succeeded. The *Coachman*, reluctant to pronounce the unpleasant sound of defeat, protracted the battle to the sixtieth round, when, completely exhausted, he was forced to yield. So much real *bottom*, manliness, and dexterity, had not been frequently witnessed before, that *Holmes* raised his character considerably in the opinion of the sporting world.

But, alas! poor BLAKE, the tough pugilist of his day, whose strength was once the terror of his enemies, and to whom a blow was of no avail, is now debilitated, from a paralytic stroke, and nearly deprived of the use of his limbs.

JACK WARR,

(Son of the late veteran Pugilist of that Name.)

FROM the renowned exploits of his father, who had so often contended in the field of glory with success and fame, great expectations were formed upon the pretensions of JACK to the pugilistic art. Under the tuition of so experienced a professor of boxing as *Bill Warr*, whose theoretical and practical acquirements, aided by considerable experience, and whose pupils had reflected such credit upon so great a master—a boy of his own rearing it was considered must prove the very acme of perfection; and that he might burst upon the world with splendour and sound pedigree, he made his *debut* in a contest with *Tom Belcher;* and although fortune did not crown his efforts with the smiles of victory, he gave such proofs of excellence and *science,* as to render him an object of attention to the amateur, and brought no discredit upon the stock from whence he sprang.

JACK WARR entered the lists with *Quirk,* for one hundred guineas, on June 5th, 1806, at Padnal Corner, Epping Forest. *Gulley* seconded WARR, and *Elias Spray* attended upon *Quirk:*—the odds were in favour of WARR, seven to four.

First round.—Considerable sparring, but both apparently shy, when at length *Quirk* gave the first hit, which was neatly returned by Warr, and both the blows made some impression. Warr fell from a slip. Even betting.

Second.—Manœuvring and sparring, both anxious to improve the opportunity; Warr made a hit, but his distance proving incorrect, rendered it of no effect, when *Quirk* put in a good blow, and followed it up by another; they closed, and fell.

'Third.—In this round the science of Warr was conspicuous; he gave his opponent two severe *facers* right and left, and likewise planted two successful hits on his body. *Quirk* made several attempts, but none of his blows told; they closed, and fell. The odds rose two to one on Warr.

Fourth.—Warr rose with great gaiety, and endeavoured to plant a blow upon his antagonist's head, which was neatly warded off by *Quirk;* but Warr, notwithstanding, put in a tremendous hit with his left hand on *Quirk's* throat, over his guard, which *floored* him.

Fifth.—Warr, elated with success, broke through *Quirk's* guard, and put in his blows, in a scientific manner, so rapidly and effectively, that his antagonist seemed in a state of stupor. Warr was now looked upon to be winning the battle so fast, that ten to one was offered; and considerable odds were sported that *Quirk* did not last five minutes longer.

Sixth.—The head of *Quirk* was much swelled, and Warr seemed somewhat exhausted from his exertions; but nevertheless he hit over his opponent's guard, which *Quirk* stopped with considerable science, although he received a severe body blow. *Quirk*, rather enraged, seized hold of Warr, who fell on his knees.

Seventh.—Rallying most determined was the order of this round, *milling* more than *science* was conspicuous—Warr gained by the rally, and in closing they both went to the ground extremely weak.

Eighth.—A most terrible round—courage, science, and bottom appeared equally on both sides—Warr tried his favourite left-handed blow; *Quirk* parried—a rally then commenced, and they stood up heroically to each other, exchanging hits, till they nearly appeared to be deprived of all motion or power to lift up their arms. The advantage was on the side of *Quirk*, and Warr fell much exhausted.

Ninth.—Warr, on *setting-to*, tried his left hand again, when another good rally took place. *Quirk* now appeared to have increased in strength, and gaining the advantage.

Tenth.—The appearance of both the combatants visibly portrayed the severe effects of each other's punishment.—This round was nobly contested, and might be said to decide the fate of the battle. Warr, still partial to his left-handed hit, tried to use it with success; but *Quirk* being now well aware of his intention, not only parried it off skilfully, but planted a dreadful blow under the ear of Warr with his left hand, which *levelled* him instantly; the effects of which were so severe upon his frame, that he lay for a few seconds utterly incapable of moving.

Eleventh.—The exhausted state of both the combatants now claimed the commiseration of the spectators—neither of them appeared capable of giving a hit; however, they closed, and Warr fell, as if dead.

Twelfth.—Warr made a desperate effort to regain his importance in the fight, and put forth all his strength to rally, but it proved of no avail, and after some slight hits were exchanged, he fell. *Quirk* was now looked upon as the winning man, and the odds were four to one in his favour.

Thirteenth.—The time being expired, (half a minute,) and Warr not being able to face his antagonist, *Quirk* was pronounced the conqueror.

It was the most resolute battle for the time it continued, eighteen minutes, and reflected considerable credit upon both combatants. The defeat of WARR was considered principally owing to his spirit and confidence of victory, which prompted him to exert himself too much at the commencement of the fight, but he was nevertheless not so much *punished* as his adversary. *Quirk* obtained the advantage by his *bottom* and superiority of strength, which enabled him to make his blows tell longer than WARR's; but, in point of *science*, the latter was much the best.

A butcher, with whom JACK WARR had some time previous an accidental *turn-up*, meeting with our hero at a public-house, in Oxendon-street, in December, 1806, claimed the superiority of manhood, but JACK, disdaining the charge with some indignation, instantly challenged him on the spot for any sum that he could muster; but the *blunt* not being at hand, the butcher declared he would fight him for a *belly-full;* and WARR, to preserve his character as a pugilist, accepted the offer without hesitation, making sure of a triumphant contest. The butcher was *a bit of a glutton,* and although not scientific, yet possessing some requisites that tend to bring a *novice,* at times, through the *piece,* threw WARR, with considerable dexterity, and repeatedly, and followed up this system with spirit. Warr suffered so dreadfully from the severe effects of the falls, that, in the course of twenty minutes, he was so much beaten as to be conveyed home. The science of WARR was conspicuous throughout the fight; and could he have prevented his antagonist from *closing* on him, the butcher would have had to tell another story: —but such is the fortune of war!

TOM CRIBB,

First known in the Pugilistic Hemisphere by the Appellation

OF

"𝔗𝔥𝔢 𝔅𝔩𝔞𝔠𝔨 𝔇𝔦𝔞𝔪𝔬𝔫𝔡!"

But who rose rapidly by his Scientific Pursuits, to the
proud and enviable Title of

THE CHAMPION OF ENGLAND,

and

In whose *Hands* it now remains, August, 1821.

"To gild refined gold, to paint the lily,
   To throw a perfume on the violet,
   To smooth the ice, or add another hue
   Unto the rainbow, or with taper light
   To seek the beauteous eye of heav'n to garnish,
   Is wasteful and ridiculous excess."

SINCE the days of the renowned FIGG, when the
Venetian Gondolier threatened, on his arrival in London, to tear the CHAMPION'S CAP from the British
brow, (but who was soon *convinced* of his error,) it has
been transferred quietly, at various times, and without
murmurs, from the *nob* of one native to another,
whose merit entitled him to its possession—but, that
a FOREIGNER should ever again have the temerity
to put in a claim, *even* for the mere contention of
obtaining the prize, much more for the honour of

wearing it, or bearing it away from GREAT BRITAIN, such an idea, however distant, never intruded itself into the breasts of Englishmen, and reminds us, in a more extended point of view, of the animating passage in the works of our immortal bard, so truly congenial with the native characteristic spirit of the country :

> " England never did nor never shall
> Lie at the proud foot of a conqueror."

But the towering and restless ambition of MOLI-NEAUX induced him to quit his home and country, and erect his hostile standard among the British heroes. The man of colour dared the most formidable of her chiefs to the chance of war ; when it was reserved for the subject of this memoir to chastise the bold intruder, in protecting the national practice and honour of the country, his own character from contempt and disgrace, and the whole race of English pugilists from ridicule and derision.

TOM was born on July 8th, 1781, at *Hanham*, a township and chapelry in the parish of Bitton, hundred of Langley and Swineshead, Gloucester, on the borders of Somerset, situate about five miles from Bristol, and it is rather a disputed point to which of the counties that are contiguous to *Hanham* this spot belongs ; therefore, whether the honour of giving birth to the CHAMPION OF ENGLAND appertains to Gloucestershire or Somersetshire remains at present undecided.

CRIBB left his native home at a very early period, and arrived in the Metropolis, when he was no more than thirteen years old, to follow the occupation of a bell-hanger, under the guidance of a relative ; but the

confined situation of *hanging bells* not exactly meeting
his ideas, and being a strong athletic youth, he preferred an out-door calling, and commenced porter at
the wharfs, during which time he met with two accidents that had nearly deprived him of existence—in
stepping from one coal barge to another, he fell between
them, and got jammed in a dreadful manner; and in
carrying a very heavy package of oranges, weighing
nearly 500 lbs. weight, he slipped down upon his back,
and the load fell upon his chest, which occasioned him
to spit blood for several days afterwards. By the
excellence of his constitution, he was soon enabled to
recover his strength from those severe accidents; and
aided by the invigorating air of the ocean, upon which,
we learn, he had the honour of serving against the
enemies of his country, that fine stamina and hardihood got improved for which the name of CRIBB, at
the present period, stands almost unrivalled.

With the *perception* of a General—the *fortitude* of a
Hero—and the *science* of a thorough-bred Professor,
TOM CRIBB has been enabled to obtain his numerous
achievements; and no pugilist whatever entered a ring
with more confidence in himself, upon all those trying
occasions, than the present CHAMPION OF ENGLAND;
his style of fighting *(milling on the retreat)* has been
somewhat disliked by several amateurs, as savouring
more of policy than manliness; but this objection loses
all its weight when put in comparison with his *game* or
gluttony exhibited in every one of his conquests; and
it must be observed, that he has had no *triflers* to
combat with—no *apologies* for boxers—but every one

who has entered the lists with him, has possessed considerable pretensions to pugilism, and most of them are of that inordinate appetite, that they must have been not only perfectly *satisfied*, but forcibly *convinced* of his superiority, ere they could have been induced to pronounce that word, so painful to issue from the lips of brave men—ENOUGH!

The names of his brave competitors render any further comment upon that head unnecessary:

GEORGE MADDOX,	JEM BELCHER, *(twice)*
TOM BLAKE,	HORTON,
IKEY PIG,	BOB GREGSON,
RICHMOND,	MOLINEAUX, *(twice)*

AND NICHOLS;*

but our love of *impartiality* compels us to state, that, notwithstanding the superlative excellence of the CHAMPION OF ENGLAND, he has, in more than one instance, been considered indebted to good fortune in being pronounced the victor: on the principle of being faithful reporters, we should "*nothing extenuate, or set down aught in malice;* but speak of one" —of whom every anecdote must prove highly interesting, and acceptable to the *Fancy* in general:

---

* In every circumstance in which the public are interested, any thing like deception ought to be avoided, and the friends of the CHAMPION acted injudiciously in withholding the name of *Nichols*, who defeated CRIBB, from the list of names which are placed under his whole-length likeness—it is calculated to mislead, and give importance to a circumstance, by endeavouring to obscure that fact, which it otherwise would not deserve. It was during the *noviciate* of CRIBB, and by no means reflected any discredit upon his conduct.

in the first contest with *Jem Belcher*, before the
strength of *Jem's* right hand had left him, the battle
was saved to CRIBB by the following manœuvre
of *Bill Warr*—the odds were five to one on *Belcher*,
and while *Gulley*, who seconded *Jem*, was offering the
above odds to *Warr*, at the conclusion of a round,
when CRIBB had received so severe a blow that he
could not come to time, *Warr*, on accepting the bet,
insisted that the money should be posted, and by
this stratagem gained more than a minute, sufficient
time for such a *glutton* as CRIBB perfectly to recover
in. And in the nineteenth round with *Molineaux*, when
the *Moor* had seized CRIBB so fast that he could not
extricate himself from his grasp, and which was
only effected by some persons breaking into the ring
to separate the combatants, during which one of the
fingers of *Molineaux* either got broke or much injured,
when soon afterwards CRIBB fell in so exhausted a state
from the severe *fibbing* which he had received, that the
limited time had expired before he was able to renew
the contest, and Sir Thomas Appreece, one of the
umpires, cried out, "*time! time!*" but his second,
Richmond, not noticing the circumstance, CRIBB recovered and won the battle.

From the placid demeanour of the CHAMPION, it
appears he was never engaged in many *skirmishes;* and
the contests in which he has proved so conspicuous,
have taken place on the principles of professed boxing,
and in some measure peculiar to himself: if then, he
may be termed a slow fighter, he is generally accounted a sure *hitter;* his skill and judgment are good; his

wind of the first quality; and supported with a *bottom* spirit never excelled. With such sound pugilistic pretensions, it cannot appear surprising that he has *milled* his way to fame and honour; and lest any more in this place might prove ill-timed or superfluous, his actions will best speak for themselves, and we shall commence with his first public *set-to* with that veteran of fistic glory,

George Maddox, on Wood Green, near Highgate, January 7th, 1805, for which see page 210. In this contest, CRIBB, being a stranger, had to contend against much ill usage and unfair treatment.

On February 15th, 1805, CRIBB entered the list with *Tom Blake*, for a subscription purse of forty guineas, on Blackheath. *Richmond* and *Joe Norton* were seconds to the former, and the latter was attended by *Dick Hall* and *Webb*. Both the combatants underwent training for a month; and betting was even, but CRIBB rather the favourite. It proved a most excellent contest, and *Blake* was not conquered without great difficulty and exertion, and continued upwards of an hour. From the scientific display of CRIBB in this battle, he began to claim considerable attention among the amateurs.

Ikey Pig, a heavier and stronger man than CRIBB, contended with him for a subscription-purse of forty guineas, on Blackheath, on May 21st, 1805. *Paddington Jones* seconded CRIBB, and the *Jew* had for his attendant *Bill Wood*. *Ikey* made good use of his strength, and *levelled* his opponent several times; but CRIBB's caution, bottom, and science proved too much

for the Jew, who gave in, much to the regret and loss
of his followers.

At Blackwater, for a subscription-purse of twenty-
five guineas, July 20th, 1805, CRIBB was defeated by
Nichols. See page 196.

Colour or *persuasion* made no odds to TOM, and he
now entered the ring with *Richmond*, for a match of
twenty-five guineas, on October 8th, 1805, at Hailsham,
in Sussex. The *solidity* of the deportment of the one,
and the *singular movements* of the other, created much
sport; and in fact it could scarcely be called a fight;
and was considered an unequal match; although an
hour and half elapsed before victory was declared in
favour of CRIBB, who was little, if any, the worse for
the contest.

CRIBB was now getting fast into notice, a pugilist
of rare pretensions, and *Captain Barclay*, who perceived those hitherto hidden qualities in him, took TOM
into training, and matched him, for two hundred guineas, with *Jem Belcher*, which took place at Moulsey-
Hurst, on the 8th of April, 1807, in a twenty-feet roped
ring. *Gulley* and *Watson* were the seconds to *Belcher*,
and CRIBB was attended by *Bill Warr* and *Richmond*
—Odds six to four on *Jem.*

First round.—Considerable science was displayed by both
the combatants upon setting-to, when Belcher planted two
hits right and left upon the head and body of his opponent,
which were returned slightly by Cribb, who rallied and
closed, and was thrown by Belcher.

Second.—Belcher put in two severe blows upon Cribb's
head and body, when the latter returned a hit, but slipped
down upon his hands in attempting to follow it up. Cribb
showed the first blood.

Third.—Several severe blows were exchanged, when Cribb threw Belcher, who planted a heavy body blow while in the act of falling. This round rather in favour of Cribb.

Fourth.—Cribb displayed good science in warding off two blows of Belcher's, when they closed and fell.

Fifth.—Belcher, with his right hand, put in a dreadful blow on Cribb's left eye, and in closing hit his opponent twice in the body, and threw him. Five to two on Belcher.

Sixth.—Cribb began to show symptoms of weakness: Belcher put in a hit, warding off which caused Cribb to fall.

Seventh.—Belcher's *punishment* was now visible on the body of Cribb, who endeavoured to put in two blows, which were parried by Belcher, and Jem returned both right and left with great dexterity, and rallied his man to the ropes, when Cribb clung to them, and fell much fatigued; Belcher also went down on his knees, but seemed in good spirits. Three to one on Jem.

Eighth.—The blood flowed profusely from Cribb; hitting and retreating neatly; when they closed, and both went down.

Ninth.—Belcher hit his adversary right and left, but only the latter told, when Jem fell.

Tenth.—Belcher commenced this round with great spirit, and gave Cribb some severe blows, without letting him have a chance, following and rallying his opponent to the ropes, when Cribb, appearing quite fatigued, fell. The odds now rose four to one on Belcher.

Eleventh.—Belcher planted two hits, which Cribb skilfully warded off, but Belcher was so rapid in closing upon his antagonist, that they both went down.

Twelfth.—A small change was now making its appearance between the combatants: Cribb seemed rather gaining his strength, while Belcher appeared rather distressed; when Cribb rallied successfully, planted a hit under Belcher's perfect eye, closed, and threw him.

Thirteenth.—Belcher, in all his contests, never showed himself to greater advantage than in this round, his skill was of the finest order, and only equalled by his courage; in closing, Belcher threw Cribb.

Fourteenth.—Both on the alert, and "eager for the fray." Belcher hit right and left, which were parried by Cribb, who returned two blows in the body; when they closed and fell. Still four to one on Belcher.

Fifteenth.—Belcher, full of gaiety, rallied Cribb to the extremity of the ring, and in struggling put an end to the round.

Sixteenth.—Cribb now convinced the spectators that he possessed considerable more *science* than they were aware of, and stopped Belcher's blows with great skill. The Knowing-Ones were, at this period of the battle, rather at a stand-still with regard to sporting their money—Cribb, it was certain, by his appearance, had received severe punishment, but not enough to satisfy any thing like his *gluttony ;* and Belcher's stamina had been considered on the decline previous to this contest, and it was apprehended that he could nor last long.

Seventeenth.—Belcher, still confident, rallied his adversary, who fell from fatigue. Two to one on Belcher.

Eighteenth.—Belcher put in some dreadful blows in the body, and a terrible thrust in the throat of his opponent, and followed him up with such spirit and rapidity, that Cribb fell violently, and quite exhausted, and to all appearance as if he would not be able to come again in time. It was in this round that Belcher sprained his wrist, and was deprived of nearly the use of his right hand afterwards. Five to one on Belcher.

Nineteenth.—Belcher slipped in making play.

Twentieth.—The combatants closed and fell.

Twenty-first.—Cribb planted two blows on his opponent's head, who slipped in returning them. It was now perceived that Belcher proved incorrect in his distances, and that several of his blows were thrown away, from the bad state of his eye.

Twenty-third.—Belcher, full of gaiety, put in a good hit, and threw Cribb a cross-buttock.

Twenty-fourth.—Cribb the most conspicuous in the round, when they closed and fell.

Twenty-fifth.—Cribb put in a tremendous blow, and in attempting to follow it up, Belcher shifted, and Cribb ran himself down :— a little disapprobation expressed, but the generality exclaimed, " Fair ! fair !"

Twenty-sixth.—The constitution of Belcher was now giving way, his strength was not able to resist the heavy *punishment* of Cribb, who hit Jem from him, and gave him a *leveller.* Cribb upon this became the favourite.

Twenty-seventh.—A well-contested round, and, notwithstanding Belcher gave Cribb a cross-buttock, it was considered in favour of the latter.

Twenty-eighth.—Belcher made a hit, which was warded off by his opponent and returned, when they closed and fell.

Twenty-ninth.—Without hesitation Cribb closed, and from his uncommon strength threw Belcher over the ropes.

Thirtieth.—Both exchanged a blow, when, with a very weak hit, Belcher went down. Five to two on Cribb.

Thirty-first.—A good round, without any particular advantage to either; though Cribb put in the most blows, yet Belcher gave his adversary a violent fall.

Thirty-second.—Both closed and fell.

Thirty-third.—Belcher, quite *game*, endeavoured to make the best of it, but Cribb rallied and threw him.

Thirty-fourth, Thirty-fifth, and Thirty-sixth.—In all these rounds Cribb maintained the superiority.

Thirty-seventh.—Belcher had scarcely any strength left to stand, and his brave opponent was not in a much better state; and from this period to the Fortieth it was little better than mere hugging, blows they could not be called, from the exhausted state of both the combatants, and they fell in an irregular manner.

Forty-first and last.—Thirty-five minutes had now elapsed, and Cribb, proving the strongest man, put in two weak blows, and rallied, when Belcher, quite exhausted, fell upon the ropes, and gave up the contest.

From the above victory, CRIBB rose rapidly into fame—his real qualities were hitherto unknown, and he had been viewed principally as a *glutton* of the first class, with a *bottom* unimpeached; but now his pretensions unfolded themselves, and the amateurs were completely surprised at his display and improvement in the SCIENCE—his *distances* were well judged, and he *stopped* with great dexterity and neatness: and had he proved a *quicker* hitter, the contest might have sooner been decided.

CRIBB was now challenged by *Horton* (who had

beaten the Champion's brother) for one hundred guineas. *Horton* had signalised himself in the vicinity of Bristol, and had improved considerably under the tuition of the *Game Chicken*; but in this contest, which took place on May 10th, 1808, Tom Cribb very soon took the *conceit* out of him; and upon *setting-to* the odds were five to four on the Champion.

Considerable interest had been excited in the *Sporting World*, on a comparison of the pugilistic qualities of *Gregson* and Cribb, when a match, in consequence, was made between those celebrated heroes of the fist, and decided at Moulsey Hurst, in a thirty-feet roped ring, on October 25, 1808. *Gulley* and *Bill Gibbons* seconded Cribb; and *Jem Belcher* and *Richmond* attended upon *Gregson*. Five to four on the Champion.

First round.—After some trifling sparring, Gregson attempted to plant the first blow with his left hand, but proving too short, it was ineffectual, and Cribb hit over his adversary's shoulder, when they closed, and in falling Gregson was the uppermost.

Second.—Cribb, full of activity, put in two body hits, right and left; when Gregson endeavoured to return the compliment, but Cribb dexterously avoided it by shifting, and put in a severe blow on the right side of Gregson's face with his left hand, which made the *claret* flow most profusely, and never ceased during the fight. Gregson, full of impetuosity, made some desperate attacks on Cribb's neck, which, if they had not been prevented from taking effect, in all probability would have terminated the contest: Cribb rallied and Gregson was thrown. Two to one on the Champion.

Third.—Gregson, full of spirit, rallied, and planted a most tremendous hit under the ear of Cribb, who retreated according to his favourite mode of fighting; Gregson, incautiously following him, suffered that severe *punishment* termed *milling on the retreat*, receiving a heavy blow on the right side of his face from every retreating step of his opponent; but still the *game* of Gregson kept following close, till he fell quite stunned.

Fourth.—Cribb went down in making play.

Fifth.—Gregson showed himself in this round to considerable advantage; his *distance* was well measured, and he put in a hit so terrific upon the temple of Cribb, that he was completely abroad, and to all appearance destitute of recollection; and, had Gregson followed up this *chance*, the battle must have been his own—instead of *sparring*, he should have kept *hitting*, while his opponent was retreating to the ropes to put an end to the round, and who had to sustain a severe rally before that circumstance was accomplished, which was effected by Cribb's being knocked off his feet.

Sixth.—The appearance of Cribb's head was truly shocking, and Gregson's face was one stream of blood; they rallied, and after exchanging hits to a stand still, Cribb was thrown by Gregson.

Seventh.—Gregson's distances were badly judged, and Cribb hit his opponent so dreadfully over his bleeding mouth that made him nearly frantic; when they closed, and Cribb received a cross-buttock. Two to one on Cribb.

Eighth.—Gregson appeared rather distressed, and Cribb *milling* away on the retreat with considerable success from Gregson's intemperate and injudicious mode of following him, who received such severe blows on his face, that he fell on his knees and was helped up. Three to one on Cribb.

Ninth.—Cribb kept the lead, and after a few hits, they both went on their knees, when a sort of hug took place, and they both went down quite exhausted.

Tenth.—The wind of both the combatants appeared distressed; when they closed and fell.

Eleventh.—Greater courage was never displayed upon any occasion than by both the combatants; Gregson attempted a most dreadful blow, but his *distance* was incorrect, and it failed; however, he rallied, and planted two severe hits on the head and body of his opponent; Cribb seemed in a state of stupor, when Gregson threw him. Seven to four on Cribb.

Twelfth.—Words cannot convey any idea of the horrid appearance of the combatants' faces—but, notwithstanding, they stood in the most determined manner exchanging blows, when Gregson went down more from fatigue than the strength of the blow.

Thirteenth.—Every exertion was made on both sides to gain the superiority—Cribb was now fast recovering his wind and strength; and Gregson suffering his passion to get the better of him.

Fifteenth.—Cribb *punishing* his opponent in first-rate style, when Gregson fell from its severe effects.

Sixteenth.—Gregson put in a blow on Cribb's head, which brought him down instantly.

Nineteenth.—Nature seemed quite exhausted in both the combatants—their blows were mere attempts to strike, and of no effect.

Twentieth.—*Game* versus *bottom*—Cribb full of heroism, and Gregson no ways destitute of valour—it was truly astonishing to witness what a pitch of courage human nature can arrive at, and, anxious of victory, the combatants seemed to forget their state, went in furiously, and both fell as if intoxicated.

Twenty-second.—On meeting, a rally took place, and strength favouring Gregson, he fairly bored down Cribb, when the odds shifted so much, and such was the general feeling, that ten to one was offered Cribb could not come again.

Twenty-third.—Never were pugilists so completely worn out, and Cribb, on setting-to, had merely strength enough to put in two feeble hits and closed : in wrestling, Cribb had the good fortune to throw his antagonist, who fell with such uncommon force as nearly to deprive him of motion. Gregson was raised and placed on his second's knee, but the *time* had expired before he was able to come again ; in consequence of which Cribb was declared the victor. It was not only the most fortunate, if not the most unexpected event in his life ; for, upon hearing the news he fell, and remained in an exhausted state for a short period.

Richmond, who it appeared had offended CRIBB, was, immediately after his recovery, challenged for fifty guineas, to be decided instantly, but his friends would not suffer such a proceeding to take place.

Jem Belcher, whose conquests had been so truly distinguished, was so grievously hurt in his mind by the defeat which he had experienced with CRIBB, that he was determined to have another trial, for the recovery of that which was so dear to him as a pugilist,

Victory and Fame. This memorable conflict took place on February 1, 1809, on Epsom race-ground, in a thirty-feet roped ring; *Belcher* was seconded by *Mendoza* and *Clark;* and CRIBB was attended by *Joe Ward* and *Bill Gibbons.* Three to one on CRIBB.

First.—Considerable *science* was displayed on both sides for a short time, when Belcher put in two hits, one of which was warded off by Cribb, but the other took effect on his body: who instantly returned, which Belcher partially stopped, and, in closing, Belcher had a light fall.

Second.—Cribb, on the alert, made play, and gave his adversary a blow on the body: Belcher rallied, and, after an exchange of hits, was thrown.

Third.—Belcher full of gaiety, and making use of excellent *science*, put in two lounging hits right and left, one of which took a dreadful effect under the left ear of his opponent, when the blood flowed in torrents. Some good hits were exchanged, but of no consequence. Cribb again threw his adversary.

Fourth.—Both the combatants made a grand display of the perfections of the art of boxing—hitting and stopping were never seen to greater advantage. In rallying, Belcher fell somewhat distressed for wind.

Fifth.—Belcher hit right and left, but his right hand appeared lamed; when Cribb rallied, and again threw Belcher.

Sixth.—Belcher, apparently distressed, retreated to the ropes to recruit his wind, where Cribb, improving the opportunity, put in some severe blows. Belcher, aware of his opponent's uncommon strength, hit out, and gave at arm's length a severe blow under Cribb's ear with his lame hand, and, unfortunately for the latter, upon the exact spot where Gregson had so wounded him—torrents of blood flowed from it; and in closing Belcher gave Cribb a severe cross-buttock. Cribb's constitution was considered so good, that the odds were four to one that he would win.

Seventh.—The *science* and style of Belcher gave him the advantage in this round, but he had not stamina to support his efforts, which operated as a check to betting in his favour. He rallied, and planted his blows successfully, and, in closing, Cribb went to the ground, but very lightly.

Eighth.—The exertions which Belcher had hitherto made, appeared now to have injured his wind considerably, and he made towards the ropes to recruit it, which Cribb perceiving followed him, when Belcher made an uncommon effort to extricate himself from the superior strength of his antagonist by rallying, and planting a few hits, but they were too feeble to make any impression on the hardy frame of Cribb : in closing much hugging took place, and, after some struggling to obtain the throw, they both went over the ropes.

Ninth.—They closed, but were separated by their seconds.

Tenth.—It was clearly seen, notwithstanding the courage and *science* displayed by Belcher, that his constitution was too weak for the competitor with which he was engaged, and that the chance of winning was against him. Cribb had been acting principally on the defensive till this period of the battle ; but now he changed the scene, went in and showed his superiority by hitting, stopping, and planting several successful blows, and finished the round by giving Belcher a severe fall. All betters as to the event, but no takers.

Eleventh.—Cribb, full of gaiety, made play, and again threw his opponent.—Belcher was losing fast every round, both his hands had forsaken their office, and Cribb kept the lead to the

Nineteenth.—When Belcher convinced the spectators in what part of him the deficiency rested, and positively fought against his nature, and stopped most scientifically every hit, till he could no longer resist the impetuosity of his opponent, who bored him completely down; yet Belcher, in spite of all his infirmities, continued the battle till the

Thirty-first.—But it was piteous to view this once renowned and brave CHAMPION OF ENGLAND only standing up to be *punished*, and that in the most dreadful manner. For the last ten rounds there was not the smallest shadow of success—the flesh had separated from his nails, and his knuckles were so miserably lacerated, as to appear as if cut with a knife : when, after a contest of forty minutes, the heroic JEM BELCHER resigned the palm of victory to CRIBB, never more to enter the field of honour.

By the above conquest, CRIBB had acquired considerable fame and eminence as a first-rate pugilist ; and his friend *Gulley* having resigned all pretensions to *prize-milling*, the envied title of CHAMPION OF ENGLAND descended to him, when he was bound in honour to protect its noble character from insult and attack; and *how* far he has fulfilled that important charge, the promulgation of his warlike deeds will best speak for themselves.

Much as the fame of the former contests of the CHAMPION had excited interest in the *Sporting World*, they were looked upon as trifling, when compared with his battle with *Molineaux:* and even those persons who had hitherto passed over boxing in general as beneath their notice, now seemed to take a lively interest in the issue of this fight. It appeared somewhat as a national concern; ALL felt for the honour of their country, and were deeply interested in the fate of their Champion, TOM CRIBB. *Molineaux* was viewed as a truly formidable rival: he was by no means deficient either in point of strength, courage, or agility, with his opponent; and, though but little known himself, his pedigree had been traced to be good: his father was never beaten; he was a twin-brother; and the family distinguished for pugilistic traits of excellence and *bottom*. In height *Molineaux* is about five feet eight and a quarter, weighing fourteen stone two pounds; while his brave opponent stands five feet ten and a half, and in weight about fourteen stone three pounds. It appears that CRIBB expected to win with ease and style; and *Molineaux* threatened to perform wonders: it was also stated by the most experienced and best informed upon the subject, that the betting upon this occasion exceeded any thing of the kind that had gone before it. Considerable odds were betted that *Molineaux* was disposed of in fifteen minutes, and it was considered safe betting that CRIBB proved the conqueror in half an hour. The day selected for this grand *milling* exhibition was Dec. 10, 1810, at Copthall Common, in the neighbourhood of East Grinstead, Sussex, within 30 miles of the Metropolis. Notwithstanding the rain came down in torrents, and the distance from London, the *Fancy* were not to be deterred from witnessing the *mill*, and who waded through a clayey road, nearly knee-deep for five miles, with alacrity and cheerfulness, as if it had been as smooth as a bowling-green, so great was the curiosity and interest manifested upon this battle. About twelve o'clock, Mr. *Jackson*, with his usual consideration, had the ring formed at the foot of a hill, (twenty-four feet roped,) surrounded by the numerous carriages which had conveyed the spectators thither, to ward off the chilling breezes and rain which came keenly from the eastward. Immediately upon this being completed, *Molineaux* came forward, bowed, threw up his hat in defiance, and retired to strip; CRIBB immediately followed, and they were soon brought forward by their seconds; *Gulley* and *Joe Ward* for the CHAMPION, and *Richmond* and *Jones* for *Molineaux*.

First round.—The first appearance of the young Roscius excited not greater attention than the *setting-to* of the above pugilists; the eyes of the spectators were stretched to their utmost, waiting for the first blow, when, after a few seconds of scientific display, the *Moor* put in a left-handed hit, but which did no execution. Cribb returned, but his *distance* was incorrect; however, he made a good stop, and planted a blow with his left hand under the eye of his opponent. A rally now ensued; a blow was exchanged by each of them, but of no import, when they closed, and Molineaux was thrown.

Second.—The *Moor* rallied with a left-handed blow, which did not tell, when Cribb planted a most tremendous one over his adversary's right eye-brow, but which did not have the effect of knocking him down; he only staggered a few paces, followed up by the Champion. Desperation was now the order of the round, and the rally re-commenced with uncommon severity, in which Cribb showed the most science, although he received a dreadful blow on the mouth that made his teeth chatter again, and exhibited the first signs of *claret.* Four to one on Cribb.

Third.—After a short space, occupied in sparring, Molineaux attempted a good blow on Cribb's *nob*, but the Champion parried it, and returned a right-handed hit under the *Moor's* lower rib, when he fell rapidly in the extreme. Still four to one.

Fourth.—On setting-to Molineaux rallied, when the Champion stopped his career by a severe hit in the face, that *levelled* him, the ground being wet and slippery.

Fifth.—The amateurs were uncommonly interested in this round, it was a display of such united *skill* and *bottom*, that both the combatants claimed peculiar notice from their extraordinary efforts. Molineaux rallied with uncommon fortitude, but his blows were short. Cribb returned with spirit, but the *Moor* knocked them off, and put in a tremendous hit on the left eye of the Champion. A rally, at half-arm's length, now followed, which excited the utmost astonishment from the resoluteness of both the heroes, who hit each other away three times, and continued this desperate *milling* for half a minute, when Molineaux fell from a feeble blow. The *knowing ones* were lost for the moment, and no bets were offered.

Sixth.—The *Moor* planted a blow upon the *nob* of the Champion, who fell from the bad state of the ground.

Seventh.—Cribb in a rally gave Molineaux a hit on the side of his head, when he went down.

Eighth.—Cribb showed himself off in good style, and dealt out his blows with considerable success and effect, but experienced, from the determined resolution of the *Moor*, that he was somewhat mistaken in his ideas of the Black's capabilities, who rallied in *prime twig*, and notwithstanding the severe left-handed hits which were planted on his *nob*—the terrible punishment he had received on his body, directed by the fine skill and power of the Champion—still he stood up undismayed, proving that his courage was of no ordinary nature, in exchanging several of the blows, till he fell almost in a state of stupor, from the *milling* his head had undergone.

This round was equal to any that preceded it, and only different in point of duration.

Ninth.—The battle had arrived at that doubtful state, and things seemed not to prove so easy and tractable as was anticipated, that the betters were rather puzzled to know how they should proceed with success. Molineaux gave such proofs of *gluttony*, that four to one now made many tremble who had sported it; but still there was a ray of hope remaining, from the senseless state in which the *Moor* appeared at the conclusion of the last round. Both the combatants appeared dreadfully punished; and Cribb's head was terribly swelled on the left side; Molineaux's *nob* was also much worse for the fight. On Cribb's displaying weakness, the *flash side* were full of palpitation—it was not looked for, and operated more severe upon their minds on that account. Molineaux rallied with a spirit unexpected, bored in upon Cribb, and by a strong blow through the Champion's guard, which he planted in his face, brought him down. It would be futile here to attempt to portray the countenances of the interested part of the spectators, who appeared, as it were, panic-struck, and those who were not thoroughly acquainted with the *game* of the Champion, began hastily to *hedge-off;* while others, better informed, still placed their confidence on Cribb, from what they had seen him hitherto *take*.

Tenth.—Molineaux now showed symptoms of weakness; but yet rallied and bored his opponent to various parts of the ring. Cribb kept knocking him about the *nob*, but he seemed to disregard it, and kept close to his man till they both went down. The Champion now perceived what sort of a *customer* he had to deal with, and that to win, judgment and caution must be resorted to; he therefore adopted his favourite and successful system of *milling on the retreat.*

Eleventh.—The *Moor*, still partial to rallying, planted several blows, but they appeared rather feeble, and did not have the desired effect; but, notwithstanding, he evinced strength enough to give Cribb a heavy fall.

Twelfth.—Molineaux, immediately on *setting-to*, commenced another rally, when the Champion put in a severe body blow, but the *Moor* treated it with indifference, and in return not only *milled* his head, but in closing threw him.

Thirteenth.—Molineaux, in boring in upon his adversary, received a severe *facer* from him, but who went down from the force of his own blow. To show the uncertainty of betting, it is necessary to state, that the odds had changed six to four on the Moor, to the no small chagrin of those who had sported their money, that Molineaux would not become the favourite during the fight.

Fourteenth.—The Moor went furiously in, and ran down Cribb without striking a blow, or without the latter being able to return one; however, on disengaging, the Champion was *levelled*.

Fifteenth.—Cribb, on *setting-to*, planted a blow over the guard of the Moor, which occasioned a most determined rally, and those persons who were fond of viewing *milling* might now witness it in perfection; no shifting, but giving and taking were displayed on both sides, till Molineaux was knocked down from a severe hit he received in his throat.

Sixteenth.—Rallying still the most prominent feature, but Molineaux went down through fatigue; Cribb appearing to the best advantage, the odds changed about till they became even, and that the Champion would win.

Seventeenth.—Both the combatants, determined to do their best, entered most spiritedly into another sharp rally, when they closed, and Molineaux not only gave Cribb a desperate fall, but fell upon him. Betting very shy, if any, it appearing to be any body's battle.

Eighteenth.—The Champion made play, and planted with his right hand a severe blow on his opponent's body; when Molineaux returned a hit on the Champion's head, who, by a blow on the forehead, hit the Moor off his legs, but afterwards fell from the strength of his own blow. Both in an exhausted state.

Nineteenth.—To distinguish the combatants by their features would have been utterly impossible, so dreadfully were both their faces beaten—but their difference of *colour* supplied this sort of defect. It was really astonishing to view the determined manner in which these heroes met—Cribb acting upon the defensive, and retreating from the blows of his antagonist, though endeavouring to put in a hit, was got by Molineaux against the ropes, which were in height about five feet, and in three rows. Molineaux with both his hands caught hold of the ropes, and held Cribb in such a singular way, that he could neither make a hit or fall down: and while the seconds were discussing the propriety of separating

the combatants, which the umpires thought could not be
done till one of the men fell down, about two hundred
persons rushed from the outer to the interior ring, and it
is asserted, that if one of the Moor's fingers was not broken,
it was much injured by some of them attempting to remove
his hand from the ropes: all this time Molineaux was gaining
his wind by laying his head on Cribb's breast, and refusing
to release his victim; when the Champion, by a desperate
effort to extricate himself from the rude grasp of the Moor,
was at length run down to one corner of the ring, and
Molineaux, having got his head under his arm, *fibbed* away
most unmercifully, but his strength not being able to the
intent, it otherwise must have proved fatal to Cribb, who
fell from exhaustion, and the severe *punishment* he had
received. The bets were now decided that Molineaux did
not fight half an hour; that time having expired during
this round.

Twentieth.—Molineaux made the most of himself, and
brought his opponent down by boring and hitting.

Twenty-first.—Cribb planted two blows upon the head
and body of his opponent, which Molineaux returned by
a desperate blow in Cribb's face; when they closed, and
the Champion was thrown. The well-known *bottom* of Cribb
induced his friends to back him six to four.

Twenty-second.—Of no importance.

Twenty-third.—The wind of both the combatants appearing somewhat damaged, they sparred some time to recruit
it, when Cribb put in a blow on the left eye of Molineaux,
which hitherto had escaped *milling*. The Moor ran in, gave
Cribb a severe hit on the body, and threw him heavily.

Twenty-fourth.—Molineaux began this round with considerable spirit, and some hits were exchanged, when Cribb
was thrown. The betting tolerably even.

Twenty-fifth.—The effects of the last fall operated in some
degree upon the feelings of Cribb, from its severity; yet
the Champion endeavoured to remove this impression by
making play, and striving (as in the former round) to put in
a hit on Molineaux's left eye, but the Moor, aware of the
intent, warded it off, and in return knocked down Cribb.

Twenty-sixth.—Both the combatants trying to recruit their
wind and strength by scientific efforts. The Champion now
endeavoured to hit the right eye of Molineaux, the left having
been *darkened* for some time; but the Moor warded off the
blows of Cribb with agility and neatness, although he went
down from a trifling hit.

Twenty-seventh.—Weakness conspicuous on both sides, and, after some pulling and hauling, both fell.

Twenty-eighth.—Cribb received a *leveller* in consequence of his distance being incorrect.

Twenty-ninth.—The Moor was running in with spirit, but the Champion stopped his career by planting a hit upon his right eye, and, from its severe effects, he went down, which materially damaged his *peeper.* The fate of the battle might be said to be decided by this round.

Thirtieth.—If any thing could reflect credit upon the *skill* and *bottom* of Cribb, it was never more manifest than in this contest, in viewing what a resolute and determined hero he had to vanquish. Molineaux, in spite of every disadvantage, with a courage and ferocity unequalled, rising superior to exhaustion and fatigue, rallied his adversary with as much resolution as at the commencement of the fight, his *nob* defying all the *milling* it had received, that *punishment* appeared to have no *decisive* effect upon it, and contending nobly with Cribb right and left, knocking him away by his hits, and gallantly concluded the round by closing and throwing the Champion. The Moor was now convinced that, if he did win, he must do it off hand, as his sight was much impaired.

Thirty-first.—The exertion of this last round operated most forcibly upon Molineaux, and he appeared much distressed on quitting his second, and was soon *levelled* by a blow in the throat, which Cribb very neatly put in.

Thirty-second.—It was almost who should—strength was fast leaving both the combatants—they staggered against each other like inebriated men, and fell without exchanging a blow.

Thirty-third.—To the astonishment of every spectator, Molineaux rallied with strength enough to bore his man down ; but both their *hits* were of more *show* than effect.

Thirty-fourth.—This was the last round that might be termed fighting, in which Molineaux had materially the worst of it; but the battle was continued to the 39th, when Cribb evidently appeared the best man, and, at its conclusion, the Moor *for the first time, complained* that "HE COULD FIGHT NO MORE!" but his seconds, who viewed the NICETY OF THE POINT, persuaded him to try the *chance* of another round, to which request he acquiesced, when he fell from weakness, reflecting additional credit on the manhood of his brave CONQUEROR, TOM CRIBB.

Great events are generally judged of by comparison;
and, however severe the conflict might have been
between *Johnson* and *Big Ben*—this battle betwixt
CRIBB and *Molineaux* was not only more formidable
in its nature, but more ferocious and sanguinary.
FIFTY-FIVE minutes of unprecedented *milling*, before
the *Moor thought* he had had *enough!!*

If any thing had been wanting to establish the
fame of CRIBB, the above contest has completely decided his just pretensions to the CHAMPIONSHIP
OF ENGLAND.   With a coolness and confidence,
almost his own, and with skill and judgment so truly
rare, that he has beaten his men with more certainty
than any of the professors of the gymnastic art; he
was called upon to protect the honour of his country,
and the reputation of *English Boxing*,—a parade of
words, or the pomposity of high-flown diction, is not
necessary to record the circumstance; however, let it
not be forgotten that TOM CRIBB

HAS DONE THIS:

and let it be remembered also, that, however partial
to his favourite system of *milling on the retreat*, he
never resorted to its scientific effects till the necessity
of the moment compelled him not to throw away the
chance; and that, for the first ten rounds of this
contest, he was the *offensive* pugilist, and, notwithstanding his game had always been well known, his
courage in this instance astonished all the spectators,
who expressed their admiration at his being ever
ready at the mark, fighting his man.

It is but candid to admit, from the excellent specimen which *Molineaux* portrayed in his contest with the CHAMPION, that the *Moor* was entitled to another trial; and the PLEA on which he grounded his fresh challenge, " *had not the weather proved so unfavourable,*" and trusting that " being *of a different colour would not operate to his prejudice,*" was a strong appeal to the liberality of Englishmen, and could not be passed over with indifference by CRIBB, who, although he had publicly declined fighting, accepted this challenge with alacrity and cheerfulness—in consequence of which, at Thiselton Gap, in the County of Rutland, a few miles from Grantham, and contiguous to three counties, on Saturday, the 28th of September, 1811, this ever-memorable combat took place, whether OLD ENGLAND should still retain her proud characteristic of conquering, or that an AMERICAN, and a *man of colour*, should win the honour, wear it, and carry it away from the shores of Britain. Never was the *sporting world* so much interested, and for twenty miles within the seat of action not a bed could be obtained on the preceding night; and by six o'clock the next morning, hundreds were in motion to get a good place near the stage, which even at that early period proved a difficult task. It is supposed that near 20,000 persons witnessed this tremendous *mill:* and that one-fourth of them were of the *highest mould,* including some of the principal CORINTHIANS of the State. VICTORY proving so long doubtful in the former combat, rendered the capabilities of the *Moor* an object of fear and jealousy on the part of the friends of the CHAMPION, who viewed

him as a rival of the most daring quality, and *one* not
to be disposed of with the common routine of *punishment.* They neither of them weighed so much as in
the last fight by a stone; and Captain *Barclay,* whose
knowledge of the capability of the human frame appears to be better than most men, took the Champion
under his immediate eye, and trained him upon a system peculiar to himself, reducing Cribb from upwards
of sixteen stone, to about thirteen stone six pounds,
yet kept his stamina unimpaired. From such patronage and protection the bets were three to one on the
Champion, and six to four that he gave the first
knock-down blow.

A few minutes after twelve o'clock, they mounted
the stage (25 feet,) Cribb springing upon it with great
confidence and bowing to the spectators : the applause
exceeding every thing of the kind. The *Moor* followed
and jumped over the railing with considerable spirit,
bowing, and was greeted with tokens of approbation,
though not of so general a nature.   Both the combatants looked well; and *Molineaux,* for a man of colour,
might be termed rather good-looking : but Cribb appeared to have the longest arms. The *Moor* seemed
disturbed, and walked the stage with hasty steps.   On
stripping, the anxiety of the multitude cannot be
described : the combatants were soon brought to the
mark by their seconds, *Gulley* and *Joe Ward* for
Cribb, and *Richmond* and *Bill Gibbons* for *Molineaux.*

First round.—A minute elapsed in sparring, when the
Champion made play right and left, and put in a right-
handed blow on the body of the Moor, who returned a feeble
hit on his opponent's *nob.* A rally now commenced, in which

a few blows were exchanged, and Molineaux received a hit in his throat, which sent him down, though not considered clean.

Second.—The *claret* was perceived to issue first from the mouth of Cribb, upon commencing this round. A most terrible rally took place by mutual consent, when the Champion planted with his right hand a severe body hit, which was returned on the head by Molineaux with his left flush. They both fought at half-arm's-length for superiority, and about six good hits were exchanged, when they closed, and, in a trial of strength, Cribb was thrown. Five to two on the Champion.

Third.—In the last rally, the right eye of Cribb was almost *darkened;* and another now commenced equally as ferocious, after sparring to obtain wind, in which it was perceived the Moor was defective, when the Champion put in a most tremendous *doubler* in the body of Molineaux, and who, notwithstanding he was *hit* away, to the astonishment of every one, renewed the rally in so determined a manner, that it created considerable agitation amongst those persons who had betted the odds. There was a marked difference in their method of fighting; Cribb hit right and left at the head and body, while the Moor aimed at the *nob* alone, and with much judgment planted several dexterous flush hits, that impaired the eye-sight of Cribb, and his mouth bled considerably. This rally continued a minute and a half, and, in closing, the Champion received a heavy fall. The superiority of the Moor's strength was evinced by his grasping the body of Cribb with one hand, and supporting himself by the other resting on the stage, and in this situation threw Cribb completely over upon the stage, by the force of a cross-buttock. To those not *flash*, the mere appearance of things was in favour of the Moor; but the fortitude of the Champion *stayed* his friends, although the betting had got down to seven to four.

Fourth.—Molineaux's wind could not be depended upon: and the head of Cribb was terrific; and although he was bleeding from every wound, he smiled with confidence, and rallied in the first style of manliness. A number of good blows were exchanged, Cribb *milling* away at the body, and Molineaux *punishing* the head. Cribb went down from a trifling blow, and betrayed symptoms of weakness. No variation in the betting.

Fifth.—Molineaux commenced a rally, and the *punishment* was truly dreadful on both sides; but the Moor had the best

of it, and the Champion fell from a hit, and received another
in the act of falling, which occasioned some difference of
opinion: but the umpires decided it to be correct, as the
hands of Cribb were at liberty.

Sixth.—Molineaux, from want of wind, lunged right and
left, but gained nothing by it, and stopped with neatness the
right hand of the Champion. Cribb now gave the Moor so
severe a blow in the body with his right hand, that it not
only appeared to *roll him up*, but seemed as if it had completely knocked the wind out of him, which issued so strong
from his mouth, like smoke from a pipe, that he was literally
gasping for breath. On renewing a rally, he behaved quite
frantic, and seemed bewildered as to the manner in which he
should conduct himself; afraid of his opponent's *punishment*,
he dared not go in, although wishing so to do, and capered
about, in an extravagant manner, to the derision of Cribb and
the spectators, hit short, and was quite abroad, when the
Champion pursued him round the stage with great success,
and concluded the round by a full-length hit, which laid the
Moor prostrate. Five to one on Cribb.

Seventh.—Molineaux, quite furious, ran in on an intemperate rally, and gained a trifling advantage; but Cribb
punished him as severe as can be described, about the neck
and jugular: after the expiration of a minute, the Moor fell
from weakness.

Eighth.—Molineaux, still desperate, rallied, but his blows
were too short, when Cribb *nobbed* him in fine style, and
fibbed him most dreadfully till he fell, the Champion having
got his head under his arm. All betters.

Ninth.—It was so evident which way the battle would now
terminate, that it was " *Lombard Street to a China Orange*"
Cribb was the conqueror. The Moor, in running in, had his
jaw broke, and he fell, as if dead, from a tremendous left-
handed blow of the Champion. Molineaux did not come
to his time by full half a minute, but Cribb wished that the
spectators should fully witness his superiority in giving away
this chance, dancing about the stage when he ought to
have been proclaimed the conqueror: and went in again,
knocking him nearly down, and then up again, and *levelled*
him.

Tenth.—It was with the utmost difficulty that Molineaux
could be brought from the knee of his second, and then
it was only to add to the severe *milling* which he had re-

ceived; but the *Moor*, still *game*, made a desperate though
unsuccessful effort, and fell from great distress.

Eleventh.—Cribb had given another *chance* away respecting
time, but the *Moor* was in a state of stupor, his senses having
been completely *milled* out of him; and upon receiving a
floorer, he was unable to be got up. Victory was announced
in a sort of a Scotch reel by *Gulley* and Cribb, elated with
success, followed by tumultuous applause.

> ————Such a noise arose,
> As the shrouds make at sea in a stiff tempest
> As loud, and to as many tunes. Hats, cloaks,
> Doublets, I think, flew up; and had their faces
> Been loose, this day they had been lost. Such joy
> I never saw before.

It appeared in the above BATTLE, that the *Moor*
had acquired *science* equal to the CHAMPION, and was
deemed as good an *in-fighter;* remarkably quick and
weighty with his left hand, and who returned on his
opponent's head, whenever he received in the body:
but no question now remains concerning the superiority
of the combatants. CRIBB having won a main, and
beat the *Moor* in *nineteen minutes and ten seconds*, when
in the former battle it continued thrice the duration;
which can only be accounted for, that CRIBB was too
full of flesh, and not in good condition; and *Molineaux*
had improved respecting *science*, but injured his stamina. The hardiest frame could not resist the blows
of the CHAMPION; and it is astonishing the *Moor*
stood them so long. He was taken out of the ring
senseless, and could not articulate; and it was thought
upon the first examination that his jaw-bone and two
of his ribs were fractured; while, on the contrary,
CRIBB scarcely received a body blow, but his head
was terribly out of shape.

All the towns upon the North road gained considerably by this contest, particularly those of Grantham and Stamford. No interruption was offered to the *mill;* and it is said, that the Corporations of the principal towns in the North solicited that the battle might be fought on their own domains ; as did numbers of the nobility residing in that part of the country.

Among the company who witnessed the battle, were the Marquis of *Queensbury,* Sir *Henry Smith,* Lord *Yarmouth,* the Hon. *Berkeley Craven,* Major *Mellish,* Captain *Barclay,* General *Grosvenor,* Lord *Pomfret,* Sir *Francis Baynton,* Sir *Charles Alton, Thomas Goddard,* Esq. Mr. *Gore,* &c. &c. and all the sporting amateurs and professors in the kingdom.

So much interest was felt in London concerning the issue of this contest, that we cannot pass it over without notice—exceeding every thing in the annals of pugilism. On Saturday night an immense crowd assembled in the front of *Richmond's* house, the *Prad and Swimmer,* St. Martin's Street, Leicester-square, to inquire the particulars, which so completely blocked up the street, that the house was shut up at an early hour ; on the next morning they assembled and gained access, and although some additional rooms were opened, half the people could not be accommodated ; and also *Bob's* Chop-house, the Castle, in Holborn, was so crowded on the Sunday evening, that several peace-officers were obliged to attend to preserve order.

On the CHAMPION's return home in a barouche and four horses, decorated with blue ribbons, on the Monday following, accompanied by an Amateur of Distinc-

tion and *Joe Ward,* he was cheered through all the towns
he passed, after the manner of an officer bearing des-
patches of a victory, so much was it felt by the people
of England : and upon the approach to his house in
White-lion-street, Seven Dials, the crowd had assembled in such numbers as to render it impassable, and
who rewarded this HERO OF THE FIST with loud and
animating plaudits, worthy of the CHAMPION OF
ENGLAND.

It was reported that CRIBB gained £400 by this *set-to,*
and his patron, Captain *Barclay,* £10,000; and that
a Baker in the Borough sported all his *blunt,* personal
property, together with the lease of his house, &c.
amounting to £1700, upon the CHAMPION. A curious
bet was also made between two sporting characters, the
winner to get *a complete suit of clothes,* shirt, &c. &c. with
a walking-stick, gloves, and a *guinea* in his pocket.

Through the kind interference of Mr. *Jackson,* a collection of near £50 was made for *Molineaux,* who by
no means conducted himself in that sort of way that a
pugilist ought to have done, who was to fight for £600,
by letting any one previously knock him about with the
gloves that had any inclination to spar with him.

It should seem that CRIBB was peculiarly indebted
to Capt. *Barclay* for his excellent condition : having
spent three months previously to the battle, at his coun-
try-seat in Scotland, living entirely by rules laid down
by the Captain, and adhering to the strictest regimen
and discipline. CRIBB, it appears, would most willingly at times have relaxed from this mode of life, had
not his patron pointed out the great advantages result-
ing from such training—shewing that the body was in-

vigorated by the prescribed means, and that nothing gross or puffy appertained to it; which was most clearly evinced in the CHAMPION, who was rendered light, firm, and free from complaint. Nothing is more obvious than by a comparison of the *trained* man with one who cannot feel or submit to the utility of it; the flesh of the former does not so soon turn black, or become inflamed with the effect of blows; while, on the contrary, the *untrained* would become blind from the hits, which the pugilist in good condition would not even show the marks of. But notwithstanding, it is said of CRIBB, that he would sooner fight *Molineaux* any time, than undergo another such a *training!*

The editor of the *Edinburgh Star* having made some comments upon the CHAMPION, which were thought rather irrelevant to his character, we insert the correspondence that passed between them, to render these memoirs as ample as possible:—"On Sunday last, CRIBB, the celebrated pugilist, arrived at Aberdeen, on a visit to a gentleman there. He is at present in training at Ury, the seat of Captain *Barclay*, preparatory to the great battle to be fought with *Molineaux*, on the 27th of September, near Doncaster. On this match not less that £50,000 are already betted, and CRIBB stakes 100 guineas of his own money on the issue. Betting, however, is at present equal. This celebrated boxer is at present the Champion of England, having fought and gained the following pitched battles, besides many casual ones, in which he never was beaten, *viz.* with *George Maddox,* Jan. 1805—*Tom Blake,* Feb. 1805 —*Ikey Pig,* May 1805—*Richmond,* the black, 1805— *James Belcher,* 1807—*Horton,* May, 1808—*Gregson,*

October 1808.—*Belcher*, 1809—and *Molineaux*, 1810. CRIBB is now only thirty years of age." Here follows the Editor's comment: "When the amount of money collected for the relief of British prisoners in France, now suffering for the cause of their country, scarcely amounts to £49,000, there is—Blush, O Britain!—there is £50,000 depending upon a *boxing match!* The Champion CRIBB's arrival, and on a Sunday, too! on a visit to a gentleman of Aberdeen, (we should be glad to know what kind of a gentleman he is,) on his way to *Capt. Barclay's* seat, where he is to go into training. This must be announced, forsooth, as if he, the *meritorious* CRIBB, did honour to the city of Aberdeen by his presence! What will the starving manufacturers of Scotland say when they read this? Shame! shame upon it."

From these remarks the CHAMPION felt induced to address the Editor with the following card:—" Mr. CRIBB presents his respects to the Editor of the *Edinburgh Star*. Mr. CRIBB saw (with what satisfaction the Editor may suppose) the paragraph relating to him in a late paper, and he will take the opportunity of soon passing through Edinburgh, to make due *personal* acknowledgments for the favour done him.——Ury, by Stonehaven, 28th July, 1811."

The above card was answered by the Editor in his paper of the 6th of August, in the following words: "If Mr. CRIBB, by *personal acknowledgments*, means any thing in his *professional* line, as we are not adepts in the noble science of boxing, we think it would be but fair to give us a little time to procure a Champion, and put him in training: perhaps, Mr. CRIBB's friend

at Aberdeen might be induced to superintend his education."

In consequence of the numerous hard-earned victories of the CHAMPION, a splendid dinner was given
at *Gregson's* Chop-house, by a large party of pugilistic
amateurs: but more especially in honour of his second
triumph over the *Moor*, when CRIBB was placed in the
chair; and his conduct, as president, was unassuming
and pleasant; receiving the approbation of several
patrons of distinction by whom he was surrounded.
Considerable harmony prevailed, and several excellent songs written for the occasion, full of point, were
most rapturously received, particularly one of *Bob
Gregson's*, (see page 358,) which was applauded to
the echo, and loudly encored. *Milling* formed the
most prominent feature of the conversation, but no
practical display of the art, to enforce their arguments.
The company did not depart till they unanimously
voted the Champion—

A SILVER CUP, *valued Fifty Guineas*,

as a memorial of the high opinion which the *Sporting
World*, in particular, held of his uniform courage and
superiority in his pugilistic combats; also on his being
induced to enter the ring (having positively declined
pugilism in general) on the score of *nationality*—his
own individual fame—and to prevent a FOREIGNER
from triumphing over the heroes of England.

The subscriptions for the above purpose proving so
ample, the sum was increased, and a silver cup of
FIGHTY GUINEAS VALUE was presented to the CHAM-
PION, at the Castle Tavern, Holborn, on Monday, the
2d of December, 1811, at a dinner appointed for that

purpose, TOM CRIBB in the chair, supported by one of the most numerous and respectable assemblages of the *Fancy* ever witnessed. After the cloth was removed, and the usual toasts of loyalty had been given, Mr. *Emery* (of the Theatre Royal, Covent Garden), who having been at a previous meeting unanimously voted to present this *Fancy Plate*, was now called upon to fulfil the wishes of the company, when the *cup* was immediately produced, the son of Thespis rose, and gave

" CRIBB—*the Champion of England!*"

and addressed the chairman to the following purport :

" THOMAS CRIBB, I have the honour this day of being the representative of a numerous and most respectable body of your friends; and though I am by no means qualified to attempt the undertaking which has devolved on me by a vote of the subscribers, yet the cause will, I am confident, prove a sufficient excuse for my want of ability. You are requested to accept this cup, as a tribute of respect, for the uniform valour and integrity you have shown in your several combats, but most particularly for the additional proofs of native skill and manly intrepidity displayed by you in your last memorable battle, when the cause rested not merely upon individual fame, but for the pugilistic reputation of your native country, in contending with a formidable foreign antagonist. In that combat you gave proof that the innovating hand of a foreigner, when lifted against a son of Britannia, must not only be aided by the *strength* of a lion, but the heart also.

" The fame you have so well earned has been by manly and upright conduct; and such conduct, I have no doubt, will ever mark your very creditable retirement from the ring, or stage of pugilism. However intoxicated the cup or its contents may at any future period make you, I am sufficiently persuaded the gentlemen present, and the sons of John Bull in general, will never consider you have a *cup* too much."

The cup, filled with wine, having gone round, the CHAMPION thus briefly addressed his patrons, " Gentlemen, for the honour you have done me in present-

ing this cup, I most respectfully beg of you to accept
my warmest thanks."

The CHAMPION having omitted to drink the health
of his patrons, Mr. *Emery* reminded him of his mistake, at the same time candidly allowing for the em-
barrassing situation of the Chairman, by observing to
the company that the feelings of the President were
too much overcome by gratitude to think of that
which he had neglected, and also to give utterance to
what he intended to have said upon the occasion;
which was well received by all present.

Chaunting then became " the order of the day," and
among the toasts and songs given upon this occasion,
considerable *originality* appeared.* Harmony reigned
throughout, and the CHAMPION, impressed with gratitude to his leading patrons, Sir *Henry Smyth*, Bart.
Capt. *Barclay*, *Shirlwall Harrison*, Esq. &c. &c. drank
their healths with marked animation and respect; and
the CUP, in being put round, upon its arrival into the
hands of Mr. *Jackson*, *Gulley*, *Gregson*, and the veteran *Joe Ward* (who acted as Vice), the company, as a
mark of esteem for their past services, loudly cheered
those celebrated heroes of the fist.

No pugilist ever retired from the *ring* with such favours heaped upon him as the present CHAMPION, and
the *sporting amateurs* have vied with each other in paying respect to his *milling* acquirements, that have been
so often seen, *felt*, and justly acknowledged; and,
doubtless, will be *long* remembered by those persons

---

* A selection of which (with some others) is introduced at
the end of the work.

who entered the lists against his conquering arm. He left the field of glory covered with honour and renown, to pass the remainder of his days in tranquillity and peace, by paying attention to his business, as a coal-merchant—which he for some time assiduously followed, and which he quitted to commence Tavern Keeper, at the *King's Arms,* the corner of King-street and Duke-street, St. James's.

Our sketch of the CHAMPION would be imperfect were we not to observe, that in disposition he is placid, condescending, and obliging, possessing a forbearance of temper that cannot be more *strikingly* illustrated than by the following circumstance, which took place a few days after the last fight. CRIBB, in passing through Fore-street, Cripplegate, was most grossly insulted by a Jew of the name of Simmonds, who, valuing himself upon his manhood, and not knowing whom he was in company with, endeavoured to give our Hero a prime *facer.* The CHAMPION, with the utmost composure, seized hold of this *mere apology,* (in his hands,) yet disdaining to inflict that sort of punishment which, had he given way to rage, from his well-known strength and science, must in all probability nearly annihilated this presuming *Israelite ;* but instead of which, he instantly compelled *Mordecai* to go before the Lord Mayor to answer for the assault. His Lordship, on hearing the case, was *struck* with the magnanimity displayed by CRIBB on this occasion, and highly praised him for his manliness of temper,—at the same time reprimanding the Jew severely for his improper behaviour. He was, however, discharged on paying the costs, to which decision the

CHAMPION, with much good nature, immediately acquiesced.

AN IMPROMPTU,

On its being said, in allusion to the late battle, that Molineaux had been " SOLD."

> The BLACK to say, at least is bold,
> That in the battle he was sold :
> If so—by *Auction*—for 'tis known,
> When he was sold, CRIBB *knocked him down!*

AN IMPROMPTU,

Occasioned by the CHAMPION's quitting his Occupation of Coal-Merchant for that of Victualler, at the sign of the KING'S ARMS.

> *Black Diamonds,* adieu!—TOM's now took to the *bar,*
>   The FANCY to *serve* with new charms—
> For a *chop* or a *glass*—to *mill* or to *spar,*
>   They'll be at home to a *peg* at the *Arms!*
> The lovers of truth, without crime, may *here* FIB—
>   On the pleasures of *sporting* can sing—
> Then, ye *Swells,* give a *turn* to gallant TOM CRIBB,
>   That he may ne'er QUIT the Arms of his KING !

If not possessing the volubility of an orator, the CHAMPION, in company, is facetious, and endeavours to render himself pleasant and sociable to those around him, with a modest and unassuming deportment.

It was under consideration to present an *emblematical* BELT to the CHAMPION. More need not be observed than, in taking leave of this distinguished Pugilist, we present our patrons with—

And Damn'd be him that first
cries Hold_Enough

Publish'd Sept.ʳ 1812   by G.Smeeton, 139 St Martin's Lane.

AN ILLUSTRATION OF THE
Coat of Arms,
ENGRAVED UPON THE SILVER CUP
Presented to TOM CRIBB,
Designed and executed at the expressed wish of the
Higher Flights of the Fancy,
AND GIVEN

As a REMEMBRANCER of their approbation of the manly
combats and pugilistic qualities of the
CHAMPION of ENGLAND.

THE CREST:
The *Bristol* Arms.

In the first quarter :

The BRITISH LION is looking down with stern regard on the *American* Flag, half-mast high (*in the
fourth quarter ;*) the Beaver, symbolic of the latter
country, hiding his head under its folds, alluding to
MOLINEAUX'S DEFEAT.

In the second quarter :
The Combatants are setting-to ; and

In the third quarter :

CRIBB is viewed in his coal barge, illustrative of his
trade.

THE SUPPORTERS
Represent the CHAMPION looking with an eye of commiseration on his vanquished opponent.

MOTTO :
" And damn'd be him who first cries, Hold! ENOUGH!"
1813.]   *Shakspeare.*

JOE WARD,

FATHER OF THE PRESENT RACE OF PUGILISTS;

Being the Oldest Professor (now living, October 1821,*)*
of the Scientific Art of Boxing.

With mirth and laughter let old wrinkles come,
And let my liver rather heat with wine,
Than my heart cool with mortifying groans.
Why should a man, whose blood is warm within,
Sit like his grandsire cut in alabaster?
Sleep when he wakes, and creep into the jaundice
By being peevish?

THE *Sporting World* have not, at the present moment,
an object of more interesting attention respecting the
SCIENCE OF PUGILISM than the above veteran. If
JOE has not personally *milled* his way to eminence in
the art, which several others have attained, he has acquired a distinguished reputation which no other
pugilist possesses, from his long and practical experience in all the VARIOUS SCHOOLS that have *flourished* and *faded* during his time; added to which, his
knowledge of the merits of the various professors,
and also in having acted as the principal *second* in nearly
all the battles of note which have transpired for the
last fifty years, places JOE WARD in the most attractive point of view. To Amateurs, the company of
JOE is not only interesting to learn the qualities and
pretensions of those men he might feel inclined to back,
but also to the young pugilist, whose inexperience points

JOE WARD.

BILL GIBBONS.

Published, April 24, 1813, by George Smeeton, 139, St. Martins Lane.

out to him the value of obtaining information, respecting the style, manner, and execution of those boxers who have *milled* their way to fame and honour, and also in avoiding those *defects* which have brought on *ruin*, defeat, and even disgrace.

The above veteran was born on the 21st of March, 1751, at Billericay, in Essex, of respectable parents, who apprenticed our hero to an engraver. JOE's seven years were passed in his Majesty's Warren, at Woolwich, and the Tower of London, in promulgating the arms of the King on cannons, guns, &c. and, in all probability, by being thus surrounded with implements of war, his mind imbibed that ardour for the " *use of arms*," which, it appears, through life he has never been tardy in using, when the necessity of the moment compelled him to have recourse to their aid. To this prominent trait in his character several of his Majesty's subjects can bear ample testimony; and also his *taste* for *engraving* upon those faces who have claimed the *finishing touches* of this most *striking* artist !

About the year 1770, we find JOE entered the lists with a man of the name of *Davis*, in Mary-le-bone Fields, for two guineas—a sort of " *kill devil fellow!*" but who was soon glad to acknowledge the superiority of WARD, although a mere youth, and inexperienced in the pugilistic art.

A locksmith, of the name of *Morris*, a good *bottom* man fought with JOE, on Lisson-Green, Paddington, for ten guineas; but who, like the former, was glad to cry out *enough*. WARD upon this occasion was seconded by *Norfolk Harry*.

In Harley-fields, JOE was called out by one *Sweat-*

man, who "had crept so much into favour with himself," on account of his superior *milling* qualities, that he fought WARD, ten guineas to ten shillings! when this conceited man experienced not only the mortification of losing his *blunt,* but also received considerable *punishment* and the contempt of the spectators for his presumption.

JOE did not long remain at peace; he was challenged by *Jack Mowet* for ten guineas, and which fight was decided in the Long Fields. It was a well-contested battle, but victory was once more decided in favour of WARD, who was seconded by *Bill Gibbons.*

On Wimbledon Common a severe battle was fought between one *Reynolds* and JOE, which continued for an hour and nine minutes, and, upon its conclusion, being considered as a *draw,* they again contested the point,

On July 1, 1788, upon a stage on the Brighton Race-Course, when the superiority of JOE was evident, who fought in the most scientific and manly style, to the complete terror of his antagonist. *Reynolds* proving destitute of *game,* shifted, and was soon glad to *give in!*

WARD, partaking of the sports at Lewes Races, was challenged by a man of the name of *Allister,* for two guineas, who was considered one of the best men in Sussex; but *Allister* was so soon disposed of by the above veteran, that upon his exclaiming, " *Is this the best man your county can boast of?*" a fellow instantly stepped up, known by the appellation of " *Jolly Rags,*" and demanded a *set-to,* upon which the ring was immediately cleared, when *Jolly Rags* received such a severe *milling* in a few minutes, from JOE's potent arm, that he was glad to cry for quarter. Both these battles were gained before WARD put his clothes on, to the no small amusement of the amateurs and spectators present.

JOE entered the lists at Langley Broom, with one *Townshend*, for twenty-five guineas a-side. This was a good contest; but the superior science of WARD again prevailed, when he was declared the conqueror. *Bill Warr* was JOE's second.

At Smallborough Green, near Hounslow, a man denominated *Great Jacobs*, challenged WARD, and who made so certain of winning, that he betted five guineas to three; but JOE was not to be intimidated either by his money or size, and seconded by his friend *Bill Gibbons*, he *set-to* without ceremony, and soon took the conceit out of this vaunting blade.

The sunshine of fortune now for a moment left our hero, who was beaten in a contest in Hyde Park, with *Jonathan Starling;* but whose defeat was occasioned by his arm being broken, which prevented him from continuing the fight. *Tom Johnson* seconded JOE.

WARD, a few years since, fought a man at Kilburn Wells, known by the title of " *Great Joe,*" *the Oxford Wagoner*, from a place called Bestre, in Oxfordshire, who was a complete terror to the road, not only from his size and weight (which was nearly 17 stone,) but from the notions entertained of his *milling* qualities. JOE, notwithstanding the remonstrances of his friends to the contrary, would fight this *Knight of the Whip*, who blustered what he could do—when WARD. without any further remarks, *set-to* with " *Great Joe,*" and in seven minutes proved, to the no small satisfaction of his friends, that *Little* JOE was the *greatest* man in actions, by *punishing* all pretensions to *milling* completely out of this insolent *chaw-bacon*. The veteran, at this period, being nearly sixty years of age, and his antagonist scarcely thirty. A dinner being given at Kilburn Wells, on the Monday following, and WARD acting as the president on the occasion, two wagoners having put up at the above inn, and learning that JOE was up stairs, one of them insisted upon joining the company, to which the landlord made no immediate objection, provided he paid 10s. 6d. the price of the dinner ticket: when *Johnny Raw* instantly threw down the blunt, and having gained admission, inquired what one of the bowls of negus upon the table came to, and was informed twelve shillings, when he ordered another to come in directly, and now declared the purpose of his errand, offering to treat JOE with a bottle of wine, for the manly courage which he had displayed in punishing his over-grown fellow-servant, and at the same time declaring the satisfaction it had given all the travellers and inn-keepers along the Oxford road, who had been continually annoyed from the insolent attacks of this *would-be* boxer.

One *Treadaway*, a bricklayer, entered the lists with JOE, at Turnham-Green, but was soon compelled to acknowledge his scientific superiority, by declaring he had had quite *enough*.

WARD being at the White Lion, Paddington, a few years since, and a trifling skirmish ensuing, a tailor, of the name of *Talbot*, who was more officious than necessary, and possessing rather more money than wit, annoyed the veteran so much, by interfering, JOE told him, if he did not remain quiet, "that for a halfpenny,

he would give him a punch on the head." The pride of
this "*ninth part of a man*" instantly took fire, and strut-
ting up to our hero, like a crow in a gutter, with a good
deal of bombastic gestures, observed he should like to
catch him at it, and if he would only attempt it, he
would give him a guinea !!! "Give me the money,"
cries the veteran. This simple remnant of *tape* and
buckram immediately handed the *shiner* over to JOE,
who directly pocketed the affront, and telling him now
to take care of himself, JOE put in such a tremendous hit upon the empty nob of poor *Stitch*, that *levelled* him in a twinkling, where he laid for a considerable
time, stunned, until awakened from his stupor by the
peals of laughter and contempt of the spectators, who
were now drinking red wine at his expense, the veteran
having ordered four bottles of port (giving the waiter
the odd shilling) as a punishment to poor Snip for his
bouncing, and to lament over his folly at his leisure,
that in future he might learn how to dispose of his
guineas on a better *suit.*

   At one of the *freaks* of the FANCY, at the late *Slender
Billy's*, in the renowned dominions of *Caleb Baldwin*,
where a prime *bruin* was the sport of the day, two great
coal-heavers fell foul of *Bill Jackling* and his *buffer*,
and who, whether from fear or some other cause, did
not resent the affront in a way which JOE expected.
The latter instantly remonstrated with *Jackling* for his
want of spirit: upon which the coal-heavers, *sans cérémonie*, fell upon JOE—a row commenced, and our hero,
who had hitherto been afraid of the *bear*, now found
himself under the animal's feet; which however had no
effect upon his nerves, for, on getting up, he soon *served*

out these customers as they deserved, to the great satisfaction of all present, but particularly to an eminent
sporting wax-chandler, who exclaimed, in the broad
accent peculiar to his country, "Ah, mon! I always
thought you only a *second*, but now I find you the best
of the *firsts!*"

In December (1812) as JOE was going through Ed-
ward-street, Portman-square, a big fellow ran after
him, threatening to give the veteran a *hiding;* a gentleman, who was passing, observed the circumstance, and
knowing JOE in the prime of his life, exclaimed, "You
rascal, there was a time when you dared not have used
WARD thus!" Upon which this *chap* made a blow at
JOE, who warded it off, and returned such a tremendous hit on the fellow's *nob*, that he fell down as if killed ;
and lay to all appearance, for a considerable time,
without any signs of life, to the great alarm of the above
gentleman, who thought the man was actually dead.
The gentleman declared his readiness to all around
him to come forward in case any thing serious occurred ;
but, upon the fellow's recovery, he expressed great
satisfaction at the *punishment* which this *hit-a-body*
had received and so justly merited.

In fact, it would require a small volume to detail
the anecdotes and laughable skirmishes of our hero, of
whom we are sorry to observe that, a few months since,
in a casual set-to at GREGSON's, he had the misfortune
to break one of his legs : but his good constitution soon
brought him through it.

Enjoying a fine green old age, JOE appears nearly
as active as when in the hey-day of youth, and *seconds*
with an uncommon degree of agility and attention.

At the zenith of his *milling days* he was in height about
5 feet 6½ inches, weighing eleven stone six pounds;
but at the present period he is somewhat heavier. As
a pugilist, few, if any, possessed more activity, and his
science, upon all occasions, appeared truly conspicuous.
Joe was looked upon as a manly fighter, and one who
put in his blows remarkably quick, and ever alert in
the fight to improve the *chance* which presented itself;
turning it ultimately to his advantage and success.
Possessing a lively eye, he seldom let the first round
pass over without *drawing the cork* of his antagonist,
and soon discovering what sort of a *customer* he had to
deal with.

In the capacity of a SECOND, he may be said, without
disparagement, to stand *first* on the list; and his judgment and discrimination in that peculiar respect has
ever been looked upon by the *Sporting World* with
considerable attention; and his long *practical* experience has stamped that opinion current. Much depends upon a good *second,* and very few of the first-
rate fighters have any sound pretensions to that character, in comparison with WARD: to recruit the exhausted—to gain wind—to infuse courage—to increase
the offering, *chance,* &c. the merits of JOE are so well
known as not to need any further comment. BOXIANA
would not have done his duty in passing them over; or
in omitting the following illustrative fact:—*Hooper,*
the *tinman,* who had often obtained victory under the
care of JOE, felt so much enraged on learning the veteran was to second *Tom Owen* against him, that *Hooper*
threatened WARD with a serious mischief, if he per-
sisted in so doing. "Never mind," cried our hero,

"I have often taught you, BILL, *how* to win; but now you shall see that I will teach *Owen* the *way* to beat you!" and which proved the fact. WARD, well knowing that it almost broke the *tinman's* heart whenever he was thrown, instructed *Owen* (who possessed more strength than art) how to acquire that qualification, but who did not know which way to commence the operations, until the few lessons that he had received from JOE, rendered him so expert and perfect, that he was *then* enabled to throw his master with ease and certainty.

We now turn aside from the qualifications of the hero, to view his pretensions as a man of taste; and in this, as in several other instances which we have portrayed, it will be found that all PUGILISTS *are not so completely absorbed by* FIGHTING, *as to prove indifferent to the softer attractions of life, in passing over the works of genius and art without admiration and attention.* If JOE cannot boast of a splendid gallery of pictures, formed of selections from the great *foreign* masters, he can sport such a collection of *native* subjects, that, in many instances, must be considered *unique.* Portraits of nearly all the Pugilists (many of them in whole-lengths and attitudes) are to be found, from the days of FIGG and BROUGHTON down to the present period; with a variety of paintings of several of the most celebrated pugilistic encounters that have transpired, and likenesses of distinguished amateurs; among whom are, Captain *Barclay,* the classic Dr. Johnson, the Duke of Cumberland (the patron of BROUGHTON), Fletcher, Reid, &c. with sporting subjects out of number; in short, a very large room is

filled from the top to the bottom; and, as a proof of
WARD's liberality in preserving the Heroes of the Fist,
many of whom must have sunk in oblivion, he has had
several painted at his own expense.   His parlour is
decorated in a similar manner; and his partiality for
pictures has gone so far, that even the tap-room contains many excellent subjects—such as the Death of
Lord Nelson, Duncan's Victory, portrait of Buckhorse,
&c. which would reflect no discredit upon a better
situation: and it must be confessed, that the FANCY
are much indebted to the exertions of JOE WARD, for
his preservation of the likenesses of so many of their
favourite heroes, and to whom, perhaps, the term may
not be misapplied by observing, that from a retentive
memory, and possessing an intelligent mind, he can
give a sort of *new life* to those departed pugilists, by
detailing their actions.

The veteran kept the GREEN DRAGON, *King-Street*,
near *Swallow-Street*, (until it was pulled down, to make
room for the new street) previous to which the Amateurs had an opportunity of verifying what has been
asserted, in viewing

WARD'S CABINET OF THE FANCY!

and where civility and good treatment gave a zest to
the other attractions of the visitor.

BILL GIBBONS,

The Ring Maker to the P. C.

In all *sports* of the FANCY, see BILL take the lead—
When hunting the Badger, or Bull of *true* breed!
With rum trotting *Neddies*, for speed or 'gainst time;
And *tykes* that will *mill* with the *primest* of *prime!*
To fight, or to *second*, 'tis to GIBBONS the same—
And a *Cove* that is *flash* to the CHANCE of the *game;*
In the *ring* truly useful—full of *spunk* at a hunt—
And a BOXER that *knows* the *true value* of BLUNT;
Tho' quite partial to *milling*—but averse to all strife,
Yet *down* to the TRICKS—and will LIVE all his LIFE!

THE Hero now before us, most undoubtedly, must
be considered as the *completest* FANCIER *in the circle,*
if not one of the oldest *blades* of the FANCY ; and however prominent his *milling* qualities may appear on the
canvass, yet they operate as mere *light* and *shade* to the
other parts of his portrait. Whether he lays any claim
of affinity to the learned historian of that name, who
has treated the world with such a copious knowledge of
the Greeks and Romans, we have not yet been able to
ascertain ; but of this we are assured, that no man has
a better knowledge of the *Greeks* and *Romans* of the
present day, or deeper *read* in their conquests, than the

Hero of this sketch. ORIGINALITY cannot be denied to him; and, in point of being *flash*, the very echo vibrates to the truth of this assertion. The Marquis of Stafford's collection of paintings to the most refined connoisseur, cannot prove a greater source of attraction than the *Sporting Menagerie* of BILL GIBBONS, to the *Fancier*. BILL may be termed a leading *asterisk* to the Sporting World; or, perhaps, more properly speaking, the *pendulum* that keeps a *certain part* of it in motion.

His levees previous to a *mill*, a HUNT, *race*, or a *bait*, upon "*the inquiring suit*," are numerous beyond description; and among whom it may clearly be seen, that the CLOTHES make *only* the difference—in witnessing the CORINTHIAN *drop* his dignity to gratify his *penchant;* the *Gownsman* put aside his cloth and his book to enjoy his favourite pursuit; and the SWEEP parting with his *scanty pittance* of *blunt*, to enjoy and participate in a *bit of life!*

In the *canine fancy*—BILL's dogs take the lead, and the stamp of GIBBONS passes them *current* for *thorough-bred* and *game*. BILL's judgment, in this respect, has never been questioned; and his decisions upon animals paid nearly as much deference to as the *fiat* of a *Lord Chief Justice*.

His BULLS that have so repeatedly attracted *Johnny Bull* and his numerous family to witness the fun, merriment, gaiety, and caricature, which they have produced by their *gameness* and *scientific* training—have rendered the object of this Memoir a character of considerable notoriety to all those who feel interested in the 𝕺𝖑𝖉 𝕰𝖓𝖌𝖑𝖎𝖘𝖍 𝕾𝖕𝖔𝖗𝖙𝖘, that, at present, we shall proceed without further prologue, by observing,

BILL GIBBONS made his first appearance in this
world, in Lloyd's Court, St. Giles's, on the 28th of
September, 1757, and, at the age of fifteen, was apprenticed out to a Coachmaker in the neighbourhood.
BILL, almost from his cradle, was much attached to
animals, and evinced judgment upon their various
shapes and sizes, which indicated the growing *Fancier;*
and at the age of seventeen, the little money he had
accumulated went to purchase a bull-dog. This
animal proved so great a favourite with BILL,
that he never went any where without being accompanied by *his partner,* (as he termed him,) and who
was the instance of making public those *pugilistic*
qualities which, in all probability, might otherwise have
been obscured from the *ring,* had not the following
adventure called them forth :—In going through War-
.dour-street, Soho, GIBBONS and *his partner* came in
contact with a drover and his dog, who started his *fancy*
upon BILL's dog, when the two animals had a fierce
set-to, backed by each of their masters; but, words
arising between them, BILL and the Drover stripped,
leaving their dogs to fight at one end of the street,
while they occupied the other part of it with a *mill.*
It proved a most desperate conflict, and, after fighting
for nearly an hour, GIBBONS was not only crowned
with the smiles of victory, but pleased to find that his
dog had also proved the conqueror.

Before his apprenticeship had expired, BILL, with
the consent of his master, commenced business for himself at the Gravel Pits.

About the year 1776, GIBBONS was challenged by
one *Jack Freegrove,* a tailor, at a public-house in Peter-

street, who valued himself on his *milling* pretensions
by having conquered a baker in a pitched battle in
Hyde Park; but whatever sharp qualities *Freegrove's
needle* might have possessed upon the *soft dough* of the
baker, BILL soon blunted its effects, and made *Freegrove* sing out for quarter.

Sam Newton, a well-known fighting post-boy, and
GIBBONS, had a few words at the Blue Posts, Peter-
street, Westminster, when they immediately went into
the street to decide this affair of honour, which was
settled *post-haste* in favour of BILL.

A dispute arising about a sixpence between GIB-
BONS and a man called *Mendoza,* a hackney coachman,
at a house kept by one Green, the corner of Brewer-
street, Golden-square, it was determined by both the
combatants, that the above *large sum* should be placed
in the hands of Mrs. Green, and as neither of them were
afraid of a little *punishment,* they agreed that whoever
proved the best man should have the *tizzy.* A ring
being made upon the stones, they immediately *set-to ;*
and after a desperate conflict, victory was decided in
favour of GIBBONS; who received the *sixpence* with
as much satisfaction as fifty pounds, now-a-days, appears to create among the *milling coves !*

In Leicester Fields, BILL sported his *canvass,* with
one Stewart, a shoemaker, where the cordwainer *napt*
it in such *prime twig,* that he soon left GIBBONS in
possession of the ring, the triumphant conqueror.

During the time of Fox's election, at Covent Garden,
when Sir Cecil Wray was his opponent—an earthen-
ware man, who resided on the above spot, and who had
gained some little notoriety in having fought *Hooper*

upon the same stage on which *Johnson* and *Ryan* had
contended, now fell in with GIBBONS; but the earthen-
ware man had one consolation on his side, that he had
not far to be taken home after being defeated by BILL.

A few days after the above rencontre, a Bristol man
attacked GIBBONS nearly on the same spot, and who
also shared the same fate as the man of *delf,* by acknowledging that he was beaten: upon which BILL
left the ground, and went to dine at Green's, in Duke-
street, Lincoln's Inn Field, but scarcely had he begun
to eat, when the Bristol man arrived and demanded
another trial, as he was not *satisfied.* BILL immediately
adjourned to Lincoln's Inn Fields; and in the course
of two rounds, completely *finished* the business, and
then returned to his dinner without being any the
worse for this singular *set-to.*

A man, known by the name of *Norfolk Harry,* a
bricklayer, and who had distinguished himself in three
or four pitched battles, insulted GIBBONS at the four-
corner ground, at the Rising Sun, Lisson Green, and
talked rather largely that he would *serve* BILL *out;*
when it was at length agreed between them, that they
should go upon the Green, and fight it out *without
seconds,* and to *pick each other up.* A most desperate
engagement ensued, when GIBBONS put in such a
tremendous hit upon *Harry's* jaw, in the eighth round,
that it was so dreadfully broken as to compel him instantly to *give in.*

At the Cart and Horses, Bainbridge-street, St. Giles's,
a match had been made between one *Hugh Lansdown*
and *Tom Magee,* for ten guineas. *Magee* had crept a
little into notice by beating *Atlen* the butcher; but

he now paid forfeit rather than enter the ring with *Lansdown*; who felt so much elated with the circumstance, that he publicly challenged any one present to fight for a gallon of beer. BILL GIBBONS being in the house, was not thus to be *bounced* out of his reputation, and instantly staked the *fourteen pence* in the hands of the landlord, and went to the Long Fields, where *Lansdown* got a receipt in full of all demands from BILL for his vain boasting.

George Lovel, a gipsy, thought he could *take the shine* out of GIBBONS, and challenged him soon afterwards to the same spot in the Long Fields. *Joe Ward* seconded BILL upon this occasion, who was not long in making the gipsy *repent* of his temerity.

In the year 1789, nearly at the close of a hot day, devoted to the OLD ENGLISH SPORTS, on Kennington Common, where a *Bull*, celebrated for his *game* qualities at the stake had been exhibited, to the amusement of some thousands of spectators, and to which place BILL had repaired with his bull-dog to fight a match against this rum *donnok*, and in the event had proved successful; a trifling row commenced, in which GIBBONS was conspicuous in preventing his brother from being insulted; when young *Darts*, (son of the celebrated pugilist of that name, so well known in the annals of boxing,) wanting to make a fight, publicly challenged any one for a *guinea*. JOE WARD instantly made a bet, and went and fetched GIBBONS from the public-house to enter the ring with him. BILL, notwithstanding he was thus taken by surprise, and rather fatigued from seconding his dog against the bull, yet, to prevent JOE's losing his money, without hesitation accepted the challenge, and a regular *set-to* commenced. It was a most terrible hard fight—both the combatants fought like heroes, and dealt out tremendous *punishment*. An hour having nearly elapsed, some difference of opinion took place between the two seconds, who instantly left their men to *mill* by themselves, affording the spectators the *nouvelle* sight of *two fights* in one ring. JOE WARD, who seconded GIBBONS, soon made the *claret* fly from his opponent's *nob*, which put an end to the battle, by the ring being broken. In a short time afterwards a new one was made, and GIBBONS immediately entered it, ready to finish the contest; but *Darts* was now blind, and the person who held the stakes returned to each of the betters their money again. The combatants getting only well *milled* for their exertions. It was curious to observe the vast difference of appearance between *Darts* and GIBBONS when stripped; the latter uncommonly fair and round, while the skin of the former was a complete dark brown colour, with flesh as close and as hard as iron, and which seemed to resist every blow made upon his rough frame.

GIBBONS had a severe fight with a disciple of Vulcan, in Shug-lane, near the Haymarket; but the blacksmith's *bellows* being somewhat damaged from the hot work in which he had been engaged, acknowledged he was defeated.

At Ascot-Heath Races, GIBBONS fought a man, designated by the title of *Whistling Bob*, who was seconded by *Big Ben*. It was a good fight, and continued for some length of time; but BILL, under the care of *Joe Ward*, was pronounced the conqueror.

GIBBONS beat one *Jack Holder*, well known as a good bottom pugilist; and he also conquered one *Clox*, a coachman, in Tottenham-court-road, near Cullington's, the Black Horse, who had distinguished himself from the superior *game* which he possessed.

BILL, in a bit of a *spree*, one night, (in Pall Mall, in company with some distinguished amateurs, with whom he had been spending the evening,) rather jolly from the juice of the grape, had a *turn-up* with a brewer's servant; but, previous to the *set-to*, GIBBONS very carefully hung up his two great coats on the rails of a gentleman's house in that neighbourhood, to prevent their being injured, and of obtaining the advantage of more room for the use of his arms. GIBBONS was not long in disposing of this customer, but on looking for his *upper togs*, found they were *brushed off;* upon which a well-known amateur, laughing, observed, *" that he should have thought* BILL *would much sooner have found* FOUR *than have lost two coats;"* to which remark GIBBONS acquiesced, by acknowledging that the " KNOWING ONE *was* done!!!"

Although a good boxer, GIBBONS never ranked as a pugilist of note, that is to say, he never entered the ring as a prize-fighter—but *milled* away, either from circumstances, row, or *turn-up*—always ready to support the true principles of the *science*, without entering the lists for money; yet, in nearly all the great contests which have taken place, the name of GIBBONS, in some capacity or other, appears prominent. His occupation, as a DEALER IN FANCIES, has introduced him to several of the first characters in the country, and who have selected from his " cabinet of rarities" some of the primest *tykes, prads, &c.* seen in the kingdom, to *grace* their mansions, and to give energy to their sports. Few, if any, can boast of such patronage as our hero—who, if report speaks true, may now smile at the frowns of the *fastidious*, that would quarrel with his calling as a FANCY MERCHANT—and looking upon "life as a jest," he may retort, in the words of the inimitable GAY, even with propriety and effect,

> Thro' all the employments of life,
> Each neighbour abuses his brother ;
> Whore and rogue they call husband and wife,
> All professions berogue one another :
> The priest calls the lawyer a cheat,
> The lawyer beknaves the divine,
> And the statesman, because he's so great,
> Thinks his trade as honest as mine.

As a *second* and bottle-holder, &c. he is entitled to much attention, and of considerable value in the ring; and it has been remarked of him by an experienced sportsman, that those who bet on the same side with GIBBONS, are seldom on the wrong *scent,* from the sound judgment he possesses in matters of this kind. Seven successive times he attended upon the renowned *Jem Belcher,* when victory crowned his efforts; and on the eighth, when that hero of heroes was defeated, GIBBONS waited upon the *Game Chicken!*

In those matters of Sport, in which the distinguished parts of the *Fancy* sometimes interest themselves for private amusement, and where the *Canaille* are pro- hibited from rudely intermixing with the COMPOSITES and CORINTHIANS, so much deference is paid to our hero's decision, that in case *nice points* might arise, the proprietors frequently act the parts of *seconds* to their own *Buffers,* and appoint GIBBONS as their Umpire; to whom applications are made by the above characters, when prime ponies, good dogs, attendance on races, or to get up any thing in good style, are wanting. From the *thorough-bred* specimens, which of late years he has produced by his *game* bulls, and celebrated bull dogs, particularly *Turpin,* any thing further must prove superfluous.

As well as contributing to the sports of the field, the bait, and ring—the public are indebted to GIBBONS for considerable amusement on the *classic stage,* as Messrs. *Harris* and *Raymond,* of the Theatres Royal, can testify. In " *Harlequin* and *Asmodeus,*" at Covent Garden, in the scene of the Spanish bull-fight, the dogs of GIBBONS afforded the audience much mirth and fun; and in the concluding scene, at the *Lyceum,* of the " *Manager's last Kick,*" to heighten the effects of the *denouement* of the piece—the united efforts of GIBBONS and *Caleb Baldwin* appeared necessary, not only by the introduction of their *neddies* and *dogs,* but the situation was rendered irresistibly comic by a *sparring-match* between them in the front of the stage. This was only intended for the first night's represen- tation; but from the satisfaction which the audience took in this *set-to,* the *Manager* was compelled to con- tinue their feats of drollery through the long run of the piece.

In taking our leave of this *Originality* of NATURE, though *down as a hammer* to what is going forward on the turf or turnpike, and mixing with sporting characters of all descriptions, we feel a pleasure in asserting, that the worst word he has to say upon any occasion is some odd phrase peculiar to himself, such as " *Burn my breeches*," &c. An oath never escapes from his lips; civility is the leading feature in his composition; and his *knowledge of* LIFE has not been thrown away upon him. Temperate in his conduct, and unassuming in his demeanour, he has reduced the game of *chance* to a certainty.——Such is the unsophisticated portrait of BILL GIBBONS:

> Search then the RULING PASSION: *There*, alone,
> The *wild* are constant, and the *cunning* known;
> The *fool* consistent, and the *false* sincere;
> Priests, princes, women, no dissemblers here!

BILL RICHMOND,

A Man of Colour, and a Native of America.

> I will a round unvarnish'd tale deliver,
> Of the *mills*, skirmishes, TURN-UPS, *spars*,
> That I have past.

THIS pugilistic hero was born at Sturton Island, at a place called Cuckold's Town, otherwise *Richmond*, contiguous to New York, in America, on August 5, 1763, under the auspices of a reverend divine of the name of *Charlton*. When Sturton Island was taken by the English, young RICHMOND engaged the attention of General Earl PERCY, (the late Duke of NORTHUMBERLAND,) who took him under his protection as his

RICHMOND.

MOLINEUX.

Published Aug: 10, 1812, by G. Smeeton, St Martin's Lane

servant, and after travelling with the Earl abroad for some time, he arrived in England, about the year 1777. The Duke finding BILL to possess a good capacity, and being an intelligent youth, had him put to school in Yorkshire, where he received a tolerably good education; and who afterwards apprenticed RICHMOND to the trade of a cabinet-maker, in the ancient city of York, where he served his time faithfully, and followed his business for a considerable time, not only in the above city, but in the Metropolis, as a journeyman, with credit to himself, and respected by his employers.

BILL's first display in the pugilistic art, which brought him into notice, was with one *George Moore*, a recruit, under Captain Connor, of the 19th Regiment, better known by the name of *Docky Moore*, who insulted RICHMOND upon the course at York, during the time of the races.   This *Docky* had been the terror of Sheffield, and had ruled the *roast* for some time in that part of the country; in fact, he was elegantly proportioned, possessing considerable strength, and all the necessary requisites for *milling;* in height about five feet nine inches and a half, and weighing fourteen stone. The friends of RICHMOND persuaded him from attempting to fight with such a man, BILL only weighing ten stone twelve pounds; the *chance* being positively against him, but he was not to be deterred: and the event proved his judgment correct, for, in the course of twenty-five minutes, our hero *punished Docky* so completely that he *gave in*, and was taken out of the ring totally blind.

On the same course, not long after the above *set-to*, RICHMOND beat two soldiers, one after the other, belonging to the Inniskilling dragoons.

RICHMOND's *milling* qualities getting abroad, a few of the lads who had a *bit of fight* in their compositions, envied his success; and one, in particular, a blacksmith, weighing thirteen stone, and in height about five feet ten inches, took the following method of provoking BILL to have a *brush*. RICHMOND was noticed in York for going smart, and appearing clean after he had done his work. BILL met this *hammerman* one evening, as he was taking a walk, who not only insulted him with opprobrious epithets, but gave him a *kick* on the thigh. Our hero remonstrated with him on the impropriety of his behaviour, and told the blacksmith, that if he wanted to fight him, he should be accommodated at the *Groves*, the next morning, to which they agreed to meet, when this *son of Vulcan* was completely *satisfied*, and acknowledged RICHMOND the best man.

RICHMOND, in passing through the streets of York, one evening, with a female under his protection, was accosted by one *Frank Myers*, with the epithets of " *black devil*," &c. and who otherwise insulted the young woman, for being in company of a *man of colour*. BILL, full of gallantry, and with a becoming spirit of indignation, requested him to desist for the present moment, but to meet him at the *Groves* on the next Monday morning, when they would settle this difference, (the circumstance happening on a Saturday night,) to which *Myers* agreed. This affair of honour being *buzzed* about on the Sunday, a great concourse of people assembled early the next day, to witness the conflict : RICHMOND was there at the appointed hour, and after suffering considerable time to elapse, and *Myers* not making his appearance, the spectators became impatien and it was judged expedient that RICHMOND and his friends should repair to the house of *Myers*, to remind him of his engagement. This *Myers* kept a bagnio, with a woman of the name of *Shepherd*, at Uggleford, to which place they went and found *Myers*, who, after some hesitation, agreed to go to the *Groves*, where he was followed by this *shepherdess* and her *flock*. The battle now commenced, and raged with fury for some time, but upon *Myers* getting the worst of it, the above *covess* and her damsels rushed into the ring to prevent their *bully* from being annihilated, and took him away. The spectators interfered, and persuaded *Myers* to return and finish the battle like a man. *Myers*, ashamed of his conduct, agreed to it, when RICHMOND soon taught him very properly to acknowledge, that it was wrong, and beneath the character of an Englishman, to abuse any individual for that he could not help—either on account of his COUNTRY or his *colour*. *Myers*, very properly, received a complete *milling*.

RICHMOND's first public *set-to* in London was with a whip-maker of the name of *Green*, of Saffron Hill, in the fields, near White Conduit-House. *Phips Medley* seconded RICHMOND, who got the whip-hand of *Green* in such good style, that in ten minutes he cried out—*enough!*

At Blackheath, on May 21, 1805, for a purse of ten guineas, RICHMOND entered the lists with one *Youssop*, a Jew. It was a well-contested battle, and the courage displayed on both sides reflected credit on the combatants, as neither of them fell without a knock-down blow: except once, when RICHMOND slipped. For the first two rounds *Youssop* took the lead; and maintained this advantage in the third round, by nearly driving RICHMOND out of the ring ; but in the fourth the scene was changed, and the superiority of the *science* of BILL was manifest, who followed up *Youssop* in the most determined manner, putting in some tremendous *facers*.   At the end of the sixth round, the countenance of the Jew was so much changed, from the severe *punishment* he had received, that he *gave in*.

From the above battle, RICHMOND'S fame, as a pugilist, had considerably increased, and Mr. *Fletcher Reid* backed him against *Jack Holmes*, the coachman, who had so nobly contested for the palm of victory with *Tom Tough*.   They entered the lists at Cricklewood-Green, a short distance from Kilburn-Wells, on July 8th, 1805, in a twenty-one feet roped ring. RICHMOND was seconded by *Tom Jones*, and *Tom Tough* attended upon *Holmes*.

First round.—Considerable *science* displayed on both sides, and *Holmes* appeared full of gaiety and in good condition ; but no blows that *told* passed between them.

Second.—A smart rally on both sides, but no falling.

Third.—Richmond very neatly put in a good blow, but fell. Two to one on *Holmes*.

Sixth.—The last three rounds nothing important transpired.

Seventh.—The combatants both on their mettle, displaying the science of boxing manfully.   The gaiety of Richmond was conspicuous, quite full of *milling*, and some excellent hits were exchanged.

Eighth.—*Coachee* appeared as if he had been driving too fast, and that he had *out-rode* his wind.   *Holmes* was distressed, but notwithstanding bets were in his favour three to two.

Ninth.—This round commenced with sparring ; but Richmond, with much dexterity, put in a most tremendous hit under his opponent's right eye, that left a severe gash, when *Holmes* fell from its severity.

Tenth.—The combatants both closed and fell. Even betting.

Eleventh.—This proved a most excellent round, and considered the best in the battle, they fought manfully, and both rallied in good style; when Richmond put an end to the round, by bringing down *Holmes.*

Fifteenth.—Of no import. *Holmes* appeared exceedingly weak, and his wind was nearly exhausted.

Sixteenth.—Both closed and fell. *Holmes* undermost— The odds had now undergone a material change. Three to one on Richmond.

Twenty-fourth.—*Holmes* was fast declining, and the rounds were nearly all hugging.

Twenty-fifth.—Richmond, full of gaiety, showed himself to great advantage, and left his antagonist little, if any, *chance* to win.

Twenty-sixth.—On setting-to, Richmond, *sans cérémonie,* levelled *Coachee;* who, however reluctant, was obliged to confess he had arrived at the end of his journey, it having lasted thirty-nine minutes.

RICHMOND now entered into a very unequal contest with *Tom Cribb.* See page 392.

BILL, for a subscription purse of fifteen guineas, fought with a countryman of the name of *Carter*, from Nuneaton, near Birmingham, on Epsom Downs, on April 14, 1809. *Carter* was much the strongest and a heavier man than RICHMOND; and who in a *turn-up* with those heroes of the fist, *Jem Belcher* and *Jack Gulley*, had convinced *them* both, that he was no TRI-FLER; and now, having expressed his fancy for a *mill* with *Mr.* RICHMOND, BILL without hesitation informed *Carter,* that he should be accommodated with a trial of skill: *Paddington Jones* and *Bob Clarke* seconded RICHMOND. Upon *setting-to,* the odds were seven to one against the *Man of Colour,* and in the fourth round the odds ran so high against RICHMOND, that twenty to one was sported that *Carter* won the battle, and ten to one that BILL did not come again. This great odds was occasioned by a severe blow that RICHMOND received on the side of his head, that rendered him nearly senseless: but BILL soon recovering from this momentary disadvantage, showed off his *science* in such good style, that in the course of twenty-five minutes, *Carter* was so *punished,* as to resign the contest. Immediately upon this being declared, RICHMOND jumped over the ropes, and caught hold of a man denominated *china-eyed Brown,* threatening to *serve him out,* (if he had not been prevented,) as it appeared that *Brown* had loudly vociferated, during the time RICHMOND was suffering from the effects of the above blow, that BILL *had got a white feather in his tail!* RICHMOND was patronised upon the above occasion by Sir *Clement Brigg,* Bart.

In seconding a baker, a few months after the above circumstance, near Wilsdon Green, a man of the same trade, weighing close upon seventeen stone, challenged RICHMOND on the spot, when a *turn-up* commenced, and in about two minutes the baker's *dough* was so well *kneaded,* that he would have no more of it at that time; offering to fight RICHMOND for £50 in a month, which was agreed to by BILL, and two guineas put down to make the bets good before that period—but the baker, it appeared, preferred losing his two *quid* than submitting his overgrown carcase to the *punishment* of RICHMOND.

BILL fought a man of the name of *Atkinson,* from Banbury, at Golder's Green, near Hendon, a bargeman, for a subscription-purse: it was a good fight, but in the course of twenty minutes *Atkinson* was perfectly satisfied the chance was against him, and acknowledged that he was beaten.

Isaac Wood, a waterman, a man of determined spirit, and not unacquainted with the principles of boxing, fought with RICHMOND, at Coombe Wood, April 9, 1809, in a twenty-five feet ring. *Wood* was attended by *Cribb* and *Cropley;* and *Paddington Jones* and *Clarke* seconded RICHMOND.

First round.—On setting-to, a little sparring took place, when Richmond put in a severe left-handed blow on Wood's jaw, who rallied, but was thrown. Seven to four on Richmond.

Second.—Wood attempted to put in a hit, which Richmond warded off and returned right and left; in closing, they both fell.

Third.—Good courage displayed on both sides; Wood commenced a rally, in which good blows were exchanged; but the science displayed by Richmond was so much superior to that of his opponent, who now was thrown, that the odds were two to one against Wood.

Fourth.—In this early stage of the fight it appeared how things were going—Richmond, in making play, planted a successful right-handed hit, upon which Wood endeavoured to rally, when Richmond stopped both right and left, and obtained the lead so conspicuously, that Wood was completely abroad, and not only punished round the ring, but thrown over the ropes. Four to one against Wood.

Fifth.—Wood, striving to appear well before the spectators, made play, and rallied in good style, when blows were exchanged for half a minute at half arm's length, but completely in favour of Richmond, who, in closing, threw his opponent. Betting all one way.

Sixth.—The *nob* of Wood now cut a terrible figure, from its punished appearance. Richmond rallied, but Wood fell from exhaustion.

Seventh.—A rally on both sides, when Wood was thrown.

Eighth.—Richmond, in not being correct in his distance, turned the advantage of this round rather in favour of Wood, who not only put in two hits, but threw his opponent.

Ninth.—In making play, Richmond slipped.

Tenth.—An excellent round, in which a good show of fighting was exhibited, the combatants contending against each other with considerable resolution and effect—hitting at full length, until they both went down.

Eleventh.—Wood convinced not only his antagonist but the spectators, that, however he might be deficient in science, he was not wanting in *bottom*—a good rally commenced; but, in closing, Richmond fibbed Wood so severely that the blood flowed in torrents, when they both went down exhausted.

Twelfth.—Wood seemed *done-up*, in respect of turning the chance in his favour, and Richmond *milled* him most terribly by three successive *facers*—then rallying the waterman to the ropes, when he went over him in a somerset.

Fourteenth.—Richmond conspicuous, and threw his opponent.

Fifteenth.—This round, though not putting an end to the contest, clearly showed how it must terminate. The courage of Wood was still good, but Richmond successfully planted three hits on his *nob*, and the waterman was not able to return; yet, notwithstanding it was going so much against him, his *bottom* enabled him to hold out till the

Twenty-third.—When Wood was again sent down by Richmond, who had run his *boat so far a-ground* that he could not come to his time, when Richmond was pronounced the conqueror. Bill appeared but little hurt.

RICHMOND again entered the lists with that brave hero of the fist, *George Maddox*, on the coast, near Margate, for 100 guineas, on the 9th of August, 1809. Five years previous to which, RICHMOND had a *turn-up* with the above pugilist, when, after contending three rounds, he resigned the contest. BILL at that time being but little known to the Metropolitan boxers, but having considerably increased in fame and *science*, this match was made to put the matter in doubt beyond all question; and it is but justice to observe, that few better battles were ever witnessed. After 52 minutes, obstinately contended, RICHMOND was declared the conqueror. (See page 212.)

A subscription-purse being made up on the *spur of the moment*, after a dinner of amateurs at *Bob's Chop House*, on May 1st, 1810, intended for *Dogherty* and *Power* to have entered the lists to obtain it, but upon the latter not being found, it was otherwise disposed of. It appears *Power* had been out spending the day, and in his way home, rather late in the evening, accidentally called in at *Bob's* to take a glass; he avers, that, being completely inebriated, on being asked to have a *set-to*, he positively denied, requesting that he might fight RICHMOND when he was perfectly sober, but being much pressed, after taking two or three glasses of wine, he accepted the challenge. A purse being subscribed, the *brush* commenced! RICHMOND was seconded by an Hon. Baronet and *Cribb*—and *Power* by a Colonel of distinction and *Bill Gibbons*. In a quarter of an hour, RICHMOND was declared the conqueror, and received the sum appropriated for the victor. *Power* attributes this defeat to inebriation, but RICHMOND asserts that he was very far from an intoxicated state, and that he, RICHMOND, laboured under considerable disadvantage in having seconded young *Cribb* for 56 minutes against *Dogherty*, but two or three hours previous to his set-to with *Power*. Considerable acrimony has subsisted between the parties ever since, concerning *superiority*, both claiming it.

It appears that RICHMOND is entitled to a respectable *niche* among the portraits of first-rate heroes of the milling art—both as a theoretical and practical pugilist; that his knowledge of the science is completely intuitive, having never received any lessons from any of the professors, but, on the contrary, has given instructions to some hundreds, not only in various parts of the kingdom, but in the very zenith of competition—LONDON. In the ring, in point of activity, he stands nearly unrivalled, and is considered to excel every other pugilist in hitting and getting away, and dealing out severe punishment with his left hand. It is also said of BILL, that for half an hour there is no danger in backing him with any of the fighting men. Although 50 years of age, (a length of years that few boxers arrive at,) his appearance to a common observer portrays no more than about 35, enjoying a good state of health, and not unmindful that it is necessary to preserve it. And what appears rather singular is, that at a time of life when other pugilists have long previously retired from the scene of action, the spirits of RICHMOND seem in such trim, that, with all the ardency of youth, he is still " eager for the fray;" and of whom there is little doubt, if he were but in possession of that quality (which must be served) *youth*—he would not be wanting of the support of the most distinguished in the *Fancy*, to become a leading boxer.

In being a *man of colour*, from the taunts and insults which he has received upon that account, particularly in his capacity as a publican, when he kept the Horse and Dolphin, RICHMOND must be considered goodtempered and placid, even to a degree that could not be expected. In one of those instances of unmerited reproach, his indignation would no longer let him remain quiet, and in a *turn-up* with the young Ruffian, at his own house, he completely *served him out*.

RICHMOND acquired considerable notoriety from his patronage of *Molineaux;* and, as far as we can learn, from the most impartial sources, his generous behaviour to that pugilist, who came to him an entire stranger, destitute of friends or money, received a very different return from what might have been expected: difference of opinion, however, may exist as to this subject, but it is certain *Molineaux* was indebted for that patronage and attention which he afterwards received from persons of distinction, entirely to his introduction by RICHMOND.

RICHMOND, after the late contest between *Molineaux* and *Carter*, challenged either of them for £100.

RICHMOND is an active, excellent second, and, from his temperate mode of living, preferring exercise to wasting his time, or injuring his constitution, by a too frequent repetition of the charms of the bottle, he has obtained the character of being a good and steady trainer, and, notwithstanding the defect in one of his knees, we are informed he excels as a cricketer.

BILL, in company with other pugilists, has exhibited his knowledge of the SCIENCE, in the Metropolis, at the *Olympic Pavilion* and *Regency* Theatres, with satisfaction and applause from numerous audiences.

In concluding this sketch, we cannot omit stating of our hero that he is intelligent, communicative, and well-behaved; and, however actively engaged in promulgating the principles of *milling*, he is not so completely absorbed with *fighting* as to be incapable of discoursing upon any other subject; in fact, he is rather facetious over a glass of noyeau, his favourite *wet* with a SWELL —and endeavours to gain his point, by attempting to *prove* that there is more certainty in his *preservation of bodies* (in allusion to his method of *training*) than either the *cobler* or *parson* in their taking care of the "*soles!* He has much more to say than many who style themselves "*Amateurs,*" but was never known to be so deficient in eloquence as when *Molineaux* experienced defeat! His experience in LIFE has taught him to be *awake* to the tricks of it; and there are few subjects upon which he suffers himself to be *lulled to sleep.* Notwithstanding many sport stylish *nobs,* it cannot be denied to him, that he wears a *head;* and although its *colour* may not prepossess the *million* in its favour, yet the liberal part of mankind will acquiesce with the sentiments of *Desdemona,* that "*the visage*" may be "*seen in the mind !*"

> 'Tis not a set of features, or complexion,
> The tincture of a skin, that I admire ;
> Beauty soon grows familiar to the lover,
> Fades in his eye, and palls upon the sense.

He seems to feel the *situation* in which he is *placed in society,* and endeavours to keep it—and in the temporary elevation of the moment, he still recollects, that however the CORINTHIAN FANCIER may closely connect himself with *milling,* there are times when he has a different *character to support,* and must not be intruded upon. BOXIANA will do his duty—and as far as the infirmities of human nature can be admitted—

neither colour, strength, patronage, or any other consideration, shall tempt him to swerve from IMPARTIALITY.

JACK CARTER,

The Lancashire Hero

WAS born at Manchester, in the year 1790, of respectable parents, who apprenticed him to the trade of a shoemaker, but JACK, being a strong healthy lad, and not liking the confinement of the *seat*, left it to give a lending hand towards the improvement of his country by commencing *navigator*, and working upon the canals in that neighbourhood. It was among those rough-hewn, hardy sons of the creation, that CARTER began to exhibit his feats of strength, by *milling* several of the best-considered men in their whole phalanx. JACK is in height about 5 feet 10¼ inches, and weighing about 13 stone; and it was the following droll and singular circumstance that brought him into notice both as a PEDESTRIAN and a PUGILIST. The navigators, in one of their moments of hilarity, proposed a *Jack-ass race*, and entered into subscriptions for that purpose, the stakes of which were held by a *Mr. Merryman*, belonging to a mountebank, who was *gammoning the flats* in that part of the country. *Mr. Merryman* was a good tumbler, full of *slum*, and could fight a bit, and who had rendered himself an attractive personage to the numerous *Johnny Raws* by whom he was surrounded. Upon the day arriving for the race to take place, no

Neddy was entered to run for the stakes, except one belonging to *Mr. Merryman:* this circumstance created
surprise, in fact, much disappointment. JACK CARTER
instantly entered himself as a JACK-*ass:* at first some
little *argument* took place, as to the oddness of the attempt, but at length it was *logically* determined that
CARTER was a JACK-*ass!* and that HE should be entered
as such : upon which they started—away went *Neddy*
with all the fleetness of a *prime donkey,* kicking and
snorting over the ground—and the JACK-*ass* set out in
fine style, amidst the shouts, loud laughs, &c. of the
multitude, who now began to bet in all manner of shapes
—CHRISTIAN against *donkey,* and NEDDY against
JACK-*ass!* The distance was four miles, producing
considerable wagers and much diversion among the
spectators. The JACK-*ass* possessing *rather* more
knowledge than the *Neddy,* made the best of his way,
leaving the *donkey* behind him, came in first, and
claimed the *stakes!* No JACK-*ass* was ever so much
caressed before for winning *a race!* but *Mr. Merryman* now treated it only *as a joke ;* observing, that he
only let *Christian* poney run to increase the sport, and
disputed his claim as a JACK-*ass.* It was certain that
all the words in *Johnson's* Dictionary would not have satisfactorily explained this *knotty point:* and there not
being LOGICIANS enough present to place the question
in a proper point of view, a nearer road was taken to
come at the *blunt.* CARTER gave *Mr. Merryman* to
understand that if he did not instantly hand over the
rag, that it should be *milled* out of his carcase. *Merryman* received this threat with a smile of contempt, entertaining an idea, that, as this JACK-*ass* had been run-

ning four miles, his wind could not be good for much —and agreed that the *fist* should decide it. A ring being formed, *Merryman* was soon made to *laugh on the wrong side of his mouth!* and he who had hitherto *tumbled* for the pleasure of the crowd, was now, in spite of his *antics*, knocked down often, and *punished* so severely, that he was compelled not only to *give in*, but to give up the money.

CARTER'S fame as a *boxer* and *racer* was soon spread abroad; and he entered the lists in a short time afterwards with a heavy strong man, a navigator, at Preston, who had gained some good battles in his time. It was a truly severe conflict, and occasioned considerable conversation in Lancashire; and CARTER obtained much notoriety in proving the conqueror. He was also matched in several races, in one of which he beat the celebrated *Abraham Wood*. At all events he left Lancashire a second-rate pedestrian; and possessing those pretensions to *milling*, it was entertained that, by time and practice, he stood a fair chance to become a leading boxer among the first-rate pugilists in the Metropolis.

It was at the Highgate Tunnel that *Bob Gregson* first met with this novelty—HE was a Lancashire man, and *that* was knowledge enough of him to recommend CARTER to *Bob*. Upon inquiry, it was also found that CARTER had hitherto proved himself a *trump;* and all that he wanted was experience, science, and introduction.—" *Thee shall have that,*" cried *Bob!* and instantly, at his own expense, took care of CARTER, and placed him under the " *Rolands*" (whose superior knowledge in the Art of Fencing, and distinguished reputation in communicating pugilistic science to their pupils, stands so high in the polite and *Sporting World*, as to render any eulogium on their talents here, perfectly unnecessary.) It is but justice to CARTER to observe, that, under such tuition, he soon made considerable progress in the art, and when it was judged a proper time to give publicity to his attempts, *Bob* introduced him at the Fives' Court. CARTER'S first *appearance* is thus described in the Morning Advertiser, Wednesday, July 29, 1812.

" SPARRING.——The last sparring exhibition took place yesterday, at the Fives' Court, for the benefit of Power, a pugilist, who, as a professor of the science, is inferior to none on the boxing list, but his exhibitions have been rare. The greatest novelty on this occasion was an exhibition between a trial-man of Gregson's, named CARTER, from Lancashire, a candidate of first-rate weight for fighting fame, and Fuller, a scientific pupil of Richmond's. A ruffianing match took place, and, not to give superiority to either, it was a match which afforded much diversion, and it will cause a considerable sensation in the sporting world. Gregson's man, who is under the best tuition, will prove a tremendous teazer, if he be gifted with the best of pugilistic favours—*game*—which remains to be tried. He is a fine weighty left-handed hitter, and, if game be in him, he can beat any thing now on the list."

With such a character, thus trumpeted forth, and so pointedly expressed, "*that if* GAME *be in him, he can beat any thing* NOW *on the list!*" it could not fail in procuring CARTER considerable popularity and attraction in the *circle* of FANCIERS; and more especially when it had been ascertained, that in his *rustic* specimens of *milling*, JACK had evinced THAT *quality;* nothing therefore remained but to put him to the test. CARTER was accordingly matched with *Bill Bone*, on

Friday, the 18th of September, 1812, near Ealing, Middlesex, which proved a severe contest for seventeen minutes, when CARTER was pronounced the victor. He was seconded by *Tom Jones* and *Joe Norton*. In the above battle his patrons thought he had made good his pretensions to *milling*, and they now looked forward in anxious expectation of placing him nearly, if not quite, at the top of the boxing list, and accordingly matched

CARTER against *Jack Power*, considered the best fighter of the day, for a stake of 200 guineas, on the 16th of November, 1813, at Rickmansworth. CARTER contended nobly for thirty-nine rounds, till he could neither move his legs or his head, he was so much beaten and exhausted.

CARTER attributed the loss of this battle to his second *(Bitton)*, who kept a *Belcher* handkerchief so close to his mouth, tending rather to deprive him of his wind, than to do every thing to increase that necessary quality in a boxer. It was a truly desperate battle— (see page 472).

If CARTER, in his battle with *Power*, did not exhibit those finished traits of *scientific* excellence which characterise the finished PUGILIST, he nevertheless portrayed that he was not destitute of the principles of boxing, and his patrons were perfectly satisfied with the *bottom* which he manifested upon the above occasion. The character of the *man of colour* had also gone before him, and since CRIBB had retired from the field of action, *Molineaux* was considered equal to any exhibitor upon the present stage. With such pretensions to public notice, a *terrible mill* was at least expected;

as it was well known that the latter could not only *give*,
but *take*, and that CARTER was no apology in either
respect.   The amateurs entertained an opinion something like a battle must have been the result upon the
meeting of those two boxers.   But whether *Molineaux*
did not like punishment since he had received such a
good *hand* and *crib* from the *Champion* that made him
lose the *game*, or whether since he had commenced *fop*
from the great liberality of his patrons, in being reduced
only to the *shadow and outline of a man*, reminding us

> How many cowards, whose hearts are all as false
> As stairs of sand, wear yet upon their chins
> The beards of Hercules, and frowning Mars ;
> Who, inward search'd, have livers white as milk !
> And these assume but valour's excrement,
> To render them redoubted—

we have not been able to ascertain, but certain it is,
Molineaux lost the character of the hero in degenerating
into the *cur*, and whether CARTER laboured under any
sort of depression from the severity of *Power*, or was
otherwise actuated, has puzzled his best friends and
supporters to find out what part of the play he acted ;
but, it is equally certain, he did not fight with that
manhood as he had hitherto done, and notwithstanding
he had gained the battle *Abraham Newland to a dump*,
yet he contrived to lose the purse ; that we cannot but
record the following circumstance, and the *Fancy* may
interpret it according to their better judgment.   Previous to the battle, the articles were read over to the
combatants, in which it stated the winner was to have a
purse of 100 guineas—when CARTER stepped up, inquiring what the " LOSER WAS TO HAVE ! ! !" *Richmond*,

who was his second, gnashed his teeth and shrugged up his shoulders; *Bob Gregson*, his friend and patron, tremblingly alive as to the event of the contest, and flattering himself that Lancashire would prove proudly triumphant on this occasion, animatedly exclaimed, "JACK, *never talk of losing, boy*—thee must win, the *chance* is all in thy favour!"

It was with the greatest difficulty that a fight was at length brought about; in fact, things had taken such a turn that no *mill* was expected to take place. However, their seconds *persuaded* them to strip—*Joe Ward* and *Bill Gibbons* for *Molineaux*; and *Richmond* and *Cooper* for CARTER. This *memorable* contest took place at *Shennington*, in Gloucestershire, six miles from Banbury, on Friday, April, 2, 1813, contiguous to the joining of four counties. Those persons who were unacquainted with what we have described, betted in some instances five to two, and three to one, on *Molineaux.*

First round.—It was the opinion of the most experienced pugilists, that such a *set-to* was never before witnessed; one "*was afraid, and the other dared not*," and two minutes were trifled away in this sort of *caricaturing,* when Carter touched Molineaux on the mouth, who *genteelly* returned it; they closed, and *the man of colour* was thrown.

In fact it would be absurd to detail by way of *rounds* any more of this "*worst of fights,*" though we readily admit that Carter was the best man after the battle began, and continued so throughout the fight. Molineaux was wretched in the extreme, and did *bolt* at one time from his second, and had it not been for Colonel and Captain Barclay, he would never have returned to the scratch, he wished so much to get away; at another period he was down on one knee, and with both hands laid fast hold of the ropes, and being hit in this situation, he roared out lustily "*foul !*" but he was given to understand that, by the laws of boxing, no one is considered down

" WITHOUT HAVING BOTH KNEES ON THE GROUND, WITH
EITHER ONE OR BOTH HANDS ALSO !"—In the 15th round
he was so terrified, that, upon being driven to one corner of
the ring, he cried out lamentably—" *O dear, O dear, murder!*"
and, but a little previous to which, he declared Carter " *had
bit him on the neck!*" and soon afterwards he repeated—" *there,
he has bit me again!*" and it was with great difficulty Joe Ward
could persuade him that it was the *knuckles* of Carter and not
his *mouth!*—This, the once brave competitor of the Champion!—impossible! *could* HE have thus degenerated? Twenty-five rounds occurred, in which *coaxing, persuading, dramm-
ing*, and *threatening*, were resorted to, in order to make the
man of colour perform *something like* fighting ! But, to the
great astonishment of all the spectators, when Molineaux was
dead beat, Carter *fainted*, and dropped his head as he sat on
the knee of his second. With all the exertions of Richmond,
it seems, he could not arouse Carter from his lethargic state,
and he thus lost the battle in not coming to *time*. His fame,
it is urged, was not only tarnished from this circumstance,
but even his *integrity* called into question. The above battle
created universal dissatisfaction.

Poor *Bob Gregson*, agitated beyond description at
seeing Lancashire (as he considered) thus trampled on
with disgrace, went up to CARTER, exclaiming "Jack,
Jack, what be'est thee at? get up and fight, man!"
But *Bob* might as well have sung psalms to a dead
horse! CARTER, some little time afterwards, raised
his head, feebly observing, " *Stop a bit! stop a bit!*"
And whether by ACCIDENT, *design,* or with an intent
to conclude this *farce* in style, we are not in the secret
to unfold, but a disciple of *Esculapius* stepped up,
and, in the twinkling of an eye, pulled out his lancet,
and bled CARTER, to the great astonishment of his
friends and the spectators in general; thus preventing,
even had any *inclination* remained on the side of CAR-
TER, to have *renewed* the fight. The latter's clothes
had hitherto been preserved, during the fight, in the

chariot of a man of distinction, but who, it is said, was so disgusted with the scene before him, that he instantly ordered them to be thrown out with disdain and contempt.

In once more taking a slight view of the *man of colour*, whatever CERTAINTY there might have been of *Molineaux* being a sound man at the core, it is strongly urged, that if his heart had been a *good one*, he must have won the first battle with the CHAMPION; however, be that as it may, since that period, he has been dissipated to excess, completely gone off in constitution, and broken winded.   One improvement appeared to have taken place—he was more temperate in *setting-to*, but he did not like to face his man, and it required no small ingenuity to get him into the ring.

POETIC RETORT

Between a " TOWN" and " COUNTRY AMATEUR" at Oxford; or, in the Phrase of the Day,
Between a *" Johnny Raw"* and a *" Knowing One!"*
On witnessing CARTER *faint away when he had won the battle, but who contrived to lose the purse, in his contest with Molineaux.*

Says Jack to Bob, " Look, poor CARTER's *hipp'd!"*
" Hipp'd, be d—d !" cries Bob, " the R—'s TIPP'D !!!"
" No, no," quoth Jack, " they *put in* too hard pats."
"*Put in*," echoes Bob, " they've PUT IN—the FLATS?"

As a boxer, and even a *scientific* pugilist, CARTER is entitled to considerable prominency: and, if viewed as a *fibber*, it will be difficult to find a better one: in point

of *hitting* and *getting away* he is little inferior, if not
equal to *Richmond*, and very good and active upon his
legs. With his left hand he deals out severe *punishment*;
and although in his former contests his right hand appeared but of little service to him, yet latterly he seems
to have rather improved in the use of it. One objection which has been warmly urged against CARTER by
many of the FANCY is, that he is soft about the head
—afraid of the coming blow—and shrinks from *punishment*; while, on the contrary, it is roundly asserted by
the other part, that if he behaves *correctly*, his *game*
is unimpeachable; and all that BOXIANA can observe
upon the above difference of opinion is, by concluding
in the words (with a trifling difference) that were first
made public concerning CARTER as a boxer, that "if
game be in him, he '*ought*' to beat any thing now on
the list."

JACK POWER,

ONE of the most celebrated *scientific* boxers in the
kingdom, is a native of the Metropolis, and descended
from Irish parents; he was born on the 8th of August,
1790, and was brought up under his father as a turn-
cock, but which calling he soon left to follow the business of a plumber. JACK'S *milling* qualities made
their appearance at a very early period of his life, for
he had scarcely turned fourteen years of age, when we
find him engaged with one *Norbrook*, a sadler, a Lancashire man, who stood six feet two inches in height,
in Tavistock Square, for two guineas. Although a

POWER.

LANCASTER.

Published May 1813 by G. Smeeton, 139, St Martin's Lane

mere boy, his knowledge of the *science* seemed so superior, as to attract considerable notice; and it was from SCIENCE alone, that he was enabled to beat a man, who possessed every other advantage over him, except a knowledge of the art of boxing.

In Bloomsbury Square, JACK fought a butcher of the name of *Jem Twist*, for three-quarters of an hour. *Twist* had hitherto been looked upon as a good *bit of stuff*, but he was now compelled to surrender to a superior POWER.

A Birmingham man, not unlike the *Chicken* in make and size, challenged JACK in Theobald's Road, when they agreed to settle the difference in the fields behind the Foundling Hospital. It was one of the most desperate conflicts in which JACK was ever engaged, and it was near terminating very seriously, as the Birmingham man was *punished* so dreadfully, that he was taken to Bartholomew Hospital, with but little hopes of recovery.

From the above display and several other skirmishes, JACK was advised to exhibit as a professor in the *ring*, and accordingly made his *debût* with *Dogherty*, in which POWER fought so well and so *game*, that *Dogherty gave-in* three times during the fight; but POWER being a new one, and *Dogherty* more experienced, it was *managed* in that sort of way, that the latter was pronounced the victor. (See page 479).

JACK next contended with one *Frere*, at Coombe Wood, on April 1st, 1809, and after a very superior display of the art of boxing for twenty-five minutes, *Frere* gave in.

At a dinner in St. James's Street, a small difference

having occurred between a tailor and POWER, they agreed to fight it out for a *guinea*, on the spot. The tailor, who was well versed in sparring, having received lessons under the renowned *Belcher*, felt *pluck* enough to enter the lists with this celebrated boxer. For ten minutes the tailor gave sound proof that he was something more than the *ninth part of a man*, by fighting courageous and well for that period : but the *science* of POWER was not to be got the better of : he stopped the blows of poor *Stitch* right and left with the utmost *sang-froid*, and putting in such tremendous blows on the tailor's *nob*, completely disfigured his face : while, on the contrary, POWER proved the conqueror, without a single hurt. On his return home, in calling in at *Gregson's*, the *Young Ruffian* and JACK fell out, and in a *turn-up*, *Fearby* was soon *served-out*, but who was so angry and dissatisfied in being thus conquered, that, strange to say, instead, as upon former occasions, of calling to his aid his potent arm, he now had recourse to the strong *arm of the law*, which paying no respect to superior *science*, proved the means of *drawing* JACK of five pounds !

POWER went down to Huntingdon to second a man of the name of *Saunders*, who was to fight a match for 40 guineas ; when an amateur of that place betted JACK that he would produce a man who should fight him for ten pounds. The bet was accepted, and a countryman made his appearance; but just upon *setting-to*, and viewing POWER from head to foot, he appeared so panic-struck, that he instantly *bolted*, and was out of sight in a few minutes. POWER laughed at this droll adventure, and pocketed the money.

Power being down at Salisbury, to superintend the *training* of a gamekeeper, belonging to —————— Biggs, Esq. of that neighbourhood; *Molineaux* had an exhibition of sparring there, at one shilling each person for admittance, where any one might *set-to* with *Molineaux* that thought proper. A *blacksmith*, well known in that quarter as a complete ruffian, and a terror to the inhabitants, entered the room, and challenged *Molineaux* to fight for 100 guineas, who replied, that he came there to *spar*, and not to *fight*—but the *blacksmith* would not be put off, and swore that *Molineaux* should have a *box* with him; upon which a sum was named, and the *Man of Colour*, under pretence of fetching the money, went to a private room in the inn, and securely locked himself up, and where no entreaties from his friends or Power could induce him to leave it. The Salisbury *blacksmith* being thus disappointed, and determined to have a *mill* at all events, upon learning Power was a professor of the *science*, instantly came up and challenged Jack, who answered he was otherwise engaged, and begged him to desist, and go about his business quietly, for that he had no intention of fighting. "*You shall*," exclaimed the blacksmith, "*you are one of the* Lunnon *fighting men, and I know I can beat thee, and will fight you for* 10*l.* 50*l.* or 100*l. and you shan't go home without a good licking.*" Power, now finding all expostulation vain, informed this ruffian, that if he would come on the next morning with any sum he thought proper, he should be accommodated. The *blacksmith*, without further ceremony, gave Power a severe blow on the head, who now seeing the necessity of the case, instantly stripped, and, in the course of fifteen minutes, so *punished* this insolent overgrown *blacksmith*, that he was carried away in a senseless state, with the loss of two of his teeth. The gentlemen and inhabitants were so pleased upon this occasion, that POWER was handsomely rewarded for his spirit.

At Moulsey Hurst, for fifty guineas a-side, and a purse, JACK entered the lists with *Joel King*, on July 16, 1811. POWER was seconded by *Clarke* and *Paddington Jones;* and *King*, by *Richmond* and *Hall*— Nine to four on POWER.

First round.—The combatants *set-to* in good spirits, and King, with considerable strength, endeavoured to put in a severe blow with his right hand, which Jack scientifically parried, and planted his ONE-TWO on the head and body of his opponent with considerable dexterity, producing the *claret*, when King fell. The bets decided concerning the first knock-down blow.

Second.—Notwithstanding the severity of the blows of Power, King was by no means shy, and again made play, putting in a severe right-handed hit on Power's throat, the left proving short: when Power, with uncommon agility, gave King such a severe left-handed *facer*, that sent him down.

Third.—Several good hits were exchanged in a rally; but the superiority of *science* manifestly appearing on the side of Power, the bets were two to one upon him.

Fourth.—Power on setting-to hit left and right, which King returned by a severe blow in the throat; when they closed, and King was again thrown.

Fifth.—King, full of gaiety, endeavoured to put in a hit with his left hand, which fell short, following it up with his right, but the *science* of Power rendered it of no effect; they closed, and King was thrown a cross-buttock.

Sixth.—King and Power both made play at the same instant: when a right-handed blow told on the head of Power; some good blows were exchanged, and this round was rather in favour of King; although he was thrown a cross-buttock by Power, who, in his haste to do it, went with his right shoulder against one of the stakes, from which he received a severe hurt.

Seventh.—Power was now fully aware what sort of a customer he had to deal with; and, to prevent the *punishment* of his opponent's right hand, adopted another mode of fighting, by getting away to hit.

Eighth.—Power, in this round, convinced the amateurs and spectators that he was a complete master of the *science*, by the way in which he treated his opponent—Jack put in a tremendous blow on King's mouth, and immediately got away; when he again repeated the dose; and kept repeating this severe *punishment* till King fell, literally covered with blood.

Ninth.—King, not dismayed, commenced a rally, and, to all appearance, had the best of it, by putting in his straight, right-handed blows with great spirit, from his better strength, but received another cross-buttock from Power.

Tenth.—The face of King exhibited a truly piteous aspect, cut and mangled in all directions; and Power put in two severe blows, one on the mouth and the other in the throat of his opponent, which brought him down.

Eleventh.—Both the combatants fell, after a good rally.

Twelfth.—Another excellent rally took place, Power exhibiting his superior *science* in the most conspicuous style, and, from the severe *punishment* he dealt out with his right hand, sent King reeling away, but who, in the most determined and courageous manner, renewed the rally with all the fortitude of a hero, and returned the hits of his opponent with the most astonishing *game*, and finally closed the round, by throwing Power.

Thirteenth.—Power, in the most scientific manner, again brought his antagonist down: who, notwithstanding, possessed so much strength and good *bottom*, that Power seemed almost incapable of giving that *punishment* to King which seemed essentially necessary to render the victory safe to Jack. However, the fight continued in most excellent style till the

Twenty-sixth.—When it was six to four. At this time the left side of King's head was so dreadfully beaten, that it was impossible to look upon it without the most commiserating sensations, but whose courage was of the finest quality, with a *bottom* never excelled, and fighting away in that manly style, claiming not only the admiration of his friends, but even the applause of his enemies, till the

Forty-sixth.—When he was now nearly reduced to a state of stupidity, from the blows he had received upon his head : and would not GIVE IN, till beat to a complete stand-still. The contest lasted 57 minutes.

By the above battle POWER's fame was completely established : and from the courage he displayed, and the superior *science* which he exhibited, fairly entitled him to rank equal with the first twelve-stone pugilist on the list.

In October, 1811, a match was endeavoured to be brought about between *Tom Belcher* and JACK; but the stakes not being made good, it went off.

Our hero now promulgated the *science* of self-defence in various parts of the kingdom with admiration and success, but who unfortunately ruptured a blood vessel, and labouring under a severe cold, reduced the state of his health considerably; and before he took time for the system to recover its proper tone, imprudently suffered himself to be matched with *Jack Carter* for 100 guineas, which contest took place on the 16th of November, 1812, at Rickmansworth, in Herts. POWER on this occasion was seconded by the Champion of England, and *Carter* by *Bitton* and *Tom Jones*.

It would be superfluous to detail the rounds of this battle, which continued *one hour and twenty-five minutes*, but suffice it to say, in no battle whatever was the *science* more finely portrayed o the *certainty* of the art so clearly demonstrated as in the above contest : and the conduct of POWER this day was above all praise. Pass ing previously a restless night, afflicted with a cough, and somewhat nervous in his habit, he entered the ring under all these disadvantages, to contend against an adversary, his superior in height, strength, constitution; perfectly in health, and not deficient in pugilistic acquirements. It was a tremendous task--a most daring attempt—and superlative *science*, and *that* ALONE, produced the victory to POWER. It required something more than fortitude, to act thus in opposition to nature, as well as considerable ingenuity in husbanding his strength, that he might be enabled to reduce his opponent to his own level. This POWER effected, when he grappled with his opponent upon superior terms: his *strength* gone, and his *science* not equal, CARTER was conquered with elegance and certainty. Upon no occasion whatever were the KNOWING ONES so completely *out of their know!*—*Carter*, although defeated, showed that he was not without *game;* but POWER completely astonished the most experienced of the FANCY!

Respecting POWER's set-to with *Richmond* (see page 453), at a sparring-match at the Fives' Court, on *Dutch Sam's* benefit, soon after the above contest, some words took place between JACK and the *Man of Colour*. Something about *a white feather* occurring, the former instantly mounted the stage, and addressed the spectators thus: "That, upon the day previous to the night when he fought *Richmond,* following his business as a plumber, in making paint, the fumes of the white lead are of so strong and poisonous a quality, that to prevent any serious effects operating upon the constitution, plumbers are necessitated to drink a quantity of *castor oil;* in addition to which, he had been drinking, that rendered him *then* unprepared—but *now*, says POWER, if *Richmond* can take out the *white feather*, as he pleases to term it, that I possess, stripping off his clothes, let him come up here, and I will fight him instantly for £50." And upon JACK's benefit, he again offered to fight *Richmond*.

In concluding this sketch, the most painful part of our duty yet remains to be performed, in being compelled to state, that no *boxer* commenced his *milling* career with a fairer prospect to arrive at the *top of the tree*, or become a *fixed star* in the pugilistic hemisphere, than JACK POWER; but, alas! possessing a gaiety of disposition which could brook no restraint : the fascinating charms of company, and the enlivening glass, proving too powerful for his youthful and inexperienced mind to withstand, he entered precipitately into excesses which produced debility and a bad state of health. In this last battle, although gaining the *victory*, he endangered his existence! In company he was good-natured and lively; and JACK was one of the most accomplished boxers of his day, viewed either as a practical fighter or an elegant *setter-to*. POWER was in height about five feet nine inches and a half—and in weight twelve stone. He turned out several good pupils.

BILL RYAN,

Son of the celebrated Pugilist of that Name.

NOTWITHSTANDING his father stood so high in the annals of pugilism, by his brave contest with the celebrated Champion, *Tom Johnson*—BILL was a much superior fighter than his veteran sire; and possessed those scientific acquirements in the *milling art*, that must have elevated him to the rank of an eminent boxer. But he was so rivetted to the *charms of the bottle*, that his constitution was soon undermined, and at a very premature age BILL paid the debt of nature. His battles were not many, but the few in which he contended were sufficient to show that he was a distinguished fighter. In both his contests with *Tom Belcher*, (see pages 336 and 339) he claimed equal attraction with that celebrated pugilist in point of science, and proved the conqueror in the first *set-to*.

With *Caleb Baldwin* (see page 311) RYAN showed himself off in good style; it was a truly severe contest between those heroes—but which was decided as *drawn*.

At Wilsdon Green, June 17, one *Clarke* entered the lists with RYAN, but the superior skill of the latter soon proclaimed him the conqueror.

RYAN's *inebriation* gained at length so fast upon him, that no dependence could be placed upon BILL even for an hour; and those who had him under *training*, without the aid of lock and key, to prevent *intemperance*, he got completely besotted.

"THE TREADWAYS:"

ALTHOUGH not the most fortunate boxers in the world, yet their efforts are nevertheless entitled to respectable mention, as, in their public displays, courage, bottom, and even judgment were not wanting. Hyde Park was the principal scene of their actions; and though not very numerous, yet some of them prominent, from their fighting against superior weight.

BILL TREADWAY is a Metropolitan, and was born on November 24, 1777—in height about five feet seven inches, and in weight 11 stone 1 lb. and at the age of nineteen, entered the lists with *Soley Sodicky*, a Jew, in Hyde Park, for twenty guineas, and contended for the prize for thirty seven-minutes, but was compelled to *give in*.

In the above Park, about a year afterwards, BILL contended with a man of the name of *Drake*, weighing fourteen stone, for twenty pounds, and it proved, we believe, the longest fight on record. They *set-to* at twenty minutes before four, and victory was not decided in favour of *Drake* till eight o'clock in the evening—occupying a space of time of *four hours and twenty minutes*.

TREADWAY fought *Coady* in Hyde Park, for twenty-seven minutes, when the latter proved the conqueror. Upon the above occasion BILL was seconded by the veteran *Joe Ward*.

In Harley Fields, a man weighing sixteen stone, known by the name of *Big Peter*, the carman, challenged TREADWAY for a guinea; BILL accepted it without hesitation, and was not long in taking the conceit out of *Big Peter*, who confessed he had had *enough*.

TREADWAY has long since left the pursuit of the *ring* for the occupation of a victualler.

TOM TREADWAY fought one *George Woodford*, near the Queen's Head and Artichoke, Harley Fields. It was a match for ten guineas a-side, and well contested, when TOM proved the conqueror. He also entered the ring with a baker on the same spot, soon afterwards, and disposed of the *Master of the Rolls.*

TREADWAY contended with one *Marshall*, a butcher, belonging to Carnaby Market, on Finchley Common, for twenty guineas a-side, denominated the " *Jaw-breaker!*" but in this instance the "*Jaw-breaker*" failed, and was beaten for his temerity.

In Mary-le-bone Fields, TREADWAY fought an African black, of the name of *Joe Lashley*, on June 13th, 1791. It proved a truly desperate conflict for thirty-five minutes, when TREADWAY was taken senseless from the scene of action. *Lashley*, during the battle, evinced great activity, skill, and game, portraying a knowledge of the art superior to most amateurs. TREADWAY never properly recovered from the effects of this severe contest.

In Hyde Park, TREADWAY engaged one *Conway*, a wheelwright, on April 22d, 1795, for five guineas a-side. TREADWAY took the lead for a few rounds, but, on receiving a severe *leveller,* the *chance* turned against him, which he did not recover during the fight, and at length *gave in.*

SILVERTHORNE.

IT appears that the above hero was introduced into the *milling circles* under the patronage of *Caleb Baldwin;* he is a coster-monger by calling, and a native of the county of Somerset. *Caleb*, no mean judge in matters of *flash*, fancied SILVERTHORNE, from the *sets-to* he had witnessed, and the slight skirmishes he had been engaged in. SILVERTHORNE was accordingly backed for 100 guineas against *Dogherty*, at Coombe Wood, near Kingston, on June 11th, 1811, and, that the business might go on well, *Bill Gibbons* assisted his friend *Caleb* in seconding his *protégé*. SILVERTHORNE the favourite seven to four. The contest continued for twenty-two minutes, and was so truly desperate, that both the combatants were bled and put to bed, being incapable of standing. SILVERTHORNE's strength brought him through the *piece*, by triumphing over the science of *Dogherty*.

SILVERTHORNE, from the above success, was matched against *Tom Belcher* for 100 guineas. (See page 340.) SILVERTHORNE is in height about five feet eight inches, weighing eleven stone two pounds. He has retired from the pursuits of pugilism, determined never more to have a *mill*, without the necessity of the moment compels him to it.

DOGHERTY

Is not only viewed as *game* a pugilist as ever stripped a shirt over a head, but as a pleasing and scientific boxer: and out of twelve trials of skill he proved victorious in nine of them.

His first *set-to* was early in June, 1806, with a Jew, at Wilsden Green, where he proved the conqueror; and, shortly afterwards, at the same place, on the 17th, he easily beat one *Wall*.

On Lowfield Common, near Crawley, Sussex, August 21, 1807, he conquered *Dick Hall;* and on his return home that day, had a *turn-up* in the road with *Jack Warr,* whom he *milled.*

George Cribb he defeated twice, see the next page.

On Epsom Downs, *Tom Belcher* conquered DOGHERTY, see page 337.

DOGHERTY fought one *Pentikin,* a Scotch Baker, at Golder's Green, Hendon, June 11, 1808, for forty-five minutes, when *Pentikin* gave in. DOGHERTY fought him forty guineas to twenty.

At Moulsey Hurst, October 25, 1808, DOGHERTY fought with *Jack Power* for an hour and a quarter. It has been considered rather a disputed point, but DOGHERTY claimed it, and got the money. It should be remembered that *Power* was but a mere *stripling* at that period.

On Epsom Downs, February 1, 1809, DOGHERTY beat a turnpike-man; and at Moulsey Hurst, on May 31, 1810, he stripped to fight one *Burns,* whose conduct not meeting the ideas of the amateurs, he brushed off.

On the 18th of January, 1811, he met with a reverse of fortune, in being defeated by *Silverthorne,* at Coombe Wood, but he was then considered in bad condition.

In November, 1811, he beat, with considerable ease, at Chichester, *Burns.*

DOGHERTY and *Bill Gibbons* once had a *turn-up* at a public-house, but the friends of both parties interfered, and *stowed* it.

DOGHERTY, for a long time, was engaged on a sparring excursion, not only in various parts of the king-

dom, but also in the sister country. On *Tom Belcher's*
arrival in Ireland, the superior *science* of that pugilist
having, it is said, taken from him a number of his
pupils, a battle took place between them. On the 23d
of April, 1813, for 100 guineas, they decided the contest on the Curragh of Kildare; when DOGHERTY
again fell beneath the conquering arm of *Belcher.*

GEORGE CRIBB,

Brother to the Champion of England.

CRIBB and *victory* have so often been coupled,
that, in attaching defeat to the name, we almost pause
for fear of being in error; but such is the versatility of Fortune, while the Champion, TOM CRIBB, has
been enjoying all the smiles of victory, and the patronage annexed to it, the junior hero, panting to emulate
the heroic deeds of his warlike brother, has encountered nothing else but DEFEAT. However unfortunate,
yet brave, and although not commanding, still deserving success.

GEORGE first entered the lists with *Horton,* near
Bristol, for a purse of fifty guineas, on September 5,
1807, and, notwithstanding the assistance of his brother
Tom for a second, he was beat in twenty-five minutes.

On February 9, 1808, he was also defeated by *Dogherty,* on Highgate Common.

On the coast, near Margate, August 9, 1809, he
entered the ring with *Cropley,* and was conquered in
16 minutes. GEORGE did not let his opponent win

THE SECOND CONTEST BETWEEN CRIB & MOLINEUX, SEPT 28,1811.

Published by Thos. Simpson, Jan.1ˢᵗ 1812.

without *punishing* him a good deal. It was considered rather an unequal match.

At a meeting of amateurs, May 1, 1810, at Bob's Chop-house, after a sporting dinner, he again fought *Dogherty*, when *Tom Cribb* also seconded his brother. In this contest GEORGE proved himself a game man, and at times overcame the superior science of his adversary; but, at the end of an hour, *Dogherty* was the conqueror, and had the £20 purse. It was a severe battle.

GEORGE fought with Isle-of-Wight *Hall*, on November 15, 1810, on Old Oak Common, near Uxbridge, when the odds were six to four in his favour, at *setting-to;* but, after a contest of one hour and nine minutes, he was reluctantly compelled to give in. He fought like a hero, and, although defeated, reflected credit on the name of CRIBB.

After his brother *Tom* had beaten *Molineaux*, on September 21, 1811, at Thisleton Gap, he entered the ring, for a subscription purse of £20, with *Ned Maltby*, a Nottinghamshire lad; it was a determined battle for the time it lasted, 13 rounds; but GEORGE was again not only conquered, but severely *punished: Maltby* was not much the worse.

GEORGE, like his brother, is a slow fighter, but spars tolerably well; is in height about 5 feet 8¼ inches, and near 11 stone in weight.

He does not appear to possess that fine *stamina* which is so conspicuous in the constitution of the CHAMPION.

JACK FORD:

A BOXER, who, it is but justice to remark, if he does not possess that superlative *science* necessary to rank with the first-rate pugilists, has *game* equal to any that has been publicly exhibited. At Bristol, he gained several hard-earned victories; but, wishing to obtain a more conspicuous character as a pugilist, he came to the Metropolis, and fought *Jem King*, at Coombe Wood, on January 12, 1812. In this contest he distinguished himself considerably, always hitting with his man, and planting his blows with his right and left hand, with uncommon severity—and never shrinking from *punishment*. Throughout the contest, forty minutes, he never once relaxed in his efforts, and, although often hit away, he still kept his legs, and was not once hit down. *King* was in every respect a hero; and did not surrender till Nature was quite exhausted. FORD, in some instances, has been compared to the *Game Chicken*. He afterwards fought *Tom Olwer*, a heavier man than himself, at Greenford Common, for 20 guineas, on October 6, 1812, for two hours and ten minutes, before he gave in. FORD is in height about 5 feet 8 inches, weighing twelve stone, and has had one of his thighs broken, which makes him limp, one leg being shorter than the other.

JOHN LANCASTER,

A VERY promising pugilist, and who distinguished himself considerably at Bristol, from whence he comes.

In all the battles he fought in that neighbourhood, he proved the conqueror, and, anxious to obtain a place in the rolls of pugilistic fame, he arrived in London, and made known his chivalrous intentions, when an opportunity soon offered at Rickmansworth, on November 16, 1812, for him to enter the lists with *Marten*, a Jew, and, after a good display of his quality, he was pronounced the conqueror. LANCASTER was much noticed, and his style of fighting approved of. He is in height about 5 feet 9 inches, weighing 11 stone. LANCASTER is an active, pleasing, and scientific fighter.

BITTON, *the Jew.*

HIS displays of the art in the *ring* have been but rare, having only fought two battles of note, with *Wood* and *Tom Jones*, when he proved the conqueror. Since which period he has confined himself to the *mufflers*, and officiating as a *second.* He is grown too heavy for fighting, weighing 17 stone, but keeps a school for the promulgation of the *science;* he *sets-to* in good style, ranking with the first *sparrers* of the day !

HARRY HARMER,

FROM Bristol, and related to the family of the *Belchers.* As a *sparrer*, he exhibits in a first-rate *scientific* style; with an attitude, it might be said, exclusively his own, that of keeping his body and head at a singular distance from his antagonist. He fought and conquered *Maltby*, a rough and hard boxer, who had defeated *George Cribb*. The *game* and excellent qualities he displayed in the above contest, rendered him an attractive boxer among the amateurs. His pedigree is good, and he is in height 5 feet 9½ inches, weighing 12 stone.

WILLIAM JAY

Born at Knaptoft, near Leicester, on the 17th of July, 1792, in height about 5 feet 10 inches, weighing 14 stone 6 pounds. In the country he *milled* away with considerable success, and acquired the reputation of a boxing hero. *Jem Allcock*, the champion of Birmingham, in a battle with Jay, struck to his superiority; and two navigators, of the names of *Cheeseby* and *Austin*, acknowledged they were conquered by his *milling* requisites. With these pretensions, he pushed forward to the Metropolis, anxious to exhibit his strength, courage, and talents, with the first-rate pugilists of the day, in order to obtain a high and permanent name in the list of boxers. He was matched with *Fuller*, at Rickmansworth, on the 16th of November, 1812: his behaviour upon that occasion made a considerable impression upon the Fancy, from the severity of his blows, and the quickness of manner in which he beat his antagonist. Great things were in future expected from him, and, had not the

CHAMPION retired from the ring,—a *few* seemed to entertain an idea that he was able to fight with *Tom Cribb*. JAY was too much elated with this success, and, in the weakness of the moment, impotently talked what he was able to perform, and that VICTORY must inevitably be the result of all his contests; while, on the contrary, *Fuller*, in defeat, (the sure school to learn experience,) viewed his defects, and thinking they might be improved, challenged JAY to another combat, and in the event defeated him, leaving JAY to observe,

" Where now are all my flattering dreams of joy."

JOE NORTON:

ALTHOUGH he cannot put in his claim to attention as a PRACTICAL *milling cove*, yet, as an "*appendage*" to the FANCY, he is deserving of notice; neither has he altogether proved himself a bloodless hero, and only been *gay* with the *mufflers !* In several skirmishes, JOE has shown activity and spirit—and the only time in which we learn that he appeared in a regular *set-to*, was with a *Sheriff's Officer*, yet he was not compelled at the *suit* of *John Doe* and *Richard Roe*, but engaged with the above catch-*pole* on the broad and unequivocal principles of *milling*, "which was the best man?" and in the contest, JOE manifested he was entitled to that appellation. But the most conspicuous part of JOE's situation in the *Fancy*, it appears, was in opening the "*Roebuck*" in Holborn, which was known under the denomination of the "*Show Shop!*" It was well frequented for some time by the amateurs, &c. and where JOE continued till the "*show went by!*" in fact, till the *Roebuck* was nearly in want of pasture. In a great number of battles of note, either as a *second* or *bottle-holder*, NORTON has taken a leading and an active part; and in that situation JOE is entitled to credit and attention; as a teacher of the *science* he is not without merit. In behaviour, interestingly civil and communicative; and very respectably connected. In fact, JOE might be termed, for the last thirty years, a living Boxing Calendar! by his having witnessed nearly all the fights which took place during that period. We cannot conclude this trifling sketch of JOE NORTON without observing, with a considerable degree of pleasure—that his humanity, care, and peculiar attention, in general, after the fight, to the LOSING MEN—is so worthy of imitation, that BOXIANA would have proved neglectful in passing over such merits.

JACK FEARBY,

DISTINGUISHED BY THE APPELLATION OF THE

" YOUNG RUFFIAN !"

IN obtaining the above title, he certainly conquered one of the best, most daring, and determined *bottom* characters, without exception, that ever appeared among the race of pugilists—SYMONDS, the old

Ruffian! (a boxer so well known, and whose unconquerable propensity to *milling* has been so copiously detailed in the preceding pages of this work, as to render any further comment superfluous.) But the best of his days were gone by when he surrendered to FEARBY. *Bill Jackling* (brother to *Tom Johnson*) was also defeated by the *Young Ruffian*. It has been observed, notwithstanding these conquests, FEARBY is more of an expert *setter-to* than a finished determined pugilist. He fell, in turn, to the conquering arm of *Jem Belcher;* and was also beaten in a contest with *Elias Spray* the coppersmith. FEARBY is nearly six feet in height, weighing about fifteen stone.

FULLER

WAS a pupil of *Richmond's*, and accompanied that pugilist in a sparring tour through some of the principal towns of Yorkshire, to promulgate the *science* of boxing. But wishing to obtain a more decided character in the art of *milling* than the *muffling* system, he manfully put the gloves aside, to use his fist, at Rickmansworth, on November 16th, 1812, with *Ill Jay.* Unacquainted with the *practical* part of the art, or presuming too much on his *science*, he indiscreetly went in at the commencement of the fight, when he got so severely smashed, as never to recover from its severe effects during the battle, but experienced terrible *punishment* and defeat in less than twenty minutes FULLER, anxious to recover this indiscretion, again entered the _ists with *Jay*, at Coombe Wood, April 6, 1813, for a subscription-purse, seconded by *Joe Ward* and *Bill Gibbons; Richmond* and *Norton* performed that office for *Jay;* upon which it was five and six to four on *setting-to*. FULLER, determined not to be *smashed* a second time, acted cautiously, and the first round occupied five minutes; and possessing the favourite system of his master, *hitting* and *getting away*, he accomplished his ends and obtained the victory. Not a single close took place during the fight, which continued forty-two minutes. *Jay* might boast of *strength*, but FULLER evinced *science*, which sooner or late must be *served*. *Jay* went blind. FULLER is a Norfolk man, and in height five feet ten inches, weighing nearly twelve stone, and by trade a copper-plate printer.

BILL DAY and BILL TOWERS.

HAVING passed over the account of the contest of the above brave pugilists, (in the early part of this work,) we now hasten to repair the omission. This fight took place on Barnet race-course, November 22d, 1784, for 100 guineas, on a thirty feet stage. DAY was so much the favourite, that ten to one was sported on him, and who felt so confident of winning, that he made a ridiculous bombast, how *easily* he *would serve out* TOWERS—and, instead of taking care of himself, was dancing about between the rounds—till at length TOWERS caught him in one corner of the stage, and held him fast by one hand, while with the other he nearly annihilated DAY, who too late saw his error, and had to repent of his vaunting. The battle continued thirty-three minutes, and DAY died in a short time afterwards, supposed from the severity of the blows.

Having arrived at the end of a most arduous and difficult journey, during which many *mile-stones* have been wanting, and *finger-posts* not to be found, to put the traveller in his right road—BOXIANA cannot take leave of his numerous heroes and tyros without humbly offering the following remarks for their consideration and attention through life, before he lays down his pen :—
" PUGILISTS! as your endeavours may stimulate you to *improve* in *science*, be not *unmindful* to increase in CHARACTER. Lift not your arm against the weak, intemperate, or the ignorant, who might *provoke* you to ridiculous combat, lest it might have a serious termination—but, in your display of the manly and

National Science of BOXING,

avoid a CROSS as you would a *pestilence!* Keep from *boasting*, as it not only shows weakness of mind, but generally ends in *disgrace!* In obtaining VICTORY, let it be procured by the most noble, honourable, and *scientific* means! However patronised, flattered, or encouraged by the HIGHER FLIGHTS OF THE FANCY, learn to keep at a respectful distance, and do not *presume* upon your merits as a boxer; above all, beware of INEBRIETY—recollect that the *stamina* once undermined is rarely ever restored, and, if *patched up* for a time, *never* returns to its pristine purity and vigour of tone!" Much more might be urged to convince and enforce, if necessary, the propriety of these remarks—but while you have a MODEL in existence the old adage is preferred, that "example is better than precept!" Therefore, BOXIANA's last words are, and he feels confident, if properly applied, they will operate more *emphatically* than a volume of advice— " PUGILISTS, look up to that MODEL, observe how he HAS, and how he DOES conduct himself in society, and endeavour to tread in his steps, to PREVENT— that, when he is gone, or retires from the promulgation of the *science*, it may not fall into *disrepute*, and HAVE AN END! that, at least, ONE may be found who can compare actions, vie in liberality, generosity, and attention to the poor and unfortunate, which will entitle him to supply the place of—JOHN JACKSON."

THE MOST ADMIRED

CHAUNTS,

Sung at the Convivial Meetings of the Fancy.

WRITTEN BY MR. LAWSON,

And sung by Mr. Emery, at a Dinner given to Cribb, at
Gregson's.

Come listen all ye fighting *gills*,
  And *coves* of boxing note, sirs,
Whilst I relate some bloody *mills*,
  In our time have been fought, sirs.
Whoe'er saw *Ben* and *Tom* display,
  Could tell a pretty story,
The *milling-bout* they got that day,
  Sent both ding-dong to glory.
          Singing fal la la, &c.

Now *Ben* he left it in his will,
  As all his *pals* declare it,
That who the *hero's* chair would fill,
  Must win it, or not wear it:
No *tainted miller* he could stand,
  Right sound must be his *cat's meat*,
Who could not bear his hide well *tann'd*,
  Was quite unfit for *that seat*.
          Singing fal la la, &c.

All nations came to claim the prize,
  Amongst them many a don, sirs;
And *Billy Ward* swore, b—t his eyes,
  He'd *mill* 'em every one, sirs.
At Bexley Heath, it happ'd one day,
  He was beaten *black* and *blue*, sirs,
By one *deep* in the *fancy lay*,
  'Twas little *Dan* the *Jew*. sirs.
          Singing fal la la &c

The *Ruffian young*, next on the list,
    Laid claim to *boxing merits*,
A mere pretender to the *fist*,
    Who dealt in *wine* and *spirits*.
His *hits* were RUM, none can deny,
    His BLACKSTRAP none could bear it,
But of his HOGSHEAD he was shy,
    Lest they should *tap* his *claret*.
              Singing fal la la, &c.

Bitton then came, a champion bold,
    And dealt some *hard* and *sly knocks;*
But yet, when all the truth is told,
    Some *rank* him with the *shy cocks;*
But prate like this we must not mind,
    A *Dutchman true* begot him,
Whoe'er has seen *Bitton behind*,
    Will ne'er dispute his *bottom*.
              Singing fal la la, &c.

Of all the *milling coves*, the crack,
    None pleases more than *Sam*, sirs,
Whose whiskers are of jetty black,
    As those of *whip Jeram*, sirs,
So neatly *fibs* the *Israelite*
    To ev'ry stander by, sirs,
Who must allow it as a sight,
    Worth well a Jew's eye, sirs.
              Singing fal la la, &c.

We must now sing of *Belcher's* fame,
    Whose race was full of glory;
His *matchless* deeds I need not name,
    You all must know his story.
He beat the best *coves* of his day,
    But few could stand before him,
For he could *hit* and *get away*,
    If not—why he could *floor* them.
              Singing fal la la, &c.

Champion of the *milling* corps,
    Next starts a true *game Chicken*,
His honours to the last he *bore*,
    But never *bore* a *licking;*
Till tyrant *Death*, man's greatest foe,
    Who mercy shows him never,
Hit poor Pearce a mortal blow,
    Which closed his eyes for ever.
              Singing fal la la, &c.

Jack Gulley made a manly stand,
  In science quite complete, sirs,
He rather chose to fight on land,
  'Than serve longer in the *Fleet*, sirs,
Where many worthies of their line,
  Like Jack for bravery noted,
Are *under hatches* left to pine,
  Nor hope to be *promoted*.
        Singing fal la la, &c.

Next rings the fame of gallant *Cribb*,
  A *cool* and *steady miller*,
Who late to Yorkshire went to *fib*
  A first-rate man of *colour*.
No matter whether *black* or *white*,
  No *tint* of *skin* could save him,
A horse's kick was pure *delight*
  To the *belly punch* he gave him.
        Singing fal la la, &c.

England's *champion* now behold,
  In him who fills the chair, sirs,
Who never yet a battle sold,
  Nor lost one in despair, sirs.
For in each contest, or *set-to*,
  Brave Tom bore off the *laurel*,
Which proudly planted on his *brow*,
  Says, " Touch me at your peril."
        Singing fal la la, &c.

Now fill your glasses to the *brim*,
  And honour well my toast, sirs,
" May we be found in *fighting trim*,
  When *Boney* treads our coast, sirs."
The gallant *Barclay* shall lead on,
  The *fancy lads* adore him,
And *Devil* or *Napoleon*,
  Leave us alone to *floor him*.
        Singing fal la la, &c.

MULTUM IN PARVO,

OR, A MIRACLE IN TWENTY MINUTES.

WRITTEN BY TOM HAZEL.

A TRUE Briton from Bristol, a rum one to fib
He's champion of England, his name is TOM CRIBB,
With white and black men, has milled all round,
But one to mill him in the world can't be found.

No curs he ever fought, but good men they all were,
Which proves him a good one, all must now declare,
For of strength he has much, and of science no lack,
And of bottom a plenty he found for the Black.

The Black's a good man, we know very well,
But Cribb is a better, and the same you can tell,
For his pluck is so lasting, and his courage so bold,
That he, Champion like, has again won their gold.

For six hundred they fought, no paltry sum,
Which by many was said, by the Black would be won;
But without prejudice to colour, and see it thousands did,
Molineaux, 'gainst his will, by our Champion was fibb'd.

Fair play to the parties was shown, you'll admit,
Though Blackee was strong, with Cribb could not hit,
And of his milling the Black has had slice upon slice,
Though giants in stature, in his hands are but mice.

Oft enough they have tried to convince 'em it's a joke,
To value the shadow of fir with the substance of oak,
Which its virtue retains for ages we are sure,
And high in perfection, when firs are no more.

CRIBB AND THE BLACK.

On the eighteenth of December, of a fight I will sing,
When bold Cribb and Molineaux entered the ring,
With hope and expectation our bosoms beating high,
While the rain pour'd in torrents from a dark low'ring sky.
                    Chorus—With hope, &c.

Tom Cribb is a British man, he's cast in British mould,
With a heart like a lion, of courage stout and bold,
A brave black man is Molineaux, from America he came,
And boldly tried to enter with Cribb the lists of fame.

The Black stripp'd, and appear'd of a giant-like strength,
Large in bone, large in muscle, and with arms a cruel length,
With his skin as black as ebony—Cribb as white as snow,
They shook hands like good fellows, then to it they did go.

The very first round they had, Cribb hit him on the head,
But received one in the mouth, and very freely he bled,
The two or three next rounds Cribb seem'd to have the b
But the black man most bravely resolved to stand the te

Then the Black he did rally, oh, how he play'd away,
And show'd our British hero some terrible hard play,
Like lightning 'bout Cribb's *napper* the blows came left and
    right,
While the Black's friends felt certain their man would win
    the fight.

Then the Black still bore on with a terrible great force,
The blows fell on poor Tom Cribb like kicks from a horse,
His friends e'en were doubtful, Cribb will lose it they did cry,
Never mind, says he to Gulley, *I'll be better by and bye.*

Look! how cautious he fights now, how his distance he does
    mind,
He's coming about, my boys, see he's got his second wind,
He's sure to bring us through, my boys, spite of all the Black's
    power,
Hark! he's come it to old Joey Ward, he can fight a good hour.

For many a hard round each the prize did strive to gain,
They had fought fifty minutes in the cold shiv'ring rain,
Belcher saw them down together, to Bill Gibbons he did say,
I'm down upon Cribb's mug, Bill, he's sure to win the day.

Now Cribb seem'd to get better and stronger every round,
And four times he fairly brought the Black to the ground,
The Black's strength forsook him, he'd not a chance to win,
He fought like a brave fellow, but was forced to give in.

Ye swells, ye flash, ye milling coves, who this hard fight did see,
Let us drink to these heroes, come join along with me,
A bumper to brave Cribb, boys, to the Black a bumper, too,
Though beat, he proved a man, my boys, what more could a
    man do?

A BOXING WE WILL GO.

Come move the song, and stir the glass,
    For why should we be sad;
Let's drink to some free-hearted lass,
    And Cribb, the boxing lad,
        And a boxing we will go, will go, will go,
        And a boxing we will go.

Italians stab their friends behind,
    In darkest shades of night;
But Britons they are bold and kind,
    And box their friends by light.

The sons of France their pistols use,
   Pop, pop, and they have done:
But Britons with their hands will bruise,
   And scorn away to run.

Throw pistols, poniards, swords, aside,
   And all such deadly tools;
Let boxing be the Briton's pride,
   The science of their schools!

Since boxing is a manly game,
   And Britons' recreation;
By boxing we will raise our fame,
   'Bove any other nation.

If Boney doubt it, let him come,
   And try with CRIBB a round;
And CRIBB shall beat him like a drum,
   And make his carcass sound.

Mendoza, Gulley, Molineaux,
   Each Nature's weapon wield;
Who each at Boney would stand true,
   And never to him yield.

We've many more would like to *floor*
   The little upstart king;
And soon for mercy make him roar
   Within a spacious ring.

A fig for Boney—let's have done
   With that ungracious name;
We'll drink and pass our days in fun,
   And box to raise our fame.
          And a boxing, &c.

SUNG AT A DINNER AT BOB'S CHOP-HOUSE.

TUNE—"*Jolly young Waterman.*"

PRAY hav'nt you heard of a jolly young coal-heaver,
   Who down at Hungerford used for to ply:
His daddles he used with such skill and dexterity,
   Winning each *mill*, sirs, and blacking each eye.
He sparr'd so neat, and fought so steadily,
   He hit so straight, and he won so readily;
And now he's a coal-merchant, why should he care,
Though his dealings are black, yet his actions are fair.

To mention the times that he's won by hard *milling*,
   'Tis useless to tell unto any one here;
For though no Adonis, he's very nigh killing,
   His arguments have such an *effect* on the *ear*.
   He hit half rounds, and he fought so steadily,
   He *mill'd* away, and won so readily;
Then why should this coal-merchant ever know care,
Though his dealings are black, yet his actions are fair.

A cove in the black line, he show'd opposition,
   So Tommy determined to give him a turn,
And Molineaux made him a bold proposition,
   But twice he has found that his coals would not burn.
   For he sparr'd so neat, and fought so steadily,
   He hit so straight, and won so readily;
For why should this coal-merchant ever know care,
While he's Champion of England, and now fills the chair.

THE END.

530896

Made in the USA